Nel mezzo del cammin di nostra vita. . . .

## Prefatory Note

The quotations on pp. 693 ff. are from *U. S. A.*, published by Harcourt, Brace and Company; copyright, 1930, 1932, 1933, 1934, by John Dos Passos. Quotations on pp. 715 f. are from *Conversation at Midnight*, published by Harper and Brothers; copyright, 1937, by Edna St. Vincent Millay. To Harcourt, Brace and Company we are indebted for the privilege of making quotations from the works of Kay Boyle, Archibald MacLeish, Carl Sandburg, and Lewis Mumford. To the Vanguard Press we are under obligations for similar privileges in connection with the works of James T. Farrell. With respect to quotations from other contemporary sources, we have cited the names of authors and their works and desire to express here our appreciation of the considerations extended to us by members of the Republic of Letters and their publishers.

C. A. B.
M. R. B.

New Milford, Conn.
Winter, 1938

# Contents

# AMERICA
# IN MIDPASSAGE

# AMERICA IN MIDPASSAGE

## CHAPTER I

### *The Golden Glow*

AFTER the long and toilsome rise, American civilization
reached, at the summer solstice of Normalcy, the
high plateau of permanent peace and prosperity — in
the general opinion of business organizers, bankers, guardians of the National Shrine in Wall Street, bondsalesmen,
grateful holders of stocks, lawyers, doctors, editors, writers,
columnists, artists, architects, actors, philosophers, economists, scientists, engineers, teachers, professors, women of the
leisure class, the aristocracy of labor, and the politicians of
the right direction. Notes of jubilee drowned the plaintive
cries of farmers and the queasy doubts of querulous critics.
According to the golden appearance of things, ingenuity

would create novelty upon novelty, gadget upon gadget, to keep the nation's machines whirling; inevitably outlets would be found for the accumulations of capital and the torrents of commodities; and employment would be afforded for laborers befitting their merits and diligence. Articles for comfort and convenience, devices for diversion and amusement were multiplying with sensational rapidity, giving promise of a satisfaction even more gratifying. Corporations were swelling in size, holding companies were rising to dizzy heights, the tide of liquid claims to wealth was flooding in. Since, it was thought, the morale of the nation was grounded in ineradicable virtues and sustained by a beneficent religion, American civilization was well fortified against all varieties of untoward experience.

Reassured by the solidity of business, educators drove ahead with plans for buildings, campuses, and endowments still more magnificent, to fit the youth of the land for entering upon the heritage prepared and guaranteed by their ancestors. Pouring out from the seats of learning, hopeful graduates, with diplomas in their hands and benedictions on their heads, looked forward in confidence to security in the professions, services, polite callings, or dainty domesticity. For consumers there were to be automobiles, radios, electric refrigerators, silk stockings, lingerie, and cosmetics, if necessary on the installment plan, with no payment down. Wherever, in the worst of excellent circumstances, unfortunates required succor, an appeal could be made to private philanthropy that the homeless might have their shelter and the hungry their bread.

This permanence and beneficence seemed doubly guaranteed by a strong government, under the watchful guardianship of nine impeccable judges soon to be housed in the resplendent Palace of Justice at the national capital. Under political institutions inherited from prudent forebears and solidified by respectful practice, the people ruled through laws of their own making, within the fixed limits of the Constitution; and as it had been it might ever be. No powerful

x

faction challenged the form of government or threatened
the vested rights of property. Nowhere in shadows lurked
a Catiline. The continental home of the nation, with its
outlying possessions, was guarded by an army and a navy
whose renown had never been darkened by defeat in war.
Relations with other governments were now pacific. Having disclaimed pretensions to larger empire, the United
States could face the future without fear of perilous conflicts
upon land or sea. Foreign trade was increasing in volume,
as loans were granted to impoverished or backward economies abroad, stimulating domestic industries, expanding
employment, swelling the coffers of bankers and capitalists
with commissions and profits, and adding the bonds of
interest to the ties of international humanity. With the
older generations still remembering the last armed contest,
and the new generation not old enough to lust after its
experience in another, the weary nations of the earth were
ready to renounce war as an instrument of national policy
and enter upon an endless age of peace. So, at least, it
seemed in the generality of opinion.

§

This generality of opinion was incarnate in Calvin Coolidge, President of the Republic. Looking out upon the
scene, he pronounced it fair and good. He had been elected
by a triumphant majority against all opposition in 1924, and
as he contemplated the coming years he saw every reason
for exulting in their promises. In his own personality he
typified the virtues which were celebrated on ceremonial
occasions as the unfailing sources of prosperity and accumulation: thrift, prudence, and simplicity. There was firmness
in his character, suggesting the granite of the Vermont hills
amid which he had been reared. And his virtues were
widely acclaimed by Americans of his generation in the
plenitude of their wealth. His crisp and homely aphorisms
excited pleasure in the drawing rooms of Park Avenue and

in the exclusive clubs of Chicago and San Francisco. Stories
of his passion for economy in private and public expenditures
were told and retold in Palm Beach, Newport, and Aiken at
Lucullan feasts typical of the golden age. When he set his
face like flint against high taxation of the rich and demanded
a reduction in public outlays, he heightened their confidence
in the future of the country and its institutions. When he
scolded critics in Congress, scorned the appeals of progressives, and braved the laughter of the amused minority, he
added to the assurance which resisted the spirit of innovation
in matters economic and political. As long as Calvin Coolidge stood on guard at the White House with the executive
veto, those who shared his sentiments could maintain their
faith in the bright image of today and tomorrow.

In case an executive veto failed to block any objectionable measure driven through the Congress of the United
States by the tumult of democracy, the Supreme Court
remained as the ultimate bulwark under the aegis of the
Constitution. Its personnel, carefully selected, offered a
guarantee of caution and conservatism. Over that tribunal presided William Howard Taft as Chief Justice, a
jurist with long political experience. As a candidate for
the presidency on two occasions and as President for four
years, he had fully certified his views to the whole country.
After a period of retirement, following his conflict with the
Progressives and his defeat in 1912, he had been elevated to
the supreme bench by President Harding. The general
conceptions of the Constitution and the rights of property
entertained by the Chief Justice were shared by three colleagues — Justice Pierce Butler, formerly a mighty railroad lawyer in the West, Justice George Sutherland, once a
leader of the Republicans in the Senate, and Justice Edward
T. Sanford, who had come to his post from a lower court.
These three had also been nominated by President Harding
with due reference to their qualifications. With them were
affiliated, in matters of essential doctrine, Justice Willis
Van Devanter, distinguished by a career of services in the

Republican party and chosen for the bench by Taft while
he was President of the United States, and Justice James
Clark McReynolds, whom President Wilson had translated from the office of Attorney General — making a safe
majority of six against almost any piece of legislation deemed
unfriendly by the leading beneficiaries of the great prosperity.

The weight thus provided for the scales of justice was
somewhat balanced by three members of the Court who
constantly warned their brethren against substituting their
economic predilections for the provisions of the Constitution.
Old and crowned with honors, Justice Oliver Wendell
Holmes led this group; he had been chosen by President
Theodore Roosevelt for the purpose of tempering the
harshness of corporation law with the humanity of jurisprudence. Akin to Justice Holmes in spirit was Justice
Louis D. Brandeis whose work in labor and social legislation
President Wilson had recognized by appointing him to this
permanent position on the bench. The third member of
the triumvirate was Justice Harlan F. Stone, elevated by
Coolidge, the youngest of the nine in point of service and
differentiated from his two colleagues by varied experiences
as dean of the Columbia University Law School, practitioner in New York City, and Attorney General of the United
States. Though these three Justices, powerful in learning
and in gifts of expression as they were, could by no means
dominate the Court, in time of sharp division they could
dissent; and again and again one or more of the three did
dissent with reasoned and pungent arguments against decisions of the majority affecting gains, profits, and incomes,
especially in respect of statutes violating the Social Statics
of Herbert Spencer. But on such occasions they could not
issue orders in the name of the Court. That function was
reserved to the majority.

While President Coolidge was in the White House and
the Supreme Court was dominated by Justices of kindred
conceptions, insurgents in the national legislature could do
little or nothing to dim the light of the fair prospect. The

elections of 1926 had given the Republicans a safe working majority in the House of Representatives. In the Senate remained the apostles of Normalcy: James E. Watson of Indiana, David A. Reed of Pennsylvania, Reed Smoot of Utah, and Francis E. Warren of Wyoming. In all the main points of doctrine President Coolidge could rely upon their orthodoxy. On the face of things there were forty-eight Republican members in the Senate, forty-seven Democrats, and one Farmer-Labor spokesman. But appearances were somewhat illusory. Among the Senators nominally of his own party, with whom the President had to work, were Smith W. Brookhart, a radical agrarian from Iowa; James Couzens, an independent millionaire from Michigan; George W. Norris, the indomitable radical from Nebraska; and Robert M. La Follette, Jr., heir of his father's devotion to democracy and a strong defender himself. The presence of these men in the Senate meant that every policy presented by President Coolidge would be mercilessly examined, if not torn to tatters in debate. But, after all, they were a minority and they could accomplish little in the line of positive action. They could combine with Democrats in pushing investigations of the oil scandal that had marred the Giant Masquerade during Harding's administration and in approving inquiries into other forms of coöperation between the Government and business enterprise; yet, while the bright hues of prosperity lay upon the cities, few people were really disturbed by incidents of scandal and corruption, as the election of 1924 had demonstrated.

§

Given his scheme of values and outlook upon life, his background and purposes, President Coolidge was obliged to devote special consideration to matters of national finance and economy. In this domain he found the situation on the whole excellent though open to improvement by the exercise of prudence.

At its peak in 1919, the interest-bearing debt of the United States had stood at the staggering sum of $25,700,000,000 in round numbers. At the close of the fiscal year in 1928 it had been reduced to $17,318,000,000. At the same time the Treasury reported that the surplus of revenues over expenditures for the fiscal year amounted to nearly $400,000,000 — of which a part was from non-recurring sources. "We are striving, as always," said the President to the federal officials responsible for budget estimates, "to pave the way for further reduction of debt and of taxes. This in itself necessitates unremitting effort to hold the level of our expenditure program." At the existing rate of debt retirement, the Treasury could count on a trivial debt at the end of fifteen or twenty years.

Moreover the present burden was offset, in the calculations of that department, by the obligations of foreign governments to the amount of nearly $11,000,000,000, all evidences of World War debts. Belgium, Estonia, Finland, Great Britain, Hungary, Italy, Latvia, Lithuania, Poland, and Rumania had delivered their bonds to the Treasury. Greece, Czechoslovakia, and Yugoslavia were on the point of depositing their pledges, and the war debt-refunding agreement with France was in process of successful negotiation. Among the great powers indebted to the United States, only Russia was set down as a recalcitrant defaulter. With debt retirement proceeding rapidly, with a surplus for the fiscal year, and with the bonds of great powers in hand or on the way, President Coolidge and his Secretary of the Treasury, Andrew W. Mellon, reviewed achievements with pride and looked forward with composure, in matters of public finance.

The sphere of business which President Coolidge surveyed at the close of 1928 likewise presented attractive prospects. Experts who watched the barometers of "free" enterprise cited impressive gains over the previous year, in check transactions, the advance of railway shares on the market, and the material appreciation in industrial stocks. The

New York Exchange reported that the volume of operations for the twelve months exceeded the total of the previous year by nearly fifty per cent and the total of 1926 by almost eighty per cent. Collaterally, brokers' loans for dealings in stocks had broken into a "new high" and interest rates were rising. It was with some justification in "facts and figures" that President Coolidge, in his final annual message to Congress, rejoiced that the country was in an "era of prosperity more extensive and of peace more permanent" than ever before in its history. To this prosperity, he admitted, there might be perils; but not while his policies were cherished and continued by the nation. "The main source of these unexampled blessings," he insisted, "lies in the integrity and character of the American people."

When President Coolidge found one sector of business enterprise, namely high-seas shipping, less prosperous than others, he suggested ways and means of amelioration. Under his guidance Congress lent the financial assistance of the Federal Government to that needy industry, by passing the Merchant Marine Act of 1928. Under this measure the Postmaster General was authorized to award contracts for the carriage of mails to all ports not covered by the coastwise shipping laws. But instead of paying shippers a fixed sum per pound of mail transported, as under previous legislation, he could now allow them a certain amount for every mile traveled on the outbound voyage from the United States, regardless of the quantity of mail on board. Although the rates varied according to the tonnage and speed of the ships, the maximum payment could run as high as twelve dollars per nautical mile. Besides making generous grants to shipowners for the carriage of mail, the Government continued the practice of lending money at low rates of interest for the construction and repair of vessels, and permitted operators to employ naval officers on leave with half-pay from active service. This Act, as a commissioner of the Shipping Board explained, offered to the shipping business the most lucrative subsidy in the world. As later investigations disclosed, the statement proved correct, indeed startlingly correct. Lest some mistake occur in the matter of lucrative returns, Congress provided that the Government should continue to operate at its own loss the "pioneer lines" that were not paying their expenses, and then transfer them to private owners as soon as a profit appeared on the balance sheets.

§

That the masses in cities and rural regions might dwell in the effulgence of the golden glow, leaders in business enterprise offered stocks and bonds to "investors" and country banks. Investment houses, often affiliated with great banking institutions, established branches all over the country, tied together by leased wires for instant communication. They organized selling forces, headed by high-powered drivers who "pepped up" salesmen by their florid orations on the "merits" of the "securities" offered to the public, and by promising bonuses and promotions for success in disposing of stocks and bonds.

Young men fresh from academic groves, Bachelors of Arts in one thing or another, were recruited by the tens of thousands and drilled into rank and file salesmen for the highways and the byways. On trains, in airplanes, and by automobile, they sped hither and yon looking for customers. To some were assigned "the big game" — men and women who could buy shares in thousand lots and bonds by the block. To others was given the task of visiting small cities and towns, dangling prizes before little bankers, and charming men and women into exchanging their cash or prime securities for the new offerings that often promised higher rates of interest and better opportunities for profits than old and seasoned paper. Flaming youth seemed to have unlimited economic opportunities at least, selling liquid claims to wealth. With banks and brokers establishing special departments to take care of women as customers, college girls found a new avenue of equality stretching out before them.

Apparently impatient over the volume of security issues that accompanied the construction of new plants and the expansion of old industries, enterprising men of affairs set feverishly about the manufacture of additional stocks and bonds by the formation of holding companies. In the field of electric power, for example, such a company would buy a controlling interest in a number of concerns engaged in the actual operation of electric plants. It did not operate itself; it merely "held." The money for this transaction the company acquired by selling its own stocks and bonds to the eager public so eloquently described in the financial columns of the newspapers. Not content with simple operations, imaginative financiers formed super-holding companies, that is, corporations which united holding companies based upon control over operating concerns. As imagination expanded, holding company was piled upon holding company until the pyramid threatened, like the Tower of Babel, to pierce the heavens. Nor was ambition limited to single industries. One financial skyscraper, through an intricate network of holding concerns, gathered under its top concern railways, terminals, trucking companies, coal mines, orange groves, real estate developments, office buildings, a hotel, a bridge, a ferry, a heat, light, and power plant, a dock, and a winter resort, in addition to a number of enterprises more difficult to classify. Nothing that Lemuel Gulliver saw in Brobdingnag, not even corn as tall as trees, was more fantastic in conception and appearance.

As the structure of a holding company rose and expanded, it was customary for its directors to "write up," that is, inflate, the actual value of the subsidiaries acquired and to issue stocks or bonds, or both, founded upon the new "values." Since, in the field of public utilities, the holding company operated usually in two or more states, it was almost entirely free from the control, such as it was, exercised by state utility commissions charged with responsibility for assuring the public that stocks and bonds represented tangible wealth or the requirements of prudent investment. So emancipated, operating hither and yon, the holding company could add almost any nominal values it liked to the real and tangible values attached to underlying property. It could float and advertise stocks and bonds resting on hopes, speculations, and other intangibles, within the loose and vague boundaries set by the law of fraud, as liberally interpreted by the courts.

Not even in the days of The Octopus had financiers been able to get control over so much property by selling the securities of their companies to the public and using the money to purchase widely scattered and numerous minor concerns. To the wealth acquired by this process was added income derived from "servicing" the subsidiaries, controlling the salaried positions in the lower companies, and dominating the purchase of their supplies. Seldom if ever had the "natural forces of free enterprise" been so freely unleashed to gather in the investor's money and lay duties on the consumer's dollar. With prosperity mounting as on the wings of the morning there seemed to be no limit to the volume of liquid claims to wealth that could be issued and sold to the public, or to the profits that could be gathered in from the sale of paper and the management of underlying properties. Financiers, bankers, brokers, operators, and manipulators walked on air, sailed the skies, exuded the optimism of everlasting progress in their line of enterprise.

While this towering structure of paper claims to property was rising higher and higher, giving gapers and gazers the vertigo, the governors of the country laid no profane hands upon it. They "let it alone" with all the severity demanded by the stiffest defender of liberty. They did not seek to regiment the financiers, to dictate to them, to interfere harshly with the market in bonds and stocks. From the point of view of free enterprise, which was bound in the inexorable nature of things, as orthodox economists taught, to "release productive forces" and make everybody as

prosperous as humanly possible, the legal conditions prescribed for business by government were ideal, or almost
ideal, especially when taken in conjunction with the tariffs,
bounties, and subsidies added to heap up the measure.
Indeed the governments of many states vied with one
another in giving business enterprise the freest range that
fancy could conceive within any bounds of government.
As practically all the corporations, super-corporations, and
holding companies, which led in this upward rush toward
the sky, derived their charters — that is to say their authority to do "business" — from state governments, politicos in
these little domains, often corporation lawyers themselves,
smoothed the path for incorporators. Although a majority
of states exercised a control more or less strict over the formation of companies, others imposed no restrictions worthy
of mention and actually invited financiers to come in and
secure authority to behave as they pleased.

Lest the advantages of the liberty available be missed by
financiers, lawyers and enterprisers in the states of freedom
advertised the merits of their commonwealths] in blatant
words. A document of invitation carried by The Scientific
American positively shouted to all whom it concerned : "In-
corporate in Arizona. Complete in 1 day. Any capitaliza-
tion, least cost, greatest advantages. Transact business anywhere. Laws, by-laws, and forms free." Another beckoned
from the pages of System : "Charters — Delaware best,
quickest, cheapest, most liberal. Nothing need be paid in.
Do business and hold meetings anywhere. Free forms." It
was on the basis of evidence clear and abundant that a witness declared before a Senate committee in 1937 : "States
have turned loose upon the other states a flock of corporate
vultures — I use that phrase deliberately and after mature
consideration — to prey upon the economy and people of the
other states." Although W. Z. Ripley, in his Main Street and
Wall Street, carefully described this procedure in detail, his
report to the nation made little, if any, impression on business men, beyond stirring up a storm of protest against his

conclusions. After all, the Lords of Creation naturally supposed that they understood corporate enterprise better than
a mere professor. At least, they could afford, in practice, to
ignore his animadversions.

The financial columns of great dailies announced in huge
headlines and flashing descriptions a wide variety of new
issues of stocks and bonds. They drew attention to the bonds
of foreign governments offered at prices to yield six or seven
per cent, or even "better." Why be content, salesmen asked,
with a miserable three or four per cent on American Liberty
bonds? If the people were squeamish about investing in foreign paper, of course they could get American real estate
bonds paying five, six, or seven per cent — first mortgage
bonds at that, guaranteed or unguaranteed, both equally
"sound" and based upon "valuations" made by reputable
firms of engineers and accountants. To investors inclined
toward an elastic rate of return, rather than fixed interest,
in order that they might share in the progressive prosperity,
stocks in bewildering array were tendered — common stocks,
Class A stocks, Class B stocks, preferred stocks of the first
and second order, all sponsored by houses of the highest
standing, with powerful New York banks as "trustees." If
the investor desired "the security of diversification" he could
buy stocks in railroads, utilities, foods, drugs, automobiles,
and all the other prime industries of America. If perchance
he distrusted his own judgment in making choices, he could
purchase shares in investment "trusts," organized by solid
old banking houses or their affiliates. These trusts were
directed by "experts" who bought the securities of ten,
twenty, fifty, or more "selected" industries and invited inex-
perienced men and women to benefit from corporate wisdom
by acquiring shares resting on fractions of many holdings.

While some of the securities so tendered were proclaimed
gilt-edged, others were more or less covertly acknowledged to
be "a bit speculative." Yet was anything really speculative
in an age of rising and endless prosperity? At all events there
were investors who wanted more than the fixed interest of a

first-mortgage bond or the modest dividend of a conservative corporation. They were eager to take a chance or their latent desires could be awakened by skilled psychologists in salesmanship. So even the oldest and most honorable banking houses or their affiliates brought out issues that might rise ten or fifteen points or might not, as events would disclose. Although advertisements of such prizes were often expressed in guarded language, the names of the sponsors obscured the warnings. Lines of fine print in the trust indenture, drawn by astute lawyers, often provided legal and moral exculpation for the issuing houses in case of a wreck.

But who read fine print, or understood its terms, if read? Nor was it always to the interest of salesmen to draw the attention of prospects to the stipulations of an indenture that reduced the equity of the stock to a position far removed from real value, indeed to a position of mere hopes founded upon possible, though not probable, contingencies. If salesmen did duly warn their customers, their side remarks must have fallen on deaf ears. Why not? After all, miracles were happening every day. Radio Corporation of America, which had once been tossed around at a few dollars a share, was at ninety-four dollars a share in March, 1928, and was destined to rise to $549 a share the very next year.

To this enchanting scene all the more appearance of solidity was given by the magic of the sponsorship. A majority of the men who led in the grand flotations and operations represented the flower of American culture, if their training in universities was an index of that culture. Certainly they were not the Daniel Drews, the Diamond Jim Bradys, the Russell Sages, and Hetty Greens of the Gilded Age, ruthless plungers, cut-throat competitors, and grim crushers of the weak who had risen from the bottom or near it, under the jungle law of tooth and claw. Of the fifty men rightly classified by Frederick Lewis Allen among the Lords of Creation as the "most powerful or influential in the Wall Street of 1929," at least forty were college men. A majority of the forty came from Harvard, Yale, Amherst, and the Massachusetts Institute of

Technology, from New England institutions, from the home of Federalism where fortunes had been augmented by the manipulation of papers since the establishment of the Constitution and the funding of the old state and continental debts. The Harvard quota, the largest of all, included such "wizards of finance" as J. P. Morgan, Thomas Lamont, George Whitney, George F. Baker, Jr., and Vincent Astor. The men of collegiate culture were, of course, often jostled by, or associated with, men who had climbed up from the bottom of the economic ladder — John J. Raskob, the Van Sweringen brothers, Clarence Dillon, and Samuel Insull, for example. But neither the jostling nor the association had tarnished the finish, the erudition, or the virtuosity of the university graduates at the top. The consideration which they enjoyed in all exclusive circles, their good taste, their correctness of dress, their respect for religion, property, and monogamy, their widely-known professions of rectitude, combined to give strength to the popular faith in the solidity, promise, and trustworthiness of their financial and business transactions.

§

Nor was the domestic scene alone fair with prosperity and assurance. To President Coolidge and those who shared his vision the foreign outlook was almost equally gratifying. Being no Caesar or Marcus Aurelius, Coolidge was neither restive with the longing to enlarge the American empire nor seriously troubled by its present size and problems. So he settled down contentedly within the ample reaches bequeathed by the navy and its affiliated interests in business and politics. The phantom of Philippine independence raised by the Democrats had been banished for all time, it seemed, by the results of the presidential election in 1920. That form of American intervention in China, known as the Open Door, was apparently working smoothly, subject to no threat of an overt nature, at least from Japan now entangled in the treaties and naval limitations of the Washington Conference.

In the Caribbean, as in the Far East, President Coolidge, as head of the navy, was able to pursue a steady course despite occasional protests by recalcitrant Senators against the use of marines — in Nicaragua, Haiti, and Santo Domingo. To such opposition he replied laconically, in terms that seemed axiomatic to those who regarded them as axiomatic, that "American lives and interests" must be protected everywhere.

That the President desired no friction with Mexico, however, was evident in the chill reception which he accorded to the importunities of interventionists who called for a war on that country in defense of American "rights." During his career in the Senate, Albert B. Fall had clamored for action in Mexico, but he was now out of the Senate; moreover he had resigned from the post of Secretary of the Interior and was under indictment for fraudulent transactions in oil consummated during his tenure of office. In the face of continued demands for strong policy from other interventionists, President Coolidge appointed Dwight W. Morrow, of the House of Morgan, ambassador to Mexico in 1927, with the expectation that he would adjust disputes by measures short of war. To protect the existing territorial American empire was one thing. To extend it by expensive adventures was no part of President Coolidge's program.

While peace reigned within the territorial empire, the dominion of foreign commerce was expanding and presumably could enlarge forever on the basis of free enterprise. From year to year, with some fluctuations, sales to other nations increased in absolute amounts, although not relatively in ratio to exportable production. The fact that commodities of export were shifting from agricultural produce to manufactured goods, with direful repercussions for labor on the land, merely confirmed the optimism of leaders in business enterprise as they forged ahead in their struggle with European and Oriental competitors. Between the years 1900 and 1930, agricultural exports fell from 66.2 per cent of the total export of the United States to 31.8 per cent of the total, while non-agricultural products, machinery and machine tools leading, rose from 33.8 per cent of the total to 68.2 per cent. In the calculation of promoters all this advance was due to the prowess of American manufacturers, bankers, and salesmen and no visible limits to everlasting expansion blurred the future. In the initiative of business men the regular politicos exulted and upon it, they were sure, the nation might safely rely.

The fact that American business men were building branch factories abroad in the staple lines of industry also lent apparent confirmation to assurance by giving Americans what was proudly called a grand "stake" in the fortunes and economy of other mighty nations. To overcome the barriers of foreign tariffs or meet the competition of cheaper foreign labor, manufacturing concerns established branches in Canada, Ireland, Great Britain, Europe, Latin America, and the Far East. If fortresses could not be taken by frontal assault, they could be occupied by boring within the walls. Besides going after foreign competitors on their home grounds, American business men bought the stocks of foreign industrial concerns, thus winning a minority voice, if not majority control, and sharing in any profits that accrued. By 1929 American private investments of the direct type in manufacturing, merchandising, mining, smelting, and other enterprises abroad amounted to the fine-appearing total of $7,477,735,000; and the structure, to the Lords of Creation, looked as substantial as the battlements of heaven.

Supplementing the billions directly invested in tangible commercial and industrial property abroad — property owned by residents of the United States — were billions invested in the bonds of foreign governments and the securities of foreign corporations. At the end of 1930 this type of portfolio investment, representing "interest capital," embraced a total of $7,204,218,000. Within its scope came national, dominion, provincial, and municipal bonds of governments in Europe, Canada, South America, Asia, Oceana, the West Indies, Mexico, Central America, and Africa. According to an official estimate as of January 1, 1931, the total of direct and portfolio investments, combined with minor items, reached the stupendous sum of $15,170,028,000. When to this aggregation was added the $11,000,000,000, owed to the Government of the United States by foreign governments on the World War account, the American "stake abroad" in the fates and fortunes of other countries amounted to about $26,000,000,000 in round numbers. Here, at least, were paper claims which accountancy viewed as a part of the national wealth, as signs of power and prosperity. "Evidences" of such claims were to be found in trust funds for widows and orphans, in the vaults of local banks, in the treasuries of universities, and in the strong boxes of American citizens who had "bought into" American economy triumphant abroad.

The billions poured from the United States into other countries enabled foreigners, financially handicapped, to buy American commodities ranging from wheat to machines by the shipload and thus gave a powerful stimulus to American production. With these billions in money went the high-powered salesmen of private concerns and the commercial agents of the Federal Government, including under the head also ambassadors, ministers, consuls, and naval attachés. As the money and men spread over the earth, the slow-going British and the still more leisurely Orientals were pushed and jostled by the representatives of American enterprise. From Copenhagen to Belgrade, from Tokyo to Singapore, from Liberia to Cape Town, and across the seas to Adelaide, loans of American money were consummated and the goods of American industries were deposited. A map of the world showing trade journeys, the stations visited, and the capital accounts registered resembled a universal commercial empire.

If it was not, like the old Roman Empire, marked by one government and one peace, with proconsuls ruling the provinces, it was at least assured the protection of the United States navy and it seemed as solid to its promoters and beneficiaries as economic and military power could make any system of human affairs. A few obscure and fretful Americans presumed to suggest the hazards of defaults and repudiations, but their warnings were as naught compared with the averment of men mighty in practical affairs that the stake abroad was founded on the integrity of business and the good faith of governments.

§

With industries humming, stocks soaring, and the empire of American trade expanding, with Europe still weary from the great blood-letting of the World War, the prospects of peace seemed as flattering as the opportunities for commercial advantage. Indeed, the time appeared ripe to effect a closer integration of "world economy" on terms satisfactory to American business. In the spring of 1927, amid the plaudits of peace advocates, a world economic conference, composed of the representatives of fifty nations, including the United States, assembled at Geneva and established, optimists said, "a landmark in the progress of international coöperation." As a representative of the Department of Commerce explained, it was "the first comprehensive gathering of the nations of the world for the purpose of consulting upon a wide range of economic problems and difficulties, with the double objective of seeking means for the removal of the obstacles in the way of the revival of general prosperity and of establishing such principles in economic affairs as would help to remove the causes for international friction and ensure world peace." The discussions of the conference covered a wide range, though on vital matters its conclusions were reserved. It recommended that the nations stop raising tariff barriers and set about lowering them, saving the "legitimate" interests of the various countries and their workers. In respect of American policy that declaration, with the qualifications, could be regarded as affirming convictions already entertained.

With the idea of providing more safeguards for the peace deemed essential to the success of commercial enterprise in all forms, President Coolidge called for an international naval conference to be held at Geneva later in the same year, 1927. Alleging that the conference might hinder the work for disarmament apparently going forward through the League of Nations, France and Italy declined to participate; but the representatives of Great Britain, Japan, and the United States did assemble at Geneva to discuss restrictions which had been deferred by the Washington Conference held during the Harding administration, namely, limitations on cruisers, destroyers, and submarines. Through many weeks the delegates argued at Geneva and then, in August, broke off negotiations without reaching an agreement on these implements of the sea power.

Although the conference did not work out according to expectations, American newspapers came to the rescue and dispelled the temporary gloom by laying the blame for the deadlock and failure on Britain. So instructed by the press, the American nation could find gratification in its good intentions and look forward to bringing Great Britain to reason at a succeeding convention. Nor was this confidence shaken three years later when a Senate investigation disclosed the lobbying and propaganda financed by American shipbuilding and other interests at Geneva for the purpose of defeating the proposed naval limitations.

If at the moment naval armaments could not be limited and relief granted to taxpayers, at any rate the glow on the horizon could be heightened by a verbal declaration in favor of world peace. And when it was made, President Coolidge declared it "the most important act" of his administration. The transaction came about in this manner. On April 6, 1927, the tenth anniversary of America's entrance into the world war, the French foreign minister, Aristide Briand, announced that France was prepared to enter an engagement with the United States outlawing war between the two nations. Although the Department of State in Washington hesitated, advocates of peace rallied to the proposal and, after mature consideration, Frank B. Kellogg, the Secretary of State, countered the French suggestion with a grand plan for widening the outlawry of war by means of a general treaty pledging all nations to pacific methods in the conduct of their relations.

After negotiations had cleared the way, representatives of Great Britain, France, Germany, Italy, Japan, the United States, and other powers signed at Paris in the summer of 1928 the document known as the Briand-Kellogg Pact, or the Kellogg-Briand Pact. Their pledge of eternal peace bound the signatories to "condemn recourse to war for the solution of international controversies and renounce it as an instrument of national policy in their relations with one another." Over their signatures, the nations agreed that the settlement of their disputes "of whatever nature or of whatever origin shall never be sought except by pacific means." This Pact the Senate of the United States ratified in January, 1929, and President Coolidge appended his signature, in America, at a special ceremony.

It was not only President Coolidge who rejoiced. To all appearances the Pact was the true outlawry or renunciation of war for which the war-weary peoples had long yearned. The language of the document was clear and luminous. Diplomats had given it their blessings and through them responsible governments had plighted their word of honor. A ritualistic solemnity had enveloped the completion of the ratification in the United States. By collateral statements on and off the records, it was true, the leading signatories laid restraints upon its terms. Great Britain, for example, reserved her special interests, France certain continental obligations, and the United States the responsibilities of the Monroe Doctrine. No method was provided for "implementing" the Pact by coercive measures directed against offenders, and hence the effort of any foreign office to apply its shining language in practice might well involve it in difficulties. Nor did the Pact proscribe in any respect a defensive war, that is, a war for the defense of national territory against invasion, or, presumably, national interests, however defined and anywhere.

But these reservations put little or no damper on the warmth of the popular enthusiasm which the Pact evoked, except among the unbelievers to whom the Pact really meant nothing at all. How could such appearances be deceptive, such dignity disingenuous, such trumpeted honor merely cynical? In the age of boundless optimism, with stocks skyrocketing every day, commerce increasing, profits soaring, the very suggestion seemed both unwarranted and invidious.

§

Although their views and actions little affected the vision of fair prospects at home and abroad, there were doubters and critics in Congress not entirely content with the theory and practice of the great promotion. Among the matters that engaged the attention of recalcitrant members, including Republicans as well as Democrats, two were of major significance — the disposition of natural resources still belonging to the Federal Government and the state of agriculture. The first presented a double aspect. Immediately involved were pending inquiries into corrupt relations among oil companies, directors of the Republican party, and officials of the Government during the Harding regime. Already the Senate investigation committee under the leadership of Senator Thomas J. Walsh had laid bare specific transactions which showed beyond question that Albert B. Fall, as Secretary of the Interior under Harding, had engineered the leasing of two great oil reserves to Harry F. Sinclair and Edward L. Doheny on terms that promised immense profits to their respective concerns. Already it had demonstrated by indubitable evidence that Secretary Fall had suddenly grown affluent after the transactions in oil and that he had received money from both of the gentlemen who had closed advantageous bargains with the federal administration.

At the very time a court of law was supplying news on the personal progress of Mr. Fall, the Senate committee was adding new chapters to the oil scandal. In February, 1928, a son-in-law of Fall was forced to confess that Harry F. Sinclair had given him a large block of Liberty Bonds and a substantial sum in cash to be transferred to his father-in-law. But, the witness insisted, the money represented payment for an interest in Fall's ranch properties which were to be used as "a gentleman's riding and hunting club." For a moment the skeptics naturally assumed that there had been some connection between the transfer of bonds and cash to Fall and the oil lease that he had granted to Sinclair. In April, 1928, however, a trial jury thought otherwise. After two hours' deliberation it acquitted both Fall and Sinclair of the charge that they had conspired to defraud the Government of the United States. Although Respectability probably vented a sigh of relief, Senator Norris, commenting on the verdict, remarked for public benefit: "We ought to pass a law that no man worth $100,000,000 should be tried for a crime. That at least would make us consistent."

The clean bill of health which the acquittal of Fall and Sinclair seemed to give to the Party of Prosperity was marred for another brief season when the Senate committee of investigation pursued the oil matter a little further and drew into its dragnet Will Hays, a high counselor of the Party. Mr. Hays had been chairman of the Republican national committee during the campaign of 1920 and had served for a time as Postmaster General under President Harding. Before the case of Fall and Sinclair had been decided in their favor — while the presidential election of 1928 was coming into sight — the Senate committee discovered, through an examination of Mr. Hays, a trail leading from the oil transaction straight to the Republican national committee that had taken charge of the campaign for the election of President Coolidge four years previously. As Mr. Hays and his brother had been of counsel for one of Sinclair's oil corporations before the quest for normalcy began in 1920, and had maintained close personal and business relations with Sinclair subsequently, the discovery was of temporary inconvenience to the guardians of law and order.

On the witness stand in March, 1928, Mr. Hays admitted that he had received from Sinclair in 1923, after the oil scandal had broken, $185,000 in Liberty Bonds as a contribution toward discharging the deficit of the Republican treasury. This was in addition to the $75,000 in cash given by Sinclair to the Republican campaign fund of 1920. In the course of its investigation, the Senate committee also received testimony to the effect that Mr. Hays had turned some of the Liberty Bonds over to prominent Republicans in exchange for cash to be placed in the party chest; and that the Secretary of the Treasury, Andrew W. Mellon, when tendered a block of these bonds, had rejected them and handed his check to Hays for $50,000 as a gift. On the Senate witness stand, Secretary Mellon explained his rejection of the bonds on the ground that "they had come to me for a purpose which did not suit me," but added that he had not, at the time, deemed it necessary to inform the Senate committee of the transaction, merely because Sinclair's bonds had been presented to the fund of his party.

Having traced oil money to the Republican treasury, the Senate committee recalled Mr. Hays to the stand and asked him point blank some relevant questions. At a meeting held in December, 1923, the Republican national committee had made preparations for the Coolidge presidential campaign that was to start actively in a few months. Did the Republican directorate then know about the receipt of the large contribution to the party funds made by Sinclair, the oil magnate? Would Mr. Hays have ventured to tell the party committee about this contribution?

To such pertinent queries Mr. Hays replied in language befitting his state of mind: "I don't think that that situation would have — I hardly know. I don't know whether that would have — the status of that investigation [the Senate committee's] would have involved, if there had been a big contribution at that time, as you say — $135,000. I don't assume that the status of that investigation was such that it would have affected the minds of the committee. I don't

know. Sinclair was regarded, I think, as a rich man. . . .
They [the members of the Republican campaign committee]
did not regard it as you [Senator Walsh] did. I assume that
must be so. I think that time — but this is far-fetched, guess-
ing at the minds of men, as Mr. Mellon said, but at that time I
rather think, as he said, that the state of mind of the committee
would probably have been one, while not of indifference, but
not of great concern, because I don't think they knew much
of about what you recognized or you thought was fact."

Although Mr. Hays' facile treatment of embarrassing questions left uncertain the degree of awareness among the members of the Republican committee, two impressive facts were
placed on record : Liberty Bonds from Sinclair had helped to
pay off the Republican deficit in 1923 and had aided in clearing
the way for a vigorous campaign to elect President Coolidge
to succeed himself the following year. The silence of President Coolidge on the point led many citizens to assume that
he could have had no knowledge of the transaction, unless
perchance, in the routine of things, Secretary Mellon had
seen fit to give him some information concerning the business. So, in the generality of Republican opinion, the President was completely exonerated.

That President Coolidge had lost neither command nor
prestige as a result of the inquiry into oil and campaign funds,
that he was not to be deflected from his fixed policies by such
revelations, was demonstrated later in the year during a contest over the disposal of federal water power at Muscle
Shoals, where a great plant had been developed for war purposes during the Wilson administration. In accordance with
his conception of sound economy, Coolidge proposed to turn
this power over to private interests, openly and on terms not
too onerous for profitable operation.

In response Congress completed on May 25, 1928, the passage of a joint resolution rejecting this program and substituting another of its own construction. The resolution provided for continued government ownership and operation of
the power plant, the addition of new units, the granting of

preference to municipal and other public bodies in the sale
of current, and use of surplus power in the experimental
development of nitrates. But this was merely an empty
gesture against the enjoyment of the golden glow. As Congress adjourned shortly after the adoption of the joint resolution, President Coolidge had an opportunity to ignore it
under the ten-day rule of the Constitution, and he took full
advantage of his opportunity. He made no direct public
comment on the measure. He did not veto it and return it to
Congress for reconsideration. He simply smothered it with a
"pocket veto" and treated the protest of its sponsor, Senator
Norris, with disdain.

§

When the cloud of agrarian unrest, larger than any man's
hand, rose above the scene so perfect to all beneficiaries,
President Coolidge was equally successful in preventing a
deluge. Unquestionably this shadow was ill-boding. Since
the collapse of war prices in 1921, agriculture had been sinking toward or below the level of subsistence, despite the fair
prospects offered by the empire of business, banking, and
investment. Between 1920 and 1933 "one farm in every four
was sold for debts or taxes." The increase of tenancy, already
long in process, was speeded up to a startling momentum. If
the loss of homes and employment, if distress and discourage-
ment, had any meaning in terms of humanity, the plight of
agriculture was certainly tragic. If urban economists knew
little about it and cared less, those financiers who watched
the failure of country banks by the hundreds every year
could not escape taking notice of rural ruin. Moreover there
were business leaders connected with farm implement industries who felt the jars of agricultural decline through their
skins if not through the study of statistical tables. Certainly
two among them, George N. Peek and General Hugh S.
Johnson, associated with the Moline Plow Company, knew
that plows could not be sold to bankrupt farmers and they
had agrarian sympathies besides. With whirlwind zeal a few

men of great energy threw themselves into the growing farmers' movement and helped bring it to a focus in the farm bloc in Congress.

By this time the tactics of the agrarians in their battle with capitalists had radically altered. Greenbackism had been smothered in 1876, free silver had been covered by an avalanche in 1896, and victory in those years had given Republican managers a strong sense of security. But inflation, attacks on banks, criticism of railway rates, and assaults on the trusts, which had brought nothing but defeats to agrarians, were now put aside by the agricultural bloc for a new weapon, for an onslaught on the whole philosophy and practice of business enterprise as sponsored by President Coolidge and the Republican directorate. Under the general theory of the business system, capitalists, farmers, and industrial workers on the whole received as their reward shares of the total product rightly and justly proportioned to their respective contributions. This assumption the agrarians now overruled. In fact at a farm conference called by Henry C. Wallace, the Secretary of Agriculture, in 1922, a resolution had been adopted directing Congress and the President to "take steps immediately to reëstablish a fair exchange value for all farm products with that of other commodities."

In short, powerful spokesmen of powerful agrarian interests repudiated the whole price mechanism of the capitalist system. They declared that in the exchanges of the so-called "free market" farmers did not receive in return for their produce an equivalent in commodity values; that the market was "rigged" against them; that capitalism was draining the wealth of the soil into the cities; that the policy of the Government facilitated the process of exploitation; and that the Government must intervene positively to put a stop to this perversion of fair price adjustments. The agrarian challenge on this level was persistent and pervasive.

And it had some support from economists of the schools, though rarely had American economists displayed the militancy of their British colleagues and demanded a complete system of laissez faire, including free trade among nations. All of them who had the courage of their convictions admitted that farmers were selling most of their great staple products at prices determined under the pressures of the world market and were buying their manufactures in the domestic market protected against foreign competition by high tariffs. That was obvious enough and the orthodox solution was to abolish the protective tariff. But agrarians knew that this entrenched privilege could not be broken, even if they desired to break it. So they adopted the view that they were robbed by a one-sided price mechanism and proceeded to formulate counter measures based on that interpretation of the American system.

Taking their cue from those protected manufacturers who sold most of their output at home behind the tariff wall and unloaded the rest abroad as best they could, the agrarians formulated their program, later incorporated in the McNary-Haugen bill, on a kindred philosophy, with variations in details. Like the beneficiaries of protective tariffs, they called upon the National Government for aid. They demanded the creation of a federal farm board endowed with large powers and supplied with a huge revolving fund of cash. With the aid of the board, they proposed to dump on foreign countries the "surplus" in several great staples and to force higher prices for the remainder in the home market. For the purpose of covering losses on sales abroad and putting a check on agricultural production, they devised an equalization fee to be paid by the farmers enjoying this form of federal assistance. To the utter surprise of urban philosophers who contemplated the pageant of industrial prosperity with satisfaction, the agrarians were able to push the McNary-Haugen bill through Congress in 1927. Metropolitan editors seemed unable to explain the phenomenon save in terms of agrarian fanaticism — as a mental disease. Recovering their self-possession, however, after the first outburst, they called upon the President to cure this evil at once and for all time by a resounding veto.

President Coolidge responded with alacrity in a long message condemning the bill in gross and detail and stamping it with a firm veto. The measure was unconstitutional, he declared. It was an adventure in government price fixing — "an economic fallacy from which this country has every right to be spared." The equalization fee deprived farmers of property without due process of law. It was, indeed, "a tax for the special benefit of particular groups" — differing apparently in this respect from the schedules of protective tariff acts. When Congress, unconvinced by the President's condemnation, repassed the McNary-Haugen bill the following year, with some changes in detail but not in principle, once more the President countered by a veto. This time he expressed his disapproval in language of increased acerbity, revealing the volcanic emotion with which he contemplated this form of government intervention in "natural economy." Yet, after the bill was vetoed, he doubtless looked upon the agrarian incident as one of the passing, if customary, inflammations of politics.

Having blocked the agrarian movement, assured domestic tranquillity, and protected American interests abroad, President Coolidge delivered a kind of farewell address to the world in a speech on Armistice day, 1928. America, he said, had saved Europe "from starvation and ruin," after the war. American citizens need not apologize "to anybody anywhere" for any failure to discharge their duty in defense of world liberty. The settlement of the war debts had been made on "the merciful principle" of ability to pay. In any event, Americans could doubtless "better afford to lose them than our debtors could afford not to pay them." As if addressing himself to advocates of the League of Nations, he declared tartly : "We have given of our counsel when asked." The United States had desired a limitation of armaments, but foreign governments would limit only the class of combat vessels "in which we were superior" while refusing limitations on the class in which they were superior. "We are against aggression and imperialism." Our overseas possessions, except the Canal Zone, are a burden, not an advantage. "We hold them not as a profit, but as a duty." Our course is set. We should pursue it "with due humility," and meet our responsibilities "in accordance with the requirements of conscience and righteousness."

§

Naturally it was in the cities that the Coolidge system shone with the brightest lustre. If agrarians grumbled over the President's veto of the farm relief bill, his popularity appeared undiminished among industrialists and financiers. In the cities it was generally agreed, in the spring of 1928, that he could have the renomination for the asking. However, as long ago as the previous summer, he had spoken the cryptic words: "I do not choose to run." Just what the words meant his friends were not sure and politicians had difficulty in interpreting them. Did he mean that he would not be a candidate again in any circumstances or merely that he did not choose to wage a personal contest for renomination? In the uncertainty, his senatorial opponents in February, 1928, adopted a resolution, proposed by Senator La Follette, protesting against a "third term." Yet so strong was the public sentiment for the President that his friends fostered a "draft Coolidge movement" even after he had requested local party managers to refrain from pressing his candidacy. Whether he genuinely preferred retirement to private life or whether he wished to set his party free to express itself on the point of another term, while secretly hoping that it would choose him on its own volition, remained among the secrets of State.

Whatever the meaning of the President's cryptic words, other Republicans certainly felt competent to wear his mantle. Among the aspirants Herbert Hoover, Secretary of Commerce since 1921, led from the very start. In the final test at the Republican convention he received the accolade as the man best fitted to preserve American institutions, sustain the empire, and continue the promotion of trade throughout the earth. Lionized as a great engineer, a successful man of business, a world-famous humanitarian, he also enjoyed the reputation of being an efficient administrator. Who among all the members of the President's entourage was better equipped to keep the heavens radiant and assure the unbroken progress of American civilization?

Moreover Mr. Hoover had the proper background for a telling appeal to forty million voters in a popular election: he symbolized the American tradition of the poor boy rising by his own initiative to the highest office in the gift of the nation. Born in Iowa, he wore the aura of the soil and typified the democracy of the Middle West. With this advantage, easily recalled for addresses to farmers, he had made his spiral ascent from lowly beginnings, through student days at Stanford University, to participation in professional and promotional enterprises connected with mines, railways, and metallurgy in Mexico, Italy, Great Britain, China, Russia, and other foreign countries. He had acquired a competence and was residing in England when the world war broke out in 1914. Either on his own motion or at the suggestion of the British government, Mr. Hoover accepted the chairmanship of a commission formed for the relief of Belgium and in that position he rapidly became a world figure. When the United States entered the war, he served the American Government in many capacities: as administrator, technician, economist, and adviser. Foreign governments also called upon him for aid.

Appointed Secretary of Commerce by President Harding shortly after the conclusion of the war, Mr. Hoover made that Department a beehive of activities associated with the promotion of business enterprise, and he sponsored a monument to his achievements in the form of a massive building to house its army of employees. Assisted by a huge staff of experts he collected information on "trade opportunities" abroad and disseminated it among American business men seeking foreign markets for their commodities. For the prosperity of domestic business he had been no less solicitous. At the same time he had escaped the animosity of agrarian leaders;

though it was privately known that he had no sympathy with farm relief of the McNary-Haugen type — that his opposition was positively violent — his official duties had not compelled him to inscribe his antipathy in black and white on the public record.

All nature seemed conspiring to make Herbert Hoover the ideal candidate to succeed President Coolidge. Here was an outstanding business man for a business empire, a vigorous exponent of prosperity through private liberty and government promotion, a man of world experience to deal with nations that had just renounced war as an instrument of national policy, a humanitarian famous from the Volga to the Yangtze. Who knew better how to keep the ways open for expanding trade, dissolve clouds of doubt and danger, and coöperate wisely with private and public beneficence in enhancing the values of American civilization? That many huckstering politicians in his party feared and disliked him, that the huge Vare-Grundy machine in Pennsylvania supported him, made little difference in the crucial hour when enthusiasm carried him to triumph in the Republican convention of 1928 on the very first ballot, with 837 votes out of 1089.

To reach the White House, however, Mr. Hoover had to run a gauntlet flanked by Democrats ardently engaged in promoting the interests of their candidate, Alfred E. Smith, governor of New York, astute in the ways of politics, and popular with the "liberals." For a while it seemed that Democratic leaders might seek victory in exploiting the malodorous oil scandals, but they soon put a soft pedal on such tactics. Neither President Coolidge nor his Secretary of Commerce, Mr. Hoover, had been directly involved in those diversions and the Democrats might find the bomb exploding in their own hands. After all, a stew was brewing in Tammany Hall and Mr. Smith had long been associated with that institution, though he had never been publicly involved in the turmoil and turpitude that had marked its history and was himself no more open to scandalous attacks than the

Republican candidate. A far greater handicap to Mr. Smith's campaign in a country overwhelmingly Protestant was his loyal membership in the Catholic Church. Even Southern Democrats found it hard to approve that religious affiliation and extremists were inclined to see in his nomination a new Popish plot.

But Mr. Smith had a certain advantage in the laurel of liberalism that wreathed his head. He had been a sponsor of social legislation in the state of New York, both as a member of the Assembly and as governor. With the help of expert advisers he had learned to clothe his natural sympathies for plain people in the language of social workers. He had defended and befriended public education. In times of public hysteria no official had been stancher in the defense of civil liberties. He had kept "red baiters" in leash and pardoned men accused of advocating radical doctrines. He had fought for the public ownership of water power sites in the Empire state, led in the reorganization of state administration, and displayed talents in the conduct of public business. Moreover he had a "humorous way with him" that caught the fancy of the crowds and, besides, he had been, from the start, an outspoken opponent of the prohibition imposed on the sale of alcoholic beverages.

Although the campaign offered to the people a choice between two distinguished personalities, the platforms of the two parties presented no sharp antithesis of policy. Both agreed that the lamp of prosperity must be kept burning and fed by the same kind of oil that had been regularly used with such success. On the old issue that had long divided the parties, namely, the tariff, there was almost perfect agreement, save in details of phraseology. The Republicans, of course, stood their ground. Echoing their old traditions, the Democrats spoke of tariff duties that would "permit effective competition, insure against monopoly, and at the same time provide a fair revenue." But these words were balanced immediately by the declaration that the measure of the tariff rate must be the difference between the cost of production at home and abroad, "with adequate safeguard for the wages of the American laborer."

In his campaign speeches Mr. Smith insured business men against "any sudden or drastic revolution in our economic system which would cause business upheaval and popular distress," and promised to protect "to the very limit . . . legitimate business enterprise as well as American labor from ruinous competition of foreign-made goods produced under conditions far below the American standard." As if to bind the assurance, the Democrats selected as chairman of their national committee John J. Raskob, a rich industrialist who poured his own money into the contest.

Of the vexatious question raised by the agrarians, the parties were wary. The Democratic platform indulged in generalities on the point and the Republicans were also circumspect. But during the campaign Mr. Smith approved the principles of the McNary-Haugen bill, including the equalization fee. Though Mr. Hoover disliked everything savoring of the agrarians' plan, including a plank endorsing farm relief which had been defeated in the Republican convention, he promised to farmers higher tariffs and the creation of a farm board empowered to deal with surpluses in some fashion. In so doing, he did not surrender, however, his opposition to crop and price controls; he simply gave his supporters in the Republican party "talking points" for the campaign.

Nor did a definite contradiction appear in the positions of the candidates and parties on the irksome question of prohibition. Both platforms promised bone-dry enforcement as demanded by reverence for the Constitution. But Mr. Smith telegraphed the Democratic convention, after the nomination was safely clinched, that he favored "fundamental changes" in the prohibition laws, which, while preventing the return of the saloon, would "secure real temperance, respect for law, and eradication of existing evils." To all such irritants Mr. Hoover responded, in language a bit vague, by declaring himself against the repeal of the prohibition amendment and promising an inquiry into abuses and methods of correction.

So it seemed that, while the two candidates agreed on the merits of the golden glow and on the necessity of warding off all storm clouds, Mr. Smith believed in enlivening the scene by assuring alcoholic beverages to all participants in American civilization who cared to establish psychological conditions favorable to a fuller enjoyment of its benefits.

Although no statistical analysis could separate the "causes" for the division of ballots in the election, it was significant that Mr. Smith carried two states in the North, Massachusetts and Rhode Island, in which the Catholic vote was numerically powerful; and lost all the "normally" Democratic states in the South, except Alabama, Arkansas, Georgia, Louisiana, Mississippi, and South Carolina. Superficially, the election had the appearances of a Republican and Protestant landslide. Yet an examination of details revealed the strength of Governor Smith's popularity. Fifteen million votes were cast for him as against 8,300,000 polled by the Democratic candidate, John W. Davis, and the 15,700,000 votes gathered by President Coolidge in the election of 1924. From one point of view this was an immense personal tribute. The huge plurality against Governor Smith was doubtless due, in a large measure, to the unusual outpouring of hitherto negligent voters. While exact information was not forthcoming on the motives of voters, that manifestation could be ascribed with some justification to the personal qualities of Mr. Hoover, to his vigorous stand against repealing the Prohibition Amendment, and to the general belief that the existing guardianship of prosperity should not be disturbed. As to the perpetuation of the golden glow Mr. Smith could offer no more assurance than Mr. Hoover; indeed, not as much assurance.

§

On assuming Coolidge's place in the White House, President Hoover likewise beheld alluring prospects of "prosperity more extensive and peace more permanent." During the campaign, he had seemed to be aware of poverty and distress

in the United States, even under the high fulfillment of industrial success, and had expressed the hope that during his
administration the remaining blots on the economic landscape would be removed by a continuance of Republican
policies thus far so happily advanced at home and abroad.
To this expectation he had adverted in his inaugural address:
"The large purpose of our economic thought should be to
establish more firmly stability and security of business and
employment, and thereby remove poverty still further from
our borders."

If that statement of the case did not concede the existence
of dire poverty within the United States, it recognized spec-
tral forms somewhere on the borders. And in keeping with
this admission President Hoover early promised, and in fact
did later invite, the coöperation of experts in economics,
medicine, public health, and social work with a view to per-
fecting "the means by which government can be adapted to
human service," especially in the "development of those processes which directly affect public health, recreation, education, and the home." Indeed all through his speeches, messages, and addresses, he emphasized the responsibility of civic
leaders and public officials for strengthening the economy and
improving the social organization upon which political and
economic institutions rest. Though often regarded as a mere
heir of Coolidge policies, President Hoover was a thinker and
actor in his own right. After six years of relative quiescence,
save in matters of negation, an unwonted stir in the White
House followed his inauguration in 1929.

Nevertheless the broad frame of political philosophy within
which President Hoover confined his operations of thought
and action in official affairs did not differ essentially from that
of his predecessor. He opposed the agrarian contention that
the price mechanism of business enterprise robbed farmers of
wealth to which they were entitled by economic efficiency
and social justice. As Secretary of Commerce, he had joined
the Chief Executive in promoting the expansion of American
trade and investment in all parts of the world with the aid of

government agencies. As President, he retained his faith in capitalism and foreign trade. He also shared the doctrine advanced by Coolidge that American dollars invested abroad and American citizens residing there were as much a part of the nation as if in the United States and were, therefore, entitled to the protection of the National Government. In the main, policies so conceived and carried out had brought and would maintain prosperity, he believed; if refined and made more scientific they would drive poverty further from American shores. But beyond such forms of intervention, assistance, and protection, in his opinion, the Government should not go. Other activities savored of "state socialism" which he spurned root and branch. Hoover's rejection of crop control in agricultural legislation and his veto of a new Muscle Shoals bill providing for government ownership and operation made his position clear beyond dispute. In other words, business men could count upon the tenacity of President Hoover's resolve to uphold what they called "free enterprise."

Toward other social questions Hoover did not assume, however, a negative attitude. Personally and as a national leader, he lent official encouragement to the efforts of private associations attacking problems of poverty, sickness, and delinquency. He created and sponsored conferences or committees on unemployment, medical care, law enforcement, economic tendencies, and social trends. On all types of civic coöperation, sometimes called "voluntary socialism," he bestowed his blessings. "Our people," he said in his first inaugural, "have in recent years developed a new-found capacity for coöperation among themselves to effect high purposes in public welfare. It is an advance toward the highest conception of self-government."

Moreover such coöperation, he thought, should receive the active support of government. "Progress is born of coöperation in the community, not from governmental restraints. The government should assist and encourage these movements of collective self-help by itself coöperating with them."

The Department of Commerce under his leadership had affiliated itself with business interests in innumerable relations. Now, as chief executive of the nation, President Hoover proposed to foster private associations and to assist them in promoting the general welfare. Quite rightly was it said at the time that the President had "the sociological outlook" and in itself this marked a certain change in the intellectual climate of the White House, if indeed not a transition to something else.

The official measures which expressed President Hoover's scheme of political thought at the outset of his administration were aimed at continuing domestic and foreign policies along lines set by his predecessors. Since the opening of the Harding regime, the Republicans had been making legislative concessions to farmers, amplifying the loan and credit system, and regulating market and stockyard practices. During his campaign Hoover had offered something more. Whatever interpretation had been put upon his words, he meant no positive government interference with production and prices. That would have been to fly in the face of "the natural and free price mechanism" upon which prosperity was supposed to depend for its very existence and perpetuity. His creed the President made perfectly plain to the special session of Congress called in the spring of 1929: "We must not undermine initiative. There should be no fee or tax imposed upon the farmer. No governmental agency should engage in the buying and selling and price fixing of products."

The outcome of congressional deliberations, amid which the administration overcame an agrarian bloc in the Senate, was the Agricultural Marketing Act of June, 1929. The law provided for a federal farm board, conferred upon it large powers, and placed in its hand a revolving fund of half a billion dollars. Among other things the board was authorized to lend money to coöperative marketing associations, to aid in coördinating the work of such associations, and to set up "stabilizing corporations" for the purpose of storing, holding, and marketing certain commodities in the interest of higher price levels. In establishing this machinery, President Hoover and his supporters rejected the old agrarian demand for some form of crop control designed to prevent the ruin of the whole structure by a flood of "surplus" commodities.

Given the nature of the new administrative machine and its powers, only one favorable condition could have prevented a failure and the waste of the half-a-billion dollars, namely, an improvement of agricultural prices on the world market. That improvement did not occur. On the contrary farm production remained on a high level, the prices of produce fell rather than advanced, and the heroic, almost frantic, efforts of able men on the farm board were in vain. Millions of dollars designed to stabilize the market passed into the hands of private operators who were little if anything more than speculators. After a year's experience with the attempt to raise prices without reference to supply, it became painfully evident in Washington that the farm board was stuck fast in a maze. Soon agrarians were pointing to their former prophecies and girding themselves for a new law designed to combine crop control with price adjustment. The income of farmers in 1931 was far far below the return of the previous year.

Second on the program was the tariff. Republican leaders had declared that the rates were not high enough and during the campaign of 1928 industrialists had paid large sums of money into the Republican campaign fund in lively hopes of favors to come. Nor were they without some justification in events. Their European competitors, partly with the aid of American investors and bankers, had rehabilitated their industries and were prepared for a vigorous price war. New times, new circumstances.

In his campaign, Hoover had advocated a special session of Congress to make "limited changes in the tariff" and deal with agricultural relief. When Congress took up the revision of the customs duties, however, it did not confine itself to limited changes. In accordance with historic practice, the framing and adoption of the Hawley-Smoot tariff bill was accompanied by bitter wrangling in Congress. As usual, Democrats loudly condemned upward revisions in general and voted discreetly on particular items, such as sugar, textiles, and steel. In the end the bill made 1125 changes in the existing revenue law, of which 890 were upward, ranging on the average from thirty-one to thirty-four per cent.

When the bill finally emerged from Congress in June, 1930, it was greeted by protests in many quarters. Finance capitalists wondered how foreign debtors could force interest and installments over the high barriers thus erected. A large body of professors, offended by its schedules, filed a formal objection against this "perversion" of economic principles deemed inviolable. Undoubtedly the measure was for the President an unpleasant dose and after signing the bill he issued a studied defense of his action that savored of apology. But whatever Hawley and Smoot thought of his plea in abatement, they could rejoice that their tariff law was placed on the books.

After helping to throw the weight of the Government on the side of higher protection for industrialists, on their plea that it was necessary for a continuance of prosperity, President Hoover turned to applying another axiom of his economic philosophy, namely, that of keeping the Government out of any business that would yield a profit. The occasion for a practical demonstration of this axiom arose in connection with a power problem inherited from the previous administration at Muscle Shoals. When the goblin of "public power" reappeared, the President immediately bent his efforts to promoting the private ownership and operation of the government's property in the Tennessee Valley. If that end could not be achieved he was determined to prevent, at all costs, the production and distribution of electricity by direct government action. Any such step, the President insisted, would imprint the bar sinister of socialism upon the unblemished escutcheon of American politics. Yet the task to which he set himself called for watchfulness and labor on his part, for Senator Norris was augmenting, day by day, the forces resolved upon public ownership and operation of the power resources and facilities in controversy.

In this struggle, President Hoover's burden was increased by the stubbornness of the men whose enterprise he sought to favor: the price offered for Muscle Shoals by private capitalists had been so low and the terms of purchase so onerous that they annoyed even conservative Senators who shared Hoover's economic philosophy. His task was further complicated by revelations brought out at periodic hearings before the Federal Trade Commission and incorporated in the ensuing reports — revelations which dealt with the propaganda and lobbying tactics of the electrical utility concerns. It was shown that they had secretly subsidized newspapers and slipped their doctrines quietly into editorial columns. They had surreptitiously hired leaders in women's clubs, college professors, and publicity experts to promote their cause. To the chests of political parties they had contributed huge sums for election purposes. The "red badge" of communism they had deliberately pinned upon their opponents to discredit men and women who refused to accept their program wholesale. Some of their undercover activities were so gross that the more reputable utility magnates were themselves flustered; and metropolitan newspapers, normally inclined to belittle congressional inquiries, felt compelled to deplore such behavior.

Making effective use of these revelations, Senator Norris delivered in the upper house documented speeches that brought new recruits to his side; men accustomed to oppose his program now shrank from the appearance of evil which even seeming to favor the utilities implied. Under his leadership, Congress again passed, in 1931, a resolution providing for government operation of the power plants in case they could not be leased to private concerns within a year and on specific terms. For a moment the radiance of the golden glow was overcast.

While the Muscle Shoals measure was still pending at the capital, President Hoover made a public statement in which he treated the whole business as trivial and chid the national legislature for giving so much time to a matter of such slight importance. Having failed to defeat the resolution in Congress, he resorted to Coolidge tactics and applied the veto when it came to his desk. The bill, he said, would help to destroy "the initiative and enterprise" of the American people — the very source of prosperity and progress. The conditions imposed would make it impossible to find a responsible lessee among the concerns that might bid for the property. Enormous and unknown expenses would be involved in modernizing the plants. The resolution had provided that members of the government control board must believe in the wisdom and feasibility of the objects contemplated by the proposal. This, insisted the President, would make it impossible to find worthy men to accept positions on the board. Having disparaged and denounced the whole project, Hoover countered it with a proposal of his own. He advised Congress to authorize the creation of a commission empowered to lease the Muscle Shoals plant "in the interests of the local community and agriculture generally."

Taken in connection with the contemporary revelations by the Federal Trade Commission, the argument and tone of the President's message raised the political temperature in Congress, but not enough votes were marshaled to pass the measure over his veto. His opponents could merely prepare to take the issue to the country in the coming congressional election.

Although Hoover pleased business interests by signing the Hawley-Smoot tariff bill and by opposing government operation of power plants using public waters, he was not an extremist. He recognized that organized labor had a place in American economy and consequently set his approval on the Norris-La Guardia anti-injunction bill in March, 1932. This project had been no part of the official Republican program, although it bore the names of Republicans. In precise language the Act declared that employees should be free from coercion by employers and should have the right to bargain collectively through agents of their own choice. It outlawed "yellow dog" contracts in labor relations — contracts binding employees not to join trade unions. It forbade federal courts to issue restraining orders or injunctions contrary to the public policy so pronounced or contrary to any of the particularized stipulations of the Act, including provisions for open hearings in which the rights of employees were to be safeguarded. Carefully drawn with the aid of legal experts, this law marked an important stage in the development of federal labor legislation in the interests of collective bargaining. As such President Hoover accepted it, despite the protests of certain manufacturers who had worked against it openly or covertly during its progress through Congress. It did not, of course, "put the Government into business," but it lent government aid to the promotion of collective bargaining in business and was therefore somewhat alien to official normalcy. Nor was it exactly calculated to sustain the pristine liberty of enterprise.

§

In the field of foreign relations deemed normal, President Hoover, generally speaking, was loyal to the policies of previous Republican administrations. Like President Coolidge, he disclaimed the intention of overt aggression against any Latin republic to the south. Just before his inauguration he made a good-will tour of South America and after assuming office he took steps in the direction of friendly cooperation. From Nicaragua, he withdrew all the marines, except a "nucleus" engaged in training native guards. In 1930 a commission was sent to study conditions in Haiti which had been under American control since Wilson's administration. On the basis of its report Hoover announced that the natives would be aided in establishing "self-government" and that in due course diplomatic forms would be substituted for dominance through armed forces. Notwithstanding a number of trying incidents in relations with

Mexico, Hoover insisted on pacific adjustments in every case. Rattling the sword was foreign to his nature and poor economic policy in addition. To allay any possible doubts, his Secretary of State, Henry L. Stimson, publicly declared that the Monroe Doctrine, "far from being an assertion of suzerainty over our sister republics, was an assertion of their individual rights as independent nations." It was only by indirection, under the Platt Amendment, that the State Department sustained the cruel and despotic regime of Señor Machado in Cuba where American bankers and investors had enormous loans and credits at stake.

In respect of the Far East no equivocation was permitted. In that sphere, the doctrines of empire and intervention bequeathed by Admiral Mahan, Theodore Roosevelt, John Hay, and Henry Cabot Lodge were preserved and developed. When Congress enacted a bill in 1932 providing for the contingent independence of the Philippines, Hoover interposed with a veto. When the measure was repassed by the requisite two-thirds majority, he must have found pleasure in seeing it rejected by the Philippine legislature. Speaking of the Philippines, Warren Gamaliel Harding had said that "we ought to go on [there] with the same thought that impelled Him who brought a plan of salvation to the earth. . . . He gathered his disciples about him and said, 'Go ye and preach the gospel to all nations of the earth.'" In his veto message Hoover re-echoed these sentiments.

When Japanese armed forces invaded Manchuria in 1931, tore the province away from China, and proceeded to organize a puppet state under the dominion of Tokyo, that other formula of American policy in the Orient, the Open Door, confirmed by the Nine-Power Pact of 1922, was invoked by the Hoover administration. In January, 1932, the Secretary of State, Henry L. Stimson, dispatched to Japan a formal note calling attention to the Nine-Power Pact which declared respect for the administrative and territorial integrity of China and reaffirmed the doctrine of equal trading privileges. The note, in addition, curtly informed the Japanese foreign office that the United States "does not intend to recognize any situation, treaty, or agreement which may be brought about by means contrary to the covenants and obligations of the Pact of Paris" — the Kellogg renunciation of war as an instrument of national policy.

This stroke of state won hearty approval from two sources. The emphasis on Open Door interventionism appealed to American economic interests in the Far East and the ringing invocation of the Peace Pact expressed the pacific sentiments so widely entertained in the United States. The combination was powerful. Yet it was thwarted by the governments of Great Britain and France which failed to support the American position. The League of Nations toyed nervously with the dilemma and ended with a weak gesture. In the circumstances Japan defied the State Department of the United States, withdrew from the League of Nations, and held fast to her pound of flesh. Yet President Hoover laid claim to an achievement: "Above all I have projected a new doctrine into international affairs, the doctrine that we do not and never will recognize title to possession of territory gained in violation of the peace pacts."

From the Coolidge regime the Hoover administration had inherited an inflexible opposition to the recognition of Soviet Russia, a confidence in the approaching collapse of its economic system, and a tenacious will to avoid lending countenance to its ideology. This disapproval of Russia's attitude toward private property was reinforced by objections to the default on her foreign debts. To the Hughes formula of official non-intercourse with Soviet Russia, Hoover steadfastly adhered — a course which affected relations with Europe in general and particular.

The Coolidge administration had also transmitted a friendly interest in the World Court and a program for joining that tribunal, the appropriate papers for which President Hoover laid before the Senate, without however pressing hard for ratification. Retaining an interest in the

League of Nations, which sprang presumably from his warm
attachment to the concert of powers, the President made a
number of amiable overtures in that direction. In proceedings of the League which bore immediately upon American
economic interests or upon humane proposals, he participated
through official or unofficial delegates or observers. In
fact he went as far as he could, safely, in helping to uphold
the prestige of the League and sharing its counsels, while
being careful to disavow, in the language of Harding's time,
all American entanglements.

The crowning act of the Hoover administration in the
line of normalcy for foreign relations was the negotiation
of the London treaty of 1930 applying naval limitations to
cruisers, submarines, destroyers, and airplane carriers as
well as to the battleships restricted by the Washington
conference. An effort to accomplish this design had been
made at Geneva three years before, while Coolidge was at
the head of affairs, but that conference was unable to reach
an agreement. At Washington in 1922 the United States
had sacrificed ships. At Geneva an adjustment required
sacrifice on the part of Great Britain, and British naval
experts would have none of it. Their obstinacy, coupled with
that of American admirals and the propaganda of American
shipbuilding interests, eventuated in a deadlock, while
Japan looked on with Oriental satisfaction. But in 1930 circumstances were more propitious. The Labor premier, Ramsay Macdonald, was then directing the British government
and, after a personal visit from the British prime minister,
Hoover took the steps necessary to assure a conference in
London.

More astute than Wilson had been in 1918, Hoover associated with the American delegation two powerful Senators
— David A. Reed of Pennsylvania and Joseph Robinson
of Arkansas, leader on the Democratic side. After about
four months of haggling at London, the American, British,
and Japanese delegations arrived at an agreement respecting
cruisers, destroyers, and submarines for a term of six years.

In addition they revised the Washington settlement by suspending the replacement program and adopting a holiday for battleship construction until 1936. To this phase of the naval holiday, France and Italy also agreed.

Taken collectively, the details of the treaty marked merely a possible restriction on the expansion of naval expenditures, not a reduction in accordance with the expectations of peace advocates. But in explaining the agreement to the country, President Hoover expressed deep satisfaction: "The most vital feature of its great accomplishments for peace is the final abolition of competition in naval arms between the greatest naval powers and the burial of the fears and suspicions which have been the constant product of rival warship construction."

Nevertheless, in carrying through his program for limiting sea armaments and easing international tension for a freer flow of world commerce, Hoover found it necessary to overcome powerful shipping and naval interests at home. When the London treaty was laid before the country and the Senate for consideration, the customary gale blew against this "surrender to Great Britain," this "betrayal of American interests." The Hearst press, abetted by a few Senators including Hiram Johnson, was especially scurrilous. The Navy League sprang into unwonted activity. It issued broadsides against the treaty, and came very near to charging President Hoover with treason in "jeopardizing American national security." The passions of the Daughters of the American Revolution were also enlisted against the project. With this opposition a number of American admirals were in hearty accord. If their position forbade them to come out openly in the press, they took full advantage of the opportunity to aid their friends quietly and to voice their dissent at hearings opened by Senate committees. Owing to the volume of vocal and printed protests, the outlook for the treaty was gloomy at first and the Senate adjourned without acting upon the question of ratification.

Then Hoover and his supporters brought their strategy

to bear on the conflict. The President called a special session of the Senate to meet in July for the consideration of the London treaty. Hearings were held on the proposal by the Senate committee on foreign relations and the Senate committee on naval affairs; and the prime interests and ideas on both sides were thoroughly explored. Under the questioning of Senator David A. Reed the issue was narrowed to its substance: the London treaty fell short of the Navy Board's requirements "only with respect to the armament of three ships" and the armament of these three ships "with six-inch guns instead of eight-inch guns."

When Admiral Jones insisted that the point of the eight-inch guns was "vital," Senator Reed confronted the Admiral with a letter he had written a year before declaring that "there are conditions under which a six-inch gun unit would be of more value than an eight-inch gun unit." Additional probing disclosed the fact that the advantages of either type of unit would depend largely upon the weather and the fighting conditions, which no Admiral could possibly foresee. When Admiral Chase opposed the treaty before the Senate Committee and insisted upon discussing technicalities, Senator Reed bored into the Admiral's mentality. The Senator asked the Admiral whether he had ever commanded the fleet. The answer was, "No." He asked the Admiral whether he had ever been to sea on an eight-inch gun cruiser or seen one at target practice. Again the Admiral answered, "No." Then Senator Reed put to him the question: "Do you know how thick the armor on its turrets is?" When the Admiral replied, "I do," the Senator shot back: "How thick is it on the *Salt Lake City* class?" Thereupon the Admiral had to confess: "I do not recall the exact thickness now, sir." Although this type of inquisition may not have been entirely just to the admirals, it helped to weaken their prestige and prepare the way for the ratification of the treaty by the Senate.

From another angle, broadsides were let loose upon the opponents of the London treaty. In 1929, while President

Hoover was preparing for the London conference, it became known through a suit at law brought by one W. B. Shearer against shipbuilding companies that he had been a kind of paid lobbyist for them at the Geneva conference two years previously. In September the President publicly condemned propaganda designed to "create international distrust and hate," called upon shipping interests for an explanation, directed the Attorney General to consider taking action in the matter, and invited a Senate committee to go "to the very bottom" of the strange business. Under a Senate resolution a subcommittee of the committee on naval affairs started an inquiry into the activities of Shearer that ran through the autumn and winter, and brought powerful personalities and interests out into the open.

The Senate inquisitors were none too keen in their searching and repeatedly failed to press revealing questions, but they spread upon the public record one of the most unsavory stories in the long history of American scandals. The investigation showed that shipbuilding concerns and allied interests had hired Shearer to represent them at Geneva, that he had done all he could to defeat any settlement there, and that after the breakdown of the conference he had been employed as lobbyist general for big naval appropriations and merchant marine subsidies. Sworn testimony disclosed Shearer preparing propaganda articles for the Republican campaign committee in 1928, calling peace advocates traitors, attacking Charles E. Hughes as a betrayer of his country, writing speeches for representatives of the American Legion and the Daughters of the American Revolution in aid of a big navy and merchant marine, serving William Randolph Hearst as a propagandist for $2,000 a month, and maintaining confidential contacts with the Navy Department. Under direct questioning, distinguished figures in shipping circles — Charles M. Schwab, E. G. Grace, and C. L. Bardo, soon to be President of the Manufacturers Association, for example — twisted, turned, confessed inability to remember, or sought to put disreputable actions in the best possible guise.

Incidentally the Shearer inquiry threw the spot-light on the interests that had lobbied for the Jones-White Merchant Marine Bill enacted during the Coolidge administration. In that "enterprise" Shearer had been employed and had served his employers faithfully. On the record of the Senate subcommittee was placed a letter from C. L. Bardo, vice president of the New York Ship Building Company, which put the lobby costs for this bill at $150,000, including $30,000 for "publicity and advertising," $26,000 for "services of experts," and $23,000 for "hotel expenses in Washington." Speaking of the undercover achievement, Mr. Bardo said in his letter: "This activity was carried on in the interests of the shipper, shipbuilder, shipowner, and suppliers of materials used in ship construction." Since heavy expenditures had been incurred in securing legislation advantageous to these interests, Mr. Bardo called upon several beneficiaries to pay the bill: for instance, the General Electric Company, the Bath Iron Works, the Worthington Pump and Machinery Company, and the American Brown Boveri Electric Corporation.

All this and more, combined with Senator Reed's grilling of naval experts, temporarily aroused a certain moral indignation in the country and facilitated the ratification of the London Naval Treaty. On July 21, 1930, the Senate set its seal of approval on the document by a vote of fifty-eight to nine. "It will renew again the faith of the world in the moral forces of good-will and patient negotiation," said Hoover, "as against the blind forces of suspicion and competitive armament."

§

For nearly ten years, it so came about, great business interests, to whose ingenuity and initiative the prosperity of the golden glow was attributed by admiring editors and publicists, pursued their course of "free enterprise" without encountering insurmountable barriers. They demanded higher tariffs and their demand was granted. They called for a material reduction in the heavy taxes on large incomes, to release money for the expansion of industry, and their argument was accepted. They besought the Government to refrain from producing electric power on the public domain and along navigable waters and distributing it directly to consumers, and their beseeching was heeded. Under the easy laws of indulgent states, they formed corporations, investment trusts, and holding companies, ever larger and more intricate in structure; they issued stocks and bonds at pleasure within the mild terms of generous legislation — without submitting their accounts and valuations to the scrutiny of federal inquisitors. They wanted to be let alone; and in all those years not a single major statute adversely affecting their rights of property was written in the law books of the Union.

Abroad as well as at home, business interests enjoyed the favor and protection of a benevolent government. Throughout the insular possessions of the American empire they reaped the benefits of preferential tariffs drawn against alien competitors. Peace they deemed necessary to the pursuits of civilian trade; for nearly ten years peace reigned; and it was sealed by an almost universal pact renouncing war as an instrument of national policy. Soldiers, sailors, and marines guarded their outposts in troublesome places beyond the jurisdiction of the United States. Ships from a powerful navy sailed the waters of seven oceans fulfilling the pledge of the Navy Department to keep the sea lanes open and promote American commerce. A corps of alert agents from the Department of Commerce scoured every nook and cranny of the world in the service of business interests, hunting opportunities for them to sell goods, lend money, and invest in foreign mills, mines, and stores. If difficulties arose, willing ministers, ambassadors, and consuls intervened on behalf of American nationals. A representative of the State Department spoke truly when he declared to an assembly of exporting merchants that the Secretary of Commerce, Mr. Hoover, "is your advance agent," and the Secretary of State, Mr. Kellogg, "is your attorney"; and he might well have added that the navy is a guarantee that your advance agent and attorney will speak as men having authority even in the distant places of the earth. In the economy of things, those who were let alone in their ways had eager and obedient servants, when, in any hour of stress, they needed aid and protection under the power and renown of the Republic. Not without visible evidence and plain reason did they pronounce their world good and look forward with confidence to its perpetuity.

# CHAPTER II

## *Dissolutions*

EARLY in the autumn of 1929, while Congress was seeking to strengthen the colors of the golden glow by raising the tariff still higher, out of the sky came flashes of lightning and rolls of thunder that were heard around the world and harrowed the guardians of the National Shrine with "fear and wonder." On September 5, there was a wild break in stocks on the New York Exchange; and Roger Babson, watcher of business indices, predicted that "sooner or later" a general crash would bring a decline ranging from sixty to eighty points. September 24, news of another sharp explosion in the market sped over the wires; the next day a check was announced; three days later a steep downward slide sent alarms in every direction. September 29, Arthur Cutten, the great plunger in speculations, a specimen from ancient times, issued a proclamation that he was "a bull on stocks" and that even twelve billion dollars in brokers' loans for speculative purposes "would not be unduly large." October 3 and 4, occurred the largest breaks of the year, followed by a few days of hesitation and a cable from London in which

Charles E. Mitchell, of the National City Bank, exclaimed in dulcet tones: "American markets generally are now in a healthy condition." The report was an exaggeration. When on October 16 a committee of the Investment Bankers Association admitted that speculation had reached a danger point and that many stocks were far above their intrinsic values, industrial and utility equities swept downward in an avalanche. For a week rallies and breaks alternated, with a drop ranging from five to ninety-six points on October 23. A great fright was creeping over the realm of high finance and brokers were calling for more margins as selling orders poured in from the provinces.

At eleven o'clock on the morning of Thursday, October 24, came a shock that was soon felt in the four corners of the earth: for a number of stocks listed on the New York Exchange no buyers could be found at any price. And on all securities, including these very stocks, member banks of the Federal Reserve system had outstanding loans to brokers and dealers amounting to $6,634,000,000 — a sum larger than the average volume of money in circulation throughout the United States during the preceding year. Evidently in this hour the "situation" was portentous for the bankers themselves. For months they had sat in their offices lending money for the great game at the National Shrine, accepting as security the stocks in which manipulations were carried on. Now the very paper in their hands was swiftly becoming valueless. But if they called their loans suddenly, they would accelerate the precipitous decline of "values" already under way.

They were, in other words, caught between two fires and some ingenious action was necessary if they were to save themselves. About noon Thomas Lamont, of the J. P. Morgan Company, summoned the representatives of four great banks to the throne room at Broad and Wall Streets, and allowed news of the event to be flashed to the press and brokers' houses from the center to the circumference of the American empire. Were Lords of Creation to assume dominion, stop the downward course of stocks, and rescue the sinking? With bated breath, victims of the pinch awaited an answer.

About 1:15 of that very day, it arrived, or something taken for an answer came. With a firm stride, Richard Whitney, floor operator for the Morgan Company, walked to the trading post for United States Steel in the Exchange and bid 205 for a large order of Steel shares, which stood at the moment at 193½. The effect was electric. Reports of the order ran out over the wires to newspapers and brokers from one end of the country to the other. Before the calming effect of this news had passed, floor traders under instructions from bankers began to make offers for stocks that in the morning of that day had found few buyers or none at all. With the swiftness of wind, stocks rallied.

A miracle had taken place under the command of the masters of economic destiny. So, at least, it appeared. After a meeting of the Federal Reserve Board in the afternoon, attended by Secretary Mellon, the Treasury announced that "business is fundamentally sound" and that the troubles were due to "bear raids." From far and wide reverberated echoes so uniform that they seemed inspired. The financial wizard of the Cleveland Trust Company, Leonard P. Ayres, poured into eager ears the explanation that the crash was a "security panic, with no economic basis. . . . A rally tomorrow is in order." From his point of observation and interest, Charles E. Mitchell saw "nothing to worry about." Not to be outdone in the transmission of glad tidings, President Hoover added his reassurance: "The fundamental business of the country, that is, production and distribution of commodities, is on a sound and prosperous basis." With a confidence omniscient, the president of the Equitable Trust issued a ukase: "There will be no repetition of the break of yesterday. I have no fear of another comparable decline."

Indeed the tone and unanimity of the auspicious chorus could not have been more perfect if all had been prearranged. The president of the American International Corporation, as if expressing the surmises of sound business everywhere, gave special thanks: "I think we are all indebted to the four gentlemen who met on the corner yesterday and through their action steadied the whole situation." In an oration that filled two solid columns of print, Charles Schwab explained that the country was prosperous and that the steel business was good. From Philadelphia came a solemn confirmation by Samuel Vauclain, of the Baldwin Locomotive Company; from Chicago, the corroboration of George M. Reynolds, of the Continental Illinois Bank and Trust Company. To such reports ostentatiously spread over the pages of the next morning's papers was added an authentic statement that a consortium of six members, representing great banks, had been formed, not to push up prices, "but to furnish a cushion of purchasing power against the recurrence of any such condition as Thursday." With the perspicacity customary in such circumstances, newspapers and stock dealers spoke affectionately of "the Big Six" as "Saviors of the Market." Heaving sighs of relief, brokers went about their business as usual on Friday morning, October 25. The market steadied and rose.

For the unsophisticated public, including brokers and speculators, the marvelous act of prestidigitation had been exhilarating, if mystifying. The Lords of Creation were in their places after all. But just what had the Big Six done? When questioned by eager reporters, Thomas Lamont replied that he did not know, although in the following January he allowed some inklings to escape. Whatever it was, the possible results became evident in a very few days after their act of thaumaturgy. As the market steadied, the bankers concerned had an opportunity to call in enough loans to save their margins of security and thus avoid heavy losses themselves, while slowly feeding into the markets the stocks they had bought, perhaps at a profit for the participants. Whether they took full advantage of their opportunity the records of history did not disclose. But one thing was certain. If "Saviors of the Market," they were not "Saviors of Mankind," for they soon refused to hold the promised "cushion" under falling prices. When the roar of the storm was renewed four days afterward, they cast off the role as "Saviors," even of the Market, stepped swiftly aside, and let the hurricane rage. Had they merely saved their own skins on October 24 ? Were they really Lords of Creation after all ? Or were they lords who deliberately declined to exercise their prerogatives ? Or were they merely bannerets and Sancho Panzas ? Had the rejoicing over their feat been merely the conquest of reason by delusion ? The haruspex of the National Shrine made no reply. On October 29, events vouchsafed the answers.

On that day, shortly after the New York Stock Exchange opened, the bottom almost fell out of the buyers' market. Only sellers appeared in force and they dumped hundreds and thousands of shares into this well-nigh bottomless pit at any prices that were offered. Down, down, down, dropped prices as the throng of brokers milled and shouted around the posts of the specialists who were supposed to have buyers for all comers. Out in the streets early editions of newspapers announced the calamity. Worried by the scare-headed reports, small holders and large rushed to increase the flood of selling orders. Over humming telephones brokers called upon their customers for more margins before it was too late. As the volume of business swelled through the day, wires were blocked with messages that could not be delivered in time to save speculators from a complete sell-out. When at last the gong rang out the closing hour, stock tickers were far behind in their reports, brokers' offices were in a pandemonium, and efforts to reach distracted victims with final news were still being made, in vain. It seemed, to use Edmund Burke's phrase, that "the architects of ruin" had completed their work. In the tumult of the day a record turnover of 16,410,000 shares was registered and the average price of fifty stock leaders fell almost forty points. Amid the repercussions of the explosion, bankers and brokers gathered in little groups, plunged to and from hurried conferences, seeking explanation, hope, and policy in preparation for the morrow.

Day after day during the remaining months of the year rallies alternated with collapses at the National Shrine, as optimism vied with despair in the bosoms of buyers and sellers. Entries chosen from the financial chronology in the American Year Book help to represent the starkness of the oscillations and the tumultuous emotions of personalities. October 30, "stocks rally as Rockefellers announce they are buying stocks." November 6, "stocks break 5 to 66 points." November 8, "trading quieter, prices lower." November 12, "violent collapse in stocks." November 13, "stocks break with great violence." November 15, "recovery in stocks." November 21, a White House conference announces large construction expenditures and Henry Ford makes a statement in Washington; "stocks advance." December 3, "Hoover's message to Congress expresses optimism, covering all aspects of trade and industry. Stocks rally while message reaches New York." December 12, "stocks decline in the widest break since November 12." December 13, "after further dip, market rallies sharply in late trading." December 19, "stocks decline in brisk trading." Through the rest of the winter declines, rallies, and dullness marked the course of fear and indecision. In the spring of 1930 decision turned to distrust. May 2, "wave of liquidation on stock exchange." May 3, "another violent break in stocks." June 6, "market weak." June 7, "another sharp break." June 8, "stocks break heavily." June 10, "recovery in stocks." For men and women whose affections were centered on such values, the alternation of faith and doubt was heart-rending. In the place of wild enthusiasm had come utter dejection. The mightiest Julius had fallen and "the sheeted dead did squeak and gibber in the Roman streets."

§

Within a few months after the first explosions on the Stock Exchange, underlying forces and realities were revealed in the events and conditions of industry, agriculture, and social living. Neither records nor figures permit, nor does the character of written discourse allow, an accurate description, a photographic portrayal in full proportions of the total drama running through four turbulent years — the scenes of unfolding distress with all the human tragedy and comedy that accompanied the gigantic pageant. Yet a part of the story was told in the cold and forbidding figures that registered those aspects of the drama susceptible of mathematical enumeration.

With some appropriateness a beginning could be made with the downward rushes of the stock market. Between September, 1929, and January, 1933, according to the Dow-Jones index of stock prices, 30 industrials fell from an average of 364.9 to 62.7 dollars per share. A group of 20 public utilities stocks dropped from 141.9 to 28.0 dollars per share. Twenty railroad stocks declined from an average of 182.0 to 28.1 dollars per share. Other indices recorded the same catastrophe. According to The New York Times index of 50 stocks (25 industrials and 25 railroads), the average price fell from 300.52 to 58.65 dollars per share. A compilation by the Standard Statistics Company (Inc.) of 421 stocks (351 industrials, 37 public utilities, and 33 railroads) based upon an index number of 100 as the 1926 monthly average, showed a decline from 225.2 to 49.1 from September, 1929, to January, 1933. According to the same source and during the same period, the index of 20 New York bank stocks fell from 357.8 to 67.9.

High among the indices of changing economic status and personal distress throughout the country were the increasing suspensions of banks. In mere financial crashes of this type there was, to be sure, little new. Between 1920 and 1929 about 5,000 banks with deposits of $1,500,000,000 had collapsed, but those failures had occurred mainly in rural regions and reflected principally the economic misfortunes of farmers and their dependent merchants. Now the normal rate of suspensions leaped upward. Between June 30, 1929, and June 30, 1930, 640 banks suspended, as against 549 for the

previous corresponding period. During the next fiscal year
1553 banks closed their doors, tying up over a billion dollars
in deposits, as compared with $345,000,000 in the previous
season. For the first ten months of 1932, the number of
bank suspensions was 1199 and the impounded depositors'
funds amounted to $605,000,000.

If this marked a turn in the tide, a promise of restoration,
as contended by financiers, the thought brought no consolation or relief to the millions of people whose savings were
caught in the vise and whose prospects of full recovery were
at best dubious. Moreover as the season of calamity advanced, banks in great cities — New York, Pittsburgh,
Washington, Cleveland, and Chicago — went under, with
detonations that sent tremors throughout the financial system. If such institutions could explode, where did safety lie
and what disaster could come next?

Scarcely less significant than banks in the generality of
economic indications were the railroads. Their tracks penetrated every region, city, and important community of the
country. Their car loadings registered in a large measure the
output of industrial plants and the movement of goods.
Their passenger receipts reflected the activities of business
life, the economic power of multitudes to travel and enjoy
leisure, and the condition of hotels, resorts, even whole towns
and regions, dependent upon travelers. And now for three
successive years, railways reported a decline in the movement
of goods and passengers and a shrinkage of earnings. Early
in the depression weaker lines began to default on their bonds
and pass into the hands of conservators or receivers. During
the first four years of the cataclysm in transportation approximately 45,000 miles of railway passed under the jurisdiction
of trustees, receivers, or bankruptcy courts. Before a positive
check appeared in the precipitous descent, great systems had
become derelicts — for example, the Wabash; the Chicago,
Milwaukee, and St. Paul; the Chicago and Northwestern;
the Missouri Pacific; the St. Louis and San Francisco; and
the New York, New Haven and Hartford. Finding their

revenues diminishing, railroad managers reduced their purchases of locomotives and materials, discharged employees by
the thousands, and reduced the working hours of operatives
kept in service. Only by acute management and with the aid
of loans from the Reconstruction Finance Corporation did
huge companies, such as the New York Central and the
Baltimore and Ohio, manage to survive. In other words a
twenty-billion dollar industry was crippled in vital parts and
the ramifications of its recession spread in every direction.

In other divisions of the economic system, disequilibrium,
as certain economists called it, superseded ideal poise. In
January, 1931, the United States Steel Corporation reported
that its earnings for the previous December were the lowest
for any month since February, 1915. In the spring of 1932
came the smash of Samuel Insull's "two billion dollar empire" in public utilities and the collapse was followed by the
flight of the magnate to Greece. In the autumn the real
estate bond house of S. W. Straus and Company in New York
City went into a receiver's hands, leaving millions in bonds
outstanding, most of them in default. This breakdown was
soon succeeded by the failure of older and more conservative
establishments of the same kind. All in all, it was estimated,
at least six billion of the ten billion dollars in "sound real
estate securities" dropped into default and millions were sold
by the victims at prices ranging from six to fifteen cents on
the dollar. In the aggregate, business failures for the first
nine months of 1932 were reported as 23,798 against 20,311
for the corresponding period in 1931 and 16,030 for the same
period of 1929.

In a survey published by the Guaranty Trust Company,
an institution not given to pessimistic statements, the workings of the American system were set forth in bald terms:
"Measured by almost any of the accepted standards of economic welfare, the year 1932, taken as a whole, was a period
of deeper depression than 1931. The production and distribution of commodities were at lower levels; unemployment was
greater; the earnings of business enterprises were smaller and

losses were larger, and commercial failures were more numerous. Prices in general continued to decline, although the
downward trend was interrupted by an advance during the
third quarter of the year. Distress among the farming population was increased by the further drastic decline in prices
of agricultural commodities." In this darkened sky, the one
star of hope to which the survey could point was a falling off
in the number of bank failures. But given the state of business and agriculture in general, this reversal of a single trend
may have meant merely that the house-cleaning of weaker
institutions was drawing toward an end. However interpreted, the fair prospect that Calvin Coolidge had acclaimed
in 1928 was sadly marred and the Lords of Creation, deemed
"the rulers of America" a short time before, were powerless
to restore its aurorean lineaments.

Upon industrial workers the dissolution of prosperity fell
with terrific weight. Even in the perfect time of President
Coolidge's prosperity, the number of unemployed, it was estimated, averaged about 2,000,000 a year. No precise figures
of unemployment were available as crashes on the Stock
Exchange followed one another with startling sharpness; but
according to the reckonings of William Green, president of
the American Federation of Labor, industrial workers were
rapidly "deflated." In April, 1930, 2,954,000 persons were
out of work; by October, 1930, the number had increased to
3,924,000; by October, 1931, the total unemployed had risen
to 6,801,000; and by October, 1932, the total stood at
10,908,000. During the first two months of 1933, the number
rose to 12,000,000, and less reliable estimates placed it even
higher. The Federal Reserve Board's unadjusted combined
index of factory employment (with the monthly average of
1923–1925 as 100) catapulted from 105.4 in September, 1929,
to 58.1 in January, 1933; and this was regarded as a conservative reckoning.

The social consequences of unemployment were quickly
registered in the clamor for relief in the great industrial
centers. A survey of 126 cities, made in 1932, representing

56 per cent of the urban population of the United States, reported relief aid to 823,894 families in May, 1932, as against 386,151 families of the previous year. Relief expenditures of New York City set at approximately one million dollars in October, 1929, rose to nine and a half millions in February, 1933. The Committee on the Costs of Medical Care reported "appalling" conditions in the South where the incomes of the people in ten southern states were so low that they were unable to purchase adequate treatment.

While industrial workers slid down hill, the descent of farmers was expedited, despite President Hoover's Agricultural Marketing Act. During the post-war decade the value of farm property decreased by twenty billion dollars; more than 450,000 farmers lost their farms; farm tenancies increased by more than 200,000; and the gross annual farm income dropped from sixteen to eleven billion dollars. Then came the crisis of 1929. Between that year and 1932 farm values suffered another decline of thirty-three per cent and the gross annual income of farmers shrank fifty-seven per cent. Between 1920 and January, 1933, the prices received by farmers for their produce fell from an index number of 205 to fifty-one. Measured by the same index the prices of goods the farmers bought dropped only from 206 to 105 during that span of years.

Though industries slumped, profits diminished, unemployment increased, and farm distress intensified, the burden of private and public debts, once deemed evidences of national prosperity and confidence, remained nominally fixed; and it was an Atlas burden. In a statement placed before the Senate Finance Committee investigating economic conditions, Irving Fisher of Yale University estimated the total debts owing in the United States in 1929 at 234 billions of dollars as compared with the 362 billions reckoned as the total wealth of the United States. According to a compilation of the National Industrial Conference Board, the total interest-bearing debt was estimated at $154,761,000,000 in 1929. This death grip on economy embraced a farm indebtedness of approximately twelve and a quarter billions, a steam-railroad debt of twelve and three-quarter billions, a total public debt of over thirty billions, a corporate debt of close to seventy-five billions, and individual indebtedness (other than farmers') of twenty-five billions. After three years of deflation and liquidation, the debt still totaled 134 billion dollars according to a study of the Twentieth Century Fund released in the spring of 1933. During the same period the national income had fallen from eighty-five to forty billions of dollars.

All these blows of misfortune were borne for many months with a remarkable fortitude. Then a definite change in temper took place in the spring of 1932. In May the railway brotherhoods presented a plea to President Hoover, containing an ominous emphasis. "Mr. President," it stated, "we have come here to tell you that unless something is done to provide employment and relieve distress among the families of the unemployed, we cannot be responsible for the orderly operations of the railroads of this country — that we will refuse to take the responsibility for the disorder which is sure to arise if conditions continue. . . . The unemployed citizens whom we represent will not accept starvation while the two major political parties struggle for control of government. . . . We are not Socialists, we are not Communists, nor are we anarchists. . . . There is a growing demand that the entire business and social structure be changed because of the general dissatisfaction with the present system. We cannot longer ignore this situation."

First in the West and rapidly throughout the country, whole communities turned to barter in the effort to provide relief and break the business stagnation; to force a resurgence in exchange of goods and services. More than 144 organizations in scores of communities in 29 states were reported by Stuart Chase to be turning to barter, to "wooden money," to self-liquidating printed scrip. As 1932 drew to a close, farmers were "on the march" to prevent foreclosure sales, to stop the production and sale of commodities until a fair

price was assured, to end tax sales, to cut down the principal
of farm mortgages, and to reduce the interest rates. The law
was either reluctant or unable to cope with them and violence
broke out here and there. In the East, industrial labor was
growing equally restless. In a statement published in the
January issue of the magazine, Nation's Business, William
Green declared: "The American trade-union movement has
been patient. . . . We gave government every opportunity
to produce a remedy. We gave management every opportunity to produce a remedy. We gave finance every opportunity. . . . We agreed to refrain from drastic action if
employers would refrain from drastic action. . . . Finally,
after three years of suffering we, the organized workers,
declare to the world, enough; we shall use our might to
compel the plain remedies withheld by those whose mis-
feasance caused our woe."

§

During the early stages of the stock market collapse, prognosticators and soothsayers in high finance, almost without
exception, from Irving Fisher of Yale University to Andrew
W. Mellon, Secretary of the Treasury, took the position that
the downward course of stocks had little or no relation to
the real state of transactions in industry and agriculture.
With droning reiteration, they insisted that "business, that
is, the production and distribution of commodities," was
sound; that only "the lunatic fringe" of speculators was
affected by the decline in paper values; and that the mass of
the people would remain secure in their homes and employments. "The nation will make steady progress in 1930,"
maintained Secretary Mellon in his words of good cheer on
New Year's Day, ". . . I see nothing in the present situation that is either menacing or warrants pessimism." From
President Hoover in the White House early in May, 1930,
came the message: "We have now passed the worst." And
in October came confirmation: "The income of a large part
of our people has not been reduced."

In the lush days of the rising market it had been generally assumed that stock prices bore a close relation to the condition and movement of actual production and distribution. Indeed the very justification for the market itself had been that it performed a vital function in bringing capital funds into business enterprise; that it served as a place for the adjustment of prices to business realities and through the knowledge and intuition of brokers kept a fair equilibrium in the relation of liquid claims to intrinsic values. Now this justification in terms of classical economy seemed to be rudely cast aside, and the conclusion was drawn by persons in high places that the stock market was a kind of "racket" where speculators had engaged in reckless operations, bearing no reasoned relations to the actual transactions of business itself. Such a verdict coming from leaders in banking, industry, and politics served to unsettle the faith of the people in the merits of the National Shrine and the authenticity of the auspices. In time this loss of faith was to plague many authors of the idea.

With their hearts chilled by repeated disappointments, pontifices among the Lords of Creation took a second line of prognosis. Industries were actually slowing down, dividends were really being passed, and unemployment was rapidly increasing. Facts sinister and brutal were visible to the blindest of prophets. Then what could be said about them? The answer made in the second line of prognosis was that industrial depression had in fact come upon the country, that there had been several such setbacks in American history, and that the nation had always come out of them into a bigger and better prosperity. "I believe," said Secretary Mellon as the year 1930 wore on, "that just as soon as much of the products in the market at present are disposed of, the business depression will better itself. Curtailment of output, without question, will correct the present condition within a short time." This rested upon actual experience and had the ring of practicality. The oil, aluminum, and other industries in which the Secretary was heavily interested were already retrenching, laying off workers, reducing the surplus on the market, and thus preparing for the correction of conditions, as correction was understood.

By the middle of 1931, President Hoover himself was convinced that the stock market gyrations revealed at least a certain unsoundness in business, a shrinkage of production and distribution, a reduction in the people's income. Speaking to the Indiana Editorial Association on June 15, he too took the second line of prognosis, with trust in Providence as a form of re-insurance. The blight of the depression, he said, "stretches from all quarters of the globe to every business place and every cottage door in our land." But "depressions are not new experiences, though none has hitherto been so widespread. We have passed through no less than fifteen major depressions in the last century. We have learned something as the result of each of these experiences. From this one we shall gain stiffening and economic discipline, a greater knowledge upon which we must build a better safeguarded system. We have come out of each previous depression into a period of prosperity greater than ever before. We shall do so this time. . . . Surplus money does not remain idle for long. . . . Whatever the immediate difficulties may be, we know they are transitory in our lives and in the life of the nation. We should have full faith and confidence in those mighty resources, those intellectual and spiritual forces which have impelled this nation to a success never before known in the history of the world. Far from being impaired, these forces were never stronger than at this moment. Under the guidance of Divine Providence they will return to us a greater and more wholesome prosperity than we have ever known."

§

Accompanying the declines and dissolutions in domestic economy were widening fissures in the empire of overseas finance and commerce that had also presented glowing prospects on the morning when President Coolidge left the White

House. From day to day came the news that foreign countries had defaulted on bonds bought by American investors with such avidity under the advice and pressure of bankers and their salesmen. By the close of 1932 more than a billion dollars' worth of bonds in American hands, it was officially estimated, were frozen, representing losses in Austria, Bolivia, Brazil, Bulgaria, Chile, Colombia, Costa Rica, Cuba, Ecuador, El Salvador, Greece, Hungary, Panama, Peru, Uruguay, and Yugoslavia. Soon billions invested in Germany were in default or in a paralysis which brought a steep decline on the market, as frightened investors sought to save something from the wreckage. Although the bonds of Italy and Poland escaped default, they staggered downward in prices amid the great fear. As European dictators closed in on the economies of their respective countries, American owners and investors entangled in fixed properties were glad to effect settlements which let them out of the debris holding some of their capital intact. With wry faces Americans who had lent money to German municipalities for the construction of model dwellings saw their bonds in real or virtual default, while millions of their countrymen still lived in substandard houses, in shacks, and in crude shanties pieced together by the unemployed.

The downward swoop in foreign commerce was likewise disconcerting to guardians of that once expanding empire. In 1929 the export of merchandise reached the towering value of $5,240,995,000 under the stimulus of lavish lending abroad. In 1932 it totalled only $1,611,000,000. Since American investors, irked by defaults on old loans, were in no mood to throw good money after bad, the outlook for lifting the export total was not encouraging. Moreover foreign governments were building barriers against the influx of goods, sometimes for purely fiscal ends and at other times for the deliberate purpose of curtailment or exclusion. France, for example, made horizontal increases against selected countries under the device of an "exchange compensation tax." In aid of such limitations other governments employed a quota system, fixing the specific amounts of particular commodities for which entry was to be allowed. Partly on fiscal and partly on commercial grounds, foreign governments also resorted to a control of currency exchanges in such a manner as to restrain the import of commodities. Building on earlier legislation of a restricted character, the British government practically abandoned its historic "free trade policy" in 1932 and went over to a general scheme of protection, under which preferences were devised for British possessions. Meanwhile Latin-American governments that had generally maintained uniform tariff fronts against all countries began to negotiate special agreements with selected countries, offering concessions in exchange for concessions — a privilege of which Great Britain was not slow to take advantage.

In other crises, a serious decline in exports had chiefly affected American agriculture, for in former times the major portion of the export had been composed of farm products. But in 1929 non-agricultural products, including manufactures and machinery, constituted far more than one-half the total export. This shift, so significant for domestic politics, had been recognized by leaders in the formulation of American policy. As early as 1926, Herbert Hoover, speaking then as Secretary of Commerce to exporters in New York, gave his interpretation of the trend: "Foreign trade has become a vital part of the whole modern economic system. . . . In peace time our exports and imports are the margins upon which our well-being depends. . . . The great problem in our foreign trade, however, is the export of goods in which we compete with other nations — but if we are intelligent we should be able to command our share of them. Our most competitive group is that of manufactured goods, and expansion of the exports of our manufactured goods is of the utmost importance to us. As our population increases we shall consume more of our foodstuff. . . . If we are to maintain the total volume of our exports and consequently our buying power for imports, it must be by steady pushing of our manufactured goods."

With the aid of American loans and the drumming agents of the Federal Government, business men had pushed the sale of "our manufactured goods." And in the crisis of the depression they, as well as farmers, were caught in the shrinkage of international trade. In earlier days exporters and importers, especially on the Atlantic seaboard, had been the chief promoters of foreign commerce, on which they thrived under the comforting phrases of classical economics. In 1930 powerful manufacturers catering to foreign markets, disturbed, if not wrecked, by the slump, joined the importers and exporters in the search for a way out of the dilemma presented by the decline in the sale of finished goods abroad. If, for example, textile industries engrossing the home market could still rejoice in the protection afforded by tariff barriers, manufacturers of automobiles, cigarette-making machinery, and typewriters, for example, had no need of it and could be vocal on the side of "getting foreign trade started again." But all their drumming could not restore the boom of former days; neither could reason nor a fairy's wand.

§

As thousands of constituents mourned over defaulted foreign bonds in their strong boxes, as receivers for banks in calamity excavated from their vaults paper in the form of Peruvian sixes or Cordoba sevens, a great clatter arose in the "provinces" where, as Dwight Morrow of the Morgans once explained, bankers had distributed such "securities." From the "provinces," the clamor reached Washington. How had this ruin come to pass? What did it all mean? Who was responsible for the downfall of "values" and "investment opportunities"? Responding to the cries of pain and wonder, the United States Senate ordered its finance committee to investigate the whole business "at the earliest possible moment," and authorized the committee to apply the penalties of the law to witnesses who failed to comply with the summons or refused to answer "any question pertinent to the investigation."

On December 18, 1931, the inquiry opened. Great men among the Lords of Creation were called before the committee and invited to explain the amazing rise and decline of foreign financing — such as Thomas Lamont, of J. P. Morgan; Otto Kahn, of Kuhn, Loeb; Charles E. Mitchell, of the National City; Winthrop Aldrich, of the Chase National; Clarence Dillon, of Dillon, Read; James Speyer, of Speyer and Company; Joseph Swan, of the Guaranty Company; and Frederick Strauss, of J. and W. Seligman. To these experts in finance were added representatives of the Departments of State and Commerce, under whose sympathetic auspices the foreign lending had been so effectively advanced, and Professor Edwin Walter Kemmerer of Princeton University, "the magic money doctor," who had helped to put "on a sound footing" some of the foreign governments whose finances were now in difficulties. If these gentlemen could not enlighten the Senate and the country, where did hope of enlightenment rest?

In the more than two thousand pages of testimony and documents, the history and existing state of things were more or less exposed to public gaze and astonishment. Despite much confusion, forgetfulness, bickering, and hesitation, several lines of relevant fact and opinion were developed. Under what conception of things had come about all this money lending from which calamities had eventuated? Were the bankers, engaged in promoting foreign loans, thinking of economic advantages for the people of the United States? Or were they thinking of something else? Otto Kahn answered categorically that the object of the promoting banker "is and must be beyond all other things America's prosperity, not merely from the point of view of a patriotic and decent citizen, but from the point of view of his own pocket. The international banker's profit, even in the case of foreign bonds, is made in this country, and not abroad." He was, in other words, not solely actuated by private interest.

While conceding that in specific cases the business of foreign lending might have been "overdone," Thomas Lamont said: "I should think that American commerce had in the long run benefited very greatly by these loans." Bankers had supplied capital to European countries denuded by war; they had aided in the rehabilitation of foreign industries; they had contributed to stabilization abroad; they had assisted in restoring "the normal course of commerce." Returning to the main issue, the effect of foreign loans upon the United States, Mr. Lamont was emphatic: "I go so far as to say that not only have they contributed very materially to the maintenance during those years of our foreign trade, but that they have contributed very materially to the capacity of the borrowing governments to enable them to discharge their obligations when due, and punctually, to the United States Government." If the bankers, in the pursuit of profits, had made genuflections to graven images, they had, it appeared, also served patriotism.

The broad and pleasing generalizations uttered by such men of expertness and authority as Otto Kahn and Thomas Lamont were allowed by the Senate committee to pass as authentic evidence, as if disposing of the issue. But when Charles E. Mitchell, of the National City Bank, declared that "foreign investments very largely control the volume of the export business of the United States," that they should have "a sound basis of desirability to the most critically patriotic of Americans," and that the banking interests concerned deserved praise, not criticism, the committee called for proof instead of assertion. Senator Couzens asked Mr. Mitchell what proportion of the billions invested abroad went into the manufacture of goods that had formerly been made in the United States. The witness confessed: "That I cannot answer, sir." The Senator then asked the banker whether it was not a fact that American capital had gone to foreign countries and engaged there in manufacturing to avoid paying their tariff duties on American goods. To this the banker responded in the affirmative. By open confession, therefore, exported capital had to some extent cut into the production and profits of domestic industries, and had not contributed to American prosperity and patriotism obviously, if at all. Following this thread, the Senator inquired "what percentage" of the total exported capital was employed in cutting down domestic business. The banker admitted that he did not know. Since it took knowledge to establish the validity of a generalization, the bankers failed to substantiate their thesis of automatic beneficence and patriotism, though they refrained from introducing Adam Smith's "invisible hand" of God to save their argument.

After the testimony of exporting bankers had raised some doubts respecting the national advantages derived from all this lending of money to foreign countries, Francis P. Garvan, speaking for the Chemical Foundation, laid before the Senate committee a list of American loans that had been made to competing chemical concerns abroad. Referring to the chemical industry specifically, Mr. Garvan gave his view of what had actually happened: "These international bankers . . . have been persistently borrowing the savings of the American people and, for the bribe of huge commissions, have been loaning these savings to the international chemical cartel, or its constituent companies, or allies, the cartel whose success is necessarily based upon the destruction of our industry and our independence. . . . Our chemical industry is faced not only in our own country, but throughout the world, with competitors whose pockets are filled with American savers' money, and, with the ability to extend long-time credit based thereon, competitors who either never intend to repay their loans, or who intend to buy them up in a depreciated market at ten or twenty cents on the dollar."

For the protagonists of the Hawley-Smoot tariff bill so recently enacted, Mr. Garvan's particular figures and specific contentions in the name of American industry were almost, if not entirely, sufficient to dissolve the overarching hypothesis of beneficence supplied by the bankers. Even for disinterested parties given to cool appraisals of policies, the facts and arguments presented to the Senate committee on foreign lending made untenable the complacent optimism and basic assumptions of the financiers. Other questions were then in order.

How had the headlong rush into money lending occurred? Who was responsible? Clarence Dillon supplied his answer: the capital exported was "surplus" capital — wealth not needed at home — and bankers had merely channeled the outward flow. Senators were not convinced. One member of the committee thought the outward flow of capital was largely due to the higher rates of interest offered by agents and bankers for foreign governments — six, seven, and even eight per cent for "gold bonds." Another member insisted that by promoting foreign loans at higher rates of interest, the bankers had perhaps contracted credit at home and exerted a deleterious influence in slowing down domestic enterprise. But Mr. Dillon held fast to his thesis: "It is a question of surplus, because this country would use its own money." That the outflow would tend to raise the domestic interest rate, he conceded, but he clung to the idea of the "surplus" to the end. In some respects this idea gave consolation to citizens who had suffered under the bankers' theory of patriotism and beneficence: the bonds in default represented surplus capital after all — money and goods not "needed" at home. If this discovery did not entirely ease the pains of bondholders, it at least made the bankers' case appear more defensible to themselves.

While the problem of beneficence and patriotism in foreign lending was being examined, a subsidiary question arose: How did it happen that so many bond issues had been offered to American investors? Some illumination was obtained by the Senate committee in the immediate hearings and a dazzling light was focused upon the question by a later inquiry into the general subject of banking and finance. That all or nearly all the exporting bankers had sent or kept agents abroad searching fervently for opportunities was already well known, but no exposition of detailed methods had been made. In quest of information on the point, Senator Hiram Johnson asked one of the investment bankers, Frederick J.

Lisman, to explain how his fraternity went about floating loans in Peru. Mr. Lisman replied that several banking houses were engaged in sharp competition to get the favors. That was, in fact, the state of affairs "all over Latin America." The purpose, continued the witness, was "to satisfy the public demand for securities." Yet it was not the sole purpose: "Bankers do not knowingly float bad loans. But the purpose is to do a good business at a profit." Incidentally it was brought out in connection with a Peruvian loan that one of the banking houses had paid a large amount to promoters who arranged the deal behind the scenes and transferred to the son of the President of Peru the sum of $415,000 for his "services" in the course of the flotation. Moreover the Senate investigation unearthed the fact that another loan had been issued for a South American republic after federal officials had pointed out the unsoundness of the transaction — a warning that came true in a default.

§

Especially pertinent to an understanding of the bankers' tactics were the revelations respecting the financing of investments in Cuba whose freedom and independence had been guaranteed when the United States began the "war of liberation" in 1898. By the opening of 1931 the direct investments in that little island alone amounted to $935,706,000, and among them were huge loans to the Cuban government, engineered by three powerful banking houses of New York City — the Chase National, the J. P. Morgan Company, and the National City. Although, for reasons of weight or none at all, the Senate committee did not explore the methods by which the Morgan Company got a share of the business, it did inquire rather closely into the operations of the Chase National group, especially into the fifty million dollar loan of 1928.

At the time the transaction was consummated, Cuba was in the iron grip of a military dictator, Machado, news of whose bloody regimen had been circulated far and wide through the press in the United States. Was Carl J. Schmidlapp, the spokesman of the Chase National interests, aware of the fact? Senator King asked him directly whether he knew that Machado had arbitrarily extended the terms of Cuban senators and congressmen and that "to accomplish his end he had suppressed all political parties and was governing by military rule?" Mr. Schmidlapp answered: "No." Did Mr. Schmidlapp know that Machado had a rather large standing army? "I had not given it a thought one way or the other," responded the banker. "I did not know what the Army of Cuba was."

With reference, however, to some details of the financing, the banker had a little knowledge. He was aware that the Chase National had employed José Obregon as manager of the Cuban branch of the Bank, first at $12,000 a year and then at $19,000, and he was acquainted with the fact that Obregon was a son-in-law of Machado, the military ruler of Cuba. He also confirmed a report in the hands of the Senate committee to the effect that a commission of half a million dollars was paid over to Obregon, as bank manager, for distribution among the participants in the syndicate connected with the flotation. Was Machado's son-in-law employed by the Chase National merely on account of his talents as a banker? Mr. Schmidlapp was not asked to develop that topic; nor did he vouchsafe specific information.

But on this point his New York house had some data. A year previously one of its representatives had written in respect of Obregon: "As we know, from any business standpoint he is perfectly useless. He has neither any ability for banking, nor has he the slightest ability in negotiating, which was something which we thought it might be possible to build him up to do. . . . From what I could gather in listening to some of the Cubans' talk is that Joe [Obregon] has very little standing with the President [Machado], and I think this is probably true. On the other hand, where the rub comes in is that if we do not pay him his salary, the President

[Machado] would have to give him an allowance, and in times as hard as these this might be fairly difficult to do." The writer of this note on the managerial ability of Obregon also informed his concern that Machado was using public funds illegally and that the State Department in Washington was "worrying" about it. With such and similar transactions the promotion of American investments had proceeded in the days of prosperity and "the free market."

§

Through the evidence elicited at the hearings on foreign loans and at subsequent inquiries, it was possible to get microscopic glimpses of pecuniary enterprise at work, but no complete and accurate picture of the whole operation was constructed. Charles E. Mitchell, of the National City, had said in explanation of his role: "Many of us have found real inspiration in the fact that in the issuance of this large volume of foreign loans we were playing a part in the development of American trade and industry. That was our first motive always." This was a lofty sentiment and it was confirmed by the testimony of Thomas Lamont and Otto Kahn. Yet neither the bankers who answered the call for information nor the Senators who heard the testimony were able to present a balance sheet covering all the transactions. They did not establish, on a basis of figures, the thesis that the sequences flowing from the multitudinous operations in foreign lending, including bankers' commissions, augmented the wealth of the United States. The bankers had operated in a system with which they were familiar, according to methods they deemed appropriate, under economic theories they accepted without severe scrutiny. That much was certain. Nevertheless no demonstration proving the case of beneficence was made. Nor was it possible to make one from knowledge available.

Other things stood crystal-clear in the record. There had been a fierce competition among rival banking houses. In the course of competition, some of them, banks of high standing in the world of finance, though by no means all, had employed politicians, or the relatives of politicians, in foreign countries, to press American money upon restive governments. Huge commissions and douceurs had been paid to the intermediaries. Adverse reports on the financial condition of potential borrowers had been suppressed and concealed from the American investors to whom securities had been offered. Warnings from experts in the service of the United States Government had been stifled or ignored. Little consideration had been given to the actual destination of American money poured into foreign countries. Millions had been spent on a great highway in Cuba, on a gilt-domed capitol in Havana, and on unproductive public works in Peru.

These things were matters of common knowledge in enlightened circles. Yet, on the whole, bankers had been indifferent to the use of funds, so long as the bonds of borrowers were drawn in correct legal terms. Nor had they paid much attention to the tyrannical acts of dictators whom they helped to keep in power by lavish contributions of American money. Bankers might buy foreign politicians and supply them with cash, but they usually deemed it none of their business to make sure that this money went into prudent enterprises to enrich the borrowing nations and thus add guarantees to the securities they offered to the American public. Though heavily involved in the intrigues of foreign politics, they conveniently forgot politics. The responsible agent of the Chase National Bank confessed himself unaware of facts known even to casual readers of metropolitan newspapers: that Machado had violated the constitution of Cuba, had suppressed all opposition, and was running in a tyrannical course, which finally led to his overthrow and flight. Innocence more magnificent had seldom been displayed by men associated with pecuniary enterprise.

The Senate committee had put the question to the Lords of Creation: How did it happen? And it had received some answers. On the basis of these responses, the Chairman,

Hiram Johnson, exclaimed that it was necessary to devise legislation "which would preclude the possibility of any such outrageous and shameful activities being indulged in again in this country, to the detriment of our people." But what kind of legislation? The committee asked Professor Edwin Walter Kemmerer, the distinguished expert in finance, for light on the problem. The Professor granted that when bonds got into the hands of commercial banks, trust funds for widows and orphans, and the endowments of educational institutions, the value of such securities became "affected with a great public interest." In view of the tales that had already been told, that much did seem obvious. Could the Professor offer some conclusions on the matter of remedial legislation? He could not: "No, sir; I have no conclusion except the feeling that something should be done. . . . I suppose in the course of a short time we will go ahead again and repeat the same mistakes." That was an admission: there really had been some "mistakes." A Senator interposed: "People forget yesterday." The Professor replied: "They may remember yesterday, but they forget the day before." Bankers had testified that the people were clamorous for new issues of bonds in the days of the golden glow. The Professor evidently imagined that in time they would be on the war path again urging bankers to furnish more "investment opportunities." Apparently history would repeat itself, till doomsday.

Unable to get any unconfused light from the science of economics or from the sociology of the banking fraternity, the Senate committee devised more "hasty legislation," of a negative character. By a statute, called the Johnson Act, Congress in 1934 made it unlawful to sell in the United States the bonds or securities of any foreign government, or its subdivisions, which had defaulted on the payment of obligations to the Government of the United States. This was not the type of legislation deemed "constructive" by economists and bankers. It left none of that freedom which permitted creditors to help in lifting good but unlucky debtors to their feet by new advances of funds. What it represented was the temper of a multitude of American citizens who found themselves either completely ruined by foreign lending or in some degree of economic misfortune as a result of the bankers' excursions into operations that "benefited the United States." News of the excursions as disclosed by the Senate committee, even though cautiously handled by metropolitan papers, reached the outlying regions of the country. A few citizens naturally inclined to forget continued to remember and nursed for a time a terrible wrath against the bankers. In fact, some caustic commentator set in circulation the frightful word "banksters."

§

Supplementing the bulky volumes of testimony and papers laid before the public by the Senate committee engaged in investigating foreign loans was a remarkable document dealing with the influence which American investments in branch factories abroad had exerted on American industry and enterprise at home. Did this capital poured into foreign countries add to or diminish the wealth of the United States? In this connection the Senate did not call the Lords of Creation before a committee and ask them to elucidate the problem. By resolution it merely instructed the Department of Commerce, which had been eagerly promoting this form of foreign enterprise, to disclose "the extent to which American capital invested in manufacturing in Europe constitutes a competitive menace, directly or indirectly, to the industries carried on in the United States." In compliance with the instructions, the Department set its experts at work on the issue presented and in 1931 they reported their findings and lack of knowledge, under the heading American Branch Factories Abroad.

This response to the call of the Senate was accompanied by a statistical elaboration that must have been impressive to manufacturers of many commodities whose outlets abroad had recently been drastically narrowed, either by American branch factories in foreign countries or by other forces less discernible. But the response was not an answer. "In view of the constantly increasing exports of the commodities figuring largely in the branch-factory movement," said the experts, "it is impossible to ascertain the effect of the branch factories on our export trade." If there was a slight euphemism in the reference to constantly increasing exports in 1931, the language was at all events explicit. Yet the experts conceded that "there is a certain amount of competition between the branch factories and the parent plants in the United States as regards neutral markets." How much? "The full extent of this competition cannot be ascertained" from the available statistics.

What of the future for American manufacturers and industrial workers affected by this outpouring of capital abroad? The Department of Commerce was as non-committal, if not as lyrical, as the bankers: "The movement is intimately connected with the general industrial development of the United States and its future progress is likely to be determined primarily by the availability of capital and the economic policies of foreign countries." Such was the capacity for insight possessed by the great Department of Commerce so heavily endowed in financial resources and so well equipped with expert personnel by Secretary Hoover and his chosen successor. Perhaps the report represented all that intelligence and knowledge could accomplish. Even if true, it instigated queries among the people's representatives on Capitol Hill and added to the perplexities and quandaries of the people themselves in the very deeps of the crushing depression.

§

While the invisible empire of investment in foreign countries was being drawn into question, doubts were rising in respect of the visible empire in the Philippines. In conjunction with the poetry of the white man's burden, manifest destiny, and moral obligation, claims had been made from the beginning that this was also a paying proposition in itself and a stepping stone to greater commerce on the mainland of Asia. At the very outset of empire building in 1898, seekers after world power for the United States had declared that the American people were producing more than they could consume, that outlets for "surplus" manufactures and farm produce must be found, and that imperial expansion would bring the necessary openings. Unless we expand, it was said, we burst. Expansion came. And after thirty years' experience, ample time for a fair test, a balance sheet of the operations containing all the economic items susceptible of "numerical expression" showed a net loss of about four million dollars a year, apart from the cost of extra naval defense. Individual interests in the United States had made high profits. The American people as a whole had not found the promised outlets for goods and taxpayers had been compelled to shoulder heavy additional burdens. Such was the outcome of all the blare, oratory, trumpeting, boasting, and pluming of the great adventure.

As the tariff legislation of the United States facilitated the import of sugar, coconut oil, copra, and other agricultural products from the Philippines into the United States in return for manufactures, it was the American farmers who felt, or said they felt, the adverse effects of empire. Manufacturers, money lenders, and merchants had profited a little from manifest destiny but farmers gradually arrived at the conviction that the experiment in expansion was carried on largely at their expense. Gradually American industrial workers reached the conclusion that they too had a case against imperialism. Out of affectionate consideration for "our little brown brothers" and for other reasons, the ports of the United States had been thrown open to immigration from the Philippines and in many divisions of industry Filipinos were cutting into American standards of living, especially on the Pacific Coast.

When the great depression deepened, the pressures of

agrarian and labor interests were exerted in Congress against the pressures of industry, commerce, finance, the State Department, and the naval bureaucracy. There had been, it was true, opposition from the former sources since the beginning of the imperial adventure, but the capitalistic interests had been able, on the whole, to win and hold the favors of federal legislation and administration, and to retain the solicitude of the Navy Department. By 1930 the tables were turning and at a series of congressional hearings a real inquest was conducted into the economic merits of empire.

Outside the committee rooms of Congress, opposition to independence for the Philippines was voiced by those interests and newspapers that had long supported the adventure in imperialism and advocated coöperation with Great Britain in European politics. The lyricism of doing good to them that sit in darkness was revived and applauded once more. The specter of Japan seizing the emancipated Islands was raised again. Responsibility for aiding Great Britain in maintaining the balance of power in the East was reëmphasized in poignant language by publicists.

That the United States could not, single-handed, overcome the naval power of Japan in her own waters, save in a long, costly, and bloody war was conceded. That Great Britain might not throw her weight on the side of the United States in such a conflict was admitted. Nevertheless to seek an escape from the pretext for this war was contemptuously described as the policy of "scuttle and run." Experts in "sea power," "Pacific relations," "international coöperation," "world affairs," and the pomp and circumstance of "grand politics" sought to educate the hinterlanders of the United States. Ingenious devices for heating patriotism and making it identical with imperialism were employed. If the attitude of the metropolitan press represented general American opinion and resolve, then the tempest raised in Congress by agrarian and labor leaders would soon subside.

But music from the chorus of imperialism failed to enchant all the politicians in Washington. In December, 1932, Con-

gress passed a bill for granting independence to the Philippines at the end of ten years on various terms and conditions,
including popular approval of the proposal in the Islands.
The following month President Hoover vetoed the bill and,
in a message to Congress and the country, reviewed the
arguments. He did not repudiate entirely the vague idea of
ultimate independence. His attention was rather concentrated on the methods of the measure in question. It might
project the Philippine people "into economic and social
chaos, with the probability of breakdown in government,
with its consequences in degeneration of a rising liberty . . .
so carefully nurtured by the United States at the cost of
thousands of American lives and hundreds of millions of
money." To the pleas of the agricultural interests in the
United States undoubtedly supporting the bill, Hoover
offered a rebuttal: "We are trustees for these people and
we must not let our selfish interest dominate that trust."
Crouching in the neighborhood was a covetous Japan. "Nor
has the spirit of imperialism," the President said, "and the
exploitation of peoples of other races departed from the
earth." Indeed seldom before had the official thesis of dollar
diplomacy been expressed in wider and nobler terms than in
Hoover's veto message. Yet it too failed to convince the
agrarians. Congress carried the measure over the veto, and
in a little more than a year after the Philippines had rejected
the first tender, a modified bill was signed by another President and placed upon the statute books of the land.

§

Amid the uproars, investigations, recriminations, alarms,
distresses, and curses that accompanied the course of the
depression, President Hoover was called upon to formulate
measures for coping with the flying debris of the crisis.
Coupled with the already existing emergency in agriculture,
the industrial calamity set for Hoover dilemmas which
Coolidge had escaped, fortunately for his reputation as a

statesman. Moreover it changed from week to week, adding the complications of development to those of the original dissolution.

Viewed from the White House, the business depression went through three stages. At first the stock market débâcle in the autumn of 1929 was regarded as affecting mainly speculators and paper jugglers, leaving American business untouched or at least fundamentally sound. The clouds would soon blow over. However, destiny willed otherwise. As the depression deepened, great banks locked their doors, industries slowed down, unemployment became obviously appalling, and misery thickened, it was conceded by the administration that something serious had happened and was happening. For this state of affairs President Hoover devised formulas and took actions deemed appropriate within the frame of his social philosophy. The depth of the depression was due, in his opinion, to the backlash of the World War. In other respects it was only another periodical crisis and would soon be merely as a tale that is told. By the spring of 1932 he was convinced that the crest of the wave was broken, that business was returning to "normal," that his measures had been effective, and that nothing novel or experimental was needed to facilitate "recovery."

In the beginning of the ordeal, none was clairvoyant enough to foresee how far the industrial depression would go, what havoc it would carry in its train — not even the President of the United States and the Lords of Creation who "ruled America." Was the market crash a harbinger of an economic breakdown or merely a drastic readjustment of liquid claims and paper manipulations? In common with economic leaders called greatest and best, President Hoover at the outset took the position that the industrial structure was sound and that the plunges of stock prices were passing flurries. Confidence in this belief seemed to be the preëminent need. Acting on that assumption, the President summoned to the White House outstanding leaders in manufacturing, transportation, agriculture, utilities, and labor organization and asked them to adopt measures of private procedure calculated to keep economic enterprises running on an even keel and wages for buying power flowing steadily. He also announced the creation of a continuing council of business men charged with the duty of watching the trends in national economy and bringing about the coöperation of interested parties in the maintenance of production on a high level.

What more was to be done by the Government of the United States, if anything? What did precedents and economic philosophy have to offer in the dilemma? Was the President merely to follow precedents or to make them? As a basis of judgment Hoover had access to records of experiences in three major panics — 1837, 1873, and 1893, as well as the teachings of minor disturbances. Two of the major panics had occurred under Democratic auspices and one under Republican authority. A little less than one hundred years before 1929, Martin Van Buren had taken office under a comforting sun of prosperity and in his inaugural address had spoken confidently of the valor of the people, referred to exhaustless resources, and paid tribute to the blessings of free institutions. Nevertheless, within a month a devastating depression started and ran for more than six years, scattering bankruptcies, unemployment, misery, and starvation in its wake. What then did President Van Buren do? First, he read the people a lecture on their follies. He told them that their troubles were chiefly due to excessive issues of bank paper and the enlargement of credit facilities, to heavy investments in unproductive lands, to the creation of fictitious values, and to "the rapid growth, among all classes, especially in our great commercial towns, of luxurious habits founded too often on merely fancied wealth, and detrimental alike to the industry, the resources, and the morals of our people."

Having read the people this lesson, Van Buren, speaking in the name of the Government, disclaimed all responsibility worthy of note for the hardships in which the people found themselves plunged. "All communities," he said, "are apt to look to government for too much. Even in our own country, where its powers and duties are so strictly limited, we are prone to do so, especially at periods of sudden embarrassment and distress. This ought not to be. The framers of our excellent Constitution and the people who approved it with calm and sagacious deliberation acted at the time on a sounder principle. They wisely judged that the less government interferes with private pursuits the better for the general prosperity. . . . Its real duty . . . is to enact and enforce a system of general laws commensurate with, but not exceeding, the objects of its establishment, and to leave every citizen and every interest to reap under its benign protection the rewards of virtue, industry, and prudence." In reality, of course, the framers of the Constitution had created a government designed to interfere extensively with economic affairs, but by 1837 the Democratic fiction of the Constitution had been substituted for the truth of the business; and only disgruntled old Federalists and Whigs were likely to challenge Van Buren's constitutional theory.

Having opened with a false premise in respect of the Constitution, Van Buren proceeded to his conclusion: "If therefore I refrain from suggesting to Congress any specific plan for regulating the exchanges of the country, relieving mercantile embarrassments, or interfering with the ordinary operations of foreign or domestic commerce, it is from a conviction that such measures are not within the constitutional province of the General Government, and that their adoption would not promote the real and permanent welfare of those they might be designed to aid."

After stoutly refusing aid to business and commerce, Van Buren, in silence, left to the strained mercies of private charity the unemployed of the urban centers, whose miseries are so graphically described in the pages of Horace Greeley's reminiscences. The example set by Van Buren, with modifications in detail, was followed by President Grant and President Hayes during the panic that began in 1873 and by President Cleveland twenty years later. Apart from proposals bearing on the Treasury, their innovations in policy consisted mainly of measures intended to contract currency and credit, as suggested by experienced bankers, and the use of federal troops in industrial disputes. Such in broad outlines was the system of theory and practice which served as a precedent and ideal for President Hoover when another great depression opened in the autumn of 1929.

But Hoover rejected this policy of negation, so foreign to the spirit of social welfare, engineering, and promotion, and embarked upon a program of positive action designed to mitigate, if not prevent, the evil consequences of the depression. Though his program, as a matter of course, came within the framework of his experience and social philosophy, it was none the less radical in its implications, for it marked a departure from the renunciation of his predecessors. It accepted a responsibility on the part of the Federal Government for breaking the clutches of the crisis and for seeking ways and means of overcoming the violent fluctuations of such cyclical disturbances. Instead of greeting the visitation with the old cry, "God wills it," or "Nature decrees it," Hoover invoked intelligence and took action in conquering the periodical "black death" which had so often disrupted industrial processes. In so doing he drew upon himself the easy criticism of those who said that he did not do enough or did the wrong thing, but such strictures in no way obscured the fact that he broke from precedents and made precedents in the discharge of his duties as Chief Executive of the United States.

§

Although Hoover developed the features of his program seriatim as the course of the depression unfolded, in their completed form they displayed economic consistency. As Secretary of Commerce, he had formulated a project for expanding the construction of public works to absorb workers discharged from private employment during industrial contraction. In accordance with this scheme, now as the President, he appealed to state and local authorities to coöperate with the Federal Government "in the energetic yet prudent" expansion of public works enterprises. Resorting to a world war precedent, he recommended, and Congress provided for, the creation of the Reconstruction Finance Corporation in 1932, endowed with the power to make loans to banks, railroads, exporters of agricultural products, and to farmers for crop production, all under specific terms as to security. Legislation easing credit for debt-burdened farmers and slowing down foreclosures was supplemented by a measure which set up a system of discount banks authorized to make loans to home owners in peril of losing their shelter. With a view to stimulating enterprise through "reopening credit channels," the discount facilities of Federal Reserve banks were enlarged and hitherto ineligible paper was admitted as the basis for advances to member banks. In addition, Hoover urged upon Congress a revision of legislation "to restore confidence in railroad bonds," to afford more adequate safeguards for depositors in banks, and to curtail federal expenditures in various directions.

All these elements of the President's program dovetailed together in a reasoned pattern that conformed to a conception of economics widely held if not dominant. Under this conception the economic entrepreneur supplies, in addition to management, the necessary capital, and his capital set in motion creates wealth — producers' goods and consumers' goods — and gives employment. To take care of an increasing population, extend employment, and raise standards of living, an appropriate expansion of capital in the form of accumulations, money, and credit is likewise indispensable to a steady operation of economy. "Normally" the provision of capital through savings and the drive of the profit motive automatically keep the economic mechanism running smoothly and in the best possible manner. Whatever the "causes" of a business depression, it is accompanied by a tightening of the money market and a slowing down of enterprise. Hence in harmony with the conception, the Government can give an impetus to the sluggish mechanism by expanding the credit facilities offered to entrepreneurs and by adding to the buying power of labor through wages paid on public works. It is true, as Democratic critics alleged, that this policy meant giving special aid to "men at the top" of the system, but it also implied the belief that the benefits of such aid would rapidly percolate to the bottom of the social pyramid. If so, would the benefits be realized in fact and be diffused rapidly enough to convince the expectants at the bottom that the remedy was sufficient?

On this question the fate of President Hoover's administration mainly turned. In the beginning many Democrats and some insurgent Republicans vigorously denied the general efficacy of the cure, though they accepted its essential features. In line with historic use and wont in politics, they harassed the administration by criticizing details and by imputing to it the primary desire to aid capitalists in banking, railway, and other enterprises. After the Democrats captured the House of Representatives in the mid-term elections, the sniping at the President grew in intensity. As the number of unemployed increased and economic distress became more acute, members of Congress insisted upon direct federal aid to the jobless and brought up proposals directed to that end. Precedents for this action they found in previous grants to sufferers from earthquakes, famines, floods, and droughts. As chairman of the American Relief Administration, Hoover had supervised the disbursement of $100,000,000 appropriated by Congress in 1919 for relieving misery in Europe and at one time the Administration had ten million pitiable Russians on its roll of dependents. In view of such examples and the rising distress in America, congressional leaders rallied in increasing force to the idea of making federal appropriations for the relief of the unemployed through state and local agencies.

Such proposals, however, did not harmonize with President Hoover's sense of propriety and he condemned them. "I am opposed," he said bluntly in 1931, "to any direct or indirect Government dole." He announced himself as equally opposed to any scheme of federal unemployment insurance and killed by a pocket veto a bill providing federal aid for employ-ment exchanges. When Congress attempted to appropriate twenty-five million dollars for relief, to be distributed by the Red Cross, administration forces were thrown athwart the effort. When Congress seemed persistent, the chairman of the Red Cross defiantly announced that his association would refuse to disburse any money appropriated to it from federal resources. Only under terrific pressure did Hoover consent to sign a bill authorizing loans to state agencies for relief work and self-liquidating projects — in July, 1932, while the pres-idential campaign was in progress. When a number of veterans, "the bonus army," poor and hungry, marched on Washington and settled there to promote "adjusted com-pensation" legislation, he employed federal troops to rout and disperse them; their tents were burned and blood was spilled. Congressional dissent from his relief policy, espe-cially in the forms made manifest, he denounced as playing politics with human misery, and to the end of his term he con-tinued to insist that direct aid for the unemployed was a duty of localities and private charities. This position, he argued, was necessary to "the maintenance of the American system of individual initiative and community responsibility."

§

Insofar as he was called upon to meet emergency problems in international relations, President Hoover also kept well within the circle of his economic philosophy. When great banking houses in Vienna fell into dire straits in the spring of 1931 and their difficulties were followed by bank failures in Germany, it became evident that Germany could not con-tinue to pay both reparations to the victorious Allies and in-stallments on the debts owed to private investors abroad. Besides the billions in long term loans made to Germany in the period of expansive prosperity, there were short term credits amounting to hundreds of millions which had been extended by British and American bankers in quest of high interest returns. Clearly the Germans had overborrowed and when pinched by the depression they could not meet their obligations.

While the contingency was painful to the creditors, it was no surprise to German economists and statesmen. For a long time common rumor in Berlin had intimated that in the next crisis foreign banks and investors would call upon their respective governments to forego reparations or public debts in the interest of private money lenders. And the crisis came in 1931. Although the United States Government had refused to admit an official connection between German reparations and payments on the debts owed by the Allies, American bankers knew that an economic connection existed or could be established through pressure politics. Indeed the whole structure of reparations and inter-governmental debts interfered with the business of bankers engaged in floating foreign loans in the United States and likewise with export and import business in general. Well aware of this obvious relation, one of them had earlier hired a propagandist to tour the Middle West and convert the hinterland to the gospel of public debt cancellation — in the interest of private debts. The forgiveness of debtors — "our Associates in the War for Democracy" — had a pleasant moral connotation and it would clear the way for more private loans and trade abroad, with compensatory commissions thereunto attached.

Having been occupied as Secretary of Commerce in promoting foreign commerce and money lending, President Hoover clung to the belief that these economic activities were indispensable to domestic prosperity. "In peace time," he had said in 1926, "our exports and imports are the margins upon which our well-being depends. The export of our surplus enables us to use in full our resources and energy. . . . The making of loans to foreign countries for productive purposes not only increases our direct exports but builds up the prosperity of foreign countries and is a blessing to both sides of the transaction." So molded by experience and instructed by his philosophy, Hoover reached the conclusion that a moratorium on inter-governmental debts would be advantageous to private recovery, when the German crisis broke over his head.

Although Congress was not in session, the President communicated with individual members by wire and, receiving favorable responses, he proposed to all the countries concerned, in June, 1931, a moratorium for one year on inter-governmental obligations. Italy and Great Britain quickly agreed. Somewhat stunned by the suddenness of the proposition, France balked for a time and insisted on coupling provisos with her acceptance. Reacting rapidly to private hopes, the prices of stocks leaped upward on the New York Exchange, only to sink back again after a second thought had come to the brokers. When Congress ratified the moratorium at its next session in December, it held stubbornly to the old contention that the public debts owed to the United States by foreign governments would have to be paid. For importers, exporters, bankers engaged in lending money abroad, and advocates of American participation in the European concert of powers this was a grave disappointment.

In the end, most of the applause that had greeted the moratorium in metropolitan centers was blanketed by complaints of Senators and Representatives from the unconverted regions. Not without a display of resentment did Congress finally ratify the temporary concession to the foreign governments and the rumor spread that the American taxpayers had been outwitted by the bankers again. An action that had been welcomed as a wise and generous gesture was now characterized in Democratic quarters as another ingenious stroke designed to aid "the men at the top," in the hope that benefits would seep down to the base of the social pyramid.

§

President Hoover's measures, taken collectively, were not swiftly followed by results sufficiently patent to silence the accumulating protest and criticism. And for bitter criticism, especially of the political type, he was ill-prepared by practice. As a promoting engineer, particularly in the Orient, he had been accustomed to giving orders to employees who obeyed with alacrity and asked no irritating questions. As the head of great international relief enterprises he had possessed large powers, dispensed huge sums of money, received the unstinted praise of multitudes whose woes he had alleviated. This is not to say that he had encountered no abuse or buffets of fortune; but certainly, until he sought the Republican nomination in 1928, his political experience had been restricted to bureaucratic administrations. With the recorded history and practice of great politics his acquaintance was not, to speak moderately, equal to his knowledge of private affairs.

Moreover, the give-and-take, the squabbles over spoils, the personal mischiefs, the hateful disagreements and equally intense love-feasts of petty politics were alien to his spirit and his conceptions of values. The ancient rule of "going along" he could not accept. He had entered high official life by the front door. The post of Secretary of Commerce had come to him as a reward for outstanding services and accomplishments in war and peace, not as a political job. With back-slapping, huckstering, and growling members of Congress he was never at ease. To strong dissent of any kind he was sensitive and he was inclined to regard even remonstrances, if pertinacious, as a form of bumptiousness. His trials and vexations were not more onerous than those of some other Presidents, but his capacity for treating them lightly or humorously was smaller than that of politicians who had battled their way upward to the White House along the arduous path of party hustle and tussle. His tenacity was little tempered by their flexibility. Entangled in his own limitations, he could not, like Lincoln, tell stories and laugh loudly when Democrats in the House hawked at him and members of his party in the Senate harassed him. He had never acquired the art of symbolizing his opponents in the lineaments of cold-blooded greed, cunning, or futility, whether they deserved it or not, and was both astonished and grieved to see himself so portrayed.

Besides suffering from the cruel thrusts of ordinary politics, President Hoover was the victim of hard circumstances — the dissolutions and heartburnings of the economic depression. No President or party had ever fully escaped the political effects of such convulsions. Though at the head of triumphant Jacksonian Democracy, Van Buren was overwhelmed in 1840 by a resurgence of the shattered and impotent Whigs. In the middle of the depression that opened in 1873, the popular verdict was against the Republicans under whose auspices it had opened, and it is highly doubtful whether Hayes was even victorious in the electoral college. Cleveland was repudiated by his party in 1896 and the Democrats were driven from office by a Republican revival.

Now, in 1932, the nemesis was to overtake the Republicans. They had been in power when the panic began and, not without some justification, they incurred the charge of responsibility for it. When the sun of prosperity rose they had generally taken credit for the event; the good fortune, they claimed, had been due to their prowess. As their candidate, Herbert Hoover had promised to continue their beneficent policies and had expressed the hope that such poverty as remained might thus be banished from the land. If the Republicans had once caused the sun to rise, why could they not do it again? If they could not, their alleged powers were delusive and their bold front was a sham. They were victims, not makers, of history. Such at least was the tenor of the popular verdict. With a thirst for alcohol rising as the depression deepened, President Hoover, an advocate of prohibition, was caught in a grip of forces too tenacious for his strength and ingenuity. If, as Phillip Guedalla has said, the final position of a statesman in history depends upon the nature of his exit from the stage, the circumstances of Mr. Hoover's departure were certainly ungenerous to his undoubted merits and talents. Necessities that could not be broken closed in upon him and his party during the onward sweep of the economic catastrophe.

§

Outside the circles of Republican theorizing and Democratic nagging, an immense upsurge of private inquiry and thought, in the fashion of American democracy, inundated the country with critical dissertations and new plans. Beyond the dispute in words lay the fact that the ponderous machine covered by President Hoover's economic philosophy had slowed down to less than half its potential speed, strewing bankruptcies and human casualties from the center to the periphery of society. Above the optimistic prophecies of trade promoters was heard the crash of foreign markets, as bonds went into default and the grand stake abroad shriveled. Over against the promises of ever-expanding outlets for American "surpluses" in the wake of empire rose mountains of "surpluses," for which no sales could be found. Furthermore the pressure of imports from imperial possessions bore heavily upon already demoralized domestic markets for agricultural produce.

From every angle of vision undeniable signs of the deepening depression thrust themselves into the range of observation — machines idle, engines rusting, locomotives weather-beaten on grass-grown sidings, ships without cargoes tossing mournfully at anchor, tractors silent in deserted fields. In that province especially assigned by tradition to women were tokens of decay: empty cupboards, ragged clothes, unpainted houses, stinking jungles of wood and tin in the very shadows of the centers of culture. Newspapers, journals and books teemed with stories of wandering men and women, boys and girls adrift, ruined homes, deserted families, leaders of finance poring over balance sheets of wrecked hopes, and, on the slabs of city morgues, bodies of suicides finding in death a security against want denied in life. Although high officials knew about these things, private citizens, especially teachers and relief workers, thrown daily into close contact with them, were acutely disturbed by them. For a time even the firm assurance of economic optimists — their faith in the "natural course," the "invisible hand," and "the long run" — was shattered.

After many months had elapsed and oft-repeated promises of prosperity "just around the corner" had grown stale, a profound searching of minds and hearts brought forth ideas never before expressed so widely in the high places of American power. Throughout the year 1931, as signs of havoc spread, the volume of indignant protests and demands mounted. On March 27, Daniel Willard, president of the Baltimore and Ohio Railroad, speaking at the fiftieth anniversary of the Wharton School in the University of Pennsylvania, laid squarely before the assembled dignitaries the problem presented by enormous productive capacity on the one side and unemployment and dire need on the other. The gravity of this condition and its challenge to their intelligence he emphasized in positive terms. The system that made it possible for five or six million people to be idle and vainly searching for work, he declared to the professors and benefactors, was unsatisfactory and had failed in one important respect. Placing himself in the position of a working man in the peril of starvation for himself and his family, the master of railway management shot a bolt of horror into Respectability by asserting: "While I do not like to say so, I would be less than candid if I did not say that in such circumstances I would steal before I would starve." Governors of law and order could scarcely believe their ears.

On June 3, 1931, Matthew Woll, acting president of the National Civic Federation which had so long combatted liberals, whether red or pink, addressed an open letter to James W. Gerard, who had recently drawn up the famous list of "sixty-four rulers of America." The appeal urged Mr. Gerard to call a national industrial congress for the purpose of framing plans for overcoming the crisis, applying economic powers rationally, and giving permanent security to the nation. "We need," Mr. Woll declared, "to meet the cold-blooded communist five-year plan with a warm-blooded ten-year plan of democratic idealism woven into the very pattern of our national fabric." In language even more pointed, Mr. Woll laid before the country in a radio broadcast the problem which Daniel Willard had presented at Philadelphia a few weeks earlier. "It is unthinkable," he exclaimed, "that America can consent to face such a problem, with all of its physical, mental, and moral endowment, and permit itself to be found sitting idly, waiting for the 'ferment' to settle, quiescent, hoping somehow we will 'muddle through.'" Rejecting the economists' confidence in the inerrant efficiency of the slow-moving price mechanism, Mr. Woll called upon the leaders of industry and labor to plan, establish, and assure an economic system of abundance and security. Time might pronounce the design chimerical, but the thought and feeling which it expressed flowed into the currents of opinion and inclination that were to make history.

A few days later, June 11, 1931, Nicholas Murray Butler, addressing the American Club in Paris, under the title of Progress and Poverty, described the revolutionary consequences of mass production in labor displacement and warned his audience that this alone, apart from the devastation of the world war, would have produced a crisis in our economic and social life. With labor unemployed, the power of consumption destroyed, and democratic forces at work in society, the western world suffered from a "lack of competent, constructive, courageous leadership, political, social, and economic." There was the puzzle. And what was the answer? "The universal answer of the office-holding class is 'Wait.'" On this form of statecraft, Dr. Butler dryly commented: "Gentlemen, if we wait too long somebody will come forward with a solution that we may not like. Let me call your attention to the fact that the characteristic feature of the experiment in Russia, to my mind, is not that it is communist, but that it is being carried on with a plan in the face of a planless opposition. The man with a plan, however much we may dislike it, has a vast advantage over the group sauntering down the road of life complaining of the economic weather and wondering when the rain is going to stop." Later in the same year Dr. Butler, in expounding the same philosophy, analyzed the chief presuppositions of orthodox economics, framed a long list of specifications for reform, and concluded with a vigorous appeal for action to fortify the foundations of our social and economic order. As if remembering the old aphorism "with what little wit the world is governed," Dr. Butler remarked ironically: "If, as Junius wrote to the Duke of Bedford, we cannot be safe, we may at least cease to be ridiculous!"

In the autumn of 1931 a special commission of the Federal Council of the Churches of Christ issued a message of criticism and proposal to be read to congregations on Labor Sunday. The document drew a gruesome picture — of men and women tramping the streets in search of work, crowding into churches and police stations seeking relief, standing in bread lines, waiting in the vestibules of charitable societies. At least twenty times since 1855 the country had passed through business depressions, it stated. Are we to endure this forever? it asked. When prosperity returns are we to drift and repeat again this story of frustration and agony? There are grave imperfections in an economic system which makes possible the awful contrast of vast fortunes and breadlines. A new conception of the position and needs of workers in the modern world is necessary, and the best minds of the nation must be applied to the reconstruction and planning of our social and economic life on sound religious principles. In a spirit of renewed dedication, the Council declared: "The facts of the situation themselves constitute a challenge to the churches to assume their rightful place of ethical leadership; to demand fundamental changes in present economic conditions; to protest against the selfish desire for wealth as the principal motive of industry; to insist upon the creation of an industrial society which shall have as its purpose economic security and freedom for the masses of mankind, 'even these least, my brethren'; to seek the development of a social order which shall be based upon Jesus' principles of love and brotherhood."

About the same time the bishops of the Protestant Episcopal Church, in a pastoral letter, proclaimed to the faithful that "the contrast between individual want and collective plenty cannot be accepted as in accordance with the will of God." The resources of the earth are unimpaired, and multitudes dependent upon doles and charity constitute an arraignment of the present economic system. Our "acquisitive society," they said, stands bewildered in the presence of a crisis precipitated not by physical catastrophe, "but apparently by the competitive, profit-seeking principles upon which, it has hitherto been assumed, general prosperity is based." Immediate relief must be given, but that is not enough. Society must see that such a crisis does not occur again. Though the Church cannot advocate a particular method, it calls upon employers "to labor for the adoption of a plan or plans which shall coördinate production and consumption, insure continuity of employment, and provide security of income to the workers of the nation. . . . The profit-seeking motive must give way to that of service." To economic distress and political unrest are added the aggravations of force in international relations: "We, with the cave man, still depend upon force, the only difference being that his club has developed into vastly more efficient agents of destruction." This, too, is in violation of Christian principles and contrary to the Christian attitude from its beginning. Throbbing with emotion, this mingled condemnation and constructive appeal rang through the Protestant Episcopal Churches and awakened echoes from Maine to California.

It was one thing for the clergy, somewhat removed from the turmoil of the marketplace and committed by faith to ethical principles, to arraign the economic order and demand measures of planning and protection against such afflictions. All this Great Business might take with a grain of salt, for it had long been accustomed to seeing men who lacked knowledge of practice indulge in theorizing. But on September 16, 1931, a distinguished industrial leader, Gerard Swope, of the General Electric Company, startled Respectability by an address on planning delivered to the National Electrical Manufacturers Association, at the Hotel Commodore in New York City, the very citadel of the Lords of Creation. In language more restrained than that of the clergy, he dwelt upon the sad plight of willing workers seeking employment, yet insisted that the presence of this condition in such periods of depression "detracts nothing from its wrongness." Then, with a deliberation evidently studied, Mr. Swope warned his brethren in business enterprise: "That industry must evolve and make effective those measures which will first ameliorate and ultimately eliminate these conditions must be the reaction of everyone who gives thought to what is taking place. Industry must do this thing, because it will surely be done." In other words, if industry did not order its household, society would act through its government. Having pointed to the handwriting on the wall, Mr. Swope put forth the elements of a plan designed to stabilize industry and employment, rationalize and purify business management, and safeguard workers against the vicissitudes of economic stresses and strains. Two months later, Mr. Swope amplified his original plan in an address before the Academy of Political Science in New York City, thus giving economists a vision of things unnoted in the classical scheme under the "invisible hand" of Providence.

At the meeting of the Electrical Manufacturers Association before which Mr. Swope laid his original design, Owen D. Young was present and spoke in support of the general purpose underlying it. His address was brief and pointed. Its staccato sentences were punctuated with caveats to the Lords of Creation. "To the insistent calls for industrial leadership in these disorganized times," he told them, "there has been a discouraging silence." Academic theses had been submitted to the country, but they were far removed from practical application. Now Mr. Swope, "after previous conference with his associates in the electrical manufacturing industry,"

submits a plan definite in terms and bearing the testimonial
of practicality. It is not free from criticism. It raises grave
questions of public and business policy. But alternatives
must be faced. Three courses are open. We can do nothing
and accept the "system of intensified individualism which,
because of its disordered action, necessarily brings great
peaks of prosperity and valleys of depression." We can place
positive responsibilities upon industry for planning and stabilization. We can acquiesce in government action, "providing
the means for employee protection through the power of taxation." These are the three positions, with some possible
compromises, which every citizen should consider. "What is
the answer? Which shall it be?" Although caution marked
Mr. Young's periods, there could be no doubt that he was
deeply moved and felt oppressed by the gravity of the
national crisis.

On the day following the publication of Mr. Swope's plan
in the newspapers near and far, industrial leaders, editors,
publicists, politicians, professors, and clergymen started a
torrent of comment and debate. Samuel Vauclain, of the
Baldwin Locomotive Works, replied tartly: "I don't believe
in it," but the judgments of business leaders were on the
whole favorable. Speaking as president of the United States
Chamber of Commerce, Silas Strawn pronounced the scheme
"excellent" and in line with plans then being projected by
his association. Dr. John A. Ryan, of the National Catholic
Welfare Conference, commended the objects of Mr. Swope's
plan as admirable, but thought that business men in general
did not have "sense enough" to form the trade associations
required by the proposal unless compelled to do it by law.
How could it be done by law "under our Constitution"?

As usual, the politicians, recognizing the dynamite in the
plan, were circumspect. Many Democrats, according to their
scheme of thought, surmised that some tinkering with the
sacred text of the anti-trust laws was in the offing, although
other Democrats promised to weigh and consider Mr. Swope's
proposition. Senator Simeon Fess, chairman of the Repub-

lican national committee, observed that the plan was "constructive" and ventured the opinion that it would be studied with care by government economists and industrial leaders. Speaking for the agrarian interests, Senator Smith W. Brookhart made caustic suggestions and exclaimed : "I am glad to see a great business manager conceding the collapse of the capitalistic system!" Whatever unfolding time might reveal — action, escape, repudiation, or oblivion — it was certain that Mr. Swope had shaken the pillars of Respectability for the season and thrown a burning brand of thought into the very center of complacency.

Meanwhile there were stirrings among the officers of the American Federation of Labor. The traditions of the Federation had been, in the main, conservative. It had accepted the imperatives of the capitalist system and within that framework had sought to win for labor what was loosely called "a fair share" of the product of industry. But now the product to be shared had fallen to about half its former volume and good trade unionists by the thousands wandered helplessly among the throngs of the unemployed, sat disconsolately on park benches, or moped in kitchens or chimney corners. Moved more by this spectacle than by any economic theories, the executive council of the Federation prepared for the convention, in October, 1931, a long report on the industrial system and measures of relief and prevention to be taken.

In this document the council rejected the academic hypothesis that the automatic workings of the price system brought justice, efficiency, and beneficence. It referred to the unequal distribution of wealth, in fact; to the lack of buying power among the people; and to the trials visited upon the country by the depression : "This unequal distribution of the nation's income throws the industrial mechanism out of balance." The President of the United States should call a national economic conference; planning and coördination should be projected by a national economic council; all the facts of business enterprises should be public property;

a federal labor board should collect statistical information on which to base constructive policies. Like organized business, organized labor shrank from a government control too stringent; yet it assigned to government a kind of directive role in stabilizing and assuring the full operation of economic processes. Although its program of action was not far removed from that of President Hoover, the Federation had ostensibly forsaken the essential principle of historic capitalism — the automatic attainment of the highest possible prosperity through the deterministic operations of the acquisitive instinct.

Without waiting for business men of Wisconsin to grapple resolutely with the panic somehow acknowledged to be associated with their system, Governor Philip La Follette, in November, 1931, summoned the state legislature in a special session. In a resonant message he presented the issues as he saw them. "We are in the midst of the greatest domestic crisis since the Civil War," he opened. "In this crisis, people are divided broadly into two groups: one opposes, and one favors, collective action to meet the emergency and to guard against its recurrence in the future." For ten years business has tolerated the deflation of agriculture. It has failed to put its own house in order. Capital has controlled our business machine and enjoyed the lion's share of the return from its operation. In 1929 "the top rung of our federal financial ladder, comprising 504 individuals," reported net incomes of over two million dollars apiece. They are not "worth" it for "the kind of leadership they have given us." Then followed a caustic etching of the contrast between concentrated wealth and the miseries engendered by the depression.

Having pictured indubitable features of the calamity, Governor La Follette submitted a program of legislation. It embraced the extension of public ownership, the stabilization of private business, unemployment insurance, the provision of machinery for community planning, a drastic revision of banking practices, and the equalization of the burdens of taxation. The struggle would be rough, the Governor told the legislators, but a government that had sent four million men to war could put five million persons to work. A government that had squandered billions for destruction could spend billions for enterprises of peace to insure a richer life. Simply stated, we are engaged in the "age-old struggle of mankind to build a better world."

In December, 1931, shortly after the legislature of Wisconsin had begun to wrestle seriously with the Governor's proposals, the United States Chamber of Commerce made public a report of its committee "on continuity of business and employment." The document was the outcome of a long study made on the demand of the Chamber for a project dealing with unemployment distress and for "a rational program of production and distribution to be initiated by business itself." While accepting the fundamental principles of capitalism, the report expressed grave doubts respecting the universality of its automatic beneficence. It pointed out the perils of speculative activity, war, and depressed agriculture. The freedom of individual action which might have been justified in the relatively simple life of the past century "cannot be tolerated today," for the unwise action of a single individual may adversely affect the lives of thousands. "We have left the period of extreme individualism and are living in a period in which national economy must be recognized as the controlling factor." The calamities of the time have been overemphasized, but the call to action is inescapable. "To an onlooker from another world, our situation must seem as stupid and anomalous as it seems painful to us. We are in want because we have too much. People go hungry while our farmers cannot dispose of their surpluses of food; unemployed are anxious to work, while there is machinery idle with which they could make the things they need. Capital and labor, facilities for production and transportation, raw materials and food, all these essential things we have in seeming superabundance. We lack only applied intelligence to bring them fruitfully into employment. This condition has led to a host of suggestions for national planning."

Though moderate in language, the report to the Chamber of Commerce was severe in its criticism of past methods in business enterprise. On the constructive side, it proposed the creation of a national economic council, under private auspices but including representation from the United States Department of Commerce. This council should employ experts of high competence, study the structure, functioning, and trends of business, lay bare the operations of the market place, and supply information for the guidance of enterprises. Under relaxed anti-trust laws, business concerns should be permitted to enter into contracts "for the purpose of equalizing production to consumption," and conducting business "on a sound basis." The formation of trade associations, the provision of unemployment reserves, private unemployment insurance, and other elements of planning, as suggested by the project of Gerard Swope, were brought under review. Immediate relief should be provided by private charity and by state and local government; proposals for federal appropriations should be opposed; but business enterprise has obligations pertaining to stabilization and continuity of employment — obligations created by a faulty functioning of the automatic system. There must not be delay, the Chamber's report insisted. "Time presses."

By the time the report to the Chamber of Commerce reached the public, a sub-committee of the Senate committee on manufactures, under the chairmanship of Robert M. La Follette, Jr., had held hearings on a bill to establish a national economic council. In the course of its proceedings, the subcommittee took the testimony of distinguished men of affairs, such as James A. Farrell, of United States Steel; Albert H. Wiggin, of the Chase National Bank; Alfred P. Sloan, of General Motors; and Charles E. Mitchell, of the National City Bank. It called upon eminent economists for their analysis and exposition of the severe contraction in business and for ways and means of mitigation and escape: upon Wallace B. Donham of the Harvard Business School, John M. Clark of Columbia University, and Virgil Jordan, formerly chief economist for the National Industrial Conference Board, for example. Spokesmen of labor, management, and social reform also laid their views before the subcommittee in language deliberately measured, yet revealing indignation at a system that permitted the stark contrast between potential plenty and evident misery and degradation. Day after day, Senator La Follette inquired and probed, seeking from great men of affairs and from close students of economy the clue to the deep mystery: How did it all happen and what is the way out?

At one end of the scale, Albert H. Wiggin answered for the philosophers of the "unconscious, automatic functioning of the markets." Is it possible to stabilize our industrial activity to any degree? "I do not think so." Did investment bankers contribute materially to the inflation and explosion in the security business? They were trying to supply what the customers wanted. Were they merely interested in the profits to be obtained from mergers and the issuance of securities under their auspices? "I should think so." Did the investment banker's incentive for profit affect his attitude toward the issuance of large security issues? "No banker intends to issue a security that is not going to be absorbed by the investing public. In other words, he is in business for profit and to make money." What is the way out? "Revival of business in the United States depends upon: (1) rapprochement between France and Germany; (2) reduced reparations; (3) reduced interallied debts; and (4) reduced tariffs."

Near the close of this hearing, Senator La Follette remarked: "Your counsel is one really of despair, then." Mr. Wiggin answered: "Human nature is human nature. Lives go on. So long as business activity goes on we are bound to have conditions of crisis once in so often." The Senator thought a moment and then commented: "The capacity for human suffering is unlimited?" The great man of affairs answered: "I think so." To clinch his contentions, Mr. Wiggin handed to the subcommittee a statement by Doctor

Benjamin Anderson, economic adviser to the Chase National Bank, who, the witness explained, is "highly respected. . . . He is a university man and a man of great intelligence. He is conscientious, and gives the truth of the situation." The learned Doctor's statement, when read into the record, proved to be a swift summary of the classic doctrine of laissez faire : let us alone and rely upon the unconscious, automatic functioning of the market. Thus an ancient code was repeated by rote and incorporated in a government document.

Against this classic theory, formulated by a learned Doctor and presented by one of the Lords of Creation, Senator La Follette set the statistics showing the functioning of the market as compiled by E. A. Goldenweiser, director of research and statistics of the Federal Reserve Board. In the form of graphic charts, Mr. Goldenweiser displayed the violent fluctuations of production and employment during the glorious age of prosperity from 1919 to 1931. As they stared at these charts, the Senators tried to see in the steep peaks and deep valleys the "equilibrium" of unconscious and automatic markets. Apparently equilibrium in reality did not conform to theory, even in a rough approximation.

By other economists, also respected and conscientious, "the truth of the situation" was presented in terms quite unlike the philosophy of the unconscious offered by the Chase National Bank. While rejecting the idea of iron regimentation in communist forms, they pointed out a long list of abuses in the capitalist system — abuses that did not square at all with the capitalist doctrine of "let us alone." Letting them alone, in fact, had not ended grave dislocations and suffering. The "unconscious" men in the market places should wake up, acquire a realistic knowledge of industrial processes, and substitute managerial intelligence for mere pecuniary interest and the automatic, acquisitive instinct. There had been reckless and ruinous financing of uneconomical projects. There is now a maldistribution of wealth that curtails buying power. Business must plan within the limits of exact knowledge ; government must deal boldly with rash banking and credit inflation and with swollen incomes and inheritances. If some economists seemed to be satisfied that this was the best possible world, others were ostensibly applying the sharp edge of analysis to capitalism, its methods, and its calamities. While the news of the hearings was flowing from the press, the reading public learned something about the kind of thinking that was going on among those in high places who were supposed to be exercising their brains.

§

As the distressful year of 1931 wore into the distressful year 1932 and preparations for the presidential campaign approached, the climate of opinion was vibrant with asserting, searching, doubting, hoping, and planning. Wherever confident citizens assembled in comfortable homes or paneled offices, the phrases of business inherited from times past ran current. Capital, the fruit of thrift and saving. Freedom of movement for capital and labor. Individual initiative, the paramount reliance. The profit motive, the source of prosperity. Restoration of equilibrium through the price mechanism. The natural order. Freedom of the markets. Business cycles. Readjustments. Best system in the world. Bigger prosperity after every panic. Recovery around the corner. No government interference. Loans from the Treasury for banks, railways, and insurance companies in distress. Charity and state and local relief for the unemployed. No starvation. The crazed public in quest of opportunities for investment. War, the cause of troubles. No limit to the suffering of humanity. I should not think so. I do not remember. I cannot recall. It may have been. To some extent, possibly. Technical correction by decline in stock prices. The American system. We may look forward without anxiety. Of such conceptions singly or in combinations was composed the thought of Respectability as it moved toward the quadrennial election geared by the Constitution of the United States to the movement of the planets.

Other words resounded in emphatic reiteration among clergymen, teachers, doctors, engineers, labor leaders, social workers, politicians, and business men who were not as certain in conviction as the members of Respectability. Our acquisitive society. Stark contrast between plenty and misery. Unbalance. Disequilibrium. Defects in capitalism. Rigid prices. Economics of scarcity. Tragedy of waste. Maldistribution of wealth. The absurdity of want amid plenty. Stealing preferable to starving. Challenges to the social order. Security of employment. Palaces and breadlines. Misery and luxury. Instability of industry. Parity of agriculture and industry. Bankruptcies and suicides. Crisis in government and economy. War on depression and poverty. Betrayal of fiduciary trust. Fraudulent securities. Control by corporations. Collective action. They guessed wrong. Economic planning. National planning. The folly of fatalism. Robber barons. Business must act. Government must act. Unendurable. Ridiculous. Insult to intelligence. Never again. Where now are the Lords of Creation?

If some of these words and phrases were intended to be coldly descriptive, all directly or by implication fanned the blaze of emotional insurgency. The recital of facts riddled the validity of old formulas. Ideas laden with revolutionary suggestions, once limited to groups obscure and unimportant, raced like wildfire from one end of the country to the other, adding intellectual ferment to the physical hardships that attended economic dissolutions.

# CHAPTER III

## *The Referendum in the Crisis*

WITH the inexorability of time the presidential election, as prescribed by the chronology of the Constitution, drew near, and politicians made ready for a great referendum on leadership, personalities, policies, measures, and the state of the nation. As the hour of decision approached, scanners of the horizon searched for portents in experience and philosophy. Despite signs of an upturn in economy, the shadows of dissolutions lay heavily upon the landscape, rural and urban. Slogans tinctured with radicalism were uttered in all parts of the country. Under powerful and respectable auspices comprehensive plans had been put forward for overcoming the ills of the panic and preventing such black plagues in the future.

In the circumstances many prophets forecast an immense diversion of political loyalty from the major parties that had long held the affections of the voters. Would history repeat itself? The panic of 1873 had been followed by violent agitations, the rise of a militant, if small, labor movement, and the rapid spread of the Greenback party. Indeed that

113

faction polled approximately a million votes in the congressional elections of 1878 and threatened to split both Republicans and Democrats. In the wake of the next crash, in 1893, had come a renewal of labor disputes, the Pullman strike of 1894, the emergence of Eugene V. Debs as a socialist leader, and the capture of the Democratic party by populist ideas and enthusiasm.

Such were some of the "lessons" from American experience available to prognosticators, but they were not the sole guides to the making of forecasts in 1932. The fate of Russia in the immense collapse of 1917 had indicated that at least on one occasion exponents of the Marxian theory had guessed right or had been fortunate in the turn of events. What had once been a mere scheme of dialectics debated in pot-houses and parlors now commanded a more general consideration, even from practical persons not at all given to speculations. According to the teachings of Marx, the economic breakdown, which started in 1929, might eventuate in something more serious than defaults, bankruptcies, doles, soup kitchens, and reform. Under his explanation of history, capitalism was not an everlasting order of things; it was a system always in process of development, marked by a growing concentration of wealth and control, by a falling rate of profit, and by periodical crises as inevitable features of its motion in time.

These crises, ran the Marxian theory, would increase in intensity and devastation until, at some point in coming years, capitalism would reach the end of its profitable expansion and the final cataclysm would occur. At that conjuncture the workers, triumphing over capitalists, would ring the death-knell of the profit system, usher in socialism or communism, celebrate humanity's "spring into freedom," and close history. Whether this prophecy was to be viewed with despair or delight, Americans were constantly told by the Marxists that the great depression was the beginning of the end. Or, if the crash did not culminate in the triumph of a Stalin, it might eventuate in the dictatorship of a Mussolini; fascists welcomed that eventuality. At all events, as the election approached, the air was charged with the feeling that strange things could "happen."

It was not necessary for voters to believe in any of the radical theories afloat to be impressed by the insistent demand for immense efforts in national planning and action to overcome the crisis and erect safeguards against its return. Leaders in churches, education, engineering, business enterprise, and the American Federation of Labor had advanced and defended more planning and less laissez faire. They had called for it in addresses, programs, and manifestoes during the previous year, 1931. They had discoursed on "our acquisitive society," the inadequacy of the profit motive, the contrast between potential plenty and actual scarcity, the necessity of industrial or government action to prevent the recurrence of such ruin, and drastic modifications in the prevailing system of economic use and wont. In 1931 Dr. Nicholas Murray Butler, responsible head of a great university, had said: "The period through which we are passing . . . is a period like the fall of the Roman Empire, like the Renaissance, like the beginning of the political and social revolutions in England and in France in the seventeenth and eighteenth centuries. . . . It is in some ways more powerful than them all; and it holds more of the world in its grip than any of them, but it certainly resembles them in its epoch-marking character." That America must "face the future" with rational plans for social security was a wide conviction, the need for which was proclaimed in the pulpit, on the platform, in gatherings of "experts," from business and professional forums, in conventions of the people, in the press. And in this ferment of opinion, pulsating with intense emotion, preparations for the national referendum on the crisis opened in the spring of 1932. But in spite of all the scanning, exploring, debating, and planning, in circles high and low, politicians betrayed little interest in theories and projects. They were primarily concerned, it seemed, with the instant need of things.

Trained in the earthly school of practice, Democratic
managers, to whom belonged the function of criticism and
opposition, felt reasonably certain that the exasperations of
the day would be ascribed to the party in power and that
victory would come to them by default, if they said little
about their intentions and made no mistakes in the choice
of a candidate or the conduct of the campaign. Under the
regime prevailing in the Solid South, many of the most
experienced and astute of the Democratic politicians were
men who had seen long service in Congress and had held
their seats despite the reverses of their party during the age
of Normalcy. Well acquainted with the demands of Southern planters, manufacturers, real estate agents, lawyers,
bankers, and cotton brokers, they were accounted hard-
headed and not given to apocalyptic visions.

The object of their hearts' desire was to oust from power
the party that had monopolized the choice places for twelve
years. And their Northern associates in the mechanics of
politics were equally eager for such a fray. Since the retirement of Woodrow Wilson, "deserving" Democrats from
Northern cities and fields had gathered few luscious plums
from the fruitful tree in Washington. As the skilled craftsmen of the trade assembled around the table of strategy,
they took some note, however, of that "lunatic fringe,"
called liberal, whose support might be necessary for the
acquisition of desirable things; but most of them could be
placated by small jobs. All the omens, then, seemed to be
auspicious for a Democratic triumph.

§

While the Democrats were gathering their forces, the
Republican convention assembled at Chicago, renominated
President Hoover and Vice President Curtis, formulated
their defensive explanation of unhappy events, and projected their program. The existence of an economic depression and widespread suffering the Republican platform

frankly admitted, and then proceeded to an elucidation of the calamity which laid little or no responsibility at the door of the party. The depression was world-wide; hence, according to the implications of the thesis, it was no mere national phenomenon to be ascribed to Republican policies. When trouble first appeared in undeniable form, President Hoover had averted many misfortunes "by securing agreement between industry and labor to maintain wages and by stimulating programs of private and governmental construction." When "the great drought of 1930" intensified the hardships of the people, they were mitigated by the mobilization of resources for physical relief, through the ministrations of the Red Cross. Under the presidential leadership a nation-wide organization was effected to grapple with the situation. Thus the general welfare had been maintained, argued the platform, by a combination of Republican management and policy with popular patience and courage — until the spring of 1931.

When the revolving earth brought the spring of that year, "the possibility of a business upturn in the United States was clearly discernible." Unhappily a series of unexpected tragedies then upset the calculations. Where could responsibility be placed? The Republican platform answered: "Suddenly a train of events was set in motion in Central Europe, which moved forward with extraordinary rapidity and violence, threatening the credit structure of the world and eventually dealing a serious blow to this country. The President foresaw the danger. He sought to avert it by proposing a suspension of intergovernmental debt payments for one year." But the strain was too great for the credit machinery of Central Europe. Disintegration continued "until in September Great Britain was forced to depart from the gold standard. This momentous event, followed by a tremendous raid on the dollar, resulted in a series of bank suspensions in this country, and the hoarding of currency on a large scale."

To avert the new perils flowing from the conduct of other

nations, President Hoover again took swift and effective action. Under his initiative the National Credit Association came into being and mobilized credit resources in aid of banks; the Railroad Credit Corporation was created; the capital of the Federal Land Banks was increased; the discount facilities of the Federal Reserve System were enlarged; and the power of the Reconstruction Finance Corporation was thrown into the breach. So a foundation was again laid for recovery. At this juncture, delays in Congress and the consideration of new and unsound measures, obviously fostered by Democrats, had kept the country in a state of uncertainty and offset much of the good otherwise accomplished. Undismayed by such carping opposition, Hoover had enlarged his program, supported loans to needy states for purposes of relief, and proposed the creation of a federal relief fund to aid states during a temporary failure of financial resources. In short, foreign governments and Democrats were the principal scapegoats.

Having dumped the causes of the national calamity at other doors, the Republicans made tenders to all interests. Financiers were informed that public expenditures were to be drastically reduced, Hoover's unbalanced budget brought into better equilibrium, the gold standard maintained, and the banking structure repaired. Moreover the depositing and investing public was remembered: federal supervision over the Reserve system was to be widened and made more stringent. Affiliates of member banks, which had led in the flotation of securities, should be examined and required to make reports, until information was developed for a more permanent solution of the problem they had presented. Home owners were to receive additional assistance. The policy of federal aid to agriculture was to be continued and broadened. Manufacturers and farmers could confidently rely upon the maintenance and extension of the protective principle. Consumers of electric power should have the benefit of federal supervision over interstate transmission of current. Labor was reminded of the many favorable laws passed under Republican auspices. That was history. For the present and future : "Collective bargaining by responsible representatives of employers and employees, of their own choice, without the interference of any one, is recognized and approved." The language of the pledge did not make it clear whether an outside organizer for the American Federation of Labor was to be banned, but at all events there was something for the consideration of labor. Moreover the platform commended "the constructive work" of the United States Department of Labor.

As if bidding for the support of Americans who adhered to the collaboration of the world powers for peace, the Republican platform proposed an ambient policy. Membership in the World Court should be accepted. The American delegation was "laboring for progress" in the reduction of armaments at Geneva. The Republican administration had acted in harmony with the League of Nations in the interests of peace. With pointed reference to Japan's seizure of Manchukuo, it had announced that it would not recognize any situation, treaty, or agreement brought about in violation of the Kellogg Pact. In continuation of this policy, Congress should enact legislation authorizing the calling of an international congress in case of any threat that the terms of the Pact would not be fulfilled. As for "our neighbors of Latin-America," they may be sure that "we have no imperialistic ambitions." Aid had been given to Nicaragua in the solution of its troubles, the number of marines stationed there had been reduced, and services of supervision over Haiti were being rapidly abridged. But the isolationists were not neglected : there had been no entanglement in the Sino-Japanese dispute during the consistent maintenance of treaty rights and international obligations, and it had been made patent to the League of Nations "that American policy would be determined at home."

Far down the line in the Republican program, after highways, crime, narcotics, and civil service, came the plank on the Eighteenth Amendment. If the sense for news values was a gauge of the primary public interest in the very throes of the depression, this plank was the most important concern of the people, for The New York Times placed the prohibition pledge of the Republicans on its first page and relegated the rest of the party document to page fifteen. Although a strong bloc at Chicago demanded an outright repeal of the Amendment, Hoover's managers forced the adoption of a middle course. The issue of prohibition repeal was to be resubmitted to the voters and repeal, if it came, was to be restricted by safeguards in favor of temperance: the Federal Government was to protect dry states against the invasion of the liquor traffic from other states and it was also to prevent the return of the saloon. The proposal, Hoover remarked, did not "dictate to the conscience of any member of the party"; it guaranteed that "in no part of the United States shall there be a return of the saloon system with its inevitable political and social corruption, and its organized interference with other states."

Having announced and justified their faith, the Republicans shot sarcastic barbs at their opponents: "The vagaries of the present Democratic House of Representatives offer characteristic and appalling proof of the existing incapacity of that party for leadership in a national crisis. Individualism running amuck has displaced party discipline and has trampled underfoot party leadership. A bewildered electorate has viewed the spectacle with profound dismay and deep misgivings." Unable to agree upon any grand policy, the Democrats in Congress, according to the Republican interpretation, had only found some unity of action around "the pork barrel." Between the helpless citizens and the evils threatened by such measures "a Republican President stands resolutely," and "the people, regardless of party, will demand his continued service." Insurgent Republicans had also given the administration anxious days and nights. They were not mentioned by name, but they were told that coherent party action was necessary for the adoption of "well-planned and wholesome" legislation. Apparently identifying the Republican party with the nation, the platform sought to impress upon Senators and Representatives "the inflexible truth that their first concern should be the welfare of the United States and the well-being of all of its people, and that stubborn pride of individual opinion is not a virtue." After a recapitulation, the platform closed as follows: "The Republican party faces the future unafraid! With courage and confidence in ultimate success, we will strive against the forces that strike at our social and economic ideals, our political institutions."

§

In his acceptance address, President Hoover spoke with evident concern of the blights that had fallen upon the country, his efforts to cope with them, and the pledges of the party platform. Here and there he commented upon and amplified its terms, strongly commending its analysis, criticisms, and proposals. After all it was his work and came entirely within his frame of social and economic reference. For the first stage of the panic, over-production, reckless speculation, and abuse of financial power had been mainly responsible; for the second, the renewed outbreak of the "insidious diseases" left by the world war. "Two courses were open. We might have done nothing. That would have been utter ruin. Instead, we met the situation with proposals to private business and the Congress of the most gigantic program of economic defense and counter-attack ever evolved in the history of the Republic. We put it into action. . . . No government in Washington has hitherto considered that it held so broad a responsibility for leadership in such times." Yet more work remained to be done. Millions were still unemployed. Farmers' prices were below a living standard. Other millions were haunted by fears for their future. "No man with a spark of humanity can sit in my place without suffering from the picture of their anxieties and hardships before him day and night." If reëlected, the President promised that he would carry forward the work of reconstruction within the limits of the American system.

Among the generalities and pledges of Hoover's address were a few words that bore upon the agricultural problem — so fateful to his career: "The farmer was never so dependent upon his tariff protection for recovery as he is at the present time. We shall hold to that." To this particular constituency these remarks were gratifying, but insufficient. In fact, to belligerent farmers they were hollow, without meaning. Farmers were demanding measures more drastic, especially control over price-depressing surpluses. What had Mr. Hoover to say on that proposition? No such scheme could come within the scope of his economic and social philosophy. "No power on earth," he admonished the nation, "can restore prices except by restoration of general recovery and markets. . . . There is no relief to the farmer by extending government bureaucracy to control his production and thus curtail his liberties, nor by subsidies that bring only more bureaucracy and ultimate collapse. I shall oppose them." To militant agrarians gathering for the fray, this was unpalatable — all the more so as coming from a President who had created a huge bureaucracy for the promotion of commerce and housed it in a costly building, who had approved lucrative subsidies for shipping and aviation. Admittedly he expressed his conviction and with courage for his words cost votes where votes were needed. "Not regimented mechanisms, but free men, is our goal," the President declared. . . . "This is my pledge to the Nation and to Almighty God."

With their interpretation of history exhibited in the platform, the lines of the drama written, and the stage set for the play, the Republicans faced the problem of presenting their candidate to the public in appealing form. This enterprise offered difficulties. For months Charles Michelson, clever and vitriolic agent of the Democratic National Committee, had been daily, almost hourly, picturing the

President to the country as a bewildered, baffled, futile man, hard of heart and indifferent to human sufferings. Nor were things going well in the councils of the President's party. Few of the seasoned veterans in Republican politics felt in perfect rapport with Hoover. Whatever ingenuity his ways revealed, it was not exactly their type of ingenuity. Stalwarts who had affection for Normalcy disliked Hoover and were free in expressing their contempt in the lobbies and salons of Washington. Other Republican members of Congress, such as Senator La Follette, Senator Norris, and Senator Cutting, had joined with Democrats in defeating or mutilating measures drafted in the White House, and their designs had encountered numerous retaliations at the hands of the President. Bringing them into line proved to be an impossibility. Yet as the bitter jealousies of Napoleon's generals were often stilled in the presence of battle and sudden death, so the antipathies among most opponents in the President's party were momentarily put aside as the managers joined in what journalists call the "build-up" of their candidate. Fortunately for the cause, Hoover's intimates were extremely loyal; in their eyes he was a great figure, unappreciated but of heroic stature — the type required by the exigencies of the trying times.

As presiding officer at the Republican convention in Chicago, the Honorable Bertrand H. Snell, leader of his party in the House of Representatives, had presented the thesis, the antithesis, the synthesis, and the deus ex machina. For many years, he said, under "progressive, forward-looking, constructive Republican leadership" the country had prospered and reveled in the felicity of security. It was true that "the invisible but ghastly pestilence of world-wide economic depression" had descended upon the land. How had that untoward event occurred under such leadership? "It is the ghost of the World War stalking over the earth." At this point, when the grand old party of Abraham Lincoln was wrestling with a fate not of its own making, the Democratic party had got control of the House of Representatives.

And with what consequences? "Uncertainty about the future increased; confidence all but disappeared; business continued to slow down. The country was thrown into a state of mind approaching chaos. No one could foretell what the Democratic majority would propose or would do next. There followed a period of anxious waiting, of trembling inactivity."

Speaking with the authority of a Representative who had witnessed at first hand the political operations in Washington, the Honorable Mr. Snell gave the country his picture of Democratic capacity. So long as they followed the guidance of President Hoover "all was well"; but, "when they started casting about for a program of their own, they became mired. They began with a blaring of trumpets." They organized a policy committee to arrange a program "to put the world back into joint." They called in their members of Congress, "all of their defeated candidates for President, and all their other master minds." Yet "not all of these geniuses combined were able to evolve a plan because no two of them could agree upon any plan." Confusion and open revolt followed the effort. "The Democratic party has as many wings as it has candidates and certainly its candidates are legion. These wings do not flap together; they flap against each other. The Democratic party is a mob of feuds and factions, unable to bring order out of the chaos in its own ranks." How could such a motley crowd maintain order in government? "The nation is to be asked to accept confusion as national policy and disorder as a rule of government." That chaos the people cannot want or endure. "They want a party in control that has a program, knows where it is going, and has the courage of leadership."

At the head of this fraternity stood President Hoover, "the pilot who keeps eternal vigil on the bridge of the ship of state. . . . No man living or dead has had to grapple with such gigantic problems at home and abroad. No man living or dead has fought world-wide economic adversity with so stout a heart and so deep an understanding." George Washington "as an engineer solved stupendous and vexatious problems for the benefit of mankind. . . . President Hoover's mind is the mind of an engineer. He first gets his facts and then he acts. . . . Sureness of decision, solidity of formation, and enduring construction by using tested materials is ingrained in the education and thought processes of an engineer. These traits are governing in all decisions on all questions. Herbert Hoover, the engineer President of the United States, is solving, and will solve, stupendous and vexatious problems, as did our first engineer President, for the benefit of our mankind. . . . With indomitable confidence and courage, with faith in our Commander-in-Chief, and with a comradeship of purpose to meet every foe of the republic, foreign or domestic, let us press onward, shouting the great American battle cry: 'Forward to victory!'"

This delineation of Herbert Hoover as "the great engineer" in the White House applying rationality to the process of government was surely dexterous and yet it did not evoke popular enthusiasm. Nor was it a complete picture of the man. Already the phrase, "great engineer," had become the subject of ribald jest among indecorous journalists. So to the rescue of Republican politicians was brought the subtler and more ingenious artistry of the man of letters, William Allen White. In making an appeal to millions of women voters and their no less sentimental brethren in search of mercy as well as omniscience, the portrayal of a giant endowed with the strength of technology was inadequate. It left the humanity of the President out of the reckoning and needed correction. The task of retouching the picture Mr. White therefore undertook in an editorial that was scattered broadcast as a pamphlet by the Republican campaign committee under the heading: "Hails Genius of Hoover." Writing at the close of the session of Congress in the summer of 1932, with the record before him, Mr. White was in command of hard facts, as well as the superlatives of his craft, and he rose to the heights of the occasion.

How had the devastating calamity come upon America? Mr. White gave his answer to the question: the President and his advisers "early last year decided that this depression was part of a world-wide phase of after-war adjustment in civilization." Against this thing, President Hoover had formulated his program. The establishment of the Reconstruction Finance Corporation was "the greatest fiscal measure ever adopted by any government in all times." Had the President failed to secure its creation "not a bank in America would be open today and our commercial system would be paralyzed." Other measures of a supporting nature had been pressed through Congress under executive leadership — for balancing the budget, effecting economy in expenditures, and saving the homes of debtors. No other President had ever won as much "in any other eight months in the history of this nation. He has won constructive, necessary legislation of a wide, important scope, and in some cases of an almost revolutionary character." It was not perfect, but without Hoover's guiding brain more errors and weaknesses would have crept into legislation. There in monolithic form stood the monument of national salvation.

Fearful that the people were unable to appreciate the man so incarnate in the deed, Mr. White sought to enlighten them further: "President Hoover's leadership is not vocal. He cannot address the American people. His strength is in conference. He cannot make public sentiment and thereby coerce Congress. Roosevelt and Wilson worked that way; so did Lincoln. But Hoover's talent is a different talent. He can convince individual men, small coteries of men, groups that can be reached by his voice, that are impressed by his sincerity, that are carried along by the resistless logic of his position. . . . Hoover cannot appeal over Congress to the masses."

So constituted by nature, the President, in Mr. White's drawing, was at the mercy of unscrupulous or less scrupulous men. "Hoover's method," he explained, "involves a struggle with individuals, with militant minorities, with mean and selfish groups that seek party or factional advantage. Moreover Hoover's method leaves the public at the mercy of demagogues. . . . So Hoover stands alone. He has fought this good fight for eight long grinding months which have torn his heart out, wracked his body, tattered his patience, but he has won. . . . He may have to wait for history to give him the laurel, but he has won it. . . . America has had no other President who has done in eight months such Herculean work for the salvation of his country as Herbert Hoover has done since December 1931. . . . Here is a rounded man, human, subject to the foibles of humanity, but strong, clean, brave and wise, a leader worthy of the times." In short, Hoover was the personification of kindness in strength, of humanism combined with rationality, the wracked and heart-torn savior of America in a time of great crisis — a picture drawn by a friend who had seen the man within the President, the victim of mean, selfish, factional, and demagogic assaults. That the portrayal was eloquent not even the most carping critics could deny. Would history accept it?

§

With the depression still in full swing and President Hoover standing firmly on his program, the Democrats made ready for the choice of their candidate. Assuming that the laurel would not wither on election day, many aspirants looked with longing eyes upon the prize of nomination. Governor Albert Ritchie, of Maryland, entertained hopes. Backed by William Randolph Hearst and Senator William Gibbs McAdoo, John Nance Garner gathered a quota of delegates for the convention. Naturally eager to remove the sting of his defeat in 1928, Alfred E. Smith cast about somewhat unobtrusively for support and his friends came to believe that in an hour of deadlock the crown might go to him. Newton D. Baker was mentioned. But in the process of capturing delegates, Governor Franklin Delano Roosevelt, of New York, early spurted ahead.

When the Democratic convention assembled, Governor
Roosevelt had the largest following — an impressive number,
though not the two-thirds made necessary by the rule of the
party. If that gave him hope, it provided no assurance.
Champ Clark had possessed a majority of the delegates in
1912, but Woodrow Wilson, powerfully aided by William
Jennings Bryan, had wrested the honor from him almost at
the moment of his victory. Failing in an effort to change the
two-thirds rule, Governor Roosevelt's managers made a
skillful maneuver behind the scenes. Delegates pledged to
Mr. Garner were shifted to Governor Roosevelt, thus guaranteeing his nomination, and by courtesy, if not by trade,
Mr. Garner was selected as the candidate for Vice President.
When William Gibbs McAdoo announced in the convention that California would vote for Roosevelt, some cynics
cried in unison: "What price California?" But after the
answer came, all was forgotten in the jollification of comradeship; or rather, almost all, for in the bitterness of his
soul, Alfred E. Smith, having failed to receive the nomination, could scarcely bring himself to support the choice of his
party.

In contrast with the Republican platform, the Democratic
pronouncement was a paragon of brevity. Save in minor
particulars, it was, however, far less explicit. Apart from a
few points, it presented no direct alternatives to the Republican promises of salvation. The Republicans had represented themselves as the victims of inexorable history not of
their own making and as heroic figures beating back the cruel
tides of adversity that flowed from other shores. As a matter
of interpretation and tactics, the Democrats rejected this
explanation of recent events and drew bold outlines of the
villain in the drama.

"The chief causes" of the unhappy state of the nation, the
Democrats declared, "were the disastrous policies pursued
by our Government since the World War, of economic isolation, fostering the merger of competitive business into monopolies and encouraging the indefensible expansion and

contraction of credit for private profit at the expense of the public. Those who were responsible for these policies have abandoned the ideals on which the war was won and thrown away the fruits of victory. . . . They have ruined our foreign trade; destroyed the values of our commodities and products, crippled our banking system, robbed millions of our people of their life savings, and thrown millions more out of work, produced wide-spread poverty and brought the Government to a state of financial distress unprecedented in time of peace." Although Republicans as such were not mentioned in this bill of indictment, they had been in control of the Government since the world war. Hence there was no doubt about the location of "those who were responsible." And, the Democrats declared, "the only hope" of improvement, of restoration, of bringing the nation back to the proud position of domestic happiness and leadership in the world "lies in a drastic change in economic governmental policies."

And what "drastic changes in economic governmental policies" were proposed by the Democrats? They fell into two groups: the one, involving a resort to old policies; and the other, departures from traditions in the form of new policies. First, there was to be "an immediate and drastic reduction of governmental expenditures . . . to accomplish a saving of not less than twenty-five per cent in the cost of Federal Government" and a call upon the states to make a zealous effort to achieve a proportionate result. Second, the federal budget was to be balanced annually and revenues raised "on the principle of ability to pay." In the pruning of expenditures, a navy and army "adequate for national defense" were to be maintained, but the facts must be surveyed to the end "that the people in time of peace may not be burdened by an expenditure fast approaching a billion dollars annually."

Paying tribute to historic Respectability, the Democrats advocated "a sound currency to be preserved at all hazards," and, remembering Populism, they approved "an international monetary conference . . . to consider the rehabilita-

tion of silver and related questions." The anti-trust laws
were to be strengthened and impartially enforced — for the
benefit of labor and the small producer and distributor. With
reference to foreign trade there must be "a competitive tariff
for revenue," a fact-finding tariff commission free from executive interference, reciprocal trade agreements with other nations, and an international economic conference to restore
international trade.

Aside from the reference to a competitive tariff for revenue,
the meaning of which was far from clear, the Democratic
platform so far presented few flat contradictions to the tenders made in the Republican pronouncement. Whatever
may have been the content of the phrase "competitive
tariff" in the minds of the authors, it offered no unequivocal
promise of a revision downward, either general or selective.

Taking up another theme which had long agitated business
men, the Democrats wrote into their platform a clause
advocating "the removal of government from all fields of
private enterprise." Thus they repudiated the socialistic
stigma and endorsed a motto which had entranced chambers
of commerce for many years. That fitted well into the project
for strengthening and enforcing the anti-trust laws in the
manner proposed by Woodrow Wilson in his New Freedom.
But, as if recalling such recent legislation as the Act for the
distribution of electric power at Boulder Dam and the approval of such invasions of the business field by the Republican platform, the Democrats added a proviso: there was
to be no competition with private enterprise "except where
necessary to develop public works and natural resources in
the common interest."

Under the head of old policy came also the Democratic
promises touching assistance for the unemployed: "We
advocate the extension of federal credit to the states to provide unemployment relief wherever the diminishing resources
of the states make it impossible for them to provide for the
needy; expansion of the federal program of necessary and
useful construction affected with a public interest, such as

adequate flood control and waterways." In no way did this pledge depart from the program initiated by President Hoover, endorsed by his party, and offered to the future. Nor was there anything new in the Democratic plank advocating " the spread of employment by a substantial reduction in the hours of labor, the encouragement of the shorter week by applying the principle in government service." Just how the reduction in the hours of labor was to be effected was left to the imagination of the voters. Certainly the language of the clause carried no implication that the thing advocated was to be realized by direct federal intervention in the processes of industry. On the contrary, the reference to a possible example set by the federal service indicated a platonic wish, rather than a specific act of Congress making a curtailment of hours mandatory throughout the nation, if necessary in defiance of the states.

Coming to "drastic changes" which they had promised, the Democrats incorporated in their platform a few items that at least implied novelty. Republican leaders had referred provisions for unemployment and old age to business enterprise itself. The Democrats left the issue to the states: "We advocate unemployment and old age insurance under state laws." This was positive and constituted the only direct bid to labor contained in the platform, apart, perhaps, from the promise to prosecute the trusts. As if recurring to the age-long effort to unite agrarians in the South and the West, the Democrats devised their offering to agriculture, cautiously and yet with inferences that might be fundamental; they favored "effective control of crop surpluses so that our farmers may have the full benefit of the domestic market" and "the enactment of every constitutional measure that will aid the farmers to receive for their basic farm commodities prices in excess of cost."

Just what did that mean in 1932? The Republican platform recognized the problem of controlling farm production and favored a national policy for diminishing the acreage under production by the withdrawal of marginal lands. Did the authors of the Democratic pledge mean that, if victorious, the Democrats would enact federal legislation providing for crop control? And what kind of legislation for farmers was deemed to be "constitutional," as the platform delimited its own promises? No clue to the reply was given until the candidate, Franklin D. Roosevelt, later put a gloss on the confession of faith by espousing the agrarians' program for effective crop control under the stimulus of contributions from the national treasury.

To the Republicans in possession of the Federal Government, the Democratic platform attributed perversions of the economic system, which had robbed millions of their savings, thrown millions out of work, and produced widespread poverty. By implication, the capitalist system itself was essentially sound. Only Republican abuses had brought on the great catastrophe. But how were such evils to be corrected and avoided for the future? The Democrats offered several panaceas. The "investing public" was to be protected by requiring all persons and concerns offering stocks and bonds for sale to file with the Government and carry in their advertisements: "true information as to bonuses, commissions, principal invested, and interests of the sellers." Though a similar proposal had been made by the Industrial Commission in 1900, under the administration of President McKinley, the dust of neglect had gathered upon it. Now the Democrats promised action and went further. They advocated the regulation of holding companies which sold securities in interstate commerce, the regulation of exchanges in securities and commodities, the severance of security and investment affiliates from commercial banks, and additional restrictions on the power of Federal Reserve banks to permit "the use of Federal Reserve facilities for speculative purposes." In line with Republican recommendations, the Democrats also proposed federal regulation of the rates of utility companies operating across state lines. By cutting off certain excrescences that had grown on the American economic system, the ills and worries of the time were to be banished, it seemed, restoration and recovery assured, and the great ideal of Jefferson, the founder of the party, attained: "Equal rights to all; special privileges to none."

Somewhat outside the circle of economic enterprise — outside agriculture, industry, and labor — stood the question of Prohibition, the burning issue of the hour judging by the salvos that greeted references to repeal in the convention at Chicago. Here the Democrats were explicit, in part: "We advocate the repeal of the Eighteenth Amendment." The Republicans had merely promised to submit an amendment allowing the states to deal with the liquor problem in their own way. The Democrats dared to flaunt the word "Repeal." The Republicans had called for legislation protecting the dry states and fending off the return of the saloon. The Democrats invited the states to enact laws that would promote temperance, "effectively prevent the return of the saloon," and bring the liquor traffic under control. The Republicans had pledged to the states the aid of the Federal Government in upholding prohibition where it existed and in safeguarding citizens everywhere against the return of the saloon. So, too, the Democrats demanded that "the Federal Government effectively exercise its power to enable the states to protect themselves against importation of intoxicating liquors in violation of their laws." Those who read and compared the language of the two platforms discovered differences in words which were microscopic rather than the sharp oppositions of black and white, except for the Democratic promise to repeal the Volstead Act.

However much or little the Democratic platform differed from the Republican program on the issues of domestic affairs, its declarations in direct matters of foreign policy certainly stuck close to tradition and practice. The tender of reciprocal trade agreements was an old Republican device that had been advocated and tried with results little more than pitiable. Like the Republicans, the Democrats favored entering the World Court, consulting with the powers on threatened violations of the Kellogg Pact and other treaties, international agreements for the reduction of armaments, and insistence upon the payment of the debts owed to the United States by foreign governments. In substance this was a vow to continue the policies of President Hoover, with such elements of Woodrow Wilson's "idealism" as had been incorporated in the old body of diplomatic formulas. Yet on one point, the Democrats were peremptory: "independence for the Philippines." For both parties that had once been an academic matter; now it was emerging from the realm of platitude into the sphere of action and hence the Democratic reiteration of the old slogan had a reality not hitherto attached to it.

§

With the country in distress, with agriculture wracked by more than ten years of ruinous prices, mortgage foreclosures, and bankruptcies, with a platform ambiguous enough for any occasion, what image of their candidate did the Democrats present to the country? By ingenious minds it was formed for the opening pages of their "campaign book." Franklin Delano Roosevelt was a descendant of early Dutch settlers on his father's side and of "equally fine colonial ancestry" on his mother's side. For capturing the Irish, Italian, and German vote that was fortunate and it offended no Anglo-Americans. Franklin was born "in a fine old home overlooking the Hudson River, surrounded by trees and looking across a field where the hay had been cut for over a hundred years. His godfather was Elliott Roosevelt, the only brother of Theodore." The fact was not mentioned but it was true that, relatively speaking, Gaius Sempronius Gracchus, younger son of Tiberius and Cornelia, was also well born. Still, "even those who know" Franklin D. Roosevelt best, "often wonder that one man can so perfectly understand the viewpoint of the dirt farmer and the city laborer, the man in the street and the one in high places — and can so quietly, impartially, firmly, uphold the rights of each and achieve a fair deal for all." That was a problem in social psychology and the Democratic image-makers supplied the solution.

The solution? "As a boy young Franklin roamed the woods, read in the well-stocked library, rode horseback, and took a child's eager interest in all that pertained to the management of a large and prosperous farm." He sailed boats on the water, traveled abroad, cycling from country to country. "At school he broke athletic records, kept up his classwork without difficulty but without enthusiasm." Evidently no academician, no bookworm, was offered to the people. "Early taught by his illustrious cousin Theodore" the lesson of good citizenship, young Franklin began to preach the doctrine. Meanwhile he "did not neglect more personal interests, and soon after graduation [from Harvard] he married Miss Anna Eleanor Roosevelt, his distant cousin and the favorite niece of the President. Theodore Roosevelt gave the bride away, dashing from a St. Patrick's day parade to the ceremony. With typical Roosevelt enthusiasm, the young wife threw herself whole-heartedly into her husband's interests." Elected to the state senate "by a strong rural vote," the young knight "won his spurs as an aggressive liberal leader" and helped to defeat an old-guard candidate for the United States Senate "to the dismay of seasoned politicians, including the famous Charlie Murphy of Tammany Hall." Made an Assistant Secretary of the Navy by Woodrow Wilson, Mr. Roosevelt had done his full part in "helping to win the war," keeping on good terms with the 125,000 workers employed on Navy projects.

After the close of the world war, Franklin D. Roosevelt was a national figure. As the nominee of his party for Vice President in 1920, he campaigned over the country "by car, train, and airplane." Stricken by the tragedy of desperate illness, he had battled his way through the trials and had emerged crippled but fit for public duties. Believing whole-heartedly "in a Progressive Democratic party," he had nominated Alfred E. Smith at the convention of 1924 and again in 1928. In aid of Mr. Smith's candidacy, he "proved his friendship . . . to the hilt by consenting to run for Governor of New York." Despite the Republican landslide he carried the state in 1928 and was even more triumphantly reëlected two years later. As Governor he "sponsored the most intelligent and constructive program for helping the farmer that the state has ever known." To labor, "organized and unorganized," he proved himself a reliable friend, by advancing a program of labor legislation. As Governor, he also strengthened the laws providing for old-age insurance, took direct action to reduce the volume of unemployment, and called an extraordinary session of the legislature to deal with the pressing issue of relief for the impoverished. He had given the consumer "a fair deal," demanded from public utilities "fair service at reasonable rates," and managed to put teeth into the state laws "that really protect the poor man, and the obscure man, whether he be farmer, small business owner, or city apartment dweller."

Now Franklin D. Roosevelt has been called to a campaign for the presidency. What will he do to cope with the cataclysmic upheavals? "Roosevelt is for fundamental measures which will prevent the recurrence of the present economic disaster. He is for a substantial lowering of the tariff — which will allow a flow of goods between countries; as well as for the building up of the home market by a reduction in the differential between the farmers and the industrial workers; and by giving the industrial workers security of wages through unemployment insurance . . . holding himself equally responsible to every section, every class, and every citizen." When tendered the Democratic nomination, he had "electrified the convention" by a spectacular flight from Albany to Chicago, broken traditions by accepting the honor then and there, and dedicated himself "to a new deal for the American people."

Beside the word-picture of Franklin D. Roosevelt as a personality and statesman, the Democratic campaign man-

agers placed an etching of his colleague in the campaign,
John Nance Garner. Mr. Garner, in the revered American
tradition, was born in a log cabin. Though an offspring of
colonial pioneers, his grandmother, born Katherine Walpole,
had descended from "the Walpoles who produced the English prime minister." After a boyhood in field and forest,
Mr. Garner made his way upward through country schooling
and a training "in the Methodist faith, to which he still ad-
heres," through "one term at Vanderbilt University," to
success in the practice of law, publishing, banking, and local
offices, and finally to a place in the Congress of the United
States. There he worked against the "autocracy" of Speaker
Joseph Cannon, wrestled with the Goliath of Finance, Andrew W. Mellon, advocated graduated income and inheritance taxes to ease the burdens of the poor and make the
rich bear their share, and served as a "watchdog of the
treasury." In Congress, Mr. Garner labored against "the
iniquitous features of the Hawley-Smoot tariff act," voted
against the Eighteenth Amendment, and valiantly sought to
"balance the budget." Acting contrary to local religious
convictions, Mr. Garner, without counting the cost, had
enthusiastically supported the candidacy of Alfred E. Smith
in 1928 as the "regular" nominee of the party. As leader in
the House of Representatives, he entered the lists against
President Hoover on the ground "that the small business man
and the individual merited as much consideration in the
way of government loans as the banks, insurance companies,
and railroads."

Their portrait of Mr. Garner as a symbol of Americanism,
the Democratic campaign managers supplemented by his
own confession of faith in the form of a letter of acceptance.
"There are just two things to this Government as I see it,"
said the candidate. "The first is to safeguard the lives and
properties of our people; the second is to insure that each
of us has a chance to work out his destiny according to his
talents. . . . In my opinion nearly all of our civic troubles
are the consequence of Government's departure from its

legitimate functions. . . . Government is not a pedagogue,
nor a parson, nor a pied piper. . . . Had it not been for the
steady encroachment of Federal Government on the rights
and duties reserved for the states, we perhaps would not have
the present spectacle of the people rushing to Washington to
set right whatever goes wrong." The economic distress
through which the country is passing cannot be wholly explained by "outside influences over which we have no control." These are contributing factors but the major causes
can be found in the legislation and policies of Republican
leaders. On the doorstep of the Republican party lie the
unbalanced budget and mounting expenditures. The Democrats? They have promised a twenty-five per cent reduction.
"That pledge will be redeemed." Their tariff plank is
"equally definite and constructive, and must have a strong
appeal to industrialists, farmers, labor, and business men who
all suffered by the wrecking of our foreign trade under the
embargo rates." There, the Democratic managers said in
effect, is John Nance Garner's explanation of the depression
and his frame of economic reference for salvation.

§

In his address of acceptance, delivered in person before
the Chicago convention, Mr. Roosevelt presented his interpretation of recent history, his analysis of automatic market
operations, and his overarching hypothesis for policy. During the period of expansion "there was little or no drop in the
prices that the consumer had to pay although . . . the
cost of production fell very greatly; corporate profit resulting
from this period was enormous; at the same time little of that
profit was devoted to the reduction of prices. The consumer
was forgotten. Very little of it went into increased wages;
the worker was forgotten; and by no means an adequate
proportion was even paid out in dividends — the stockholder
was forgotten." Where did the corporate surpluses go?
"First, into new and unnecessary plants which now stand

stark and idle; and secondly, into the call money market of Wall Street, either directly by the corporations, or indirectly through the banks. Those are the facts. Why blink them?" In the hour of lamentation, the Republican administration had come to the aid of the interests at "the top of the pyramid," on the old assumption that benefits would leak down to those at the bottom. In reality, "never in all history have the interests of all the people been so united in a single economic problem. . . . Statesmanship and vision, my friends, require relief to all at the same time."

According to this economic interpretation, the managers of the unconscious, automatic market had consciously and willfully manipulated it, and the Republican administration had sprung to the aid of the men at the top. "And there we are today!" exclaimed Mr. Roosevelt. What now is to be done to cure and avoid? Governments must economize. The Eighteenth Amendment must be repealed though the return of the saloon must be prevented. Daylight is to be let through securities offered to the investing public. The avenue to employment is to be partly opened by well-planned public works as self-sustaining as possible. Agriculture is in a slough of despond. "Final voluntary reduction of surplus is a part of our objective," but emergency measures are necessary to repair the immediate damages. "Such a plan as that, my friends, does not cost the Government any money, nor does it keep the Government in business or in speculation." So far as the actual words of the farm bill are concerned, "the Democratic party stands ready to be guided by whatever the responsible farm groups themselves agree on." For mortgaged home owners and farmers, credit is to be eased. The "primary responsibility for relief rests with localities now, as ever"; yet the Federal Government has a continuing responsibility that will soon be fulfilled. In these terms Mr. Roosevelt set forth his view of "the recent history and the simple economics, the kind of economics that you and I and the average man and woman talk." "Woman," it seemed, was not to be forgotten either.

While laying emphasis on domestic economy, Mr. Roosevelt took into account its contacts with world commerce. Republican leaders of the nation had erected "an impregnable barbed wire entanglement around its borders through the instrumentality of tariffs which have isolated us from all the other human beings in all the rest of the round world." On their part, the Democrats had made their tariff offer and Mr. Roosevelt approved: "I accept that admirable tariff statement in the platform of this convention. It would protect American business and American labor." Leaving aside specifications of the protection to be afforded, Mr. Roosevelt continued: "By our acts of the past we have invited and received the retaliation of other nations. I propose an invitation to them to forget the past, to sit at the table with us, as friends, and to plan with us for the restoration of the trade of the world." Yet agriculture is to have "a reasonable tariff protection; . . . the same protection that industry has today." Thus, although the Democratic managers had been careful in their portrait to remove all academic taint from their candidate, he himself seemed to proclaim the formula of historic internationalism so assiduously and stoutly propagated by the schoolmen — that dream logic belied by all the tariff acts of the leading nations since the fateful year 1918. However, the dream logic of Mr. Roosevelt was safeguarded by qualifications — protection for American business, American labor, and American agriculture.

§

When the parts of the two major platforms bearing upon specific economic issues were superimposed and all were rearranged with reference to any scheme of economic thought and corresponding reality, their similarities were striking. They presented essentially the same structure, the same elements, the same interpretation of American culture and history. Both accepted as permanent the continuance of the prevailing ownership and distribution of real and intangible property and promised to take the government out of business. Both accepted the imperative of the profit motive as the prime motor in setting and keeping real property in action to produce wealth, with the contingencies of opportunity, risk, losses, and insecurity inseparably attached. Both assumed that the automatic pressure of competition would prevent "artificial" prices, hold down "exorbitant" profits, and estop perilous concentration of wealth. Both assumed that a "fairly" just distribution of wealth would occur through the automatic and unconscious operation of the price and wage mechanism in the marketplace, sustaining the continuous circulation of commodities and the equilibrium of economy. The perdurance of all American culture, including mores, folkways, and ethical sentiments, was likewise taken for granted by the two platforms; in other words, there would be a continuity of what John R. Commons called "duty, performance, forbearance, and avoidance" on the part of those who possessed little or no real or tangible property under the prevailing system of tenure, use, and wont. No doubt, duties, performances, forbearances, and avoidances were as necessary to functioning economy as property, real and intangible, but owners could count on nonowners fulfilling these obligations without making sociological disturbances.

In formulating their articles of faith, therefore, the makers of the two platforms departed from the political philosophy bequeathed by the Fathers of the Republic, rejected even the implication of development, and adopted the equivalence of the schoolmen in economics, who knew no history or excluded it from their conception of reality as injecting irrational vagaries into the symmetry of rationality — the "natural" order. James Madison had foreseen a time when the great mass of the people would be without property of any kind; when the statesmen of America would find all their wisdom tested. Thomas Jefferson had contemplated the arrival of that contingency. Daniel Webster had propounded a similar philosophy of politics and economics. But neither the Republicans nor the Democrats took note of it in making their platforms, if indeed they had ever heard of it.

Their conception of things allowed for no development in American history, making fundamental alterations in the distribution of real and intangible property, effecting an increasing concentration of control, adding to the number of tenants and sharecroppers, drawing in its wake a rising population of industrial workers and white-collar employees. There were no inexorable tendencies in American history, no tendencies as real and ruthless as the operations of the price mechanism, reshaping from top to bottom the configuration of actuality with which politicians were supposed to deal. Judging by the intimations and implications of their platforms, both parties believed that American history had been closed; that the future, near and distant, would repeat some period of the past unnamed; that the function of politics was to "recover" and "restore." What situation? That of 1928, 1914, 1896? To this question there was no answer, for "practical politicians" apparently deemed it irrelevant.

Yet there were stresses and strains in the perfect system of equivalence and equilibrium. Idle workmen and women on breadlines and dispossessed farmers could see and feel them. Even many scholastics admitted as much privately, if not publicly. From what sources had sprung dislocations in the symmetry of the automatic? If the platform makers were to be accepted as authorities, the main sources were four in number. Some willful men had violated the rules of the economic game by seeking to avoid the discomforting effects of competition, by refusing to hand out their rewards of profit to consumers and wage earners. This was, however, a passing phenomenon not inherent in the economic system, a kind of evil spirit that could be vanquished by legislation. A second source of disequilibrium was the economic breakdown in foreign countries, which threw obstructions into the smooth-running machinery of the American equilibrium. Akin to crashes in foreign economies was war — a strange thing presumably unconnected with the forms, operations, and passions of domestic and foreign economies. The fourth source of disturbances in the equilibrium was the willful intrusions of government into the mechanism of private economy — into the "natural" circulation of goods and into the "natural" operations of the price and wage system in the domestic and world market. Both party platforms promised to beat back these intrusions, more or less, but the Democratic platform especially emphasized this interpretation of the disequilibrium and in substance implied that the policies and actions of the party, if victorious, would be encompassed by that frame of reference.

§

With the platforms so drawn and the issues so formulated, the campaign of the major parties ran along in customary channels. The great debate, if at times heated, never roared up into a thunderous dispute. It was marked by no such frenzy and violent language as the contest of 1896, waged in the midst of a depression less devastating in its social effects. The Democratic candidate awakened no fears comparable to those raised by the militancy of William Jennings Bryan. No turbulent strikes, such as the Pullman struggle of 1894 or the Pittsburgh upheaval of 1877, frightened the John Hayses and Henry Cabot Lodges of 1932. In contrast a strange calm reigned everywhere, as if the memory of Sam Adams, Daniel Shays, and John P. Altgeld had perished from the earth.

The Republican candidate, Herbert Hoover, spoke with gravity, in a style sober and dignified, sometimes lacking in limpidity. In the nature of things, he was compelled to take the defensive. After all, whatever mighty things he had in fact accomplished, the plague of the depression still lay heavily upon the country, despite some evidences of lifting. That was not an achievement to which he could convincingly point with pride. He could say that without his labors things would have been far worse, but there was little popular appeal in that observation. Men of large affairs, the Lords of Creation, were able to appreciate the theory and practice of his administration and his program for the future. Yet even they were not united. Many, if not all of them, had been engaged in stock pools, manipulations, and "churnings," and Hoover had openly ascribed a large part of the country's troubles to their activities, especially to their efforts to make money by selling stocks "short." As a result Hoover had few ardent friends in Wall Street, which was supposed to be the nerve center of the economic system that he was striving to resuscitate.

On the Democratic side, the candidate also carried on a decorous campaign with touches of geniality rather than the vindictiveness of the crusader. This seemed in keeping with Roosevelt's character and it was good strategy besides. With encouraging reports coming from every direction, his party managers knew that their chief problem was to avoid "making mistakes," that is, declarations too precise and likely to alienate voters by clarifications and specifications. Only one major point in his platform did Roosevelt amplify by a commitment affecting the resentments and designs positively cherished by millions of voters, namely, the control of surpluses in agriculture.

After the veto of the McNary-Haugen farm bill and the failure of President Hoover's Farm Board to stem the downward flux of prices, a group of men in the Department of Agriculture had evolved a plan for balancing the agricultural output. In the autumn of 1931 M. L. Wilson, of the Montana State Agricultural College, had launched a campaign to enlist the support of business men and farmers for a scheme of control known as "the domestic allotment plan." Under this scheme there was to be no dumping of surpluses abroad; nor any government interference with the open market prices, such as Hoover had sponsored at a great cost to the Treasury and with negative results. On the contrary, under the domestic allotment plan, farmers were to cut surpluses by paring down production, and were in return to be given benefit payments, in addition to the open market prices —

payments proportioned to each producer's share of the domestic consumption of the commodities listed as human food.
By the summer of 1932 a multitude of business men, especially merchants relying on a local trade and manufacturers
of farm supplies, had become convinced that this domestic
allotment plan was the only hope for barring the road to ruin.

As Governor of New York, Roosevelt had taken a genuine
interest in agriculture and had devoted messages and addresses to the exposition of agricultural difficulties in his state.
But the domestic allotment scheme applied particularly to
the producers of great staples in the West and South, rather
than to dairy and miscellaneous farming in the East, although the latter too was in a semi-paralyzed state. To most
stock brokers, men of affairs, and other members of the
middle class in the East, this agrarian project was as mysterious as Egyptian hieroglyphics. Perhaps, generally speaking,
they looked upon it as an invention of "crack pots," a
device of farmers to get something that did not belong to
them under the American Economic System, but its contours
gave them no sleepless nights.

Eventually, compelled by his function as campaigner to
examine innumerable proposals and hear all views, Roosevelt
gave careful consideration to the domestic allotment plan as
presented to him by Rexford Tugwell, then professor of
economics at Columbia University. Having explored the
details of the project, Roosevelt decided to support it openly.
In September he went into the very heart of the agrarian
West and in a ringing speech at Topeka, Kansas, he espoused,
in general terms, the very principles of crop control which
were soon to be written in the terms of the Agricultural
Adjustment Act. At last the agrarians had broken through
the barriers of equivocations and had won a definite commitment on their program. Like a forest fire the news spread
among farm leaders in village, hamlet, and field. Without
unduly affronting capitalists and trade unionists, it was to
bring a deluge of rural votes in the Middle West, the old
stronghold of Homestead Republicans.

Any trepidation started among men in high places by Roosevelt's acceptance of a positive agrarian program was offset in part by a statement from William H. Woodin included in the Democratic book of faith. This document had a peculiar significance for the discerning. Mr. Woodin was the president of the American Car and Foundry Company. He was so intimately acquainted with the J. P. Morgan Company that his name was included in its "preferred list" of friends who received opportunities to buy stocks at prices below those paid by the "investing public." This fact was not known outside the inner circle in 1932 and was not revealed to the country until after the election; but it was doubtless no secret to the Morgan associates when Mr. Woodin issued his campaign manifesto. The document itself was skillfully designed to allay the "fear" that Roosevelt's policies were inimical to big business. The suggestion, explained Mr. Woodin, was absurd "unless by big business is meant bad business"; and certainly no man in a high place admitted that he was engaged in bad business, as innumerable congressional investigations made plain. "By tradition and training," as Mr. Woodin set forth the personality of the candidate, "he is antagonistic neither to the rights of invested capital nor to the rights of those whose capital is their industry, self-respect, and ability to produce. To his thinking there is no distinction to be drawn between the classes and the masses."

Although caution and moderation marked the campaign conducted by the two major candidates, there were charges and counter-charges, rumblings and grumblings that must have left their impressions upon public sentiments after the election had passed. On behalf of the Republican party it was drummed into the heads of the people who listened that the triumph of the Democrats meant more ruin in American economy. While the Democratic campaign book assured big business that it had "absolutely nothing to fear" from Roosevelt's policies, Democratic spellbinders made such savage assaults on "the wickedness of Wall Street and magnates in finance" that some voters were doubtless led to expect material changes in the system of acquisition and enjoyment. In this expectation they were confirmed by the vituperations of two manipulants who had enormous followings: Senator Huey P. Long of Louisiana and Charles E. Coughlin, priest of the Little Flower in the diocese of Detroit. Both were ardent supporters of Mr. Roosevelt's candidacy. The Senator fulminated in the South against great riches and reiterated one theme: "Share our wealth." In the North, Father Coughlin concentrated his wrath on bankers, capitalism, and communism and demanded a government currency having the semblance of fiat money. While the Democratic candidate put no official seal of approval on the philosophy of these preachers to the multitudes, he derived electoral benefits from their audiences; the hopes and alarms which they raised entered into the tumult of emotions associated with the national referendum.

Given the formulations of the major parties and the character of their campaigns, given wide-spread unemployment and actual misery among industrial workers, the signs seemed propitious for socialists and communists of all schools and persuasions to make, if not an immense diversion, at least a larger showing than in any previous contest. The United States, they thought, might be entering the final crisis which would pave the way for their triumph. They knew, to be sure, that the main body of labor in the United States was unorganized and that orthodox trade unionists wanted a larger share of the profits, not an overturn of the capitalist system. But in the turmoil of 1932, when even skilled craftsmen were tramping the streets, socialists and communists could imagine that "objective realities" had altered the psychology of American industrial workers and prepared them for a break with the past.

Although the great majority of socialists in the United States had one faith and one prophet, they disagreed among themselves over the precise interpretation of the Word according to Karl Marx and the right line of tactics to be followed. Above all they were divided over the methods of practice. Would the triumph of labor over capitalism come everywhere in a crisis, through violence, and by means of a dictatorship? If so, it was argued, then this must be the universal creed and appeal. Or were tactics appropriate for the despotism of the Tsar wholly inappropriate in the United States, with its democratic institutions and freedom of discussion?

True to tradition established when it was founded in 1900, the Socialist party rejected the dogma of automatic violence and endorsed political methods for achieving its ends. Yet even the Socialist party, in presenting Norman Thomas as its candidate, accepted the hypothesis that if labor encountered violence from the other side a response in similar terms might be a historic necessity. Inclined to spurn Socialistic tactics as supine, Communists chose other devices. But they were split into factions, for the unity of their creed and procedure had been shattered by the victory of Stalin and the downfall of Trotsky in Russia. Hence Communists failed to present "a united front" behind the candidate of the Communist party, W. Z. Foster.

Whatever issues, if any, were decided by the referendum, the numerical result was overwhelming. The total popular vote rose nearly three millions above that cast in 1928, showing, even when increase of population was discounted, that strong currents of popular sentiment had been set in motion. The tables of the preceding election were almost reversed. Hoover received 15,758,901 votes and carried only six states — Connecticut, Delaware, Maine, Pennsylvania, New Hampshire, and Vermont. With a popular vote of 22,809,638 Roosevelt carried forty-two states. A detailed analysis of the balloting by counties revealed that, on the whole, the old centers of disaffection which had supported William Jennings Bryan in 1896 threw their weight to Roosevelt in 1932. It also revealed the fact that counties and cities which had long been set down in the statistics of politics as "rock-ribbed Republican" experienced upheavals that were almost volcanic. For example, every county in Indiana that had given Bryan a majority in 1896 went Democratic in 1932, and other counties that had been reckoned as Republican since the civil war shifted over into the Democratic column. Despite this crack in the alignment of the major parties, the combined Socialist and Communist vote, with women nationally enfranchised in the meantime, was only 987,000 in round numbers as against nearly one million cast for Eugene V. Debs in 1912.

After the storm of the campaign had blown over, many citizens who had voted for Roosevelt doubtless had visions of things to be done by the incoming Democratic administration. In some respects the Democratic mandate was emphatic, especially with reference to the agrarian program. In other respects it was clouded by uncertainty. The concatenation of federal actions later known as "the New Deal" was not forecast in its entirety; nor were several parts of the coming program foreshadowed at all. It could not be correctly said, therefore, that the country had voted for a New Deal any more than it had voted for the emancipation of slaves in 1860, or for a war on Spain and imperialism in 1896. Indeed, the American electorate had seldom, if ever, voted for anything positive. Yet, as in the case of Lincoln's election, startling events occurred between the November poll and the March inauguration — events which conditioned, if they did not make necessary, actions not contemplated in the referendum.

## CHAPTER IV

## *Detonations*

AMID the celebrations of victory, Democrats prepared to divide the spoils, in accordance with a venerable tradition. Having watched history "repeat itself," Senator George W. Norris described the process: "The professional politician is mainly interested in jobs. He deals in political jobs and sells them across the political counter much as the merchant sells calico and boots and shoes." The practice covered petty posts in villages as well as lucrative places in city, state, and national governments, and nothing in the Democratic campaign of 1932 presaged any substantial interference with the normal course. The platform, it is true, contained a few pledges that could be interpreted as commands; the candidate had committed himself to the agrarian program and given hints of action in other directions. But equivocation was always possible in fulfillment, and Roosevelt was generally regarded as "an amiable man" who would not ride too hard when entrusted with the reins. Had the American financial system been as sound as Hoover alleged during the campaign, had there been no mighty dislocation in economic forces at home and abroad since the summer of 1932, had history stood still or proved reversible, the administration of Franklin D. Roosevelt might have pursued an unvarying routine as Democratic politicians expected. The lush spoils of office might have been distributed with customary rejoicings and sore disappointments; a number of mild "corrective" statutes might have been placed upon the books in a leisurely fashion; and the era of the New Freedom might have been in some respects duplicated.

§

Unknown, however, to the makers of small politics, perhaps known only to a few men on the inside of financial operations, a swift and apparently inexorable shift had been taking place in the incidence of liquid claims to wealth, especially bank deposits. As Berle and Pederson later pointed out, in their illuminating study of Liquid Claims to National Wealth, the very term "liquid claims" was relatively new in economic thought despite the fact that "from 1900 onward these claims had constituted a larger and larger percentage of the fixed or non-liquid wealth of the country." Between November, 1929, and November, 1932, an immense collapse had occurred in the values behind those claims called stocks and bonds, and thousands of banks, mostly small in size, had been caught in the roaring flood of bankruptcy. Nevertheless, banks in general, particularly large institutions in the great cities, had seemed to stand like rocks of Gibraltar, sentinels of power looming high in the dusk of the little gods. Business was sinking, unemployment was mounting, misery was spreading. But mighty banks revealed no flaws. In round numbers their resources amounted to seventy-one and a half billions in 1928, seventy-two billions in 1929, seventy-four billions in 1930, and over seventy billions in June, 1931. What their ledgers showed on June 30, 1932, while the campaign was in progress, the public did not know for, contrary to custom and significantly, the announcement of the official figures was long withheld — a delay lasting until January, 1933. After all, what preoccupied persons, engaged in ordinary politics or in deriving history from memoirs, ever paid any attention to the statistical tables of financial reports dealing with changes in intricate economic relations?

As a matter of fact, between June 30, 1931, and June 30, 1932, bank resources had dropped from seventy billions to fifty-seven billions, and bank deposits had declined about twelve billion dollars. This new configuration of liquid claims had come about through innumerable individual actions, each perhaps conscious, resulting in a general economic situation which no one had foreseen, deliberately willed, or purposely effected. If some persons had dimly divined an approaching pinch, the public certainly had no suspicion of it in June, 1932, or on election day in November of that year. Individual bankers knew only too well that the value of the papers in their portfolios was shrinking as railways went into the "hands of custodians," to use the phrase more polite than that of plain bankruptcy, as real estate mortgages plunged into default, and as the golden certificates of towering holding companies shriveled like autumn leaves in a fire. Individual depositors were also aware that they were withdrawing deposits to meet expenses as the days of unemployment and unprofitable business went on. But the sum of individual actions, the totality of banking resources, was beyond the knowledge of the generality, and perhaps even of the Lords of Creation. If a few leaders in finance suspected that trouble was coming, they were disposed to take comfort in a transcendent faith: the "invisible hand" makes public good out of private transactions consummated in the interest of individuals.

In the circumstances, as the campaign drew to a close, little attention was paid in the country at large to the news on October 31, 1932, that the governor of Nevada had proclaimed a banking holiday for twelve days in order to save a chain of banks in the state. Their real estate assets were frozen and their depositors were withdrawing money. Although for the moment an avalanche was averted in Nevada, neighboring states became nervous. Was it a local disorder that could be insulated? Or was it the beginning of a general dissolution? In the shouting of the election, the event received scant notice east of the Hudson River where, some imagined, the history of America was all made. Artists in coloring and makers of beautiful letters in Greenwich Village could still cash checks on metropolitan banks, if they had balances.

But even the illuminati must have been alarmed when in January, 1933, newspapers published figures compiled by the Comptroller of the Currency showing a steep drop in banking resources and bank deposits. Certainly "men in high places" and such politicians as gave attention to public business suffered dizzy spells as they ran their eyes down the columns of digits, mere ink and yet so fateful in terms of human life and political management. It may have been "silly," as Henry Seidel Canby, expert in polite letters, once remarked, to make "the attempt to interpret even business solely by statistics of supply and demand, profit or loss." Even so, the "inside development of the American nation" between January, 1932, and March, 1933, was not to be "found in American novels and plays," as Mr. Canby intimated in using his broom on "the economic interpretation of history." At least, some of it was registered in the reported shrinkage of liquid claims to wealth during the fifteen months previous to the inauguration of Franklin D. Roosevelt on March 4, 1933, and news of the disagreeable fact jarred complacency from Montauk Point to Catalina Island.

While the detonations of the report by the Comptroller of the Currency were still reverberating, their oscillations were accelerated by the figures of the quarterly release made by the Reconstruction Finance Corporation on February 3, 1933. Here, too, were indisputable statistics associated with supply and demand, profit and loss. They showed that the Corporation had authorized, between February, 1932, and December,

1932, loans to 5,582 banks and trust companies and that the loans actually made during the period amounted to $850,000,000. Next on the list of borrowers from the Corporation stood the railroads. Powerful lines as well as powerful banks were evidently in trouble, for it was not the function of the Corporation to assist concerns that could carry their own loads. Now it began to dawn upon the people that banks were in serious straits and that railways, whose bonds were stacked in the vaults of savings banks, universities, foundations, and insurance companies, were struggling for existence and positively gasping for credit. Beyond cavil, vital parts of the American System were far from "sound," according to any conception of that term, and depositors hastened to withdraw from banks more money for expenses and hoarding.

In the meantime, banking "incidents" multiplied in the provinces. On January 20, 1933, the legislature of Iowa enacted a law authorizing the Superintendent of Banking to assume the management of any bank and operate it for a year without instituting a formal receivership. This was also a sign of the tornado, as afterwards discovered, but the country, accustomed to the bankruptcy of rural banks in the era of Coolidge prosperity, could easily regard the event at the moment as just another episode. Although Iowa was a part of the Union, who in the high places of the omniscient and omnipotent East gave much thought to acts of the Iowa legislature? Nor did the press of the financial metropolis appear to be seriously disturbed when on February 4, 1933, the governor of Louisiana, hearing that certain banks in New Orleans were in peril, proclaimed a general banking holiday. Yet that was also another straw in the wind. According to a story in circulation the dictator of the state, Huey P. Long, had once prevented, at the point of a pistol, a group of bankers from going into liquidation. His political power was still unbroken in February, 1933. Then why did he eventually allow things to come to a dire pass among the bankers of his state? Perhaps, after all, the emotions of a dictator

were futile before a stampede of events to be interpreted in
economic terms. Still, as far as the nerve centers of the
industrial Northeast were concerned, Louisiana, like Iowa,
was far away and Confidence might act as insulation.

Hopes arising from that source were dashed, however,
when news that could not be pushed far back into financial
columns announced that the governor of Michigan had proclaimed on February 14, 1933, a banking holiday for a week
throughout the state. Yet circumspection marked both the
proclamation and the press reports: the action had been
taken for the purpose of enabling "some of the larger banks
in Detroit to meet the situation." In the ordinary course,
this might have passed as an adequate explanation. But
coming on top of the Comptroller's report from Washington,
the revelations of the Reconstruction Finance Corporation,
and explosions in Nevada, Iowa, and Louisiana, the news
from Michigan jangled the American System from center to
periphery.

From state to state banking holidays spread, for no one in
authority seemed to want the "automatic and unconscious"
operations of the marketplace to follow the process of liquidation to its logical and cleansing finality, in preparation for an
upturn. Still, as proclamations of banking holidays rattled
from state capitals like shots of machine guns, the strong
banks of New York, Chicago, Philadelphia, and other great
centers continued to operate, their grim walls showing no
fissures. Could they withstand the drain of their correspond-
ent banks and weather the gale without government intervention? That question was definitely answered. At 4 : 20
on the morning of March 4, 1933, the governor of New York
declared a limited two-day moratorium and when nine o'clock
arrived the doors of banks in great centers of finance remained
shut. Throngs collected in the neighboring streets vaguely
hoping for — something.

So it came about that, when President Hoover rode along
Pennsylvania Avenue with Franklin D. Roosevelt to the
inauguration, the huge mechanism of American finance had

almost ceased to function. In forty-seven of the forty-eight
states, banks were either closed completely or, with few
exceptions, were doing business under severe restraints as to
the withdrawal of deposits. By the hour for beginning the
interpretation and application of the mandate received in
the preceding November, profound alterations had been
made in the resources and functioning of banking interests.
Whatever the cause, no matter where the responsibility lay,
facts, real facts, fraught with brutal consequences, threatened
the nation with cataclysm. Philosophers, psychologists, and
public relations counselors could no more conjure them away
than could the bankers and politicians who stood aghast in
their presence. Lords of Creation, Pillars of Society, Peers
of Respectability gathered for hurried and whispered conferences amid the magnificence of their clubs and offices.
Home owners, bond holders, "investors," bank directors
brooded over defeated calculations. Silent crowds of the idle
and unemployed flooded and ebbed through the streets of the
cities, wondering, puzzled, and bewildered, rather than revolutionary in spirit. If, as Ralph Waldo Emerson had said,
"Whiggery is the great fear," the banking collapse of March,
1933, awakened another great fear — one that staggered the
heirs of Whiggery and everybody else. No words, spoken or
written, could fully describe the confusion and fright. Those
who went through it were powerless to enclose their sensations in a rationality of language that could reproduce it in
the feelings of succeeding generations.

§

For the frightful crisis in banking affairs, men in high
places had, as always, an explanation which was also in the
nature of an alibi. Francis C. Sisson, president of the American Bankers Association, had formulated the escape in an
address to his assembled colleagues during the previous October : "The blame for this situation rests with state laws and
public supervisory agencies, not with legitimate members of

the banking fraternity." Although the word "legitimate" opened to them the path for a successful flight, the implication of the formula was clear and positive: government, not the bankers, must bear the blame. And in a sense that was true. Since the days of Andrew Jackson, under the theory of states' rights and laissez faire, banking had been left largely under the supervision of state governments and the multiplication of local banks had been encouraged. Bankers had successfully prevented the Federal Government from establishing control over the currency through a public bank of issue in Washington and, tenaciously clinging to the Jacksonian tradition, the Congress had refused to give a semiprivate corporation a position of centralized dominance. Under this policy, or lack of policy, a reckless struggle for business had long prevailed among thousands of independent banks, despite the creation of a national banking system during the civil war and the subsequent strengthening of that separate device. The truth was that for more than a hundred years bankers had distrusted the politicians and the politicians had distrusted the bankers, both with good reasons in theory and experience.

Out of this antagonism had come a condition of highly competitive banking, in which a large number of state and federal institutions, singly or in small combinations, fought for depositors and borrowers in accordance with the Darwinian conception of life and society, transplanted from England and enthusiastically advanced in the United States during the gilded age, while the economists steeped in that philosophy were insisting that all economic activity except consumption is production. Banks were established in small towns where the amount of available business did not justify the venture. Federal banks were given the power to issue notes on the basis of paper securities and thereby inflate the currency on the shaky foundations of tenuous claims to wealth. In the thirst for profits, loans were made on real property at swollen values, on the bonds and stocks of pyramided corporations at fantastic valuations; and billions were poured into the stock market to finance speculation in paper tokens which fell little, if any, short of pure gambling in unknowable futurities. Presumably each banker was partly conscious of what he personally was doing but there was no conscious control over the entire process — either in the hands of the Federal Government or of a single national corporation. And it so happened in the more or less blind competition that Adam Smith's "invisible hand" of Providence failed to effect an outcome in the "general interest." When, in the contraction of resources and deposits, the results of millions of individual transactions came together in a total process, the consequence was a convulsion. That much was painfully evident, whatever the correct apportionment of "blame."

Perhaps even then the part of the public that possessed any knowledge of banking or did any thinking on the subject might have accepted the bankers' explanation and alibi — "all the blame rests on government," if other relevant facts had not been exhibited contemporaneously. According to the official thesis of the bankers, constantly reiterated, their transactions, though motivated by the natural desire for profit, were collectively in the public interest, that is, they helped to sustain and to promote the production and distribution of real wealth. Did the private conduct of the "legitimate members of the banking fraternity" correspond in reality to their official thesis? Did practice conform to theory? While everything had been going smoothly such questions might have seemed impertinent to bankers, but grueling adversity now suggested an inquiry.

Moved by curiosity, if nothing more, the Senate of the United States passed, in the spring of 1932, a resolution instructing its committee on banking and currency to make an investigation "with respect to the buying and selling, and the borrowing and lending, of securities upon the various Stock Exchanges," and to report on the subject. Although sponsored mainly by dissidents, the resolution had support also among the more conservative Senators. President

Hoover himself had been harrowed and vexed by "short selling" on the exchanges, which seemed to be arbitrary and likely to arouse more fear among the people, multiplying the physical afflictions of the times. Hence the resolution was carried through the Senate despite the usual cries against "rocking the boat" and "making attacks on private rights guaranteed by the Constitution."

Acting under its instructions the Senate committee opened its hearings on April 11, 1932, and held periodical sessions until June 23, producing at each hearing sensational evidence bearing on the official thesis of the bankers. For reasons deemed sufficient, the committee suspended its operations on June 23, remained quiescent during the campaign season, and then resumed proceedings early in 1933. Through the rest of the year, the committee pursued its searching inquiry — after February 21, with the assistance of a skilled prober, Ferdinand Pecora.

In the course of the investigation the committee called before it once more the veritable Lords of Creation and asked them to explain to a tormented public how the stock and banking crisis had really happened. Representatives were summoned from the mightiest banks and the most Napoleonic brokerage houses: for example, J. P. Morgan and Company; Kuhn, Loeb; Lee, Higginson and Company; National City; Dillon Read; and Chase Securities Corporation. Before the committee appeared the famous figures of the legitimate banking and trading fraternity, keepers of the National Shrine now a bit tarnished by wear, while accounting experts examined their books and files of correspondence.

From day to day, in restrained and yet sagacious tones, counsel and members of the committee asked witnesses to verify documents, to authenticate matters of record, and to explain just how the practices of bankers and traders conformed with the official thesis that all lawful acquisitive actions redounded to the public interest. Never before in the history of the country had the anatomy, morphology, intelligence, morals, and functioning of the banking and stock-trading business been so fully laid bare to national gaze and understanding. Even the metropolitan papers, accustomed to treat congressional investigations with contempt or to "play them down" by relegation to inside columns, were moved to place reports from the committee rooms on their front pages under startling captions. Some odors simply could not be confined. So, during the months previous to the inauguration of Franklin D. Roosevelt and during the tempestuous weeks that followed, the nation was literally rocked by revelations, confessions, admissions, and even apologies from the highest men in the highest places — the Lords of Creation, the men who, according to James W. Gerard, "ruled America."

In the voluminous testimony and documentation incorporated in the bulky volumes of the committee's report, the story was told of just what bankers and traders had been doing, under their official theory of serving the public interest. No economist saw fit to integrate all the revelations of transactions so recorded into a system of institutional economics and contrast them with the hypothetical fictions of schoolmen, but fragments of the capitalist system in operation were made so vivid by the Senate committee's exposition that even country bankers could grasp their significance, as they looked ruefully at their blocks of defaulted bonds and their piles of depreciated stocks. In the hearts of the millions of "investors," with unsystematic minds, who had gambled in stocks during the frenzied days, particular items from the committee's investigation awakened poignant emotions and outraged feelings. They were cut to the quick as tales of special stock pools and raids — Kolster Radio Corporation, Indian Motorcycle, Anaconda Copper, German bonds, and Radio Corporation — blazed into the front pages of their favorite and trustworthy newspapers. All this exposure, no less than the sight of closed banks and the experience of personal losses, contributed to the tumult of opinions and passions in the sweep of which the Roosevelt administration began its work and moved forward to its future.

Page after page of sworn testimony showed that mighty
men among the Lords of Creation had formed "pools" for
particular stocks and bonds, run up the prices of securities,
poisoned the news of financial columns by the bribery of
reporters, drawn unwary sheep into the pen of bulls and
bears and sheared them as the bottom fell out of liquid
claims to wealth. Theoretically the stock exchange had been
viewed and celebrated as an unconscious marketplace where
the prices of stocks and bonds found, or tended to find, their
"natural" level, as sellers offered and buyers purchased
securities according to their individual judgments on values.
Insiders had long known about pools and manipulations to
their own advantage but, in the days of the Golden Glow,
ordinary investors, sober or frenzied, had vague, if any, ideas
relative to that subject. On the whole the impression reigned
that "legitimate members of the banking fraternity" had
nothing to do with such manipulations, in fact discountenanced them as injurious to sound business. But after the
Senate committee started its inquiry, innocence gave way to
knowledge and a sense of double outrage developed — over
personal losses incurred at the game and the prestidigitation
practiced at the expense of simple, if greedy, players.

A few examples will illustrate processes too vast for a
description short of the original full hearings. In 1928 the
earnings of the Kolster Radio Corporation dropped in the
direction of zero and the directors were disquieted; but a
way of flight from ruin by unloading the wreck upon the
public was quickly discovered. Rudolph Spreckels, chairman of the company and chief stockholder, called in the aid
of George Breen, "the hero of a hundred pools," gave him
options on Kolster stock, and set him in motion. Mr. Breen
thereupon engaged the interest and cupidity of a number of
prominent stock brokers and hired a newspaper publicity
man to prepare the people for another opportunity to "invest
in America's prosperity." In a short time news of "highly
favorable developments" in Kolster business was circulated
among brokers and insinuated into the financial columns of

the press. With "public interest" receptive, Mr. Breen and his enlisted brokers started "the big push" — buying and selling huge blocks of Kolster stock, all the while managing to raise the price as eager watchers rushed to share in "a good thing." In the course of this "unconscious and automatic" market operation, the price of stock was lifted from seventy-four to nearly ninety-six, over twenty points, as the insiders gradually sold out their holdings. When they withdrew from "the killing," Kolster stock slid down to its "natural" value, reaching five or six dollars a share in December, 1929. Then in January, 1930, the bubble burst; the company went into the hands of receivers.

About two years after the wreck, the Senate committee exhibited to the country the outlines of this transaction in institutional economics. The naive public had lost millions of dollars in the "business" adventure. Mr. Spreckels had received more than nineteen million dollars for stock that proved to be worthless. One company of brokers collected $182,760 in fees from operations. The hero of the pool, Mr. Breen, reaped a profit of $1,351,152.50, according to his own testimony. The publicity expert's reward was $40,000 — a small sum for such effective labors; yet, as he had ventured no money at all in the "enterprise," his entrepreneur's risk had been negligible.

Perhaps the most diverting feature of this demonstration in productive economy was Mr. Breen's elaborate defense of the process and his own action. It had all been legitimate. He had not manipulated the market. He had merely sought to "stabilize" it, he declared. Since, however, the stock under his care had risen twenty points and then fallen to almost nothing within a year, his adroitness in the art of maintaining an economic equilibrium was, to say the least, not impressive. In fact, his stabilization theory, when presented to the Senate committee, was received with raucous laughter. And for Lords of Creation, in a time of political uncertainty, laughter was as inauspicious as anger.

If the Kolster Radio farce could be discounted as a play

# ERRATUM

The insertion of the name of Mr. Harry Guggenheim in connection with the statements made with reference to the Anaconda Copper pool, page 163 of the book, was due to error and we wish to express our regret for the mistake in reference to him.

THE MACMILLAN COMPANY

on a small stage, the same could not be said of the pool in Anaconda Copper, the earnings of which had fallen in 1927–1928. In this experiment in stabilization the very paragons of private and public virtue participated — John D. Ryan, Harry Guggenheim, Thomas E. Bragg of a Stock Exchange firm, and Charles E. Mitchell, head of the National City Bank and its investment affiliate. With the aid of his institutions, his colleagues, his brokers, his high-powered selling agents throughout the country, Mr. Mitchell bought and sold Anaconda stock, churned the market, ran up prices, "stabilized" the boiling market somewhere between 60 and 135, and sold out to "investors." Before many months passed Anaconda stock plunged downward to about four dollars a share. The public's losses were estimated at $160,000,000 and the profits of legitimate members of the banking fraternity were correspondingly large, temporarily at least. Although the Senate committee did not elicit from proud witnesses all the details of the public services rendered by the pool, or even get an admission that there had been a pool, its discoveries were as salt rubbed on the wounds of thousands of investors who had once believed the glorious yarns spun by the National City's agents and "investment counselors." Discounting all allegations of deliberate conspiracy against the public, substituting the word "stabilization" for "manipulation," still there seemed to be justification for Arthur M. Wickwire's phrasing in the Weeds of Wall Street: "The Anaconda crushes its prey."

Akin to the formation of a pool was an operation known as price pegging, which took place especially in connection with the flotation of new issues of stocks or bonds. Its immediate purpose was to hold up the price of a security to the offering figure until the distributors had succeeded in selling the issue to the investing public, for a drop under the offering price or even weakness made prospective customers skittish. Such an operation was well illustrated by the case of the German bonds issued on June 12, 1930, through a syndicate under the leadership of the J. P. Morgan Company. The

inside of this business transaction in "the automatic and unconscious" market was unfolded by the Senate committee
early in its inquiry. The witness was Richard Whitney,
president of the New York Stock Exchange and head of a
brokerage house — destined to an assignment in Sing Sing
prison a few years later.

Under insistent examination, Mr. Whitney explained the
process to the lay public. From June 12, the day of the
public offering, to July 2, 1930, the syndicate operated in
the market, buying and selling the German bonds and keeping the price on a level with or above the offering price of
ninety. This operation Mr. Whitney's house had carried on
"under order . . . through J. P. Morgan and Company."
On July 2, after the syndicate had disposed of the entire
issue to investors, it "pulled the plug," to apply the characterization of the Street, and let the securities take care of
themselves. Almost immediately the price sagged below
ninety, and on the day of Mr. Whitney's explanation the
German bonds were selling at thirty-five or thirty-six cents
on the dollar.

To the undiscriminating public, especially that portion
which held the depreciated German bonds, this looked very
much like a pool. To those experienced in the art of practice,
as distinguished from the logic of theory, on the contrary,
it was not a pool; nor was it in any way unusual. Indeed,
Mr. Whitney made it clear to the Senators from the "provinces" that it was "an absolutely usual and customary
method of merchandising and distributing securities." Although men familiar with the folkways and mores of business readily agreed, innocence was appalled to read about
it in the morning papers. The factual description of the
operation, coming so shortly after the collapse of this "prime
security," made a galling impression upon holders of the
"sound, gold bonds." The public learned how the selling
agents who had given investors the privilege of personal
suggestions in June, 1930, had been working for a syndicate
which was holding up the price temporarily by operations in

the market, that is, until the bonds were unloaded and the plug could be pulled. Mr. Whitney would not concede that his market transactions had made an "artificial" price; his purpose had merely been "to maintain a price." But again the audience at his hearing failed to understand, and in a few days the laughter of wiseacres, even in far-away village stores, was rising over the new phrases: maintaining a price, rigging the market, pulling the plug, protecting investors, and letting prices find their natural level.

The effervescence provoked among small investors by the news of stabilization, pools, price maintenance, and plug-pulling was almost turned into venom when they received a detailed explanation of another practice in "the automatic and unconscious market," known as "the cut in." This short and pointed phrase meant "giving our inside clients a chance to buy our securities at a price below that offered to the public." In the nature of things every great banking house had its heavy depositors, borrowers, and friends. Among the friends might well be old schoolmates, neighbors, members of the same social set, as well as directors of other banks and corporations able to reciprocate by extending similar privileges. In the nature of things also a few of the friends might be men high in the councils of the political parties — either casual acquaintances or leaders with whom contacts had been made in the "natural course" of transactions or otherwise. All this had been customary and conventional from time immemorial. Even corner store magnates had received from the village bank considerations not extended to hard-bitten farmers and penniless proletarians. Nevertheless the anatomy and morphology of the system had never been exposed until the Senate committee performed deft operations on it in the presence of the assembled representatives of the entire press, all on edge to peep behind the curtain.

Although the system was general, the Senate committee chose to illustrate it specifically by examining the practice followed by the House of Morgan. Its counsel and agents in searching the files of that firm came across lists of distin-

guished American citizens who had been given opportunities
to buy securities at prices below those reigning in the marketplace. Partners of the House, despite pertinacious questioning, refused to admit that the lists had any special significance apart from the regular business of merchandising and
distributing securities. Their more generalized explanation
was that the lists contained the names of men of means who
could well afford to participate in the risks and advantages
of investment. Just how and by whom in the House of
Morgan and under whose final authoritative decision the
lists were perfected, the witnesses failed to make clear. Some
individuals there enrolled were personal friends. For what
reasons other names were placed on the list witnesses were
at a loss to explain. In several instances they could not recall
any reasons. Certainly, they insisted in substance, there
was nothing sinister in the lists, no design to influence anyone, especially any of the politicians who appeared on the
books. It was, as they saw it, merely business, normal business, and their sincerity on the witness stand seemed transparent. They objected to calling the lists "preferred" or
even "selected." They chose to describe them simply as
"lists."

Without emphasizing the refinements, explanations, and
purifications introduced into the evidence by the Morgan
partners, managing editors blazoned on the front pages of
their papers the names of influential men chosen from the
Morgan "lists" — with supplementary annotations. In
skeleton form the registers presented to readers of newspapers made an imposing schedule of personalities that
could be arranged in the following order:

Charles Francis Adams, former Secretary of the Navy under
  President Hoover
Newton D. Baker, former Secretary of War under President
  Wilson
Bernard M. Baruch, philosopher general of the Democratic
  party
Charles D. Hilles, co-manager, with J. Henry Roraback,
  of the Republican party

J. R. Nutt, former treasurer of the Republican National
Committee

William H. Woodin, then Secretary of the Treasury under
President Roosevelt — the business leader who in 1932
had assured good big business that it had nothing to
fear from The Chief

Norman H. Davis, Ambassador to the World under President
Hoover and under President Roosevelt

William G. McAdoo, former Secretary of the Treasury under
President Wilson and Senator from California

Henry E. Machold, former chairman of the Republican party
in New York and a utility magnate

Frank L. Polk, Under-Secretary of State under President
Wilson

Silas H. Strawn, former president of the United States
Chamber of Commerce and distinguished Republican
leader in Chicago

Owen J. Roberts, Republican from Pennsylvania, Associate
Justice of the Supreme Court of the United States,
appointed by President Hoover

General John J. Pershing, Commander of the A. E. F. in the
War for Democracy

Wallace B. Donham, head of the Harvard School of Business

John J. Raskob, chairman of the Democratic National Committee, recent manager of Alfred E. Smith's campaign

John W. Davis, former Democratic candidate for President,
counsel for the House of Morgan

Calvin Coolidge, former President of the United States.

Selected and annotated names from the Morgan "lists,"
crowned by fitting headlines, fastened attention upon the
ways of the Street. No qualifying elucidations could overcome the immediate effect of the news. In vain did George
Whitney, Thomas Lamont, and other partners from the
House of Morgan, courteously and modestly explain that
they had no thought of political influence in selecting such
friends of the House for investment opportunities. Hour
after hour Morgan partners, under the glare that blazed on
witnesses, responded in well-modulated, never angry or
impatient, voices to questions about the list and its implications. Special circumstances, never political, they contended, were sufficient to account for the appearance of each

name in the lists; the thought of political influence or any other kind had never occurred to them. If in a tabulation, political connotations were attached to the selected names, that was purely fortuitous — no part of any design framed by the House of Morgan. Charles Francis Adams just happened to be the father-in-law of a young Mr. Morgan. Calvin Coolidge had voluntarily sought the advice of the House in solving his investment problems. Senator McAdoo had been merely a warm friend of a former partner. Newton D. Baker was simply a man of Cleveland — the home of the Van Sweringen Brothers for whom the Morgans had done a large, if not profitable, business. Giving such men advance opportunities was just business, customary business.

In time, perhaps, the patient elucidation of the Morgan partners might have overcome the insinuations and innuendoes of the doubtful and the cynical. But the effect of their even-tempered exegesis was partly vitiated by what seemed to be lack of knowledge on their part which was not convincing to a public stung by losses into incredulity. When Mr. Pecora asked Mr. George Whitney whether John J. Raskob had something to do with the Democratic National Committee, the witness replied: "I don't follow such things." Mr. Pecora inquired of him whether Henry E. Machold had not been chairman of the Republican committee in New York for many years and Mr. Whitney replied: "Why, I don't know, Mr. Pecora. You seem to be suggesting that we have these listed with their political offices. Well, I don't know." Was not Silas H. Strawn president of the United States Chamber of Commerce? In response, Mr. Whitney confessed innocence: "I really don't know." Why had J. R. Nutt subscribed to Allegheny stock through the Morgans when he was a friend of the Van Sweringens in his home town? Mr. Whitney: "I don't know, sir. I just don't know." Rarely did Mr. Whitney appear to find knowledge of such matters in his mind. When informed by Mr. Pecora that Cornelius N. Bliss had once been treasurer of the Republican national campaign committee, Mr. Whitney responded: "So I heard." To astounded reporters who knew the answer to every question of the kind, Mr. Whitney's want of familiarity with political events and personalities seemed almost miraculous. How could so distinguished a citizen be so slightly informed about matters of public interest and common knowledge? How could great men in the House of Morgan be so great and yet apparently so limited in acquaintance with practical affairs?

If the introduction of other evidence had not intervened, the explanations of the Morgan representatives respecting the so-called "preferred" lists, coupled with protestations of artlessness in matters political, might have been more generally accepted. However, other evidence was presented and suspicions regarding protestations of devotion to "sound banking practices" were raised by the revelation of a letter, dated February 1, 1929, to one of the gentlemen on a "list," William H. Woodin, at the moment of the Senate hearing May, 1933, Secretary of the Treasury under President Roosevelt. This letter from a member of the Morgan House, written to Mr. Woodin in 1929, gave him the privilege of purchasing 1,000 shares of Allegheny stock. It explained that the stock "is not the class of security we wish to offer publicly" and that the House was giving some of "our close friends" a chance to buy shares at the cost to the firm, namely twenty dollars a share. By way of special assistance, the Morgan partner furnished Mr. Woodin additional information: "I believe that the stock is selling in the market around $35 to $37 a share, which means very little, except that people wish to speculate. . . . There are no strings tied to this stock, so you can sell it whenever you wish. . . . We just want you to know that we were thinking of you in this connection." After this letter had been placed in the record, Senator Townsend asked the Morgan witness, Mr. George Whitney, when he sold most of his own Allegheny shares and received the answer: "I really do not know. I sold some, but I do not remember how many." Thereupon the committee's counsel placed before the witness a copy of his income tax returns for 1929 disclosing that he had sold that year 8,145 shares at a profit of $229,411.32.

When the text of the letter and reports of the hearings pertaining to it reached the pages of newspapers, they formed for the public a definite image of the kind of business transacted by the House of Morgan. The partners again sought to show that this was merely one among numerous transactions which had proved to be sound for investors and that it could easily be distorted. Yet the Morgan Company had sold privately to its close friends a stock of such a dubious character that the House would not sponsor the paper publicly. It took cognizance of the fact that "people wish to speculate." It informed Mr. Woodin that he could have the stock at twenty dollars a share, that it was selling at from fifteen to seventeen dollars above that price, and that he could sell his allotment whenever he wished to do so, clearing by the transaction perhaps $15,000 or more. In short, the stock was not good enough for the Morgans to issue openly, but it was being fed out privately to the speculative public and close friends of the House were given an opportunity to make "easy money" by unloading on the people who "wish to speculate." That may not have been the Morgans' notion of themselves, but it was an image that appeared to conform to the evidence they had presented. Even Walter Lippmann protested, with chaste restraint: "The testimony has shown that at least in the period under investigation, that is to say, in the years of the great boom, the House of Morgan had not only not exercised a wise restraint upon the speculative craze, but participated in it and profited largely by it."

Besides forming pools, pegging prices, and giving favors to close friends, legitimate members of the banking fraternity, with notable exceptions, had used high pressure methods in inducing the "people who wish to speculate" to keep up their activities. One Chicago investment house, which had sold large blocks of Insull securities, paid for a radio program of instruction delivered to the people in their homes. The program was conducted by a soft-voiced broadcaster known to the radio audience as "The Old Counselor." On inquiry it was discovered that "The Old Counselor" was a professor in Chicago University who was paid fifty dollars a week for his services of instruction and that "everything he delivered" was written in the office of the investment bankers who were unloading "securities" which proved to be almost if not entirely worthless. Far out on the Pacific Coast, another professor acted as an old counselor to the people, by making broadcasts praising the securities of a New York real estate house that later went into bankruptcy and ruined thousands of small investors who had sought safety in its "first mort-gage gold bonds."

These disclosures, coupled with revelations of the ways in which electrical utility companies had employed professors in their propaganda, led to questions about the character of scholars in the universities. Querulous curiosity also ex-tended to political matters when it was discovered that the program conducted by the Chicago professor known as "Old Counselor" had opened with an introductory address by a Republican member of the House of Representatives, at the time chairman of the banking committee, and that the Honorable Member had rendered this service at the request of the head of the investment house engaged in selling Insull securities.

Whatever the effect of revelations respecting the salesman-ship of a few professors, it was trivial in comparison with the excitement aroused by an exposition of the methods em-ployed by stock manipulators in "poisoning" the "financial news" of reputable papers. Early in the Senate committee's proceedings, Fiorello H. La Guardia entered its chamber with a trunk full of papers and presented sensational evidence to the effect that deceiving the public by false news had been a regular part of the market proceedings carried on by insiders. From evidence in the possession of Mr. La Guardia the public learned that pool operators, in preparing what was euphoniously called "balloon ascensions" for people who wished to speculate, had paid large sums in cash or stocks to financial writers on newspapers of the highest standing.

When one of the gentlemen implicated in such phases of business enterprise was asked to explain his methods, he replied: "I employed newspapers." The counsel for the Senate committee sought to correct him: "You mean writers, I suppose." His response was illuminating: "I don't know what they were. I would give them a copy of an article and sometimes it was in the paper and sometimes it wasn't." Canceled checks issued to writers for their labors in behalf of balloon ascensions showed that reporters on the papers representing the Cream of Respectability had so stooped to serve private interests: the Wall Street Journal, the Evening Mail, the Financial American, The New York Times, The Herald Tribune, and The Evening Post, for instance. Thus even great publishers had been deceived on occasion by their own employees. While in justice to themselves and their readers, they immediately got rid of their unfaithful servants, millions of readers were introduced to the hidden potentialities of financial "news."

In the examination of the National City Company, the affiliate of the National City Bank, the structure and methods of high-pressure selling were uncovered in detail. The men associated with this institution were no mere operators in particular pools and deals. They had a grand system, at the head of which stood Charles E. Mitchell, long deemed a titan of the "legitimate" banking fraternity. The National City Company had divided the country into nearly seventy districts and had established offices in all the important centers of business. The several parts of this empire were tied together and united with the main headquarters in New York by more than eleven thousand miles of private wires. Salesmen in the respective districts were stimulated to high tension by "sales contests" in which large prizes went to the agents who sold the most shares or bonds of particular issues. A special division of the Company combed the automobile registrations, tax lists, and other evidences of property ownership for "prospective customers" or, as things often turned out, prospective victims. By this process new names were constantly added to the roll of persons upon whom selling agents could call in search of investors; in one year, 1928, at least 122,000 new "opportunities" were furnished to the selling force.

Among the securities relentlessly pressed upon prospective customers was the stock of the National City Bank in small or large lots. From day to day the National City Company sent "flashes," or telegraphic dispatches, to its agents, instructing them in the matter of objectives and procedures for the immediate future. In one of those flashes, called "Loaves from Crumbs," headquarters advised its salesmen to observe whether clients had small balances in their accounts accruing from other transactions and, if balances were discovered, to induce such clients to buy one or more shares of National City Bank stock. In any particular case the balance might be less than the amount required for one share. In that instance, salesmen were informed: "You can have the customer put up the remaining cash. If you will continue this practice, it will not be long before each client and you will be agreeably surprised by the shares of the National City Bank stock that he will have accumulated. By using the crumbs of cash resulting from exchanges to buy the new stock of the National City Bank and continuing that practice as opportunity arises, you will work these crumbs into a loaf of substantial size with consequent advantages to the client, the National City Company, and yourself." The advice was frequently taken. Customers bought shares at figures ranging as high as $579 and later were surprised, not agreeably, by seeing them fall to twenty-five or thirty dollars a share. Indeed one day after Charles E. Mitchell had described this type of business to the Senate committee, many former clients in the room declared that they had lost all their savings in helping the Company to make loaves from crumbs.

§

If the bankers' description of their high-pressure selling system actually seemed formal when inscribed in the records of the Senate committee, their operations had a human interest which was illustrated by the injection of a customer or, it would be truer to say, a victim of the bankers' new legitimacy. Some of "the people who wish to speculate," as the Morgans explained the frenzy of the time, were not in truth desirous of embarking upon a career of speculation. One of them was Edgar D. Brown, of Pottsville, Pennsylvania, to whom M. R. Werner has given literary immortality in his volume on Privileged Characters. Mr. Brown had by careful management accumulated about $100,000, partly invested in sound government bonds. Suffering from ill-health, he decided to leave his home town for California. Who was to look after his property during his absence? While pondering that question, he chanced upon an advertisement in a magazine of national circulation, suggesting that anyone about to take a long trip would do well "to get in touch with our institution." This tender of assistance made to the public came from the National City Company. The idea seemed excellent. Here was a great company advertising in a great magazine. So Mr. Brown answered the appeal to reason and very soon a district representative of the Company called upon him in the beneficent guise of an investment counselor. After taking an inventory of Mr. Brown's securities, the counselor wrote to headquarters about the prospects. That was the beginning of a beautiful friendship with the National City Company.

Being an American, Edgar Brown of Pottsville, Pennsylvania, was not averse "to making a little money" by having papers shuffled to and fro in the market, but he was also cautious. At first he insisted that the Company buy bonds for his account and no common stocks. The customer was to be pleased. The Company sold his prime securities, bought bonds yielding a higher rate of interest (of which

the Company had plenty on hand), and induced him to
borrow money from its twin concern, the National City
Bank, at the market rate, for the purpose of buying more
high-yield bonds. For a time all seemed to go like a whirlwind — on paper; Mr. Brown appeared to have his capital
doubled or better — on paper. Then the high-yield bonds
began to decline as plugs were pulled out or the cruel truth
about foreign bonds crept around in esoteric circles. Mr.
Brown was alarmed. Thereupon his investment counselor
from the National City Company carefully explained: "That
is your fault for insisting upon bonds. Why don't you let me
sell you some stock?" Mr. Brown consented. Exactly how
the transition in finance was made does not appear in the
record. Mr. Brown swore that he had never told the counselor to buy any particular stocks. But, whether his memory
was faulty or not, Mr. Brown soon found "his" Company
buying stocks for "his" account fast and furiously, churning
them up and down and around and around, and selling him
the "favorite" securities of the Company, which was active
in syndicates and pools. For a time that seemed to go well,
although Mr. Brown had difficulty in keeping track of his
papers in the flurry of the great commotion.

Although Mr. Brown was now enjoying the salubrious
climate of Los Angeles, he apparently kept his eyes on the
stock market reports and discovered in September, 1929,
that the prices of his "securities" were dropping. In some
trepidation he visited the Los Angeles branch of the National
City network for the purpose of saving what he could by
selling his liquid claims to wealth. On his arrival at the
office of the Company, he was besieged by many counselors.
"I was surrounded at once," he told the Senate committee,
"by all of the salesmen in the place, and made to know that
was a very, very foolish thing to do. . . . I was placed in the
category of the man who seeks to put his own mother out of
his house." Local counsel was supplemented by a telegram
from his counselor in Pennsylvania, who got his address in
some mysterious way: "National City Bank now 525. Sit

tight." Despite the advice, Mr. Brown continued to urge upon the Company the sale of his stock, only to be informed by his counselors that he was foolish and that the market would rise, despite the troubles of the day. Sales pressure, he learned, did not work in reverse. The Company refused to sell his stocks as long as he had a chance to save something from the wreck.

While Mr. Brown of Pottsville, Pennsylvania, and Los Angeles, California, was still beseeching and vacillating, the bubble burst in Wall Street on October 29, 1929. Then the National City Company, without stopping in the hurry to consult the restive client, sold his Bank stock at $320 a share, in good time "to get out" itself. It also disposed of his securities and paid off his debts at the National City Bank. In the final moments of affliction, his Company could obtain no more loans for him to save the paper on which he had been told to "sit tight." After the storm was over, Mr. Brown found himself at the bottom of the economic ladder, where he had started in his youth, entirely stripped of his savings. His status he graphically described in a letter to the New York headquarters of his Company: "I am now 40 years of age — tubercular — almost totally deaf — my wife and family are depending on me solely and alone and because of my abiding faith in the advice of your company I am today a pauper." The chief of headquarters may have laughed or cried, but he lent Mr. Brown no more money. Down and out Edgar Brown made his way back from the sunny climate of California to Pottsville, Pennsylvania, where old friends found an appropriate place for him, "clerking for the poor board."

§

While engaged in forming pools and syndicates, giving "our friends" inside opportunities to buy stocks below the market, buying the affections of newspaper reporters, and turning droves of salesmen loose on prospective customers, some legitimate members of the banking fraternity came to the conclusion that their services to their own institutions were so valuable as to warrant extra compensation over and above the stated salaries. In many cases the special rewards took the form of bonuses voted by grateful directors. In the case of the National City Company, the process was regularized and standardized by the establishment of a "Management Fund" for the benefit of low-salaried executives, most of whom received about $25,000 a year. The Fund was supplied by pouring into its chest a fixed percentage of the Company's earnings. Semi-annually the high officers assembled around the Fund and each one wrote on a secret ballot just what proportion of the total amount each of his respective colleagues should receive, leaving his own name off the list. On the basis of the ballot, the Fund was divided. As Charles E. Mitchell was the head of the National City Bank as well, he deemed it advisable to create another such Fund for that institution. Between 1923 and 1930, the Combined Funds so divided amounted to more than nineteen million dollars. And it happened in the balloting of appreciative colleagues that Mr. Mitchell received on the average about one-third of the distribution.

On the witness stand before the Senate committee, Mr. Mitchell explained this system prevailing at the headquarters, to which Mr. Brown of Pottsville, Pennsylvania, had appealed in vain for aid. The Fund was a valuable device in personnel administration, Mr. Mitchell thought, for it helped to hold the loyalty of executives who might otherwise have been dissatisfied with $25,000 a year and have accepted more attractive posts in other financial institutions. "It establishes," he said, "an *esprit de corps* and an interest in one officer in another officer's work that is to me most noticeable." Indeed, in appreciation of his services to the National City institutions, Mr. Mitchell's own salary, apart from the Fund, had been raised from $100,000 a year to $200,000 in 1931, amid the debris of the depression. To Senator Couzens, the total picture looked peculiar. He asked Mr. Mitchell whether giving each individual officer "a split" had not inspired "a lack of care in the handling and sale of securities to the public." To this insinuation the banker replied: "I can readily see from your point of view, that that would seem so. . . . At the same time I do not recall seeing it operate that way." Thereupon, the Senator diagramed his view: "You would not see it. Only the customers would see it after they had gotten their securities." Perhaps Mr. Brown, of Pottsville, Pennsylvania, lately of California, had already seen it. At all events, the directors of the National City institutions retired Mr. Mitchell from his dual post, after the facts that they had long privately known had become public property.

§

The perfect meeting of Simplicity and Respectability occurred, however, in the Kreuger and Toll affair which was reviewed in the Senate committee's chamber on January 11 and 12, 1933. That enucleation of the difference between the economic practice of business men and the economic theory of the schoolmen was especially dramatic on account of the personalities entangled in the transactions, the number of shorn investors involved, and the hundreds of millions drawn into the whirlpool. Moreover it made an international uproar. European investors, bankers, lawyers, accountants, and manipulators, as well as American counterparts, had been caught in the ascension, explosion, and descent. The central figure of the drama, once revered as the Grand Symbol of the Age, and then damned in suicide as the most gigantic liar and swindler of all ages, was Ivar Kreuger, appropriately a specialist in an incendiary product — the inflammable match — among other things.

In European countries the humble match had been seized upon by impecunious governments as a source of indirect revenue collected through a public monopoly. The article was in universal use. By monopolizing it, a government could add to each pack of matches a tax so small as to be almost impalpable and yet yield enormous sums in the aggregate. Furthermore a beggared government, in need of immediate millions, could collect in advance by issuing bonds against the revenues to be obtained from matches — for ten, twenty, or thirty years. In the United States, where matches were used by prodigal citizens in billion quantities, they formed a big item in industrial production. On the continent of Europe the match was so important that the fate of statesmen might hang upon its potentialities for revenue.

With a genius little short of the miraculous, Ivar Kreuger divined the possibilities of the match, among other things, on two continents. From one end of Europe to the other, he approached poverty-stricken governments with offers of huge loans to be secured and liquidated through public monopolies. To befuddled premiers, dictators, and secretaries of treasuries, casting feverishly about for money with which to pay bills, arm soldiers, and build battleships through painless taxation, he seemed a veritable godsend, a wizard, a wonder-worker. Wherever he went in Europe the doors of chancelleries and treasuries flew open to receive him. The biggest and mightiest welcomed him, dined in state with him, bowed to his lightest wish. To ordinary business men, who had to seek letters of introduction, wait unnoticed in antechambers, prostrate themselves in quest of opportunities to sell goods or float loans, Ivar Kreuger was more than a wizard: he was the Supreme, Invincible, High Potentate among the very Lords of All Creation — the most brilliant star in the universal firmament of business. Compared with Kreuger, Montagu Norman of the Bank of England or J. P. Morgan, the American Napoleon, dwindled into an obsequious courtier seeking favors in the very Throne Room of Sovereignty. When Kreuger came to the United States to deal in matches — and other things — he came as a conqueror to command. And he did command.

With his bases of action and manipulation in Sweden, France, Holland, and the United States, Kreuger organized at least 140 companies, some independent, others interconnected, all tied into his personal network. Among his many concerns, the Kreuger and Toll Company and the International Match Corporation were of special interest to American investors and speculators. Through these concerns about $250,000,000 worth of debentures and participating debentures were issued in the United States and their securities were listed for trading on the New York Stock Exchange.

In the indenture for a fifty million dollar issue of "secured sinking fund gold debentures" of the Kreuger and Toll Company, devised in March, 1929, a special provision allowed the Company to substitute new stocks and bonds for stocks and bonds originally pledged as security for the loan, provided that the par value and interest returns on the substitutes equaled 120 per cent of the debentures and the interest requirements. Obviously this clause permitted Kreuger to substitute "shaky bonds" for good bonds, if the substitutes had the requisite par value and were at the moment paying their interest. But the provision which assured to Kreuger this liberty of shifting securities underlying the debentures was explained on the ground that it was necessary for the conduct of so great an international business, with changes taking place constantly in its relations with governments. Perhaps it was. Even so, the original bonds posted as security were dubious to any banker with insight, for they included such paper as Latvian six per cents, Greek eight and one-half per cents, and Ecuadorian seven per cents; and in the course of time Kreuger substituted Yugoslav bonds for bonds of the French Republic.

The sponsoring house for a huge block of these debentures was Lee, Higginson, and Company, founded in Boston in 1848 and regarded as one of the soundest and most conservative banking houses in the United States. Although it had established a branch in New York City, it was such a pillar of Boston honor and intelligence that it commanded respect and confidence throughout the country. The partner of the house most intimately associated with the flotation of the debentures was Donald Durant who, after leaving college, had worked his way up from the position of "office boy" to that of high responsibility in the Company. Was Mr. Durant "acquainted with the mechanism and legal conditions under which the security business is conducted generally abroad"? He had had, he replied to the inquisitor, "something to do indirectly with various issues for foreign companies, but had never had any experience with the operation of an office abroad."

Since the underlying securities for the debenture issue were foreign government papers, the counsel for the Senate committee asked whether he was "fairly well acquainted with political conditions abroad." Mr. Durant answered that he had never pretended to be an expert on political conditions. They were important? "Perhaps important in the getting of foreign issues, of foreign Government bonds, but the bond speaks for itself as an obligation," he contended. Mr. Durant was a director of the Kreuger and Toll Company which issued the debentures in the United States? Yes. Had he attended any meetings of that Company? None between 1929 and 1932 — the year of the flotation and the year of the disaster.

But the Lee, Higginson Company did not issue the debentures without aid. It was assisted by "participating houses" with imposing lists of directors — Kreuger and Toll; Clark, Dodge, and Company; Brown Brothers and Company; the Guaranty Company; the National City Company; Dillon, Read; and the Union Trust Company of Pittsburgh. Among the directors of these sponsoring houses loomed such impressive figures as Jerome D. Greene, John Henry Hammond, C. H. Sabin, P. A. Rockefeller, James A. Stillman, N. F. Brady, Richard B. Mellon, and David A. Reed. Around the nucleus of powerful participating houses were grouped members of the syndicate which sold to the American public the Kreuger and Toll five per cent "secured sinking fund gold debentures." The bare list of syndicate members, including no references to their directors, filled almost six pages of fine print in the Senate committee's record. It embraced such magnates of business as Lehman

Brothers, the Manufacturers Trust Company, the J. P. Morgan Company of New York City, the Union Trust Company of Cleveland, the Mellon National Bank of Pittsburgh, the Shawmut Corporation of Boston, the First National of Detroit, Cassatt and Company of Philadelphia. In all, there were more than three hundred active sponsors, participating in the operation of selling and in the profits arising from the success of the venture.

Distributed geographically, the members of the syndicate fairly well covered the continental domain of the United States from Bangor, Maine, to Seattle, Washington, from San Francisco, California, to Miami, Florida. Indeed nothing short of the entire list of cities and towns in which one or more banks and other responsible concerns offered Kreuger and Toll debentures to their customers could convey a correct impression of the magnitude of the enterprise: Daytona Beach, Jacksonville, Miami, Tampa, Atlanta, Baltimore, Jersey City, Newark, Albany, Auburn, Buffalo, Cooperstown, Elmira, Geneseo, Glens Falls, Gloversville, Jamestown, Johnstown, New York City (more than seventy firms), Ogdensburg, Rochester, Syracuse, Troy, Utica, Watertown, Canton (Ohio), Cincinnati, Cleveland, Columbus, Dayton, Toledo, Youngstown, Braddock (Pennsylvania), Erie, Masontown, Norristown, Philadelphia, Pittsburgh, Sharon, Wilkes-Barre, Charleston (South Carolina), Norfolk (Virginia), Richmond, Washington (D. C.), Bridgeport (Connecticut), Hartford, New Haven, Bangor (Maine), Portland, Boston, Lowell, Pittsfield, Springfield, Providence, San Francisco, Aurora (Illinois), Champaign, Chicago, Evanston, Moline, Peoria, Quincy, Rockford, Indianapolis, La Porte, South Bend, Clinton (Iowa), Davenport, Des Moines, Muscatine, Sioux City, New Orleans, Detroit, Jackson, Kalamazoo, Lansing, Minneapolis, Saint Paul, Kansas City, St. Louis, Lincoln, Omaha, Lead (South Dakota), Sioux Falls, Memphis, Dallas, Houston, Salt Lake City, Seattle, Spokane, Beloit (Wisconsin), Janesville, Madison (four banks), Milwaukee, and Monroe.

In each of these places, one or more institutions enjoying public confidence offered the securities of Kreuger and Toll to friends, acquaintances, and prospects. To widen the network, banks and investment concerns in large cities allowed correspondents in surrounding regions to share in the general distribution. Given such favorable circumstances, the big sale was a complete success and widows, orphans, colleges, and investors by the thousands, as well as speculators, found themselves in possession of "secured sinking fund gold debentures."

Shortly after the syndicate withdrew its support and the plug was pulled in the spring of 1929, Kreuger and Toll securities seemed to waver. They crumbled in the great crash of the autumn. Still, the Lee, Higginson Company had a certain faith in the "equities" and in January, 1932, when Kreuger and Toll American certificates were selling at six cents on the dollar, the Company sent out a circular, entitled "An Undervalued Security," which contained the following suggestion: "Taking into consideration facts alone and not general apprehension unsupported by facts, they represent, in our opinion, an interesting commitment from the standpoint of price in relation to intrinsic value. . . . Unless one lacks all faith in the future of the world, and in the preservation of its economic structure, it seems obvious that these assets will not continue to be valued as they are at the present time" — one prognosis that proved to be correct. Ivar Kreuger evidently had a similar faith or some kind of faith in the world, for in the same month, January, 1932, he arranged with a New York brokerage house to borrow a million dollars, secured by Kreuger and Toll stocks, for the purpose of "stabilizing" the market. A representative of the house declared to the Senate committee that the Lee, Higginson Company had knowledge of the arrangement. Whether it did or not in fact, the brokerage house churned the market in accordance with the contract signed by Kreuger. It was engaged in churning when the dénouement came about two months later.

On March 12, 1932, Ivar Kreuger died suddenly in Paris where directors of Kreuger and Toll, including Donald Durant of Lee, Higginson, had assembled for a meeting with him planned to discover, among other things, the meaning of some mysterious transactions now suspected. When the news of Kreuger's death reached Mr. Durant, he cabled his partners in New York: "For partners only Oak died very suddenly today not public yet please say nothing until announced here." And before Kreuger's death as a suicide was announced in the United States, European speculators unloaded a large amount of Kreuger paper on American "investors."

After the news broke in New York and all the capitals of the world, lawyers, accountants, security-holders' committees, and other interested parties started an exploration of Kreuger's companies, accounts, transactions, and "miracles." Forty volumes could scarcely hold the documents and findings. The evidence contained in their pages placed Kreuger among the most colossal manipulators of all times, ancient and modern. His financial reports and balance sheets on which American business men had trustingly relied were peppered with fraud; his reported earnings were three, four, or five times above his real earnings. During a period of eighteen years the actual operating profit of one group of filiates, for example, was apparently about 150,000,000 kroner, before interest on bonds, and yet dividends amounting to 668,000,000 kroner had been paid. Neither the height nor the depth of Kreuger's operations could be fully reckoned. Investors merely knew that they had lost heavily.

How had it been possible for Kreuger to secure formidable statements, declarations, balance sheets, and other "evidences" of "intrinsic values" upon which trusting business men in America had relied in urging prospects and customers to invest in his secured sinking fund gold debentures? With great ingenuity and display of details, the mystery was explained to the Senate committee by an accountant who had investigated about 140 of the wizard's concerns. Kreuger had formed two companies for the special purpose of fixing up the

reports that "demonstrated" his high financial standing —
the Continental Company and the Dutch Kreuger and Toll.
"Those," explained the accountant, "he kept well under his
thumb with creatures of his own in charge, and auditors,
and he knew that he could get a certificate from them at any
time of anything he wanted. And that is where he buried his
stuff. . . . The whole structure was honeycombed with
irregularities."

As if unable to take it all in, Senator Costigan inquired:
"They were clearing houses for manipulation?" To this the
accountant laconically replied: "Well, they were sinks."
Reluctantly, a representative of the New York Stock Exchange admitted that he and his colleagues responsible for
listing Kreuger "securities" on the Big Board had accorded
to a foreigner privileges not granted to Americans and had
been snared by "the greatest swindler of all time." Sponsors,
leading bankers, managers of the Stock Exchange, men who
had been supposed to know what they were doing, all stood
naked under the sign of their defeat — Credulous Ignorance
— from Bangor to Seattle, from San Francisco to Dallas and
Miami.

§

Capping the testimony displaying lack of insight and mistakes in judgment were disclosures showing that great bankers had not been paying federal income taxes in recent years.
Here again their activities were entirely "legitimate." The
law levied taxes on capital gains and permitted deductions
for losses. When the promoting bankers were making large
profits, they paid large taxes on incomes. When they incurred losses, they deducted losses from earnings. If their
losses exceeded earnings for the year, they owed no taxes to
the Government. Under the law, losses had to be realized;
that is, the holder of a $1000 bond which fell to $60 could not
deduct his loss unless he sold his bond and "took his loss" in
fact. Presumably it was the intention of the lawmakers that

losses so established should be bona fide; in other words, that
the seller should actually dispose of his bond in the market
and be permanently rid of it.

Yet under the terms of the law a practice had grown up of
selling securities to friends and relatives, deducting the losses,
and then buying back the same paper at the expiration of a
few months at or near the same price. In keeping with this
practice the owner of a home or a farm might have sold his
property to his wife at a loss and taken the loss out of his
income tax, if he had thought of it and the revenue officers
had accepted the transaction as bona fide. But small investors, unlike bankers and manipulators, were not all
familiar with the niceties of the law and, when they read in
the newspapers that many Lords of Creation had paid no
income taxes at all in 1930, 1931, and 1932, they found difficulty in making fine discriminations.

Within the letter of the law, the devices employed in incurring losses that could be deducted from incomes were
various. Albert Wiggin, of the Chase National Bank, had
three "personal," or "family," corporations to which he
could sell or from which he could buy securities, as occasion
might suggest. He also had similar corporations chartered
in Canada. If he was about to make a profitable sale of
stock, he could transfer the transaction to one of his Canadian
corporations and thus show no taxable profit actually arising
within the jurisdiction of the United States. By employing
such legitimate methods, Mr. Wiggin, as he remarked,
"saved" a tax of $440,000 on a profit of $4,000,000. Charles
E. Mitchell, of the National City Bank, was so adroit and
multifarious in consummating transactions of this kind that
legal action was brought against him by the Government.
With the aid of Max Steuer, called the Prince of Juries, Mr.
Mitchell convinced twelve men tried and true that all had
been lawfully done; but the Government later recovered
large sums from him in the form of back taxes. Otto Kahn
testified that he had reduced his taxes for 1930 by selling
securities to his daughter and had bought them back a few

months later. He had cut his taxes and yet remained, financially speaking, in possession of the same property — all as permitted by the letter of the law.

A similar elucidation of the perfectly legitimate process was made by another expert in finance. At the end of the year 1930 this expert sold certain shares publicly in the market. His wife borrowed money from him on her personal note and bought a similar amount of these shares. "There was no agreement nor any understanding between us," he testified, "that I should any time later on repurchase these shares from her or any of them. I intended the sale to be a complete and final disposal of these shares, and she understood it to be so. . . . I was advised that under these circumstances I was fully within my rights in deducting from my income return for the year 1930 the amount of the loss sustained." A few months later, however, things seemed to be "slipping." Indeed they might get worse. "I talked to my wife about this, and we both felt that it was not wise that she should continue to carry this debt against stocks. Therefore, I purchased the stocks from her on April 8, 1931, at the original price and she thereupon paid her loan. The note was surrendered and marked 'paid.'" All this was entirely proper within the terms of the law and accepted as such by the Treasury Department of the United States under President Hoover. Yet, when millions of investors were smarting under their losses and income-tax payers were learning of their own carelessness in taking advantage of their rights, such revelations by the Senate committee had a tendency to aggravate, rather than allay, popular irritations.

§

The innumerable transactions disclosed by the Senate committee, taken collectively and arranged with reference to any coherent theory of political economy, did not seem to square with doctrines of business long taught in the schools and accepted by the Mentors of Society as good always and everywhere. Since the time of Adam Smith it had been widely held that legitimate business transactions, under the invisible hand of Providence, had kept economy in motion, produced and distributed wealth, and redounded to public welfare. This broad principle had been worked out into a system, an American System, which bankers and men of affairs were supposed, at least by professors and school children, to observe in practice. Its elements could be simplified in the following terms. Individual industry brings earning. Thrift effects savings. Savings supply capital. It is the function of capital to set enterprise in motion, under the profit incentive. Enterprise in motion creates and distributes wealth in the form of valuable goods. Bankers lend their depositors' money on sound securities to aid capital in setting enterprise in motion, and they float securities for the same purpose. Business men to whom such funds are lent manage real property employed in production, with fiduciary consideration for investors entitled to reward for thrift and saving. The stock exchange is a place where bona fide securities are listed after examination and where investors are furnished a true and open market for buying and selling securities at their intrinsic or natural level. The participants in this System know what functions they are performing. Presumably, they know what they are doing and, as Thomas W. Lamont phrased it, they regard their transactions as in the main "wholesome." For about fifty years this was the general conception of the System, expounded by economists, popularized in public schools and Sunday schools, celebrated by men of affairs at banquets, and repeated by business and professional women at some of their conventions.

In many respects the practices described to the Senate committee offered strange contrasts to the pure word of this theory. Untold billions had been accumulated, not by labor and thrift, but by organizing holding companies, investment trusts, corporations, pools, price manipulations, and balloon ascensions on the basis of inside knowledge — knowledge withheld from stockholders and the general public. At the same time "poisoned financial news," bought and paid for by the insiders, had been concocted to mislead investors. Untold billions in capital had been used, not to set enterprise and labor in motion, but for purposes far removed from the creation of real goods. Billions had been collected to form holding and investing companies which merely bought stocks in going concerns at inflated values, often from and through insiders. Millions had been employed to get control over industries and railway companies with a view to making a profit in fees, commissions, and purchases, rather than to enlarging their real capital — plants, trackage, and terminal facilities.

Millions had been diverted to consolidating banks and other concerns through stock purchases and directorships, thus increasing the powers of control and manipulation. Banks had been lending money in the boom years but not merely for the purpose of enlarging plants and setting wealth-creating enterprises in motion. They had lent money to big speculators in the stock market, to the creators of hidden pools, to the organizers of mergers bearing no relation to any increase in real capital, that is, to plant extension or more efficient operation of existing plants. Many a business man supposed to be safeguarding his investors' interests had been found wrecking the property over which he was supposed to preside, speculating in the market in the securities of his own concern, forming secret pools against stockholders and investors. Eventually Lords of Creation whose superior wisdom and knowledge the populace had been taught to respect were forced to confess publicly that their System did not harmonize in practice with the theory of business enterprise: "Let us alone and we will produce wealth, distribute prosperity, and employ the idle."

Pools, syndicates, plug pullings, balloon ascensions, poisoned news, "favors to our friends," high-pressure salesmanship, management funds, and bonuses had not come inexorably out of the automatic, unconscious market. Schoolmen droning economics in the classrooms might still hold that

such activities were productive because they were not forms
of consumption; but participants in the deeds were not asleep
at the time. Wide-awake and astute men, with the aid of
wide-awake and astute lawyers, had *ex proprio motu* and with
full knowledge, created and operated such devices for their
own end — making a profit. Such undertakings did not
spring from the realm of the unconscious. The men who carried them on doubtless had little inkling of the distant consequences or total outcome of their labors. Probably they
had learned from history just what statesmen and historians
had learned — nothing or at best very little. Nevertheless
the evidence presented to the Senate committee made it indisputable that these men had done all these things deliberately. They had their explanations, justifications, homilies,
and moralities to unfold in a way that, in their opinion, ab-
solved them from responsibility for the misadventures and
reverses of their operations. Some of them seemed to have
only hazy ideas as to the meaning of pools, balloon ascensions,
and other practices known even to the errand boys of the
Stock Exchange. Yet none of them contended that their
acts had been performed unconsciously or automatically.

According to an old maxim, every idea which gets possession of civilization begins as a rank heresy and ends as a crass
superstition. Could it be that the once heretical American
System had become a superstition? At all events clergymen,
professors, editors, columnists and other promoters of law
and order, from circles which had long defended the System
on the basis of its Theory, now began to question its Practice
in vigorous inquiries. Some of the promoters of law and order
were obviously horrified by the Senate findings with respect
to the things which the Paragons and Pillars of the System
had been doing. Even such well-poised commentators as
Walter Lippmann and Mark Sullivan were moved to deviate
slightly from their fixed line in discussing the course of events.
And misgivings expressed in pulpits, on the platform, and in
the press seeped down to the listening and reading multitude.
The inside history of their heroes and their investments had

repercussions among farmers and other homeowners in peril of losing the very roofs over their heads. Through the tabloids, if through no other channels, the derelicts of industry got inklings of errors in high places affecting their own struggle to keep soul and body together. If, in moral standards and lust for money, the people in general were akin to the Lords of Creation, that possible resemblance merely burdened them with the sting of a common defeat. Judging by critical comments, the spirit of black distrust was succeeding the spirit of unquestioning faith.

§

It was fortunate for the possessors of good things in 1933 that William Randolph Hearst had reversed the role filled by his yellow press during the opening years of the century. Once he had thundered against plutocrats, railway magnates, stock gamblers, monopolists, and the "Plunderbund." In flaming editorials his papers had scourged "the money changers in the temple" with the vigor and wrath of ancient Jewish prophets. Indeed he had gone so far as to permit one of his writers to hint at assassination as a method for disposing of one major leader of the time. By 1933, however, for reasons best known to himself, he had shifted over into the conservative fortress. He had supported Coolidge and dined with him in the White House. He had approved the Democratic candidate in 1932, for there was little in the Democratic platform or campaign speeches to which he could take exception. Appealing to the populace for readers, he had advocated large expenditures for public works to give employment and he had condemned President Hoover's opposition to direct federal grants in aid of the idle and the hungry.

In the main, Mr. Hearst's emotions were conservative in 1933. Instead of turning his engines of denunciation against the possessors of special privileges, he employed them in defending things he had formerly denounced and applied his energies to pillorying and flaying critics and doubters as

"Reds." The most charitable explanation of this reversal was that Mr. Hearst had grown old. Certainly that was enough. Voltaire had once remarked that the strength of the English church rested upon the fact that it made no man a bishop until he had become so aged that avarice was his sole motive. At all events Mr. Hearst, who had formerly made men tremble over their possessions, now seemed to tremble himself. And the country witnessed the spectacle of the man whom Theodore Roosevelt had charged with being an accessory to the death of President McKinley transformed into the man praised, wined, dined, and flattered by the spiritual descendants of Marcus A. Hanna, the paragon of conservatism in the age of McKinley.

Though the Hearst press swung to the side of "yellow" reaction, it would have been a marvel of history if no leaders had arisen to express the sentiments and resentments of the multitudes who were unemployed or fretted by deposits frozen in banks, homes or farms in peril of foreclosure, bonds in default, stocks evidently worthless. It would also have been a marvel if no demagogues had taken advantage of the opportunity to elevate themselves into places of influence and authority. Both appeared upon the scene and it was not always easy to distinguish the one from the other.

From ancient times, it is true, a connotation of evil had been associated with demagogues. In the fourth century before Christ, Aristotle had called the demagogue the man who flatters the people as the sycophant flatters the tyrant. The people were "too ready" to listen to him — "the worthless fellow" opposed by "the better class." At least the demagogue was a trouble-maker. "Revolutions in democracies," declared the Greek philosopher, "are generally caused by the intemperance of demagogues who either in their private capacity lay information against rich men . . . or coming forward in public they stir up the people against them." Yet Aristotle did not regard the demagogue as an evil genius springing out of a vacuum, with no justification or right on his side. "Constitutional governments and aristocracies," he explained, "are commonly overthrown owing to some deviation from justice in the constitution itself."

In classic theory, therefore, it had not been entirely a case of black against white — the villainy of the demagogue against the excellence of "the better class." The judgment of subsequent history likewise had been mixed. Jefferson, the hero of agrarians, had been denounced as a demagogue and atheist by "the wealth and talents" of his time. Nor had the planting aristocracy looked upon Lincoln and his "greasy mechanics" as the symbols of perfect chivalry. With historic lines of demarkation so loosely drawn it was impossible in 1933 to make a distinction universally acceptable. Nevertheless, if violence of language and the promise of impossible gifts were the signs of demagogy, then the United States had three masters of the art engaged in whipping up opposition to the Lords of Creation and their System — Huey P. Long, Father Charles E. Coughlin, and Dr. Francis E. Townsend. Each in his way was a man of singular power. Each addressed himself to a special audience and employed his own language and symbols of martial array. But, if the character of their following was the test of their intention, all appealed to misery and discontent with the economy and government of "the better class."

Huey P. Long, son of a poor farmer, born in 1893, belonged in origin to the class upon whose support he depended for power. By energy of will and strong native talents he had made his way through a toilsome youth and meager education to a position at the bar. Early in his career as a lawyer he had encountered the Standard Oil Company, and its ruthless obstruction, he said, had kept him from entering the millionaire circle. Had he been taken into the fold of the mighty his annals might have been those of many a poor boy who had marched from poverty to riches. Be that as it may, Mr. Long became an inveterate foe of the "corporate interests" and their politicians in Louisiana. Gathering strength in the progress of his denunciations, he managed to find a place for himself on the state commission charged with the regulation of public utilities. In 1928 he was elevated to the office of governor by a large popular vote.

As if learning from Machiavelli, Governor Long sharpened and turned against his foes the weapons they had employed against him. He brought the state legislature under his dominion. He drove his opponents out of office, by "ripper" legislation when necessary. Their places he filled with his obedient servants — some of them men whose vision of a political heaven was a kingdom in which corruptionists enriched themselves according to the formula of the Orleanist monarchy in France.

Whatever the character of his council, from start to finish the Governor remembered his constituents, so long neglected by "the better class" which he had evicted from political dominion. Under his direction the public school system was strengthened, free books were provided for pupils, farmers and villagers were "lifted out of the mud" by a network of improved roads and bridges, and the state university of Louisiana was raised to a higher standard of proficiency. Naturally all this improvement cost huge sums of money and to meet the bills the Governor laid heavy taxes on corporations and public utilities while exempting small homesteads from public levies. Even his irreconcilable foes had to acknowledge that, despite his ruthless methods, the Governor had materially aided poor whites and negroes in their galling struggles with ignorance and poverty.

Reaching out like Alexander for new worlds to conquer, Governor Long entered the campaign as a candidate for the United States Senate in 1930 and was elected. By this time he had attracted national attention and started to work out his economic program for the country. "I had been in the United States Senate only a few days," he said, "when I began my effort to make the battle for a distribution of wealth among all the people a national issue for the coming election." At the Chicago convention, Senator Long took special note of one sentence in Franklin D. Roosevelt's acceptance speech: "Throughout the Nation, men and women, forgotten in the political philosophy of the Government of the last years, look to us here for guidance and for a more equitable opportunity to share in the distribution of national wealth." This became Senator Long's keynote: "Share our wealth." With his wonted vigor, tireless and almost superhuman, he threw himself into the campaign for the election of Governor Roosevelt to the office of President, assailing the rich as despoilers of the people and demanding legislation that would strip them of power and force a new distribution of wealth. Just how this reallocation was to be effected, the Senator did not make very precise. His citations from the Old Testament seemed to indicate that he imagined it possible to divide railways, industrial plants, and corporate property as the ancient Jews had divided land and cattle. Yet, if his economic theory was somewhat obscure, there was no doubt about the effectiveness of his appeal and the magnitude of the following he secured.

Soon after President Roosevelt assumed his duties in the Spring of 1933, Mr. Long opened his barrage in the Senate. When he spoke, he ridiculed, snapped, gesticulated, and bellowed. News that he was to address his colleagues and the nation brought huge crowds to the galleries. Rarely had a Senator lashed out with such fury at banks, bankers, stock brokers, investment houses, and the Lords of Creation in particular and general. No invisible ties imposed caution upon his tongue. Dominant over his own local machine, sustained by the spoils of office and the perquisites, he could spurn the peace-offerings of corporations and "the better class" in his state. Senators of his own party, less secure in their seats, knew this and, as he scourged the money changers, named names, or made insinuations, they sat silent in their places, some aghast, others afraid.

When the Senate committee engaged in investigating stock exchange practices disclosed the fact that President Roosevelt's Secretary of the Treasury, Mr. Woodin, had been on the "preferred lists" of the J. P. Morgan Company, Senator Long made an impassioned speech declaring that "the

Treasury Department of the United States should be ousted from the House of Morgan." After Collier's Weekly had begun a war on him, Senator Long entered the chamber of the Senate committee, subjected Thomas W. Lamont to an inquisition, and sought to show that Mr. Lamont's ownership of stock in a concern that controlled Collier's Weekly had some connection with the attack published in its pages.

Shaking his finger at the witness, Senator Long persisted in his effort to drive Mr. Lamont into a corner and make him confess that through his financial interest in the Crowell Publishing Company he had exerted pressure upon editorial policies. Again and again, Mr. Lamont explained that his relation with the concern as a stockholder was merely financial and that he had not influenced in any respect the nature of the articles printed in its various publications, not so much as an article·in the Woman's Home Companion or the Farm and Fireside. Again and again he patiently informed the Senator that he was not even familiar with editorials and articles which had appeared in the pages of the Crowell magazines. "I haven't control of any of those papers, Senator Long," Mr. Lamont insisted quietly. "You see, Senator Long, my connection with the Crowell Publishing Company is simply a financial connection . . . I hold such stock as I hold in that company for the purpose of the dividends that I gain through it, I hope." When thus informed that the witness was interested in the dividends rather than in the intellectual output of the industry, Senator Long hurled at Mr. Lamont the retort: "I see. Thank you," provoking hilarity among the reporters and auditors in the chamber.

To the end of the hearing Mr. Lamont preserved his composure. Without raising his voice, he tried to make the Senator believe that the connections of the House of Morgan or its partners with men who happened to be in politics or the publishing business was incidental to financial transactions and in no way designed to influence political or editorial convictions or policies. Between the things which Mr. Lamont explained and the things he said he knew nothing about, Senator Long swelled in exasperation until he reached the point of explosion. In every respect the scene was indicative of a change in popular temper : a member of the House of Morgan had been treated with indignity by a Senator of the United States, a thing inconceivable in the age of the golden glow.

The second mighty malcontent of the season, Father Charles E. Coughlin, priest of the Royal Oak parish in the diocese of Detroit, pastor of the Shrine of the Little Flower, built up his dominion of power largely through the radio. Branching out from a local station over which he delivered sermonettes on religious and moral subjects to his parishioners, Father Coughlin organized a radio league of his own in 1930, bought time on other radio stations, and delivered a series of broadcasts on political and economic issues, in which he named names and fumed at men in high places. Swiftly he gathered an immense audience. One of his outbursts against President Hoover, it was reported, brought 1,200,000 letters from his auditors. Denunciations of the Morgan Company, Andrew W. Mellon, Ogden Mills, and Eugene Meyer as "the four Horsemen of the Apocalypse" evoked cheers from the hundreds of thousands. When great banks closed their doors in Detroit early in 1933 and the streets of the city were jammed with men and women crying for their money on deposit, Father Coughlin loosed a torrent of invective against bankers and politicians. Inasmuch as enormous audiences listened to his addresses, his stinging monologues "made news." So the press felt compelled to repeat them for its multitudinous readers and the nation fairly writhed under the priest's brazen denunciations.

Although Father Coughlin held rather close to Senator Long's keynote, his program contained distinctive elements. Being a Catholic, he employed for his coverage the humane sentiments expressed in the noblest encyclicals issued at Rome on social questions. The special objects of his censure were bankers, brokers, and "their politicians." The emancipation from their despotism was to come from "a living annual wage, nationalization of banking and currency and of natural resources, private ownership of all other property, control of private property for the public good, government banking, congressional control of coinage, steady currency value, cost of production plus a fair value for agriculture, labor unions under government protection, recall of non-productive bonds, abolition of tax-free bonds, social taxation," and other devices.

These proposals, it was evident, stemmed largely from the creed of American populism, with its attachment to the direct owners of small properties and its enmity for high finance and large enterprise. They were familiar, but in this case familiarity did not breed contempt, for auditors by the million heard with rapture their own desires so lustily stated. Clearly addressed to small home owners, debt-burdened farmers, and laborers — to men and women struggling on the verge of subsistence — the appeal penetrated every region and substratum of society. Commanding an audience so large and so constituted, on doctrines so formulated, Father Coughlin at first threw his weight on the side of the Roosevelt administration. He was among the councilors invited to Washington and stood ready to cheer as well as to scoff. How much havoc he could play with party regularity in 1933, none of the adepts could divine and as the months of the year slipped by they had to walk warily.

Less imposing in personality, no orator at all, was Dr. Francis E. Townsend, the third mighty malcontent who brought heavy pressure on Washington as the Roosevelt administration picked its way, now resolutely, now cautiously, amid the broken fortunes of the depression. Dr. Townsend was a quiet, soft-voiced physician of humble origins. For long, weary years, he had served poor patients generously in the Black Hills. At length, in search of a milder climate, he had migrated to Long Beach, California, where he found a minor post in the department of health. When the panic struck the nation in 1929, he and his little family were safe enough themselves but the sights and sounds of the catastrophe were too much even for his schooled patience. Through his window, one day, according to his own account, he saw three old women sorting over the contents of a garbage can in the street, searching there for their daily bread. Like Paul on the road to Damascus, Dr. Townsend beheld a sign and heard a call. With the wrath of an indignant prophet, he loudly cursed a world in which old women were compelled to search for food in the wastes of a city — so loudly that his outburst lifted his wife to her feet in alarm. This was America, land of the free and home of the brave, the land of great wealth and rugged individualism — indeed! Under the stress of tumultuous emotions, Dr. Townsend evolved a simple plan of salvation.

About his scheme there was nothing revolutionary, nothing as radical as the program of Senator Long or the proposals of Father Coughlin. It called for no knowledge of Marx's dialectics or Spengler's technics; nor of the automatic market or marginal utility. Aged people simply ought not to starve or resort to garbage for their bread. An old-age pension, Dr. Townsend thought, would prevent that, and many states had pension systems, of a kind, already in effect. It should, however, be a generous pension — two hundred dollars a month; no less. But that could not stand alone. The country was in financial straits and industry was running on a low level of production. Consequently Dr. Townsend had to add another drive to his system: each recipient of a two hundred dollar pension must spend it all within a month. Such an enormous stream of cash would set all sleeping enterprise in rapid motion, he thought, keep it in motion, and stimulate new enterprise. The aged poor were to be saved from disgrace and poverty; the problem that had baffled the world's statesmen was to be solved swiftly and painlessly. With economic energies engaged at full blast, the revenue for the pensions could be painlessly derived, by a sales tax, a transactions tax on consumption. The wealth of the rich would not be threatened. Consumers would pay and the American System, unchanged in form, would run at top speed.

In vain did economists try to explain voluminously that the transactions tax would really fall upon the poor whose buying power was already scant and that a pension of even thirty dollars a month would cost four billion dollars a year. Dr. Townsend retained his fixed idea and in the highways and byways preached his gospel of economic salvation. From one end of the land to the other, Old Age Revolving Pension clubs were formed by the thousands and members assembled in conventions. Contributions were collected in dollars, dimes, and pennies. Old men and women, believing that pensions were almost at hand, sold their earthly possessions and emptied the returns into the treasury for the good of the cause. Very soon the whole country was laid out into districts, each with its directing headquarters, and a central office was established in Washington, well-staffed by publicity experts. Petitions to Congress were drafted and it was alleged that at least twenty-five million signatures had been secured before much time had elapsed. As the movement acquired enormous funds for propaganda, it recruited orators, manipulators, and clever managers of the news.

Having organized an immense constituency, the Townsendites concentrated a heavy pressure on the politicians. Candidates for Congress were questioned privately, heckled at public meetings, and driven into commitments. While the uproar was at its height, the directors of the movement could claim a strong nucleus of followers in the House of Representatives. In many districts even conservative Republicans had to make bows of approval. Added to the noise raised by Senator Long and Father Coughlin, the shrill voices of the aged poor deepened the tension of the national capital as the Roosevelt administration formulated its policies, while taking account of the necessities likely to be presented in coming campaigns.

§

Domestic anxieties were augmented in the spring of 1933 by foreign news. At the end of three years the detonations of the panic appeared to be expanding rather than diminishing throughout the world; but in the general wreckage communist Russia forged ahead, enlarging production and employment, while capitalist nations blundered around aimlessly. In 1933 the Soviet Republic brought to a close its first five-year plan with a paean of triumph, and announced the opening of the second concerted effort on a scale more vast. The arch-conspirator, Leon Trotsky, with his feverish designs for a quixotic world revolution, had been expelled, his faction suppressed, the Stalin regime consolidated, and the demonstration of efficient socialism in one country acclaimed as in progress. From any point of view the spectacle was impressive. The left-wing intelligentsia in the United States now spoke knowingly of five-year plans realized, not romantically of utopian dreams as of old. The middle classes were moved to mild curiosity at least and read the New Russian Primer by the thousands. If the red-baiters in turn were stirred to greater activity, that could be interpreted to mean that communism was really on the march. Even President Hoover had felt compelled to refer to five-year plans, if only to discredit all planning as Bolshevik in origin and intention. Marx had emerged from a hole in a corner and hovered as a hope or a menace over places high and low.

Still, Russia was far off and could be discounted as a bit oriental in its ways and values. Besides, communist formulas — for instance, law of capitalist development, thesis, antithesis, and synthesis, inevitable breakdown of capitalist economy, dictatorship of the proletariat, and the spring into freedom — had a strange sound in most American ears. The phrase "materialist dialectics" was a puzzle propounded in drawing-rooms for sheer entertainment. Had the preachers of ideology been confined to the Kremlin or the banks of the Volga, the rolling reverberations of their voices might have faded away unheard in Jersey City, in the Rocky Mountains, in sunny California. It so came about, however, that while the celebration of Russia's first five-year plan was in process, nearer events in central Europe announced the triumph of another ideology, equally dogmatic and equally Bolshevik in method, whose rise to power could not be ignored in any part of the United States.

For fifteen years Germany had been struggling through the mess left by the war, under a constitution that was in many respects a model for the world. Despite endless difficulties and the harsh impositions of the Versailles Treaty, sober and steady Germans had managed to keep their political machinery running, especially with the aid of lavish loans, long-term and short-term, from American and British capitalists. But the old military party, tolerated and favored by the Weimar republic, continued to smart under the stings of defeat, and found it more pleasant to discover scapegoats in democrats, socialists, and Jews than to accept the disconcerting fact of its own failure. Militarism still lived and its devotees became positively frantic as they contemplated their impotence. To the unrest of the officer class was united the violence of war veterans from the trenches. They chafed at the restraints of civilian life, even when they could secure regular employment, and they turned to murder and civil war during discouraging days of enforced idleness. All through the years which Coolidge found so blessed with prosperity, German veterans unadjusted to civilian life had been drawing together in the National Socialist Workers Party under the direction of a powerful demagogue, Adolf Hitler.

In opposition to this growing military concentration, German democracy developed only factionalism, betraying confusion in purpose and method. Cursing democracy in terms as lurid as those employed by Hitler's Nazis, Communists fought Socialists in the streets and occasionally voted with Hitler's party in the Reichstag. Frightened by communism and socialism alike, great landlords trembling for the safety of their estates and capitalists anxious over the future of their heavy industries cast about for any port in the storm. Terrified ladies made lavish contributions to Hitler's exchequer. So, when the full fury of the economic panic broke in Germany in 1929, there was no democratic unity to cope with the gathering forces of reaction. Backed by his marching men, Hitler, in January, 1933, came to terms with Franz von Papen on "a national concentration" representing landlords, heavy industries, and Catholicism, foe of all "irreligious" radicalism. From a conference with President von Hindenburg, now in the last stages of senility, the two conspirators emerged with a commission to form a government composed of Hitler as chancellor, von Papen as vice chancellor, and a cabinet weighted by landlords and big industrialists.

Within two months Germany had slipped into despotism. On February 4, a month before the inauguration of Roosevelt in Washington, von Hindenburg signed a decree prohibiting public meetings and silencing the press. A few weeks later the Reichstag building, dedicated to the German people, was gutted by fire — perhaps an event symbolizing Nazi contempt for democratic institutions. February 28, Hindenburg suspended all the fundamental rights guaranteed by the Weimar constitution, imposed severe penalties on open opponents, and put the country into a state of siege. Although Hitler's party received less than a majority of the votes cast in an election on March 5, it was able, by unity of will, to ride rough-shod over the divided opposition. March 23, a docile Reichstag met and enacted legislation which in substance put an end to the last pretences of constitutional government and placed a formal sanction on government by dictatorial decree — government by despotism. Now terrorism moved swiftly. All opposition parties were suppressed. Trade unions and coöperative societies were destroyed. Jews were barbarously persecuted. Liberal critics, even of the German race, were beheaded, shot, or imprisoned. Like Mussolini's Fascists, Hitler's Nazis began their march over "the rotten corpse of liberalism and democracy," as they termed it — a march that was to end in tyranny, armed to the teeth, triumphant, invincible at home, feared abroad. "Let contemptible democracies beware!" ran the cry along the Berlin-Rome axis.

Meanwhile, across the Pacific, the fire lighted in China by Japanese militarists continued to burn. The efforts of President Hoover and Secretary Stimson to quench it had been without avail. Great Britain and France had refused to join them in united action against the violator of the Kellogg Pact. Almost without let or hindrance the Japanese consolidated their position in Manchukuo, pressed westward and southward, operated around Peiping, made "deals" with local war lords, and bombed their way down toward the Yangtze. In Tokyo all the old Liberals who had coöperated with the League of Nations and sought an orientation toward the Anglo-Saxon world were driven from power. Some died. Others were assassinated. A few fled. The remainder with rare exceptions took refuge in silence. Their last line of defense had been destroyed in 1924 when the Congress of the United States passed the Exclusion Act, slammed the door in the face of the Japanese nation, making no effort to spare its feelings. Like a bolt from the heavens had come the answer. "Asia for the Asiatics!" rolled the war shout from Yokohama to Dairen. With their power and prestige enhanced, militarists and navalists took charge of the government in Tokyo, polished their weapons, and prepared to tear up four-power pacts, nine-power pacts, and all the other kinds of pacts that stood in their way. The little candle of democracy, which had flickered in the national capital of Japan, sank into a dying sputter. Over this development, Rome and Berlin at least could strut. Was tyranny, one of the oldest forms of government, to be the last?

During the closing months of his administration, President Hoover watched the course of events with growing anxiety. His defeat in the election had left him with no mandate for action, and inability to fathom his successor's plans added to his perplexities. In domestic affairs the tension of the economic distress remained taut. In foreign affairs the question of the inter-governmental debts was pressing. Great Britain and France asked for a re-opening of the settlements, and France prepared to default on her obligations. The disarmament conference at Geneva was in a state of suspended animation, and on its idle talk Germany had heaped ridicule. A world economic conference had been called and experts were laying out the agenda, but the prospects for "appeasement" were slight. The Hoover-Stimson doctrine applied to Japan in the Manchukuo affair was hanging in mid-air and the Council of the League of Nations was maneuvering for an escape.

In an effort to bridge the gulf, President Hoover, after the election, invited Governor Roosevelt, his successor, to confer with him on the issues of the moment and on November 22, 1932, they held a desultory discussion without arriving at a program of joint action. The following January, Secretary Stimson took up the matter of foreign affairs with Governor Roosevelt. Apparently he gained the impression that the incoming President would adhere to the policy of refusing to recognize territorial changes made in violation of the Kellogg Pact. Later in the month President Hoover and Governor Roosevelt again conferred in the White House, and again failed to arrive at any major decision. Although a statement was issued to the effect that the incoming administration would be glad to discuss the debt question and other matters with British representatives, the pronouncement merely confirmed a platitude. Admittedly the conference was futile. If the misadventure gave President Hoover an opportunity to shift some of the responsibility for the banking crisis of February upon his successor, Governor Roosevelt was able to retort that it would have been folly to assume responsibility without power.

§

Such, in bald outline, with meager illustrations, were the maladies and tumults surrounding the Roosevelt administration when it entered upon its duties in March, 1933, and began to thread its way in the maze. Banks closed. Unemployment increasing. Grievances deepening. Uncertainty

spreading. Farmers, tenants, and share croppers groaning.
Bread lines lengthening. "The better class" bewildered and
bespattered by the revelations of congressional inquiries. Investors full of wrath over the duplicity of their former counselors. Malcontents sowing the wind. Communists jeering.
Fascists sneering. Old-line Democrats in Congress bewildered by problems and spectacles never yet beheld in a world
they never made. Republican managers reduced to helpless-
ness. A majority of Senators and Representatives committed
to only one positive program — the hoary program of currency inflation in some form. The country and the national
capital beset by alarms. The optimism of 1928 succeeded
by pessimism. There was, to be sure, more good humor and
less hatred than the amount of distress suggested, but even
merry-makers could scarcely escape thought of the vortex.
Was the crisis merely another episode in the long history of
calamities — a passing shadow? Or was it the beginning of
profound changes in American life? With the future veiled,
only guesses and surmises were possible on March 4, 1933.

# CHAPTER V

## Reformation and Salvation

THRUSTING immediately at the fright induced by stresses and strains, President Roosevelt, in his inaugural address on March 4, 1933, called upon "a stricken Nation in the midst of a stricken world" to put aside fear and move forward to the conquest of the depression "as a trained and loyal army willing to sacrifice for the good of a common discipline" under the leadership that had just been placed in his care. This could be done in accordance with the terms of the Constitution, which "is so simple and practical that it is possible always to meet extraordinary needs by changes in emphasis and arrangement without loss of essential form." It was to be hoped that "the normal balance of Executive and legislative authority" would be wholly adequate to cope with the task that confronted the country; but the "unprecedented demand and need for undelayed action may call for temporary departure from that normal balance of public procedure."

Unequivocally the incoming President described the sweep of the depression, ranging from the collapse of economic values to despair among "a host of unemployed citizens." There was no doubt about all that. "Only a foolish optimist can deny the dark realities of the moment. . . . Plenty is at our doorstep, but a generous use of it languishes in the very sight of the supply." Guilt was implied and the President passed judgment. "Primarily this is because rulers of the exchange of mankind's goods have failed, through their own stubbornness and their own incompetence, have admitted their failure, and have abdicated. Practices of the unscrupulous money changers stand indicted in the court of public opinion, rejected by the hearts and minds of men. . . . They know only the rules of a generation of self-seekers. They have no vision, and when there is no vision the people perish. Yes, the money changers have fled from their high seats in the temple of our civilization. We may now restore that temple to the ancient truths. The measure of the restoration lies in the extent to which we apply social values more noble than mere monetary profit." Thus the sentiment of dedication was sweetened for sinners by the idea that the primary scapegoats were the money changers — from whom investors had bought Allegheny common, Kreuger and Toll secured, sinking fund gold debentures, and other symbols of wealth in the riotous days of the prodigal son.

There must be a program. "There must be a strict supervision of all banking and credits and investments; there must be an end to speculation with other people's money; and there must be provision for an adequate but sound currency." That was an echo of Woodrow Wilson's New Freedom, especially soothing to the heirs of populism. But President Roosevelt did not stop with currency reform. "Our greatest primary task is to put people to work." There must be a wiser use of our great natural resources, a better balance of industry and agriculture, an increase in the value of agricultural products, protection for mortgaged homes and farms, a curtailment of government expenditures, a unification of relief work, and national planning for public utilities that have a definitely public character. In foreign relations we must follow "the policy of the good neighbor." No efforts will be spared to restore world trade by international adjustments. Yet such trade relations, "though vastly important, are in point of time and necessity secondary to the establishment of a sound national economy. I favor as a practical policy the putting of first things first." In such terms the President's program was outlined.

The next step from talking was action. We must act; we must act quickly. We must act together. We are dependent upon one another; we must give as well as take. We must bend to discipline, for without discipline "no progress is made, no leadership becomes effective. . . . This I propose to offer," pledging the supremacy of the larger good. "With this pledge taken, I assume unhesitatingly the leadership of this great army of our people dedicated to a disciplined attack upon our common problems." The Constitution permits it, for it is so framed that the Government can meet every stress. Measures required by the stricken nation will be laid before Congress, and proper efforts will be made to secure a speedy adoption.

In case Congress fails to adopt or devise appropriate measures and the emergency continues to be critical, "I shall not evade the clear course of duty that will then confront me. I shall ask the Congress for the one remaining instrument to meet the crisis — broad Executive power to wage a war against the emergency, as great as the power that would be given to me if we were in fact invaded by a foreign foe. . . . We do not distrust the future of essential democracy. The people of the United States have not failed. In their need they have registered a mandate that they want direct, vigorous action. They have asked for discipline and direction under leadership. They have made me the present instrument of their wishes. In the spirit of the gift I take it."

In supporting the constitutional provision for a strong President, Hamilton, long before Roosevelt's day, had said in the sixty-ninth number of the Federalist: "Every man the least conversant in Roman history knows how often that republic was obliged to take refuge in the absolute power of a single man, under the formidable title of 'Dictator.'" The provision had been tested in war in 1861 and 1917. Now it was to be tested in time of peace. Or was it? Could an invocation of force command the energies of the nation for constructive purposes, for the building of a civilization? The future lowered over the present.

"This is a day of national consecration." With these words President Roosevelt had opened his inaugural address — words which were, in the process of editing, omitted from the definitive edition of his works published five years later. Having begun on this note, and having disclosed his resolve to act, to wield great powers in an attack upon calamity, the President, in bringing his address to a close, called for divine aid: "In this dedication of a Nation we humbly ask the blessings of God."

The ideas, "consecration" and "dedication," peculiarly fitted the popular mood of the hour. They suggested that the task to be undertaken had a sacred character; they throbbed with religious fervor. For centuries the preacher, Hebrew and Christian, in calling sinners to account, had reminded them of their wickedness and pointed out the narrow way leading to righteousness. Things had been done that should not have been done. Things that should have been done had been left undone. After years of reckless living, the nation had fallen upon evil days. A consciousness of sin was abroad in the land. The future was uncertain and even greater adversity might be hidden behind the morrow. "People are like . . . little children quarrelling, crying, and then straight-away laughing," Marcus Aurelius, Emperor of the Romans, had said in the second century of the Christian era. On March 4, 1933, in the United States, they were quarrelling and crying. They might be laughing again, as soon as a ray of prosperity broke through the clouds; but at the moment they were grieved, afraid, and repentant. Even the voice of the opposition presses and benches could be neither scornful nor ribald in the presence of the débâcle or of the Chief

Executive scourging the wicked and seeking a road to the promised land.

Without waiting for Congress to assemble on March 9 to consider the state of the nation, in accordance with his official summons, President Roosevelt squared away for action on the Sunday following his inauguration. His advisers found sanction for government by decree in the unrepealed provisions of a war statute, enacted in 1917, giving the Chief Executive almost plenary control over foreign exchanges, gold, silver, and currency. Under the authority of this legislation President Roosevelt issued, at one o'clock in the morning of March 6, an order closing all the banks in the United States from Monday, March 6, to Thursday, March 9; and on the day of expiry he extended it "in full force and effect until further proclamation." During the holiday all banking transactions were suspended, except those specifically authorized by the Secretary of the Treasury, with the approval of the President.

This decree, completing the closures already made under state authority, was designed to stop runs on banks and maintain the status quo until new legislation could be enacted by Congress — legislation safeguarding "sound" institutions, providing more currency, and establishing procedures for salvaging as far as possible the banks that were really in financial straits. If any lawyers were inclined to ask what constitutional authority the President had over state banks in time of peace, their question had no practical effect. With amazing unanimity, national leaders rallied to the support of the Executive's proposals. A conference of governors assembled at the White House on Monday, March 6, threw aside political affiliations, expressed confidence in the President, and urged all the people to coöperate with him "in such action as he shall find necessary or desirable in restoring banking and economic stability." On the instant the Constitution of the United States had acquired an extraordinary flexibility and the rights of sovereign states over banking had been, for practical purposes, abrogated.

When Congress gathered in special session on March 9, the Chief Executive was cautious. He did not propose anything specific and radical, such as nationalizing banks of issue. He merely laid before Congress a message calling for blanket authority over banks and the draft of a bill conferring it. With an alacrity suggesting spontaneous combustion, excited Representatives and Senators rushed the draft through the two houses and placed it on the President's desk before the close of the day. Neither Lincoln in 1861 nor Wilson in 1917 had been granted drastic powers with so little haggling and bickering. That "democracy can act," in accord with its normal processes, in a crisis, had been conclusively demonstrated.

The new legislation gave the President authority in time of war or "any other period of national emergency" to resort to extraordinary measures in respect of currency and banking. It empowered the Treasury to compel the surrender of all gold coin, bullion, and gold certificates in exchange for other coin or currency issued under the laws of the United States. Conservators for national banking institutions were provided. National Banks were allowed to raise cash by the sale of preferred stock, and arrangements were made for permitting both national and state institutions to borrow from the Reconstruction Finance Corporation. Steps were taken to expand the currency for immediate needs in the form of "circulating notes" issued to Federal Reserve banks on the basis of federal obligations and other prime paper.

In appearance the Act was an emergency measure, but President Roosevelt was looking beyond the exigencies of the day. In his mind it was "to mark the beginning of a new relationship between the banks and the people of the country." The Act was not the nationalization of banking and currency that had been demanded by one wing of Jacksonian Democracy. It drove no money changers from the temple. On the contrary it gave the support of public credit to bankers while establishing the supremacy of the Federal Government over gold. Time was to amplify the meaning.

Under the authority of the emergency legislation, during an inquiry into the soundness of institutions in difficulty, the Secretary of the Treasury permitted the gradual resumption of the banking business. By the end of May nearly thirteen thousand banks were reported open without restriction. As they held almost ninety per cent of the total amount on deposit throughout the United States, it seemed that the immediate emergency had passed. Viewed superficially, the remaining problem was one of determining the fate of state and national banks yet in a dubious position. Nevertheless other fiscal events of major significance for American economy were soon set in train.

Among them was the modification, if not the abandonment, of the gold standard as the basis of the monetary system — a violation of the fundamental principle written into law in 1900, four years after the "battle of 1896 for the salvation of the country." By the legislation of 1900 a certain weight and fineness of gold was made the foundation of the American dollar and all other currency was made exchangeable in terms of gold. Two essential elements were embraced in the system : gold, a privately owned commodity in general circulation, was chosen as the substance on which the dollar rested and all paper money could be freely exchanged for that precious metal. While gold certificates issued by the Government had a certain priority, possessors of other paper currency could nominally demand gold in exchange. The "free" movement of gold thus established for internal economy was also extended to international transactions and gold circulated "freely" among the nations in the operations of their commerce.

Although this gold system, as far as the United States was concerned, was little more than thirty years old, it had become embedded in American business thought and in popular psychology. Actually it had acquired some of the characteristics of a fetish, a sacred thing, absolutely indispensable to the functioning of industry and commerce on any level of efficiency. To touch it or to threaten it was to profane the very altar of Fortune. It was true that Great Britain, the modern originator of the gold standard for universal purposes, had abandoned it, or at least cut loose from it, but the major portion of American economists seemed to regard the British revision as a temporary procedure, and in any case no guide for American policy.

Whether Great Britain had been "forced" off the gold base or had voluntarily "gone" off made little difference. The fact remained and it impinged upon American policy. Either from necessity or as a matter of policy, the United States gradually followed the British example in some respects, as the Chief Executive became convinced that gold was not, after all, a veritable pillar of heaven. "Gradually" is the correct word, and "in some respects" must be attached to it. The very closing of the banks on March 6, 1933, impaired the gold standard, for citizens could not then demand gold for any gold certificates which they held. The gold standard was further impaired when the banks were reopened, for they were forbidden to pay out gold or gold certificates. Another step was taken on April 5 when the President issued an order prohibiting the hoarding of gold and requiring the delivery of all gold coin, bullion, and certificates to Federal Reserve banks on or before April 28, with minor exceptions for industrial and other purposes. A supplement to this measure, in August, prohibited all private holdings of gold and all private transactions in gold. Thus two phases of the gold system were destroyed, namely, private ownership of gold coins or bullion and free transactions in that metal.

With transactions in gold hampered by the banking crisis and forbidden by executive order, Congress faced the issue of public and private contracts calling for payments in gold values. Previous to 1933 it had been a practice of governments and private concerns in the United States to stipulate that their bonds and other evidences of indebtedness which they sold were payable in gold coin "of the present standard of value." Obligations running into the billions contained this "gold clause." After March 6, however, it became impossible to fulfill all such contracts.

Of course, fulfillment had always been a mere matter of theoretical probability. Now it had become even theoretically impossible. President Roosevelt recognized the fact. Congress agreed and by a joint resolution, effective June 6, 1933, it folded the mantle of law over the fact and the theory. It declared that the right to require the payment of gold obligations in gold was "against public policy" and that such obligations could be lawfully satisfied by payment in any coin or currency "which at the time of payment is legal tender for public and private debts." Looking to the future, Congress prohibited the issuance of new obligations containing the gold clause. In short, in the emergency, one of the "most sacred elements" in public and private contracts was swept aside by national legislation. Had the spirit of Daniel Shays returned or was there a necessity that knew not law?

While "the eternal foundations of sound economy" seemed to be dissolving like vapory figments of the imagination, the agrarian interests in Congress grew bolder and made a concerted drive on the retreating Old Guard of the Gold Army. The ghost of 1896 had not been buried after all. The Senate and the House were crowded with members who could recall Bryan's picture of mankind crucified on a cross of gold; but for forty years advocates of inflation and free silver had been baffled by the protagonists of sound money. Now in an hour of crisis their victory seemed to be in sight. If it had not been for the opposition of President Roosevelt, they might have exploded the gold works then and there.

In the circumstances they were able to do no more than declare their sentiments and confer upon him powers to be used at his discretion. Appropriately, they incorporated their principles in the farm relief law of May 12, 1933, known as the Agricultural Adjustment Act. Their main purposes were declared to be to offset the effects of depreciated foreign currencies on American foreign commerce, to maintain a parity among the currency issues of the United States, and to meet the economic emergency by an expansion of credit.

For the attainment of these ends, the President was authorized, not commanded, to use the Federal Reserve System in purchasing and holding obligations of the United States in an aggregate sum of $3,000,000,000. If this device could not be applied, then the President might direct the Treasury to issue three billion dollars' worth of legal tenders for the purpose of meeting the maturing obligations of the Government or purchasing its obligations in the market. Attacking their principal foe, gold, the agrarians empowered the President to reduce the weight of the gold dollar by fifty per cent at most, and to fix the weight of the silver dollar at a definite ratio to the gold dollar. Notwithstanding the defeat of efforts to force the coinage of silver at the ratio of sixteen to one, the President was authorized to accept a certain amount of silver from foreign debtors and issue silver certificates against it. Later the silver faction was able to force through a measure declaring that, in the monetary system of the United States, silver shall constitute one-fourth in value as against three-fourths in gold, and directing the Treasury to buy silver within a certain price range per ounce, store it, and issue silver certificates. Nevertheless its declaration of sentiments was in fact largely academic — a threat, not an achievement — since President Roosevelt did little or nothing under the inflationist sections of the Agricultural Adjustment Act.

After all, William Jennings Bryan was dead. A Kerensky might be on the horizon of fervid imaginations, but no Bryan was there any more. When Congress recovered from the first shocks of the crisis and came to formulating the Banking Act of 1933, conservatives took the lead and steered close to their well-known headlands. An inducement was made to bring more state banks into the Federal Reserve System, by permitting federal banks to open branches in states which gave a similar permission to their own banks. Stricter supervision was established over banks, holding companies, and affiliates, and banks were required to cut loose, within a year, from affiliated security concerns. In this way, it was hoped, some patent abuses in the investment business would be eliminated. With a view to holding down speculation, while providing accommodations to business and commerce, the Federal Reserve Board was given large powers over the purchase and sale of eligible paper by member banks. To remove fears and lure money out of hoards, a temporary scheme for insuring deposits up to a certain amount was put into effect.

Despite some alarms on the right, the Banking Act of 1933 was conservative from start to finish, from the standpoint of agrarian inflationists. The limited power to issue currency was still vested in private hands. Banks of issue were not nationalized. Private banking was not confined to commercial business. The original compromise between centralization and states' rights was preserved in its essential features.

A search for some overarching hypothesis of consistency to explain the various currency and banking measures led to the White House rather than to Capitol Hill. In Congress every action took the form of an adjustment of interests. The Chief Executive, on the other hand, gave out a series of statements that had the merits of a certain congruity, especially in relation to the basic rights of property. He was seeking, he declared, to "restore commodity price levels," to facilitate the payment of public and private debts "more nearly at the price level at which they were incurred," to effect a balance in the price system "so that farmers may exchange their products for the products of industry on a fairer exchange basis." The question whether the measures adopted would accomplish the posited ends might be debated, but here at least was a clear objective. Beyond these adjustments in the price system, President Roosevelt looked to stabilization — the establishment and maintenance of a dollar "which will not change its purchasing and debt-paying power during the succeeding generation." In appearance this was the time-worn scheme for overcoming the calamities of depression by currency manipulation, but other measures of the administration made it plain that the day for pure and simple reliance on any such device had passed.

In the process of seeking to raise the price level and stabilize it, President Roosevelt had to take account of international aspects of the currency system. Here, too, he was positive as to objectives. He declared that the dollar had too long been at the mercy of accidents in international trade, the internal policies pursued by other nations, and political disturbances in other continents. "Therefore," he said, "the United States must take firmly in its own hands the control of the gold value of our dollar. This is necessary in order to prevent dollar disturbances from swinging us away from our ultimate goal, namely, the continued recovery of our commodity prices. . . . My aim in taking this step [of buying and selling gold] is to establish and maintain continuous control. . . . We are thus continuing to move toward a managed currency." Whether it was possible, in fact, to manage the domestic price system and at the same time cushion it against the shocks of foreign-trade oscillations was a matter of dispute among schoolmen. Nor was it easy, if at all feasible, to find out whether multitudinous practices did indeed conform to the controlling hypothesis of policy. Even so, the departure from the conception of the "free" market, national and international, with gold as the unit of exchange, seemed to close an epoch.

While making much ado over the alleged expulsion of money changers from the temple and the revision of the currency and banking system, Congress turned to public finance. "Our government's house is not in order," President Roosevelt declared to the special session called in March, 1933. He reminded it of the Democratic promise of economy and warned the members that "too often in recent history liberal governments have been wrecked on rocks of loose fiscal policy." Well aware of log-rolling propensities among Senators and Representatives, he demanded and received a broad authority to reduce payments to war veterans and to cut, within certain limits, the salaries of government employees. Proceeding under the provisions of the Economy Act, the President effected changes, consolidations, and reductions which, it was estimated, would bring savings amounting to nearly a billion dollars in the next budget. Collaterally, federal revenues were raised by new taxes, on legalized beer, gasoline, new capital stock, and excess profits. After conventions in the requisite number of states had ratified, in December, 1933, the twenty-first amendment, repealing prohibition, Congress joined state legislatures in a scramble to derive heavy revenues from alcoholic beverages.

Taking the position that emergency peace expenditures, like war expenditures, constituted a class in themselves and should be at least partly financed by bond issues, Roosevelt proposed to set up a double budget. Outlays for emergency purposes were to be met by borrowings, and the budget of ordinary or current expenditures was to be balanced by curtailments in expenditures and increases in revenues. As a matter of fact the Government of the United States had never possessed a budget which clearly separated capital outlays from current running expenses. From the beginning Congress had made appropriations from tax revenues to pay for roads, waterway improvements, lighthouses, buildings, and other public works of various kinds. Some states and many cities had established the distinction and had regularly borrowed money for public improvements and emergency outlays, often making provision for meeting interest and installment charges as they fell due. But Congress had not followed these examples. Nor had the Government of the United States ever set up a capital balance sheet, showing on the one side the federal debt and on the other its real and intangible properties which could be deemed offsetting assets. For example, the money borrowed for the Reconstruction Finance Corporation was properly placed under the head of federal debt, but the securities pledged by private concerns with the Corporation as collateral undoubtedly formed assets of some value that belonged, with equal propriety, on the credit side. Accordingly, there was a promise of more realistic finance in Roosevelt's proposal. However, he did not work it out in detail or apply it with precision. Despite all the pledges, mounting deficits marked the dealings of Congress and the Administration.

In connection with the "purification" and readjustment of the financial system, Congress laid its hands on the National Shrine in Wall Street by extending federal control over the issue of certain types of securities for which a high degree of market freedom had hitherto existed. The scheme of control was embodied in the Securities Act, approved May 27, 1933, and later given a more permanent form in the Securities and Exchange Act. In part the legislation expressed the indignation of investors and speculators who had suffered losses in the pools, peggings, balloon ascensions, and other operations of the great boom. In part also the law had a bearing upon banking, currency, and the functioning of economy in the broadest sense of the term.

Although it was not easy to draw the legal line between "honesty" and "fraud" in security transactions, between sober judgment and absurd hopes, the revelations of past transactions made by the Senate committee on banking and finance created an overwhelming sentiment in favor of additional protection for investors. Irrespective of the intention, the drafting of merely protective features was difficult. The determination of the kinds of new liquid claims to wealth that actually represented real wealth called for prognosis no less than diagnosis. Additional complications sprang from the fact that banking was entangled in the process of issuing stocks and bonds : many liquid claims in the form of securities were employed as the basis for the expansion of the currency by members of the Federal Reserve System. That the raising of capital funds by the sale of securities bore some relation to the forms and operations of industry was also undeniable. Was it possible, by positive restrictions on the freedom of the market, to compel banks and sellers of securities to discharge the function which they had been supposed to perform : that of acting as mediators between investors and productive enterprises in need of capital goods? The situation was perplexing and Congress struck out pragmatically.

After exempting from the operations of the Act a long list of securities, such as government bonds and commercial paper of limited scope, Congress stipulated that other securities must be registered with the Federal Trade Commission, later the Securities and Exchange Commission especially created. In all cases registration was to disclose specific information respecting the nature, sponsorship, and substance of the paper tendered to the public. Among the items of information required were the names, addresses, and functions of the persons connected with the "issuer" of the security, including directors and officers of the corporation concerned, underwriters, persons owning more than ten per cent of the stock, salaries paid to officers and directors, and commissions paid to participants.

From personnel, Congress turned to substance. It called upon the issuer for information respecting the funded debt already outstanding, the amount and purpose of the security offered, properties to be acquired by the capital raised, material contracts arising in connection therewith, balance sheets, profit and loss statements, and articles of incorporation. Subject to exceptions and modifications, foreign securities were brought within the same frame of control. For the benefit of investors, essential parts of the information filed with the Commission were to be made matters of public record. Remedies at law were provided against participants guilty of making untrue statements or concealing facts essential to the broad purposes of the Act. Heavy penalties were set for persons who transgressed the law, subject to judicial safeguards in case of violations due to justifiable conditions or the fallibility of human judgment. To protect American holders of foreign securities, Congress provided for the creation of a semi-private Corporation of Foreign Security Holders empowered to look after the interests of investors whose paper was in default.

During the debates on the original bill in Congress and outside, protests were lodged against the severity of the restrictions proposed against violations of the liberty long enjoyed in pecuniary transactions — the liberty deemed essential to dynamic enterprise. In the light of available information respecting the spoliation of investors in the age of Coolidge prosperity, few critics were brash enough at first to demand complete laissez faire in the grand style. Yet many were ready to insist that the restraints of the bill would deprive industry of needed capital, paralyze the enterprise of bankers and initiators, and slow down the process of recovery. In the theory of business enterprise, room had always been made for the element of risk; the mechanical laws of economics did not work perfectly; at the side of or in the interstices of the network composed of going concerns lay possibilities of chance that might result in either profit or loss.

Indeed there were a few economists who maintained that, in the regime of corporate management, this operation of whirling Fortune's wheel was the chief function left to the business man. If losses ensued, they must be accepted. If the divination was correct, new and great enterprises might rise, enriching individual promoters and adding to the sum total of national wealth. It mattered little that the modern devotee of Fortune used other people's money. It was the function that counted.

Vibrating between the idea of economic law and the conception of economic chance, with freedom for business ingenuity and risk, Congress tossed to and fro over the terms of the securities bill. In the end it declared that numerous economic activities traditionally regarded as a part of the free system should be forbidden, but that some leeway should be granted to pecuniary enterprise under the protection of the courts. When the provisional legislation was recast in the Securities and Exchange Act of 1934, its restrictions were tightened and enforcement was entrusted to a special body, the Securities and Exchange Commission.

§

All the modifications in banking, currency, and security legislation left untouched a question of wider and deeper popular interest: What about unemployment and poverty? At no time during the formulation of these modifications did the Roosevelt administration itself take the ground that such cleansing and readjustment of system would be automatically followed by a speeding up of industry and agriculture to the highest possible tempo. Theorists and practitioners who considered this subject were divided on the prospects. Without designating the time and place at which any free and automatic market had actually maintained the highest possible level of economic activity, one group maintained that some of the restrictions imposed by the banking and security legislation really impeded the proper flow of capital into the production and distribution of goods. Another group, squaring its economic philosophy with the New Freedom of President Wilson, was inclined to insist that, with abuses and excrescences cut off, the industrial mechanism would speed up under its own momentum.

But other ideas were afloat and other interests were vocal in the political forum. Free market or no free market, millions of unemployed on the ragged edge of awful hunger and local officials struggling with the cruel realities of human wretchedness clamored for "relief." Price mechanism or not, business men, represented by the United States Chamber of Commerce, demanded the right to balance production and consumption and to eliminate the unfair practices so obtrusive in the competitions of the marketplace. Farmers had received their pledge in the campaign and were impatient for redemption. While all the ideas and interests were interrelated, each set had its particular defenders and proceeded on its own assumptions as to the nature of American economy and things deemed desirable.

Could the idle be put to work? For unemployment and pauperism on such a large scale, respectable economic theory had no systematic place. In the realm of gentility a primary assumption had long prevailed to the effect that, in the main, idleness and poverty were due to defective minds or bodies, or to congenital improvidence; and in the current saying, as in other popular aphorisms, there was an element of truth. But with ten or twelve million people unemployed and many on the verge of hunger, if not actually starving, the situation was bothersome even for aphorists and economists. If phrase-makers were willing to let nature take its course, as doing nothing had been rhetorically described, politicians were in no position to adopt the maxim. As elected persons they had a public responsibility of some kind that was not imposed on private persons, for instance on the issuer of Kreuger and Toll secured, sinking fund, gold debentures. Being politi-cians, presumably they had to be on guard against undermin-ing the national morale — the very foundation of govern-ment and economy.

In dealing with unemployment and immediate relief, President Roosevelt and Congress had before them other considerations bearing upon the central issue — how to put people to work by prying economy out of the slough and setting it in motion. Time and again in history governments had done little or nothing while multitudes died in famines and floods; for example, in Russia and China. If, in the theory of experts, a repetition of such allegiance to "natural law" was possible in the United States, no such probability appeared in the calculations of politics. With little or no positive guidance from theoretical economics of any repu-table school, the President and Congress sought to grapple with the scheme of things entire, under the pressure of powerful interests, right, left, front, rear.

The legislative measures and executive actions which fol-lowed in swift succession during the spring and summer and autumn of 1933 showed a resolve to prevent starvation, if necessary even by the dole so generally abhorred. Neverthe-less there was a growing recognition of the fact that the rigors of the law for paupers in the historic style were inappli-

cable. Even legal provisions for the immediate relief of the
destitute, save hurried grants for food and clothing, expressed
more than the traditional righteous psychology of alms giving
associated with the stigma of pauperism. Two or three million unemployed persons might deserve nothing, but the
suspicion of total depravity and disgrace could hardly apply
wholesale to twelve or thirteen millions. Brushing aside the
warning against "pauperizing" the people, Congress enacted
the Emergency Relief law, approved May 12, 1933, which
made available half a billion dollars to aid the states in coping
with their relief obligations. Under the terms of the Act, the
Federal Emergency Relief Administration was established
and $250,000,000 granted to the states — a part to be pro-
portioned to each state's outlay for the purpose and a larger
part to be allocated to the states on the basis of their requirements without reference to their own expenditures. Besides
distributing money in aid of relief, the Emergency Administration bought huge quantities of food and clothing that
"glutted the market" and distributed them through the network of state and local agencies in all parts of the country.
"While it isn't written in the Constitution," President Roosevelt explained, "nevertheless it is the inherent duty of the
Federal Government to keep its citizens from starvation."
Though the proposition violated an earlier dictum by President Van Buren and had a strange ring for constitutional
lawyers, in that hour of alarm even Respectability had little
patience with black-letter lore.

To the main body of the American people, however, doles
were detestable. Something frightful lurked in the prospect
of ten million citizens sunk in the morass of permanent pauperism, sustained by meager grants of money and commodities. Subsequent familiarity with the horror, coupled with
the high cost of providing honest work, might induce willingness to accept the dole, but in 1933 opposition to the very
idea was almost universal. "Work, not doles!" was the cry
heard on all sides. In response to this preference, Congress
sought to create work under public auspices. By the Unem-

ployment Relief Act of March, 1933, it authorized the President to employ citizens in constructing and maintaining works of a public nature in connection with the natural resources of the country. Under this authority the Citizens Civilian Conservation Corps was organized and more than 300,000 young men, housed in well-built camps, were set to work combating forest fires, soil erosion, floods, and plant pests, planting trees, making trails, and cutting fire lanes on the public domain — state and federal. In November, 1933, with employment still lagging, President Roosevelt created the Civil Works Administration, allocated to it $400,000,000 for the coming season, and instructed it to provide occupations for about four million people on highways, community projects, and other hastily devised activities, ranging from social work in nursery schools to traveling theatrical performances. When charged with employing people on wasteful and futile undertakings, representatives of the administration replied that the hostility of business enterprise to all forms of public competition made it impossible to utilize the unemployed in the creation of wealth. If there was irony in the paradox, there was practical economics as well.

§

If large-scale pauperism and permanent doles were to be avoided, industry and agriculture had to be operated at fuller capacity. Of this the Chief Executive and Congress were fully aware. So, while trying to meet the obvious and menacing needs of millions unemployed, they sought to adjust the "unbalanced" economy of the nation, prod it into swifter motion, stabilize it, and aid it in providing opportunities for earning a livelihood "in the normal channels of private enterprise." In the realization of this broad purpose, two great statutes were enacted and put into force: the farm relief, or Agricultural Adjustment Act of May 12, 1933, and the National Industrial Recovery Act of June 16, 1933. Although it was later the fashion in uninformed circles to ascribe these measures to academic theorists and to characterize them as "hastily drawn," the facts in the case belied the imputation. Each measure in truth conformed to some kind of economic theory — the theory of hard-bitten practitioners.

The provisions of both statutes had behind them accumulations of precedents. What is more: academicians did not make the precedents or dictate the provisions. The Agricultural Adjustment Act, for example, had been in process of formulation for years; only a few detailed specifications were wanting in the spring of 1933. Except for the labor section, the National Industrial Recovery Act embodied the system of thought officially set forth by the United States Chamber of Commerce; and representatives of that powerful body participated actively in the drafting of the bill. It was in keeping with the facts, therefore, to say that the two statutes gave legal expression to the economic doctrines of organized agriculture and organized business enterprise. The section of the Recovery Act accorded to labor could scarcely be regarded as an exception to this rule, for it was written to forestall special legislation in that line, rather than to establish new policy in labor relations. In the original draft no such provision was incorporated; labor was at first left to fend for itself. Only when Congress seemed on the verge of enacting a thirty-hour bill did the draftsmen of the Recovery Law bring themselves to accept collective bargaining in industry. The sheer truth was that agriculture and business were striving to break through an impasse which they had created for themselves or, more accurately, which history had prepared for both.

For farmers, the Government was to enlarge buying power by an adjustment of prices and production. Lest there be a misunderstanding of their economic theory, the authors of the Agricultural Act set it forth explicitly in Title I. Their purpose, they said, was to establish and maintain a balance between the production and consumption of agricultural commodities and to assure appropriate marketing conditions.

The balance so determined was to be of such a character that it would "reëstablish prices to farmers at a level that will give agricultural commodities a purchasing power with respect to articles that farmers buy, equivalent to the purchasing power of agricultural commodities in the base period." For tobacco the base period chosen was from August, 1919, to July, 1929, and for other farm produce from August, 1909, to July, 1924.

In this underlying conception of agricultural prices there was an element as old as the republic. When Federalists and Jeffersonian Republicans were battling over power, John Taylor of Caroline County, Virginia, had contended in an elaborate treatise that high finance, with its tariffs, bounties, and " paper," violated the laws of " natural exchange " and created a constant unbalance against agriculture. After the lapse of more than a hundred years an effort was being made to redress the unbalance, real or imagined, by employing the powerful instrumentalities of the Federal Government. The Federal Marketing Act of the Hoover administration had honored the theory and accomplished no favorable results. Another tack was to be taken now.

The devices adopted by the Agricultural Adjustment Act were simple. The prices of "basic agricultural commodities," such as wheat, cotton, field corn, sugar beets, and pork products, were to be raised by curtailing production and controlling market operations. Production quotas adjusted to effective demand were to be established on the basis of statistical calculations. For the purpose of holding output within the limits of the quotas, each farmer affected was to make his pro rata reduction and in return for his action receive a subsidy from the Government precisely determined by the degree of the curtailment. Nominally there was no compulsion. Practically the inducement was sufficient to bring about almost universal compliance. Such, in substance, were the mechanics of the Act, with many variations in detail and many stipulations collateral in nature. Of necessity the project would cost money; provisions for revenue were therefore incorporated in the statute itself — unhappily for the sponsors of the bill, as they learned three years later when the Supreme Court declared the law invalid. Chief among the sources of finance were taxes on the processing of commodities, such as grinding wheat into flour, taxes on domestic products grown in excess of quotas, and customs duties on certain imported farm commodities. To all appearances, at the time, the statute was "water-tight" and the funds were assured for enforcement.

At last producers on the land were to try out a reform devised to fit their interpretation of things. Although millions of farmers were affected by the law and a great diversity of agricultural and processing interests was drawn within the scope of its terms, the Agricultural Adjustment Administration put the statute into force with extraordinary swiftness and universality. Throughout the country, at farmers' meetings in villages and counties, agents of the Administration explained the complexities of the Act, determined the reduction quota of each producer, drew up the contract, and had it duly signed. Field agents visited the farms listed in the program, surveyed the land taken out of cultivation, checked up on other adjustments, and made sure that changes in crop rotation or land uses conformed to the terms of the law. After all these preliminaries were over, the Agricultural Administration in Washington scrutinized the millions of reports and sent checks on the Treasury to farmers for their compliance with agreements.

Nothing just like it had ever been done in the history of American agriculture, not even in the midst of war. In times past, steel barons had cut production by "dinner table agreements," but the sheer act of swinging millions of farmers into serried lines was little short of magic, at least to the theorists of farm individualism. The insularity of regimentation was also overcome. Through a combination of cotton and tobacco with corn and wheat a union of Southern and Western hearts was effected, such as Calhoun and the statesmen of the planting system had sought in vain to secure nearly a hundred years before. However viewed, the mere accomplishment was a tribute to the skill and power of the Secretary of Agriculture, Henry A. Wallace, George N. Peek, head of the Agricultural Adjustment Administration, and their capable assistants.

Before the Agricultural Adjustment Administration, under the direction of Mr. Peek, could set in full operation the elaborate machinery for organizing the production of farmers, Congress sought to grapple with the problem of the idle industries and unemployed workers. How could employment be provided and wage levels maintained? In the search for an answer, Congress came to grips with two formulas for dealing with the issue. Spokesmen for labor, with Senator Hugo Black of Alabama in the vanguard, proposed to reduce by law the hours of work per week throughout the country, while upholding the wage levels. From one point of view this was a project for dividing the existing amount of employment. The second formula for economic salvation was that devised by the United States Chamber of Commerce. Under its interpretation of events, the long-drawn-out economic distress was mainly due to savage competition which destroyed profits all around; and the exit from the dilemma lay in balancing production with effective demand while establishing "fair competition" or "fair trade practices" under the authority of the Federal Government. Both formulas rested on the assumption or conviction that Congress could, in point of constitutional law, nationalize trade and labor practices under its power to regulate interstate commerce, or, as the liberalizing lawyers put it, "the flow of interstate commerce." More than one statute resting upon that general prerogative had been enacted in times past and sustained by the Supreme Court. Doubts still entertained on the question of its validity were set aside in favor of action.

As a result of a compromise both formulas were employed in drafting the National Industrial Recovery Act — a measure for a limited type of national planning, approved by the Chief Executive on June 16, 1933. Although the two operating theories really implied a restriction of production, the first section of the Act proclaimed the grand purpose to be the acceleration of productive enterprise. It referred to the "widespread unemployment and disorganization of industry." It declared a national emergency to exist. How the automatic, self-adjusting market of capitalist economy could ever be "disorganized" Congress did not attempt to explain in the preamble nor in the body of the law. It accepted disorganization as fact. Indeed, at the moment, it did seem to be a fact.

Having announced the emergency, the first section of the Act set forth the economic objectives of Congress: "to remove obstructions to the free flow of interstate and foreign commerce . . . to provide for the general welfare . . . to induce and maintain united action of labor and management under adequate government sanctions and supervision, to eliminate unfair competitive practices, to promote the fullest possible utilization of the present productive capacity of industries, to avoid undue restriction of production (except as may be temporarily required), to increase the consumption of industrial and agricultural products by increasing purchasing power, to reduce and relieve unemployment, to improve standards of labor, and otherwise to rehabilitate industry and to conserve natural resources." In commenting on the purposes of the Act, Roosevelt referred to its emergency features and to the objective of planning "for a better future, for the longer pull."

A breach had been made in the predominant theory of a successful economy. Undoubtedly a mosaic of many ideas, the opening section of the National Industrial Recovery Act broke with the economic assumptions that had long prevailed in Congress. For many years a few students of technology had been insisting that the going economy of the United States fell far short of the total productive capacity available in the scientific and natural resources of the country. Thorstein Veblen had underlined the thesis. But to most theorists this truth, so obvious to those with eyes to see, had seemed

esoteric as compared with the habitual recitations of schoolmen in economics; while Congress, representing "practical"
persons, had proceeded on a tacit assumption that the anti-
trust laws merely reaffirmed the law of gravitation in business
enterprise. Hence it was a daring intellectual adventure
when Congress recognized that "the present productive
capacity of industries" was not fully utilized. A second
interruption was made in use and wont by the declaration
that an increase in "purchasing power" would lead to an
increase in the consumption of industrial and agricultural
commodities. Had not academicians taught their pupils
that, in the automatic and unconscious operations of things,
the wages of labor were rather naturally adjusted to the
contributions made by labor to the total production of
wealth? Strange phraseology had crept into a statute of
the United States.

The practices of industry were to be codified and controlled. In giving effect to the alleged purposes, the Recovery
Act authorized the formation of associations, or groups, in
each trade and industry. Such organizations were to be
truly representative and open to all individuals or concerns
entitled to membership. Any association properly organized
under the Act had the authority to adopt "a code or codes
of fair competition for the trade or industry or subdivision
thereof." A code duly drawn, after affording the interested
parties ample opportunity to be heard, went to the President
for his scrutiny and when approved had the force of law for
all members of the industry in question. To expedite the
process of industrial organization, the President was empowered to draft and impose a code upon any trade or industry that failed to establish its own constitution. Recognizing the fact that it would take time to devise codes,
Congress also authorized the President to license business
enterprises and enter into arrangements with individuals or
concerns willing to put into immediate effect accepted standards of hours, wages, working conditions, and fair trade
practices. In short, Congress conferred on trades and indus-

tries the right to organize; gave the President authority to bring into line the laggards that failed to exercise the right; and permitted him to recognize officially individuals and concerns which conformed to the new standards of work, wages, and fair competition.

Under the terms of the Act, a code for a trade or industry had to contain certain features. It set the business practices for the entire group and might provide for a uniform system of accounting and reporting. It could even go to the extent of prescribing the use of plants and equipment and indirectly the prices of goods and services. Although price fixing was not expressly authorized, a certain amount of price adjustment flowed inevitably from the agreements as to hours, wages, and competitive actions. So far the code fit the formula proposed by the United States Chamber of Commerce.

But in carrying the bill through Congress a concession was made to organized labor: a special clause of the law (Section 7-a) provided that every code, agreement, and license should contain three conditions respecting industrial workers. Employees were to enjoy the right to organize and bargain collectively, to designate their own representatives, and to be free from interference by employers in the choice of their agents. No employee could be required to join a company union or to refrain from affiliating with an organization of his own choosing. Within the scope of the code each employer had to comply "with the maximum hours of labor, minimum rates of pay, and other conditions of employment, approved or prescribed by the President."

However, in placing legal or political restraints upon the economic war of all against each and each against all, Congress encountered two danger signals: international competition and the antitrust laws. Beyond the horizon was the cheap labor of teeming millions in Europe and Asia. How could American cotton spinners paying a dollar a day or more in wages survive a flood of imports from Japanese mills where working girls were paid twenty-five cents a day or less? For this contingency, a Democratic Congress, without so much as a salute to free trade, made provision, by empowering the President to restrain or forbid the importation of goods and articles which rendered "ineffective" or "seriously" endangered the maintenance of any code or agreement. Thus domestic economy was sheltered against "cut-throat" competition from foreign sources. Next came a consideration of the Sherman and Clayton Acts, prescribing the law of competition at home. With scarcely a shudder among the congregation of faithful trustbusters in the national legislature, a clause was incorporated in the Recovery Act exempting codes, agreements, and licenses duly adopted and approved "from the provisions of the anti-trust laws of the United States." For more than forty years statutory supplements to "the laws of nature" had been on the books. Now they were to be set aside — for the emergency anyway and the immediate life of Title I of the Recovery Act, namely, two years.

At last the path was cleared for an experiment in the kind of national planning proposed by the United States Chamber of Commerce. To supervise and press forward the gigantic process of organizing trade, industry, and labor, the National Recovery Administration was established under the direction of General Hugh Johnson, who combined a limited amount of homely wisdom with the irritating methods of a drill sergeant. Leaders in commerce, industry, and trade unionism rolled into Washington. Amid much confusion and table pounding, codes were drafted, approved, and put into effect. Wrangles within and between trade associations were heard and decisions rendered. To every individual and concern that complied with the terms of the appropriate code an emblem — the Blue Eagle — was awarded. Like a sudden rash, Blue Eagles burst forth in the windows of shops, on the walls of factories, and in the advertisements of merchants.

As demonstrations of good-will and a determination to set business going, monster parades were held in large cities, headed by political and economic dignitaries. Blaring bands and cheering throngs greeted the new day of national cooperation in "breaking the panic's back," putting people to work, and restoring profits to enterprise. At Washington, labor boards, advisory boards, code authorities, and mediation boards were created to scrutinize or administer the millions of details. The whole country was laid out in districts, recovery boards were established in the states, and local bodies were organized — all to promote "the fullest possible utilization of the present productive capacity of industry." Within a year, more than four hundred codes were completed and put into effect, covering about ninety per cent of American business enterprise and approximately twenty-two million wage and salary workers. Considered merely in itself, this was a gigantic manifestation of human effort directed to the achievement of economic ends on a national scale.

§

At the same time, as if convinced that these great measures for lifting agriculture and industry out of the abyss were insufficient to set economy in rapid motion, Congress sought to stimulate the process by authorizing public works of social value. Such enterprises, it assumed, would make heavy demands upon the stagnant construction industries and they in turn would supply the wages to augment the buying power of industrial workers. Thus the wheels would keep turning round and round and round. In this scheme there was no abrupt departure from custom. In fact, since 1929 state and local governments had resorted to public works as a form of activity designed to break the jam of economic quiescence. In the blueprint stage or on the horizon of engineering thought were innumerable projects for such activity under public auspices.

But state and local governments were hampered by constitutional and statutory provisions respecting the floating of loans and the letting of contracts, which either imposed blockades or long delays upon generous and rapid enterprise. Only the Federal Government possessed unlimited borrowing power and could put workers and materials in motion without encountering a tangle of legal barriers. Although it had to watch for any obstacles which the Supreme Court might discover in the federal Constitution, the country was not disposed at this time to enter upon fine-spun debates over the theories of juristic probability. Powerful interests, therefore, including the Hearst press, representatives of heavy industries, and spokesmen of the workers, urged the Roosevelt administration to take action — immediate, bold, and wholesale action — in spite of the burdens already thrown upon the Treasury.

Among the projects in public works long pending in Washington was the development of water power in the Tennessee Valley — a potential for easing the burden of labor and raising social standards, if only under the guise of war necessities, navigation, and flood control. Efforts to turn over the Muscle Shoals plant to private interests had been defeated. Efforts to develop it under public auspices had likewise been blocked by executive veto. But George W. Norris, who had led the tedious campaign for public ownership, development, and operation, was still in the Senate, as resolute as ever in defending his program. In the spring of 1933 his advocacy had been strengthened. Having deserted the Republicans during the campaign of the previous year to support the candidacy of Roosevelt, Senator Norris met a hearty welcome at the White House. Moreover Roosevelt, while governor of New York and as a candidate for the presidency, had indicated that he would seek the development of power resources under public auspices for two purposes: to force a reduction of electrical rates and to make electricity available to millions of Americans yet unserved. When Senator Norris now found Democratic members of Congress setting up hurdles in his path, he could rely upon executive assistance instead of rebuffs. His reliance was reinforced by the fact that the utility interests had, in the main, supported President Hoover for reëlection and vigorously opposed Roosevelt on this very issue. With little difficulty, therefore, the bill for the development of natural resources in the Tennessee Valley was rushed through both houses of Congress and signed by the President on May 18, 1933.

Knowing well that their measure would be challenged by utility interests in the federal courts on constitutional grounds, the draftsmen of the Act made due obeisance to constitutional authority by opening with an appropriate declaration of purposes. Among other things the Act was designed "to improve the navigability and to provide for the flood control of the Tennessee River." For that approach there were precedents in conservative legislation and judicial decisions. Strict constructionist Democrats had denied their weight, but few if any Republicans had ever entertained doubts on that score. Another purpose of the Tennessee Valley Act was "to provide for reforestation." For that, also, there were accepted Republican examples; Republican leaders had engineered through Congress the Appalachian Forest Reserve Act of 1911 which appropriated money for the purchase of lands for forests "with a view to protecting the navigability of streams." A third purpose of the Tennessee Valley Act was "to provide for the national defense" by the creation of a corporation to operate "the government properties" at or near Muscle Shoals. If the Supreme Court of the United States turned its back on precedents touching the navigability of streams, flood control, and reforestation, it was not likely to withhold from Congress the power to prepare for war. On that point even Virtue and Respectability had no reservation.

To accomplish the purposes of the Act the Tennessee Valley Authority was created and endowed with extensive powers. The Authority was composed of three members, all required to "profess a belief in the feasibility and wisdom of this Act." It was authorized to issue securities; to construct dams, reservoirs, power houses, transmission lines, and incidental works on the Tennessee River and its tributaries; to contract with commercial concerns or produce fertilizers and ingredients; to coöperate with agricultural experiment stations and farmers; and to produce, distribute, and sell electric power to private corporations, individuals, states, counties, and municipalities. In arranging for the sale of power to private concerns for redistribution, the Authority was required to make sure that the electrical rates to ultimate consumers were reasonable, just, and fair. Throughout the austere lines of the statute ran the note of a general purpose: that of "fostering an orderly and proper physical, economic, and social development of said areas," reserving to the Government of the United States the right to take full possession of the whole enterprise in the event of war.

Here, within the scope of a single statute, were fused in one project activities for which there were individual precedents scattered from the old Muscle Shoals plant to Boulder Dam and Alaska. If any particular item in the law was novel, it was the Authority's power to build transmission lines and sell current directly to individuals, and the utility interests regarded this as especially dangerous. Step by step they had been compelled to allow public regulation of their rates and services, then public construction of plants, and subsequently public operation. Now they faced public competition in the sale of electric power. It was with difficult maneuvers impending that the Tennessee Valley Authority, consisting of Arthur Morgan, David Lilienthal, and Harcourt Morgan, began work in the summer of 1933.

In some respects the Tennessee Valley development stood alone. It had its own history. Doubtless it would have come in one form or another had there been no depression emergency. It gave expression to a movement of ideas and interests which was broader in scope and really inspired the Roosevelt administration in laying out its general program of public works. Authority for the program was contained in Title II of the National Industrial Recovery Act, which empowered the President to establish a Federal Emergency Administration of Public Works and to supervise the Administrator in executing a comprehensive scheme of public enterprises. For the realization of the blueprints the enormous sum of $3,300,000,000 was appropriated by Congress.

Under the immediate direction of Harold Ickes, Secretary of the Interior and Public Works Administrator, allocations of money were made to certain classes of federal projects and to a number of undertakings planned by state and local governments. Among the allotments were grants for two giant power plants — one, the Grand Coulee on the Columbia River, approximately seventy miles west of Spokane, and the other at Bonneville, Oregon, about fifty miles east of Portland. Although far less comprehensive than the Tennessee Valley development, these engineering exploits included the generation and sale of electric power, the improvement of navigation, flood control, and the provision of water for reclamation. Whether considered as devices for stimulating construction industries and employing labor or as power projects, they raised in the Far West conflicts of interests akin to those evoked at Muscle Shoals.

Departing more radically from national precedents, the Public Works Administration responded to an appeal from a small but active minority that had made "housing the people" an issue. By decree, it created in June, 1933, an Emergency Housing Division and authorized it to promote the clearing of slum areas and the erection of low-cost dwellings. In October, a Housing Corporation was created and given power to proceed on its own motion, buy land in cities, and build houses by direct action. For this purpose it could exercise the right of eminent domain and condemn land if necessary to cut extortionate prices. In addition to carrying out its own projects, the Corporation could enter into relations with municipalities and semi-public housing corporations, allot funds to them on specific conditions, and encourage them to substitute modern dwellings for slum tenements. Thus under government propulsion building industries floundering on the borders of disaster were to be stimulated to production and at least a few blots on American civilization removed.

Over the whole business, especially over direct federal action in condemning land and building houses, hovered the usual "grave constitutional doubts," but blighted cement, brick, and lumber industries and idle masons and carpenters probably gave little heed to the agitations of lawyers when they saw the prospects of profits and employment offered by federal housing activities. Their eagerness was too exigent to permit fine discriminations in jurisprudence.

While Congress was discovering the well-known frightfulness of living conditions in cities, its attention was drawn to another familiar fact, namely, that in large sections of rural and mining regions degradation in housing was, if possible, deeper and blacker. In various respects the problem of rural housing was more baffling than that of slum clearance. A low-paid urban worker could at least spend some money each month for rent. The stranded farmer's or miner's family, unemployed and living in a shack, had little or nothing to spare for a landlord or a government housing authority. Embarking upon rural housing projects was evidently highly experimental, and Congress was mindful of the hazards. Without attempting to be specific, it allocated in the National Industrial Recovery Act the sum of $25,000,000 for the purpose of "aiding the redistribution of the overbalance of population in industrial centers . . . for making loans for and otherwise aiding in the purchase of subsistence homesteads." This authorization, which set a precedent for the later Resettlement Administration created in 1935, was followed by the construction of a "model village" in a decayed mining region of West Virginia and by other experiments of the kind. Whatever could be said for or against them they certainly revealed difficulties and helped to educate the educators and well-wishers.

Far more conventional in economic thought were the major allocations of the Public Works Administration to federal and local projects. These included grants for highways, bridges, office buildings, hospitals, schools, tunnels, soil erosion control, rivers and harbors, the construction of buildings for the Army and Navy, and the improvements of the lighthouse and airways services. States were spurred to activity along these lines by the formation of local committees, the offer of loans on easy terms, and outright gifts amounting to a certain percentage of the cost of each enterprise. Within little more than a year, at least 17,000 projects, scattered from Porto Rico to Alaska, had been approved and had received allotments of funds. The Administrator reported that ninety-nine per cent of the counties in the Union had at least one project, that nearly 700,000 persons were directly employed on public works, and that probably 1,400,000 were engaged in supplying materials for the enterprises under way. There had been an impatient, almost frantic, demand for action. Alfred E. Smith had called for a dictator to cut red tape and set things in motion. Amid confusions, uncertainties, and uproars, the Roosevelt administration displayed energy in directions so numerous as to be astounding to old-fashioned politicians.

§

While striving to relieve farmers, industrialists, and urban workers by stimulating production, the Federal Government came to the aid of debtors in town and country. From all sections came the call: "Credit, credit, credit!" During the Hoover administration, Congress had adopted the policy of saving home owners from "the natural consequences" of their debts. For that purpose it had created the Home Loan Bank System but had limited the Bank to transactions with lending institutions, which were in about as much trouble as the debtors themselves. Dissatisfied with results achieved under this legislation, the Roosevelt administration went directly into the money-lending business and formed contacts with individual debtors. By an act approved June 13, 1933, Congress established the Home Owners Loan Corporation endowed with a capital of $200,000,000 and authorized to issue bonds to the amount of two billion dollars. The Act also provided for the formation of Federal Savings and Loan

Associations, for thrift and home-financing societies, organized on coöperative principles. In accordance with its instructions, the Corporation took over mortgages on homes at lower interest rates and extended the time for payments on principal to a longer term of years.

At the moment, real estate values were so low that many mortgages on real property were selling at prices ranging from eight to twenty cents on the dollar. Bondholders were frightened within an inch of their lives. Even foreclosure, in a multitude of cases, meant slashes in the bondholders' liquid claims. Home owners heavily in debt were overwhelmed by anxiety. Banks and mortgage institutions trembled for their own safety. In the circumstances a chorus of praise welcomed the decision of Congress to hurl the Federal Government into the money-lending business. But when the prospect of private profits began to take the place of certain losses, the praise could be forgotten and condemnation substituted.

Deviating less from precedents were the activities of the Roosevelt administration in relieving farmers oppressed by debts. During the first administration of President Wilson, Congress had instituted a farm loan system, and the business had been extended under Republican auspices as agricultural prices sank in the market. Confronted by a crisis still more acute in 1933, Congress authorized federal land banks, by the Farm Relief Act, to issue bonds in the amount of two billion dollars, purchase farm mortgages, exchange bonds for mortgages, and make new loans at a rate not to exceed four per cent. Under later legislation Production Credit Corporations, Production Credit Associations, a Central Bank for Coöperatives, and regional Banks for Coöperatives were established, the formation of thrift and self-financing organizations among farmers was encouraged, and the credit of the Federal Government was placed at their disposal. By an executive order, the scattered agencies of the Government concerned with farm mortgages, loans, and credits were consolidated under the Federal Farm Credit Administration and the multitudinous activities of agricultural financing were integrated into a coherent and powerful system.

When all the details of legislation and administration were brought into a scheme of theory and practice, it became evident that the major portion of farm financing was passing out of the hands of private banks and institutions into the control of government agencies which maintained direct contact with individual farmers and farmers' associations. Although slow in coming to a focus, this development really marked a departure from historic traditions and methods. From the adoption of the Constitution until 1916, farmers had relied upon banks, mortgage institutions, and local money lenders for credits and loans. As the researches of James O. Wettereau disclosed, the first Bank of the United States, so hated by the agrarians, did little "to befriend the agricultural man." Its successors, whether national or state, had operated on the theory of "charging all the traffic will bear." In a large measure the finances of great insurance companies had been built upon farm mortgages as "premier securities." But the structure of private financing had long been crumbling, especially after the advent of Woodrow Wilson's New Freedom, and the downward swing in agriculture that followed the close of the world war shook it from top to bottom, as thousands of rural banks broke down. By 1933 thousands of farms were not worth the nominal value of the mortages recorded against them and in such circumstances even foreclosure offered little consolation to creditors.

After the private financing of agriculture had ceased to be safe and profitable, interested money lenders — individuals and institutions — were willing, indeed eager, to shift the onus of the dubious business to the Federal Government. It was now difficult, if not impossible, to collect eight, ten, or twelve per cent on a farm loan. Millions of dollars' worth of farm mortgages in the vaults of banks and insurance companies had defaulted on interest and principal and were on the way to extinction. Collection by foreclosure, even with the posse comitatus of the sheriff available to supply force, encountered physical and moral barriers. Sheriffs and governors might invoke the agencies of state power, but they could not compel anyone to buy the property of his neighbor auctioned off under the hammer of the law. Often by agreement farmers arranged that no bid above a trivial sum should be offered for livestock or a farm sold under duress; and, when the debt collector had followed due process to the end, he found himself in possession of a few dollars in "full satisfaction" of a claim for hundreds or thousands of dollars. Since the system of private economy had failed to work according to the canons of autonomism, private and institutional losers joined farmers in the demand for "relief." For the time at least, money lenders, insurance companies, endowments, and universities preferred a three per cent Federal Farm Mortgage bond to a six or eight per cent private mortgage in default and steadily sinking in value. Facing the probabilities of a total loss, High Respectability lodged few protests in 1933 against "putting the Government in the farm credit business."

§

Despite minor dissents and controversies over details, the country as a whole rallied enthusiastically to the support of President Roosevelt during the spring and summer of 1933. Companionship in misery and fear almost turned politics into a love feast. Powerful business leaders coöperated with the administration in a spirit of cheerful compliance contrasting sharply with the hostility which they had displayed toward Bryanism, Progressivism, and the New Freedom. It seemed that the concussions of the crisis had shaken their assurance in themselves and their system. The old program of "letting nature take its course" had lost its glitter. They themselves had always made use of government whenever advantages could be obtained by that method; the Coolidge and Hoover administrations had favored them by special policies and had let them alone in most of their major operations. Yet catastrophe had come upon them, under the most beneficent auspices. In the spring and summer of 1933 the Lords of Creation were distraught and for the moment had no rallying point save the Chief Executive of the nation. In due time they were to turn upon him with unrepentant anger, but in the opening months of his administration they were contrite, thankful for favors, and eager to serve. Although by late autumn an opposition composed of discordant elements began to emerge from the fog of turbulent activities, it had no program. It could harass the outposts of the New Deal but could not take the citadel.

The second session of Congress, which opened in January, 1934, the first under the Twentieth Amendment altering the date of its annual meeting, kept on the same course, despite the rumbles of vexation. Its numerous acts bore the stamp of interventionism, not of a return to "free enterprise." Government control of agriculture was increased by a mandatory Cotton Control Act which fixed the production of that commodity and made provision for enforcement by a heavy tax on output in excess of quotas. Additional relief was granted to debt-burdened farmers by the Frazier-Lemke law imposing a moratorium on foreclosures and easing the terms of settlement for debtors. Federal regulation of utilities was fortified by the creation of a Communications Commission empowered to control telegraph, telephone, and radio concerns, which had been loosely supervised hitherto by the Interstate Commerce Commission. Agrarians of the old style, who still pinned their faith to free silver, forced the President to accept a measure requiring the purchase of silver in amounts necessary to keep that metal equal to one-fourth of the monetary stocks of the Government. It also authorized him to call all silver into the Treasury, and this action he took later in the year. Although conservative Senators called the bill a form of legalized robbery, Congress ordered a transfer of the title to all gold in the Federal Reserve System to the Federal Reserve Board. This measure it supplemented by an act fortifying the earlier provisions for the insurance of bank deposits. Designs for the control of investment and stock selling processes were strengthened by the Securities and Exchange Act. To administer and apply the general principles prescribed by the law, a Commission was established, with an experienced stock speculator at the head.

Two bills passed by Congress widened the area of what was coming to be called "social legislation" — a relatively strange phrase in federal jurisprudence. One, the Railway Pension Act, instituted a pension system for railway employees and made levies on carriers and workers to supply the funds. The second, entitled the National Housing Act, was built more on hopes than substance. In conception, it represented mainly the views of bankers, real estate promoters, and the building interests. In performance, its chief outcome was to place the credit of the Government behind the construction and repair of dwellings. Severely criticized by housing reformers and little used by the supposed beneficiaries, the measure served as a kind of stop-gap rather than as a charter for rehousing activities on a national scale. More permanent in effect, perhaps, than the terms of the Act were the revelations of wretched housing throughout the United States and the awakened sense of public obligation manifest in the discussion of the bill.

In turning from domestic affairs to matters impinging on relations with other countries, Congress vacillated in its economic theory. Agitated by reports from the Senate committee that had investigated the methods employed by bankers in floating foreign loans and had inquired also into the sources of immense losses in that field, Congress again applied interventionism — a kind of punitive remedy. By the Johnson Act of 1934 it forbade, within American jurisdiction, the sale of securities of foreign governments which had defaulted on payments due to the Government of the United States. If, as was said at the time, the law was conceived in resentment rather than cunning, it undoubtedly expressed a determination to control the freedom of enterprise that had formerly reigned in the flotation of foreign loans. A mandatory bar of law stood between bankers and investors in the United States and renewed operations in the money markets of many foreign countries. Good money was not to be thrown after bad in an effort to rescue desperate debtors.

Yet the very Congress that wrote the protective tariff provision into the National Industrial Recovery Act and passed the Johnson law veered in the direction of freer trade by devising the Reciprocal Trade Act of 1934, designed to promote foreign commerce. In this case, as in previous legislation, supreme confidence was placed in the Chief Executive. The Trade Act empowered the President for a term of three years to make trade agreements with foreign governments, and, within limits, to change existing import duties and restrictions. With a view, it was alleged, to keeping "politics" out of the transactions, trade agreements so negotiated were to go into effect without the consent of the Senate. This arrangement was undoubtedly a wholesale transfer of law-making and treaty-making powers to the Executive Department, and yet such "delegation running riot" inspired no effective protest among professional guardians of the Constitution. A frontal assault on the tariff seemed to be out of the question, especially for an administration engaged in raising wages and prices at home. There was more promise for "tariff reform" in sapping and mining — a little, not much. What the ingenuity of the State Department could effect under the terms of the Act lay hidden in the uncertainty of things.

§

The word "never" is to be used sparingly in history. It could be said with due respect for the record, however, that never before had Congress in the course of two years enacted legislation running so widely and deeply into American economy. Perhaps it would be no exaggeration to declare that all the federal legislation from the establishment of the Constitution down to the inauguration of Franklin D. Roosevelt in the spring of 1933 had not flouted so materially the presuppositions of "free enterprise" and the doctrine of laissez faire.

How did this happen, and what was its meaning? Was it, as heated imaginations suggested, a revolution or the beginning of a revolution? Or did it merely bring to a closer focus theories and practices long in process of development, without marking a sharp break in the course of events? Was it an illustration of Edmund Burke's dictum that greater changes may be effected in society by accretion and accumulation over a period of years than by a sudden revolution radically executed? Or was it a tempest in a teapot that would subside when wheat sold again at a dollar a bushel, if it should do so again, and the United States Steel Corporation resumed the payment of dividends? As always, where freedom of opinion is permitted, diversity of opinion raged over such fundamental questions.

On the verdict to be reached, history threw some light. Behind each statute of the New Deal legislation lay a long series of agitations, numerous changes in the thought and economy of American society, and pertinent enactments. Except for certain sections of the National Industrial Recovery Act, not a single measure passed by Congress in 1933 and 1934 was without some more or less relevant precedent; and this Act, in departing from the philosophy of antitrust individualism, reflected conceptions that had been associated with the apparently inexorable concentration of control in industrial economy. Had there been no profound dislocations connected with the panic, the movement of ideas and interests in this economy would have continued, unless history itself came to an end. But the depression had introduced fear, uncertainty, and distress, had cut established connections loose from customary points of contact, had shaken many rigid opinions, and, to use a metaphor, had made social relations more fluid. Where everything seemed afloat, particular interests gained more liberty of action and found more companions in misery ready to coöperate. When industry was prosperous, it could defy or hold the agrarians in check.

REFORMATION AND SALVATION

When both branches of economy were in peril of ruin, industrialists and agrarians were readier to make concessions,
truces, and combinations that rendered possible the flood of
far-reaching legislation.

In this legislation was there anything revolutionary? If
by revolution is meant the overthrow of one class by another,
a sudden and wholesale transfer of property, then all the
New Deal laws combined effected no revolution. Nor were
they intended to do so. The Agricultural Adjustment Act
deprived no farmer, planter, or wheat-raising corporation of
land. The Recovery Act stripped no industrial concern of its
tangibles. The two laws were designed to set agriculture and
industry in motion without changing property holdings or
property relations. The former did little or nothing for
tenants, and nothing at all for mere laborers on the land.
Indeed, by forcing the curtailment of crops, it reduced employment for farm laborers. If the Recovery Act made a
gesture in the direction of collective bargaining, it merely
referred to a principle easily violated by obstinate practice.
In saving distressed banks, the Government saved depositors.
The departure from the gold standard enriched gold-mining
concerns. Concessions to silver swelled the profits of interests
engaged in extracting that metal, thus giving value to property once stagnant or of no value. The credit and money-
lending legislation was framed to protect the holders of railway, bank, and real estate securities against grievous losses,
and to enable debt-burdened farmers and home owners to
avoid the stringent processes of liquidation.

And all this was done by placing the credit of the Government, that is, the collective public, under disaster-ridden
private enterprises, by adding billions to the national debt,
by shifting the major portion of the burden to indirect taxes,
including heavy excises on alcoholic liquors after the repeal
of the Prohibition Amendment in December, 1933, and by
postponing, in an effort to avoid, a day of reckoning. If a
change in things was thus effected, it was the change of tying
private interests more closely into a single network and mak-

ing the fate of each increasingly dependent upon the fate of all. From the process a revolution might develop, but that would be another historical illustration of events outrunning purposes, of mankind building better or worse than it knows.

The business was too complicated, however, for any neat theory of revolutionary dialectic — the overturn of one class by another until the final day of the communist spring into everlasting freedom or the totalitarian jump into the thousand year period of the corporative state. When history was conceived not as handsprings into liberation but as the movement of ideas and interests in time, with occasional broad jumps occurring, then the events of 1933 and 1934 seemed merely to mark the dissolution of once firm assurances and a modification of many theories and practices.

Whatever the near or distant outcome might be, the New Deal legislation did indicate fundamental doubts respecting many ideas, long current, as good always and everywhere in American society. It marked a general surrender of the doctrine that poverty and unemployment come only from the improvidence of the poor and that the persons affected must take the consequences of their futile and evil lives. It repudiated the Darwinian law of the jungle by seeking to eliminate through concerted action — mutual aid — innumerable practices of competition once deemed right and just, including the shifting of capitalists' strains to labor in the form of wage cutting. For more than forty years, statesmen and demagogues alike had sought by antitrust acts to intensify the ruthless struggles of competition, on the assumption that such conflicts in economy were wholesome and that the downward pressure of competition on labor was of no concern to the State or Society.

Besides casting off the formulas of economic Darwinism, New Deal legislation brought forcibly into national thought a recognition of persistent agrarian claims, affecting the conception of a balanced economy. For more than a hundred years philosophic agrarians had insisted that capitalism and its price system, with or without the protective tariff, worked against agriculture, exploited it, drained the land of its bone and sinew, failed to do justice to labor on the soil. For more than a hundred years economic thought had been steadily growing urban in outlook. To quote a European wag, it was the work of asphalt flowers. But the crisis of 1933, the Agricultural Adjustment Act and supplementary measures thrust agrarian economy into the center of national policy.

With the powerful aid of the Government, farmers were at last enabled to imitate industrial practices in time of depression, namely, to curtail production, reduce losses, and turn laborers adrift to shift for themselves. As Secretary Wallace conceded, this was the economy of scarcity with a vengeance, but if the medicine was good for industrialists it might be good for farmers. Although it brought forth wails of disgust from urban editors, publicists, and propagandists, it called popular attention to the fundamental principles of capitalist economy and suggested a general revision. If an economy of abundance, that is, general prosperity, was ever to be established in the United States, both industry and agriculture would have to undergo some kind of transformation, escape from the bondage of the so-called "effective demand," from the periodical restriction of production to meet reduced buying power.

On a final balance sheet struck at the close of 1934 it was only in the matter of banking and currency that New Deal legislation offered the possibility of resolvent implications. The gold standard, with the interchangeability of currencies, was abandoned. For this formula, Respectability had waged a hot campaign in 1896. Then it had deemed the gold standard so nearly a command of God and Nature that few words could be too bitter or vile enough to characterize opponents. In 1933 the everlasting gold foundations slipped out from under the economy of society, leaving it very much as it was before, if no more happy and secure. By other enactments Congress declared that banks, investment houses, and stock exchanges could not be relied upon to keep business enterprise in motion, to protect the public against exploitation, and to fulfill the moral obligations of fiduciary trust. That, too, was a blow to Respectability's sense of private virtue. Had it not been for the opposition of President Roosevelt as a guardian of vested rights, Congress might have gone far beyond these measures. According to the reports of seasoned newspaper men in Washington, a large number, perhaps a majority, of the Senators and Representatives were prepared, in the spring of 1933, to abolish stock exchanges, nationalize banks of issue, and reduce the substance of fixed claims to wealth by a huge inflation of the currency.

Had the restraining hand of the Chief Executive been released, a conjuncture of physical distress and financial maladies might have culminated in that form of revolution known as inflation. The immense structure of fixed debt, public and private, with its heavy claims on the returns of real property and the wages of labor, might have been pulled down close to the earth, if not entirely liquidated. But by maneuvering, by accepting powers without using them, President Roosevelt helped to prevent that convulsion. In so doing, he probably interpreted correctly the popular judgment; for in the congressional elections of 1934 the active voters, contrary to the mid-term tradition, increased the Democratic delegations in the House and Senate, diminished the strength of the Republican opposition, and seemed to approve the course which things had taken under the management of the Chief Executive. The returns of the balloting divulged no evidences of an overwhelming demand for a program more radical or for a retreat upon the way thus far chosen. It was with renewed confidence, then, that Roosevelt announced to Congress on January 4, 1935, a broader scheme of action touching the wiser use of natural resources, social insurance, and security of homes.

By that time, however, the immense strain thrown upon the nerves, sentiments, and acquisitive instincts of individuals had begun to snap the bonds of coöperation imposed by fear, law, and administration. Indeed for that strain the people had been ill-prepared by knowledge, understanding, and acceptance of responsibilities; and their leaders, especially those trained in schools and colleges, had been no better prepared. From decade to decade it had been revealed in the census returns of industry, agriculture, and labor, that the self-sufficing homestead and community were dying and that all the interests, occupations, properties, and callings of the nation were being drawn into a tighter and tighter web of economic interdependence. The commodities and articles produced in each center or region were scattered broadcast throughout the Union in exchange for goods of use and consumption. The complete independence of the farming family that satisfied all its own wants had almost vanished. For isolated individualism, always overemphasized in American thought and teaching, was substituted an interlaced system of exchange and mutuality correctly described as collectivism.

Yet the very word that described the fact excited horror among editors, professors, teachers, school superintendents, public mentors in general, and their disciples, who, in accordance with immemorial practice, repeated by rote the axioms and maxims received from high instructors. The mental imagery of the past was employed to combat the present and the future. So the deep-seated propulsions of private interest found sanction in the phrases of Respectability for a drive to the very end of acquisition.

For a brief season, in the spring of 1933, fear — blanched fear — held these propulsions in leash and counseled unity and coöperation. This counsel was incorporated in an open letter directed to the governors' conference by a committee of representative citizens on March 6 of that year. "We are convinced," said the signers of the manifesto, "that there is throughout the nation a spontaneous spiritual uprising of confidence and hope in our chosen leader. The nature of our national crisis calls for an expression of this confidence in the combined voice of the people to show that they are behind him, alert and vocal and united in heart. Prompt and decisive action of a national scope, and in several directions, is necessary to prevent economic collapse throughout the land.

254 AMERICA IN MIDPASSAGE

The ordinary operations of government that prevail and are suitable in time of prosperity with normal conditions may be too slow to meet adequately this emergency and avoid the danger of this economic avalanche carrying all before it." In this spirit the citizens' committee appealed to the governors and the Congress of the United States to support the President and our institutions, "thus enabling the whole people to declare in unison their confidence and faith in our President." That would, they asserted, "constitute the people's appeal to the patriotism of Congress, which we know they possess, in common with all, to coöperate with the President in taking such action as will guarantee economic stability, restore confidence, and thereby relieve unemployment and widespread distress."

This memorandum and appeal, framed during the great fear, was signed by William Green for the American Federation of Labor; Louis J. Taber, master of the National Grange; Edward O'Neal, president of the American Farm Bureau Federation; His Eminence George Cardinal Mundelein; Dr. Harry Emerson Fosdick; Rabbi Stephen Wise; Alfred E. Smith; Newton D. Baker; Dr. Nicholas Murray Butler; H. G. Harriman, president of the United States Chamber of Commerce; Daniel Willard, president of the Baltimore and Ohio Railway; and Walter Lippmann, publicist. In a few months some of the signers were to turn against President Roosevelt and his prompt and decisive actions "of a national scope," and denounce legislation of Congress apparently enacted to "guarantee economic stability." But in March they all joined in the "spiritual uprising of confidence and hope."

However interpreted, the appeal and the revolt had a bearing upon the nature of the great upheaval. Were the signers only united in support of the President until banks and financial institutions had been saved by the outpouring of public credit? Or did they deem his prompt and decisive actions "of a national scope" to be inappropriate guarantees of "economic stability?" Or were they alarmed by subsequent measures framed to "relieve unemployment and widespread distress?" Whatever the answer, the distinguished signers of the appeal for national solidarity evidently believed in March, 1933, that the crisis was national in scope and that national measures alone could cope with it; and in this belief they had a solid basis of facts evident to open eyes.

Nevertheless the high tension of unity reflected in the appeal steadily relaxed after the banks and financial institutions of the country had been saved, at least for a time, by the actions of the Roosevelt administration. Nowhere dominant was there a program of concerted and defensible unity, inspired by strong resolve and informed by realistic knowledge, to continue, expand, and apply effectively the recognition accorded to the collective character of American economy. Nowhere available was there a scheme of tested thought and moral principle to sustain such a program. Nowhere available was there a body of tried, trained, and loyal public servants to fill all the top positions of administration required to discharge skillfully the functions so suddenly imposed upon the Government of the United States. Nor did the President seem able, during the uproar and haste of the time, to draw together all the duties so suddenly assumed, assure efficiency, and explain to the nation the fullness of the designs taking shape in Washington. In such circumstances bustle and improvization characterized political action. Either because too much was undertaken or the requisite abilities were lacking or the strain was too great for private interests, the devices adopted by the administration began to disintegrate, the acquisitive instinct seized upon its opportunities for satisfaction, individualists called "chiselers" fell upon the spoils, and the "spontaneous spiritual uprising" of March, 1933, dissolved. A large part of the economic, intellectual, and moral leadership that had rallied to the New Deal melted away. The "brain trust," composed of a few intimate advisers, disbanded. Still, President Roosevelt continued to command a majority of voters.

## CHAPTER VI

*Interplay of Court, Congress, and President*

AT the center of the national stage, President Roosevelt enacted his role of leadership and, during the early months of his administration, through the power he symbolized and the force of his personality, he commanded a public affection rarely bestowed upon a national figure in America. Even in time of war a President of the United States had not been accustomed to such enthusiastic coöperation from his party and his political antagonists. In the eyes of the unemployed, the poverty-stricken, the debt-harassed farmers and home owners, he was a Prince in shining armor leading the hosts of justice against the powers of darkness and confusion, a Prince devoted to peace and humanity. Neither on grounds of broad policy nor on the basis of personal antipathies did his critics marshal an imposing opposition. In crucial matters they followed his leadership. Such non-conformity as they mustered was sporadic, not organized. Such independence as Congress displayed ran, in the main, to details rather than principles. Cordial to the press, endowed with an ingratiating voice for fireside dis-

256

courses to the people over the radio, the President, during these months, seemed to hold the entire nation in the spell of his magnetism. Actions deemed mistakes by the captious were treated as the normal errors of a human being who was trying, with courage and resolution, to bring the nation out of economic distress and spiritual defeat. In the circumstances, President Roosevelt overshadowed all other personalities in the Government and all the Lords of Creation in the country.

§

At the other end of Pennsylvania Avenue, during the season of executive preëminence, sat the Supreme Court attending to matters relatively small and receiving slight consideration from the multitudes engrossed in saving their very skins. Nevertheless experts knew that the laws which went through Congress touched economic matters of vital interest and could easily be employed to raise constitutional issues. Astute lawyers were conversant with the conflicts taking shape and early began to speculate on the outcome. Had the Government pressed its cases to a decision at the autumn term of Court in 1933 the atmospheric pressure of calamity might have carried it to victory. But for many reasons, trial was postponed, perhaps above all from lack of time rather than fear of the result. Not many laymen, possibly, supposed that the Supreme Court would venture to pull down the pillars of the great fabric erected, as alleged, for the salvation of the country. Nor did all students of law. In a searching analysis of constitutional and economic complexities, Professor E. S. Corwin indicated the perils that lurked in judicial intervention of the old style, entitling his volume, significantly, The Twilight of the Supreme Court. And for a moment, the Supreme Court was content with an undramatic role. In two cases involving state legislation of the reformist type, the Court, though sharply divided, betrayed "liberal leanings" in 1934. It sustained a Minnesota statute placing a moratorium on mortgage foreclosures and a New York statute

empowering a commission to fix minimum prices for milk —
laws designed to ease the worries of debtors and farmers in
the new mode. Evidently constitutional law was viable in
both meanings of the term.

However encouraging these decisions were to the administration in Washington, the two state laws upheld by the
Court did not cut very deeply into accepted economic predilections, despite the vigorous complaints of the four dissenters — Justices Sutherland, Van Devanter, McReynolds,
and Butler. Nor, save by implication, did the two decisions
lend countenance to the legislation recently enacted by
Congress. To watchers concerned with the future, only one
thing seemed sure : since the judges were divided in opinion,
Chief Justice Hughes and Justice Roberts held the fate of
the Court, if not the New Deal, in their hands, and they
were not devoid of political acumen and experience.

As governor of New York and as the Republican candidate
for President in 1916, the Chief Justice was familiar with the
problems of power, the sweets of victory, and the bitters of
defeat. He did not cherish the illusion that the Constitution
is as unequivocal as the multiplication table. Far from it.
He had once publicly declared that the Constitution is what
the judges say it is and, despite the context which explainers
tried to use in glossing over the confession, the statement,
with or without the context, meant just exactly what it set
forth in intelligible English. The Chief Justice also knew
that the Court could sustain the New Deal legislation by
reference to the liberal doctrines of Alexander Hamilton and
John Marshall or annul it by reference to the narrow doctrines of Thomas Jefferson and John C. Calhoun. Previously,
he had referred, in secular discourse, to the wounds which the
Court had inflicted upon itself in the Dred Scott case, the
Legal Tender cases, and the Income Tax case. In brief, the
Chief Justice was sagacious, appreciative of the hazards implicit in decision either way, and not unmindful of the statesman's role in the unfolding drama.

When in February, 1935, the Supreme Court came to

grips with legal issues presented by the resolution of Congress abrogating the gold clause in private and public securities, it equivocated and was by no means categorical in its reasoning. By a five to four vote it sustained the proposition that the gold clause, in respect of railway bonds, could not be enforced and that the payment of interest and principal in legal-tender currency was sufficient. When the holder of a federal gold certificate demanded coin in accordance with the Government's pledge, the Court replied that he had demonstrated no actual damage at the moment and that the Court of Claims could not entertain his suit. When the holder of a Liberty bond demanded his gold as promised in the instrument, the Court gave him a double-barreled answer: the provision of the law overriding the gold obligation of the bond is unconstitutional, but the "plaintiff has failed to show cause of action for actual damages." If no compliment to the Roosevelt administration, the decisions were no comfort either for those defenders of the gold standard who insisted on a judicial order compelling the Treasury and corporations to discharge their gold obligations in accordance with the terms of the contracts. Part of the resolution of Congress is valid, said the Court in effect, and part of it is invalid; for the moment, if ever, nothing can be done to enforce the unconstitutional part.

For die-hards who wanted from the Court a paralyzing blow at the monetary policy of the New Deal, these decisions were disappointing. At best they offered only rays of hope — feeble rays. In their effect upon practice, as distinguished from jurisprudence, they were mere verbal concessions. Furthermore, the whole business was clouded by confusion in judicial reasonings. Although a majority of the nine judges agreed on the decisions, the majority were not united in agreeing with the opinion of Chief Justice Hughes on the most fundamental issue up for determination, namely, the power of Congress to abrogate the Government's gold pledge. Addressing himself to this question, Justice Stone declined to accept two primary propositions put forward by the Chief

Justice in bolstering up the conclusions which the majority affirmed. That left four judges united on the opinion of the Court in the particular instance. And on the other side there were four dissenters — the historic four, Justices McReynolds, Butler, Sutherland, and Van Devanter. Speaking for them, Justice McReynolds, with pungent sarcasm, charged Chief Justice Hughes with using "mere generalities or multitudes of words to distract the mind," characterized the "repudiation of national obligations" as "abhorrent," declared that the Constitution was now destroyed, and referred to "Nero," the royal prerogatives of old France, and the near "wickedness" of the administration's monetary policy. Although his printed opinion was more restrained than his oral discourse from the bench, it was blunt and furious enough to irk the majority of the judges as well as the celebrants of an alleged victory in the White House.

§

A few months passed, while speculators in jurisprudence scanned the heavens for omens. In May and June, the Supreme Court declared its twilight to be a dawn, by holding major acts of Congress null and void. Its decisions scattered consternation in New Deal circles, made the President angry, and encouraged his opponents to come into the open for a direct assault. According to a legend, it had been the custom for Louis XIV to remain in the background during a war until his generals declared a fortress on the verge of surrender, and then to ride fully caparisoned to the front in time to receive the honors. In the spring of 1935 the Supreme Court so thoroughly shattered the New Deal fortress that even little men felt that they could safely ride into the breach. Any supposition that the Supreme Court felt itself incompetent to govern was now waved aside. To all appearances, the eminent tribunal intended to employ its engines of sovereignty in handling the national crisis. It had failed at this business in 1857, reversed itself in 1871, partly succeeded in 1896; it might be more fortunate in a fourth grand effort.

The first of the three destructive decisions declared invalid the Railroad Retirement Act, which had provided a system of pensions for railway employees — an installment of the social security program already announced. Justice Roberts delivered the opinion of the Court. Before his elevation to the bench, he had lifted the curtain on his basic social philosophy in an address in 1923 to the Trust Division of the American Bankers Association, by declaring: "The business man in America today feels that he is doing business with a minion of government looking over his shoulder with an upraised arm and a threatening scowl. . . . Are we to go into a state of socialism, or are you men, and men like you, prepared to get out, take off your coats, and root for good old-fashioned Anglo-Saxon individualism?" Certainly the Railroad Pension Act ran counter to that well-known brand of "Anglo-Saxon" philosophy, and Justice Roberts found that the Constitution of the United States also ran against it. The Act, he said, was invalid. It denied due process of law, "by taking the property of one and bestowing it upon another." It violated the interstate commerce clause of the Constitution. It had no "reasonable" relation to interstate traffic or to efficiency in operating railways. Flashing through the austere texture of his jurisprudence were gleams of Justice Roberts' faith in individualism. A pension system would destroy rather than promote the loyalty of employees. It was "an attempt for social ends" to insure "a particular class of employees against old age dependency" and, therefore, invaded the rights of property. This credo was underwritten by a wealth of citations and discriminations.

In the position thus taken Justice Roberts was sustained by the four Justices who had thought the Constitution destroyed by the decisions in the gold cases. Against him were ranged four dissenters — Justices Stone, Brandeis, and Cardozo, and Chief Justice Hughes. The burden of delivering the dissenting opinion was assumed by the Chief Justice.

In an argument that equaled in vigor the discourse of Justice
Roberts, he posited axioms similarly cogent but with different
social content, drew diametrically opposed conclusions
respecting the meaning of the Constitution as applied to the
Railroad Pension Act, and sustained his reasoning by citations as thoroughly apposite. Turning abruptly on the
majority, he declared: "The gravest aspect of the decision
is that it does not rest simply upon a condemnation of particular features of the Railroad Retirement Act, but denies
to Congress the power to pass any compulsory pension act for
railroad employees." In making this assertion the Chief Justice did not correctly anticipate history; but in the spring of
1935, the decision of the majority on the Railroad Retirement
Act seemed to sound the doom of every "attempt for social
ends" to insure any class of employees against old-age dependency. The barrier raised was so high that, apparently,
nothing short of a constitutional amendment could hurdle it
and this was out of the question.

The division of opinion that marked the railway pension
case vanished when the Supreme Court came to the Frazier-
Lemke Farm Moratorium Act of 1934. Without hesitation,
eight colleagues agreed with Justice Brandeis in declaring the
statute void. Although the law, loosely drawn, had been no
official part of the administration program, it reflected the
desperate plea of debtors for relief from the letter of the bond.
Unanimous also was the opinion of the Court in the Humphrey case involving the power of the President to remove
federal officers without regard to stipulations imposed by
Congress, in respect of qualifications.

The issue in the Humphrey case was an old one. Since the
establishment of the Constitution the nature of this power
had been debated by lawyers. Practice likewise had varied.
Yet competent authorities had regarded the matter as settled
by the Meyers case in 1926, when Chief Justice Taft upheld
the removal power of the President and went out of his way
to indicate that the prerogative was almost unlimited in its
range. But the Chief Justice had then seen the problem

from the standpoint of the Chief Executive as well as of the Court, and at the moment Calvin Coolidge was safely installed in the White House.

Now in 1935 the political scene presented many new aspects and dissenters of 1926 joined newcomers in declaring that President Roosevelt could not oust a member of the Federal Trade Commission at will. The member in question, a good Republican, had been outspoken, even acrimonious, in denouncing policies espoused by Roosevelt. In taking this course he felt safe, for the law under which he held office prescribed specific conditions for removal. And the Court sustained his view. President Roosevelt, it said, could not retire Humphrey merely because they differed over policies, over a mere interpretation of the officer's duties. Friends of the President contended that he had been "tricked" by the official, that the two had agreed upon a friendly settlement, and that the Commissioner had then dared the President to remove him. Whatever the verdict on that charge, the Supreme Court narrowed an executive prerogative which many legal experts had long held to be a part of the President's constitutional authority. But the public did not get excited about this contest.

Far different was the reception accorded to the Schechter case, May 27, 1935, in which the Court unanimously agreed that the National Industrial Recovery Act was null and void. When this case reached the Court, enthusiasm for the Act was dying and difficulties of enforcement in detail were harassing the administration itself. The Act was assailed by business men who had originally sponsored it, by foes of corporations, and by a number of labor leaders. As things had developed, none of the interested parties affected by the law had been able to reap all the expected advantages. The substitution of coöperation in industry for tooth and claw had proved to be a Herculean undertaking without the mastery of a Hercules. A demand for a return to a free-for-all competition, out of which the statute had sprung as a protest and mode of escape, surged through the country. If not as unanimous as the decision of the Court, the demand was potent. In the climate of opinion so prepared, Chief Justice Hughes, with the support of all his colleagues, brushed the Recovery Act and its symbol, "the Blue Eagle," into the waste basket, with an air of finality almost imperial in its sweep.

In the opinion that supported the decision, the Chief Justice seemed to block every loophole for the regulation of procedures, hours, and wages in industries by federal law. He was not content to declare that the code-making provisions of the Act violated the doctrine of the separation of powers; that they transferred the law-making authority from Congress to the President and trade associations. Had he so limited his range, Congress could have corrected this error by modifying the statute, in accordance with many earlier decisions sustaining the quasi-legislative powers of boards and commissions. As if determined to make a complete disposal of the business, the Chief Justice, with equal force and assurance, destroyed the hours and wages provisions of the Recovery law. The determination of hours and wages in such local industries, he asserted, does not "directly affect" interstate commerce, cannot be brought about by Congress under the commerce clause, is left to the states under the Constitution. In 1931, two years before the Blue Eagle burst upon their vision, some chicken dealers had been charged with violating the federal antitrust laws by running a "racket," and the Court had held that the chicken business did affect interstate commerce. However, in the spring of 1935, the chicken business did not look the same to the judges.

News of the decision in the Schechter case startled the country. For the first time in many months the Supreme Court of the United States crowded the President of the United States off the front page of the daily newspapers. "Wall Street Hails New Deal Defeats!" shrieked a headline announcing gratification from the precincts of the National Shrine. After the report of the decision broke in the afternoon, stocks spurted upward as if the great day so longed for in the Street had come at last. The night closed in. "Regimentation" seemed buried in its darkness. But the next day came word that business men were not unanimous like the Court. New England textile manufacturers were not exulting whole-heartedly in the prospects of a free play for the low-wage mills of the South. On behalf of the American Federation of Labor, William Green issued a warning that wage-slashing under the ruling of the Court would be a signal for a series of strikes. Telegrams poured into the White House asking the President to save all that he could of the Recovery Act under the recent edict from the Palace of Justice. The day following the decision of the Court, stocks which had jumped upward shot downward "in the second heaviest trading of the year." Evidently the news of the business resurrection by judicial fiat had been exaggerated.

§

Four days later, President Roosevelt met the representatives of the press. The wonted smile had gone from his face. Off the record he gave reporters a history of judicial intervention in policies that bristled with insinuations. For the benefit of the public he stated that the Supreme Court had interpreted the Constitution in the light of the "horse-and-buggy days." He expressed a fear that the decision of the Court in the Schechter case had jeopardized the Agricultural Adjustment Act, the Securities and Exchange Act, the Social Security bill, and other social legislation then pending. In measured words he referred to the Dred Scott decision as an important factor among the events that precipitated the civil war. "With some asperity," reporters noted, the President observed that the Court "seemed to recognize mining as an instrument of interstate commerce when it supported injunction suits against miners, although the shoe was on the other foot when the question of miners' wages and hours was raised." At the close of the press conference, the inference was drawn that the President contemplated not a civil war but a constitutional war, "if the Constitution made his federal program for regulating economic conditions impossible." No special shrewdness was required to discover that then and there President Roosevelt had made up his mind to counter, in his manner and time, the destructive blast that had rolled down from the Palace of Justice.

Yet events urged caution. In speaking of the Supreme Court with asperity, in referring to its horse-and-buggy doctrines, he had touched an American holy of holies. Though conservative tradition admitted that Congress could be cursed as a "gang of criminals," or the President as "a law-breaker and a communist," the tradition commanded awe in the presence of the Supreme Court. If President Roosevelt was not well acquainted with its mandate on May 31, 1935, he was made conscious of it in a very few days. Soon after his opinions on judicial opinions became known, the Liberty League, an organization of rich men and women, formed to "save the country," issued a ukase against him personally and his leadership and against all tinkering with the sacred text. Not to be outdone by the Liberty League, Senator Borah, whose forgotten speeches were sprinkled with scathing reflections on the judicial process, delivered an impassioned oration against President Roosevelt's constitutional reasoning, defended what he called the handiwork of "Hamilton, Madison and Jefferson," and demanded the maintenance of the Constitution as interpreted by the Supreme Court. Telegrams of criticism from people who could afford to pay for them flooded the President's desk.

The opposition to his legislative policies now had a higher intellectual and moral coverage than mere economic argument — the coverage of the Constitution. Many critics of the administration who, for various reasons, had shrunk from direct assaults on explicit measures of the New Deal, could now put on shining armor in defense of the Constitution as expounded by the Supreme Court in destroying New Deal statutes. With the campaign of 1936 approaching, an appeal to the voters was in sight. The Democrats had fulminated

against the Supreme Court forty years before and had been
overwhelmed at the polls. It was true that the Republicans
had also assailed the Court in 1860 and had triumphed in the
election; but it took long memories to recall that incident.
Bemused, if not frightened, by the experience, the President
relapsed into silence as the storm over the Constitution continued to rage. Whether Chief Justice Hughes was a tactician
might be debated. That the Chief Executive had been one
could scarcely be denied.

While the President kept his own counsel on the issue of the
Court, Congress went forward with his legislative program.
Before closing its session in August, 1935, it passed a sheaf of
bills extending the scope of the New Deal. It modified and
strengthened the Agricultural Adjustment Act. It enacted
the Social Security law providing for a system of national
old-age pensions and insurance. Despite the positive warning of the Court in the Schechter case, Congress enacted the
Wagner-Connery Labor Relations bill and the Guffey-Snyder
Bituminous Coal bill — both regulating industrial processes,
on the assumption that they "directly" affected interstate
commerce. For the railway pension law declared invalid by
the Court, a new pension law was substituted. Since pensions
could not be assured under its authority over interstate commerce, Congress shifted the base of the new law to the taxing
power. The new statute was doubtful in the light of some
judicial decisions, but a chance was taken, and the railways
finally accepted its principles. In a similar spirit, the Farm
Mortgage Moratorium Act was revived, drastically amended,
and placed on the books in new form. Thus the Democrats
went ahead legislating. If some of them desired to settle
back, enjoy the sweets of office, and lay the responsibility
for quiescence on the Supreme Court and the Constitution,
the majority favored continued experimentation. So more
acts of Congress were to be carried up the marble steps to the
throne room of the Palace on Capitol Hill.

§

When the Supreme Court reassembled in the autumn of 1935, expectancy was on tiptoes in the capital and the country. Weeks passed. From decision day to decision day, crowds eager for news turned away from the Palace of Justice in disappointment. It was rumored that the Justices were engaged in heated controversies and could come to no agreements on crucial pending measures. Not until January 6, 1936, was public curiosity gratified by an official announcement. On that day the Court, by a vote of six to three, declared null and void the Agricultural Adjustment Act, the law for which agrarian leaders had labored so long and so zealously.

The opinion of the Court was delivered by Justice Roberts. He conceded that Congress had the power to tax for the general welfare; in fact the Constitution said so in plain English. But the power to regulate and control agricultural production was a right reserved to the states and Congress could not spend the money raised by taxation to effect such a purpose. Having excluded Congress from interference with agriculture in the states, Justice Roberts painted a frightful picture of what might happen in case Congress were allowed to do any such thing. "It would be possible," he insisted, "to exact money from one branch of an industry and pay it to another branch in every field of activity which lies within the province of the states." In the manner sometimes honored by violation, Justice Roberts disclaimed all thought of passing upon the wisdom or merits of the Act; he merely "squared" the law by the Constitution and found it invalid — perhaps too long or too short or too crooked.

From the interpretation and application of the Constitution put forward by Justice Roberts there was vigorous dissent by Justice Stone, supported by Justices Cardozo and Brandeis. According to a report current in Washington deemed fairly authentic, Chief Justice Hughes originally believed the Agricultural Adjustment Act to be valid and finally went with the majority for the purpose of avoiding another close division, five to four. Such splits, already numerous, were producing doubts in the country respecting the very operating hypothesis of the Court, namely, that it was unaffected by the merits of statutes and was merely expounding the Constitution with unerring accuracy. At all events, as in many other cases in which the Chief Justice found himself aligned against the liberal constructionists, he assigned to a colleague the task of writing the opinion agreeable to Justices Butler, Sutherland, McReynolds, and Van Devanter. Whether this action represented courtesy or an ingenious maneuver, certainly the Chief Justice was not impervious to the cutting and blistering dissent read to the majority and the country by Justice Stone.

Point by point, Justice Stone followed the argument of the majority opinion, analyzing it with Ciceronian pertinacity. Under his conception of intellectual operations, it seemed a flagrant contradiction in terms to say, as Justice Roberts did, that Congress had the power to tax and spend for the general welfare and then defeat that power by applying "limitations that do not find their origin in any express provisions of the Constitution" — limitations "to which other expressly delegated powers are not subject." Justice Roberts had contended philosophically that the Adjustment Act invaded powers belonging to the states. Justice Stone replied by citing practices — a long list of federal expenditures for schools, roads, vocational rehabilitation, unemployment relief, financing agriculture, industry, and commerce, and other activities clearly within the powers of the states. Must these functions also collapse under the principle now advanced by the majority? Justice Roberts had referred to hideous abuses that might arise if the principle of the Agricultural Adjustment Act were sustained, if the exercise of such powers of government were not kept in check. This contention, Justice Stone replied, "hardly rises to the dignity of an argument."

Taking up the time-honored theory repeated by Justice Roberts that the Court merely declares the law and cannot err, Justice Stone replied that judicial power may be abused, that "Congress and the courts both unhappily may falter or be mistaken in the performance of their constitutional duty." Apparently referring to an inarticulate premise in Justice Roberts' argument, Justice Stone said prophetically: "Courts are not the only agency of government that must be assumed to have capacity to govern. . . . Interpretation of our great charter of government which proceeds on any assumption that the responsibility for the preservation of our institutions is the exclusive concern of any one of the three branches of government, or that it alone can save them from destruction, is far more likely, in the long run, 'to obliterate the constituent members' . . . than the frank recognition that language, even of a constitution, may mean what it says: that the power to tax and spend includes the power to relieve a nation-wide economic maladjustment by conditional gifts of money."

Although Justice Stone's opinion was pointed enough to make the victors wince, it was after all just a dissent. They had carried the day. In his argument before the Court against the Adjustment Act, George Wharton Pepper had closed with the exclamation: "I pray Almighty God that not in my time may 'the land of the regimented' be accepted as a worthy substitute for 'the land of the free.'" The prayer, if it had little to do with constitutional law, vibrated with the animus of the opposition. Mr. Pepper was and had long been a close personal friend of Justice Roberts; they had studied together as young men in the University of Pennsylvania, had risen together in the economics and politics of Philadelphia, and had served as colleagues in the councils of the Republican party. Indeed, Mr. Pepper had urged President Hoover to appoint Mr. Roberts to the Supreme Court and had warmly supported his confirmation. In the circumstances cynics had been inconsiderate enough to suggest that a nice sense of judicial propriety would have led Justice Roberts to refrain from writing the opinion of the Court in response to the fervid plea of his bosom friend and former political associate. But the suggestion was hypercritical and implied that a judge must necessarily be influenced by what he knows as a man and feels as a friend. In any case, the power of the Court had been vindicated and the triumph over "regimentation" had been magnificent — in the particular matter and for a time, if not for eternity.

Owing to the sweeping language of the Court in overthrowing the Agricultural Adjustment Act, there was no possibility of getting around the decision by minor modifications of the original text. Yet neither President Roosevelt nor Secretary Wallace made adverse comments for public benefit, with or without "asperity." That they had not accepted defeat, however, became evident on January 8 when the President announced his determination to attain justice for agriculture and gave out an official statement to the effect that his administration would continue the Agricultural Adjustment program or "its equivalent." Within a short time, agrarian lawyers found a loophole in the judicial barrier, and on February 29, 1936, the President signed the Soil Conservation and Domestic Allotment Act, instituting a form of crop control under a more constitutional name. Crop adjustments were called soil-erosion adjustments — to "normal domestic human consumption" as determined by the Secretary of Agriculture. As in other matters of federal and state coöperation, the states were to enforce the law temporarily, subject to the supervision of agents from the Department of Agriculture.

§

With the agrarians theoretically prostrate under the Constitution and, according to political calculations, powerless to force an amendment of the text in their favor, one great enterprise of the New Deal seemed to lie in ruins. Having disposed of the Agricultural Adjustment Act, the Supreme Court then took up the program for the Tennessee Valley and the development of water power resources under the jurisdiction of the Federal Government. Congressional control over navigable streams and falling waters on the national domain was indisputable, if readers of law could believe legal

words. Neither navigable rivers nor public lands were yet
regarded as objects of private property with which individuals might "do as they please." But could the Government
itself utilize these power resources, build hydro-electric plants,
construct transmission lines, and sell current directly to consumers? Or was it compelled by the Constitution either to
let its resources go to waste or turn them over to private
corporations for development? These questions had been
argued directly or by implication before the Supreme Court
in a Tennessee Valley case and after a tedious delay that
tribunal rendered an opinion, on February 17, 1936.

Like the effort of agrarians to influence economy with
special reference to their concerns, the attempt of the Federal
Government to develop its power resources had involved a
perennial conflict of interests. It had been marked by
acrimonious debates on the floor of Congress, by voluminous
investigations of utility companies, their practices, and their
propaganda, and by rhetorical contests in newspapers and
magazines. Billions of dollars had been drawn into consideration, and the prospects of gathering more billions in private
profits had been placed in jeopardy.

During the campaign of 1932 Roosevelt had endorsed
public ownership of public power resources and direct government action in their development. In so doing he had openly
defied a great industry. Taking into account existing utility
interests and the potentials of future expansion, the economy
of power production overtopped in dollars and cents the
assessed valuation of all the farms between Maine and
California. Therefore, if less visible to the eye, the issue
presented by the Tennessee Valley case was scarcely less
significant, in material terms, than the problem raised by the
Agricultural Adjustment Act; and the following enlisted by
the electric power companies, if more concentrated, was
probably as active in politics as the agrarians.

In the strange involution of legalistic processes the case
presented to the Supreme Court in the Tennessee Valley
litigation came not from a private company claiming to be

damaged by federal competition. It was raised by certain holders of stock in a corporation that had made a favorable contract with the Tennessee Valley Authority for the purchase of electric power produced by its plants. Hence the case propounded two questions. Do these plaintiffs have interests adversely affected and enjoy the right to a hearing and adjudication? If they have a standing in the Court, does the Government of the United States have a constitutional right to build the Wilson dam and enter into a contract with the Alabama Power Company for the sale of surplus energy from the plant and for other auxiliary purposes? Three possibilities confronted the Court. It could dismiss the stockholders' plea as offering no true case for consideration, thereby postponing the day of judgment. It could assume jurisdiction and give the narrowest possible range to its decision. Or, after assuming jurisdiction it could, for practical purposes, settle the general question of public power development. Often the Court had traveled outside a particular case and prepared the way for broad rulings against the Government. Logically, if not psychologically, the reverse process was possible. Using the immediate Tennessee challenge, the Court could emancipate the Government for the pursuit of its avowed power policy.

Over the first of the questions the Supreme Court was divided five to four. The Chief Justice, who wrote the opinion, was supported by Justices Butler, Sutherland, Van Devanter, and McReynolds. He took the position that the plea presented a true case and that the Court should hear it. Justices Brandeis, Stone, Cardozo, and Roberts dissented, contending that the plaintiffs had no standing in court and that by according them a standing the Court opened the door to all kinds of collusive actions on constitutional grounds. Having assumed jurisdiction, however, the Court considered the second question and by a vote of eight to one decided that Congress had the power to construct the Wilson dam for war purposes and other constitutional ends and to sell surplus power to the Alabama Power Company. Nevertheless in its opinion, the Court hewed close to the narrow line and gave no hint that the fundamentals of the New Deal power program were valid. Though hailed in the White House and recorded in the press as a victory, the decision in itself was at best a dubious victory. In fact it could be considered as a defeat for the administration in that it flung wide the gates for endless litigation and left ample room for invalidating the essentials of the Tennessee Valley program whenever a broader question was raised for adjudication.

Any pleasure produced in the Executive Mansion by the alleged victory in the Tennessee Valley case must have been cooled by the arguments against the Government in the Guffey-Snyder coal case, which closed on March 11; and completely dispelled by a forthright decision against the validity of the law rendered on May 18, after two months of wrangling in the council chamber of the Supreme Court. Like the Tennessee Valley Act, the Bituminous Coal Act affected powerful interests and was the outcome of a long struggle to adjust them. For years the coal industry had been "sick." The competition of oil and hydro-electric plants had injured its markets. The relentless rivalry of mine owners had transformed their business into a cutthroat fight for survival and price slashing had kept the market in turmoil. Warfare among owners and sellers was accompanied by attempts of labor to prevent wage reductions and unemployment, by efforts to uphold standards of living already low and precarious, by strikes, riots, injunctions, strife with coal and iron police, intrigues, and bloodshed. Again and again the diseased industry had been investigated by public commissions. Again and again the conclusion had been reached that nothing short of collective action in the public interest could save it from wreckage, could lift it even partly out of the quagmire of the depression. Everywhere that the coal empire extended, throughout vast sections of the country, from Pennsylvania to the west, south, or north, in all the coal states, the same scenes of misery and degradation were reported. In despair, owners and miners alike had turned to Congress for help and state officials had contributed their pleas. Had there been no politics in coal, the informed opinion of the nation on the need for collective action might have been almost unanimous.

It was in line with no less than nineteen government hearings and investigations of the coal industry that Congress framed the Guffey-Snyder coal bill, which sought to stabilize the industry, adjust production to effective demand, equalize and steady prices, and substitute amicable arrangements with labor for dragging, costly, and sanguinary strikes. In the place of economic violence there was to be coöperation, with protection for the public interest; mutual aid was to mitigate the war of each against all. Familiar with this economic background the Government marshaled a battery of talents to sustain the validity of the Coal Act before the Supreme Court. On the legal side it engaged John Dickinson, Assistant Attorney General, Professor Edward S. Corwin of Princeton University, and Professor Thomas Reed Powell of Harvard, three of the profoundest students of constitutional history and law that the country could boast. Their capacities were supplemented by the ingenuity and knowledge of experts from the Bureau of Mines, especially Frederick Tryon, whose grasp of technical problems was wide and firm. The brief prepared and the argument presented were accordingly an exceptional combination of jurisprudence, economics, and technology. And a dramatic touch was added to the pleadings by the fact that Mr. Dickinson, assigned to deliver the oral argument, was a descendant of a member of the convention that had framed the Constitution of the United States in 1787.

After disposing of the legal preliminaries, the Government's brief devoted seventy-seven pages to "the legislative background" of the Coal Act, accompanied by a large graphic map showing the far-reaching interstate flow of coal from the mining regions affected to all parts of the country. Could anyone deny that every great coal-producing unit covered by the law depended on interstate commerce and was enmeshed in a national net of coal economy? From economics the brief turned to constitutional law. The Act employed the taxing power of Congress to bring producers into coöperation. Was that permissible? In a long schedule, counsel for the Government listed examples of the use of the taxing power for other than mere revenue purposes, and showed how the Supreme Court had repeatedly sustained such actions. Could Congress exercise one of its undoubted powers for a purpose not expressly set forth in the Constitution? The contention that it could not, answered the counsel, "is a fallacy which was early sought to be introduced into our constitutional thinking by opponents of a protective tariff and was answered conclusively and exhaustively by Mr. Justice Story." That was the truth of the matter; and it was a genial hint to at least four members of the Court who were committed to the proposition that a protective tariff was constitutional — a use of the taxing or regulating power for purposes not explicitly mentioned in the Constitution. Perhaps the counsel thought that a love of logic might overcome a love of something else — and resentments as well.

Supplementing the taxing power granted by the Constitution to Congress was that of regulating interstate commerce. On this point the Government brief heaped up citations showing that in many cases, especially under the antitrust laws, the Court had brought under the rubric of interstate commerce various actions connected with local industries that affected the flow of such commerce or burdened it. When miners had struck and tied up local production, they had been set down as interfering with interstate commerce. In such cases industry had not been insulated against federal action and placed entirely under state authority. Again and again strikes had been held to be within the scope of the Sherman Anti-Trust Act or of federal commerce power, on the ground that they were designed, as the Court had once said, to "control the supply entering and moving in interstate commerce, or the price of it in interstate markets." If Congress could act to enforce competition and restrain strikes, why could it not act to promote coöperation and bring about collective bargaining? Such in sum and substance was the Government's central question.

In addition to providing for coöperation among owners and collective bargaining in labor relations, the Coal Act contemplated the establishment of prices, within limits. Recently Justice Roberts had declared in the name of the Court that a New York statute authorizing the fixing of prices for milk was valid; that it did not violate the due process clause of the Fourteenth Amendment. It seemed, then, to counsel for the Government, that, in authorizing the establishment of prices in the coal industry, Congress did not violate the due process clause of the Fifth Amendment limiting federal power.

In support of this proposition they referred to the milk case and to the considerations advanced by Justice Roberts, "which made price fixing for that industry a reasonable and hence legitimate exercise of governmental power and consistent with due process." In his opinion sustaining the New York law, Justice Roberts had employed economics. "During 1932," he had said, "the prices received by farmers for milk were much below the cost of production. . . . The situation of the families of dairy producers had become desperate and called for state aid similar to that afforded the unemployed, if conditions should not improve. . . . Milk is an essential item of diet. . . . The prevalence of unfair and destructive trade practices in the distribution of milk, leading to a demoralization of prices . . . , unrestricted competition aggravated existing evils . . . , the normal law of supply and demand was insufficient to correct maladjustments detrimental to the community." After quoting these passages from Justice Roberts' earlier opinion, counsel for the Government cited parallel passages from official sources showing an almost identical condition of affairs in the coal industry. Logic might carry the Court over from milk to coal.

On the other side, counsel for the plaintiff rested their case largely on legal grounds and gave little attention to economic

or technological matters. They insisted that the coal industry was an intrastate affair and did not come within the scope
of interstate commerce. For this contention they also had the
support of some judicial decisions and applied to their case
the opinion invalidating the National Industrial Recovery
Act and the Agricultural Adjustment Act. The use of the
taxing power for purposes other than revenue-raising, they
maintained, violated the Constitution. For that also there
were judicial precedents. Passing over economic considerations, the counsel branded the Coal Act as an attempt to
establish a planned economy, to unload the troubles of the
coal industry on the Federal Government, to institute federal
control of economic life, and to promote the interests of coal
operators and miners as against the rest of the nation. As far
as the arguments against the Guffey-Snyder law were concerned, the coal industry might have been in a flourishing
state, owners and miners well content, and the Federal
Government merely trying to interfere with a sound economic
order for the purpose of regimentation. Beyond that the
opposition deemed it unnecessary to go. If the reasoning of
the Court in the opinion which invalidated the Recovery Act
still appealed to the Justices who indulged in it, then the Coal
Act, which established "a little NIRA," was also invalid.

Nevertheless when the decision was reached in the coal
case, the Court was not unanimous. Indeed it was split three
ways. A majority composed of five members declared the
entire Coal Act null and void. Congress had provided in the
law that the price-fixing and labor sections were separable
and that the nullification of one need not abrogate the other.
Speaking for the Court, Justice Sutherland refused, however,
to accept the dictum of Congress. He found the two sections
to be so entangled that when the labor provisions were thrown
out they carried along the price-fixing provisions. In respect
of the labor provisions, he was categorical: "The [labor] controversies and evils which it is the object of the Act to
regulate and minimize are local controversies and evils
affecting local work undertaken to accomplish that local

result." But Chief Justice Hughes was not entirely satisfied. Although he went with the majority in nullifying the labor provisions of the Act, he separated from them in the matter of the price-fixing provisions. For the latter he found constitutional warrant. If nothing could be done for labor under the Constitution, something might be done for mine-owners in the way of regimenting their prices. Wages might be local but prices even at the mine's mouth might be a part of interstate commerce.

To the surprise of logicians who had read the opinions of the Court in the National Industrial Recovery case, Justices Stone, Brandeis, and Cardozo dissented all along the line in the coal case, and insisted on postponing the consideration of the labor provision. In the former case all the Justices had apparently agreed that the regulation of wages was a local matter, under the authority of the states, not Congress, and had implied that the regulation of industry was also local. In this case three Justices united in sustaining the validity of all parts of the Coal Act properly before the Court. Justice Cardozo wrote their opinion. Dealing with the economics of the issue he said: "Overproduction was at a point where free competition had been degraded into anarchy. . . . There were strikes . . . with the accompaniment of violence and bloodshed and misery and bitter feeling." The price-fixing provisions of the law, he held, were clearly within the power of Congress to regulate, promote, and protect the flow of interstate commerce. As a matter of hard fact, "the complainant has admitted that 'substantially all' (over 97½ per cent) of the sales of the Carter Company are made in interstate commerce." Turning to the labor provisions of the Coal Act, Justice Cardozo drew attention to the fact that the issue was not before the Court. "What the code will provide as to wages and hours of labor, or whether it will provide anything, is still in the domain of prophecy. . . . The complainants have been crying before they are really hurt." The validity of the labor clauses he desired to postpone to the day when it could be properly reviewed.

When the three-forked thunderbolt fell in the Court room on May 18, 1936, one thing was clear amid the confusion: the Court had nullified the entire Coal Act. Lawyers for the plaintiff rejoiced. Foes of the New Deal were convinced that one more spike had been driven into the coffin of this spectre and that preparations could be confidently made for the funeral services after the autumn election. Gloom settled over the lawyers for the Government. The Court had informed them that the high and rock-ribbed barrier of the Constitution stood in the way of the "progress" they were promoting. In the White House, silence reigned. Was it the silence of resignation or the calm of meditation and planning?

Everything done that day was not done in the Palace of Justice. Masters in the coal industry and governors of great coal states had favored the Coal Act and were still resolved to overcome the anarchy of the business by coöperative processes. Labor too had a continuing interest. The hard-bitten leader of many a coal battle, John L. Lewis, did not embrace the victor in jurisprudence. "It is a tragic and ominous commentary on our form of government," he said, "when every decision of the Supreme Court seems designed to fatten capital and starve and destroy labor." And, unlike the opinions of the Supreme Court, Mr. Lewis' opinion was not mere law, logic, and rhetoric. A few months later it took the form of a $469,870 contribution from the United Mine Workers of America to the campaign fund for the reëlection of President Roosevelt. However powerful they were, whatever their inclinations, members of the Supreme Court could not duplicate that performance.

§

As things stood on the afternoon of May 18, 1936, the regulation of wages and labor conditions in industry appeared to be a right reserved to the states. Two weeks passed. On June 1, the Supreme Court, by another five to four vote, declared invalid the New York State minimum wage law for women. The opinion of the majority, written by Justice Butler and approved by Justice Roberts, who had upheld the power of New York to fix milk prices, was so comprehensive in its terms as to close the door against all wage regulation, state or federal. On his side Justice Butler produced a load of authority. He cited decisions of the Supreme Court nullifying previous state wage laws and invalidating an act of Congress that provided for minimum wage standards in the District of Columbia. The fact that the New York law immediately under consideration varied in terms from the other statutes which had been set aside made no difference in his reasoning. In the District of Columbia case, Justice Butler said, "it was held that Congress was without power to deal with the subject at all." And the ruling in that case applied also to state laws however conceived or framed to accomplish the same purpose. Such statutes, too, violated the freedom of competition and contract — in relation to employment guaranteed by the Fourteenth Amendment. The prescribing of minimum wages for women "would unreasonably restrain them in competition with men and tend arbitrarily to deprive them of employment and a fair chance to find work." If a strict respect for the immediately relevant precedents cited was controlling on June 1, 1936, then Justice Butler's decision and opinion reposed on strong foundations.

But Chief Justice Hughes, in this instance, did not accept the version of the majority. He found the ends of the New York statute legitimate, the means appropriate, the Act constitutional. This contention he rested mainly on the ground that the law differed in principle and administration from minimum wage laws previously held invalid by the Court. Hence the New York statute could be sustained without repudiating and reversing earlier doctrines of the high tribunal. "The constitutional validity of a minimum wage statute like the New York Act," he stated, "has not hitherto been passed upon by this Court." The Chief Justice pointed out the features which distinguished the District of Columbia law from the Act immediately under consideration: "We have here a question of constitutional law of grave importance, applying to the statutes of several states in a matter of profound public interest. I think that we should deal with that question upon its merits, without feeling that we are bound by a decision which on its facts is not strictly in point." Turning from the technicalities of the law, the Chief Justice referred to "the seriousness of the social problem" presented by the statistics of low wages and to the heavy burden thrown upon the taxpayers by the necessity of supplementing wages by payments from the public relief agencies. The issue might be, theoretically, one of mere law to the majority; to the Chief Justice it presented aspects of humanity.

Justices Stone, Cardozo, and Brandeis agreed with the Chief Justice in upholding the statute before them but declined to make the difference between the New York law and the District of Columbia law the basis of decision. For these dissenters, Justice Stone wrote the separate opinion. "I attach little importance to the fact," he declared, "that the earlier statute was aimed only at a starvation wage and that the present one does not prohibit such a wage unless it is also less than the reasonable value of the service." He did not think that "the vague and general pronouncement of the Fourteenth Amendment" required any such fine-spun distinctions. "There is grim irony in speaking of the freedom of contract of those who, because of their economic necessities, give their services for less than is needful to keep body and soul together." The language of the Amendment did not prevent legislation deemed reasonable and appropriate for dealing with any of those matters of public concern with which it is the business of government to deal. Is the principle of the New York law reasonable? This question Justice Stone answered by citing the legislation of Congress, of seventeen states, and of twenty-one foreign countries, including Great Britain and the four Commonwealths. Such a legislative demonstration "precludes for me any assumption that it is a remedy beyond the bounds of reason."

How, then, could the majority of the Justices take the opposite view? Justice Stone answered: "It is difficult to imagine any grounds, other than our own personal economic predilections. . . . The Fourteenth Amendment has no more embedded in the Constitution our preference for some particular set of economic beliefs than it has adopted, in the name of liberty, the system of theology which we may happen to approve." The New York statute was reasonable. The Fourteenth Amendment, unless twisted to cover a system of economics, did not forbid it.

There were, moreover, among the Court's own rulings, many precedents to sustain the Act. Justice Stone cited them, laying special emphasis on the Nebbia case in which Justice Roberts, a short time before, had upheld a New York law that authorized the fixing of prices for milk. This decision certainly allowed government interference with freedom of contract and the autonomy of the marketplace. In his judicial opinion Justice Roberts had said that, as far as the Fourteenth Amendment was concerned, "a state is free to adopt whatever economic policy may reasonably be deemed to promote public welfare and to enforce that policy by legislation adapted to its purpose." Surely, if a state could interfere with freedom of contract in buying and selling milk, it could interfere with freedom of contract in the matter of buying and selling the labor of human beings confronted with the problem of keeping soul and body together.

So it seemed to Justice Stone. The declaration and decision in the milk case, he thought, should control the Court in the wages case. "They are irreconcilable with the decision and most that was said in the Adkins case" — the District of Columbia case. "They have left the Court free of its restriction as a precedent, and free to declare that the choice of the particular form of regulation by which grave economic maladjustments are to be remedied is for legislatures and not for the courts. . . . We should follow our decision in the Nebbia case and leave the selection and the method of the solution of the problems to which the statute is addressed where it seems to me the Constitution has left them, to the legislative branch of the government." In substance Justice Stone took the reasoning of Justice Roberts in the milk case at face value, applied it to wages as well as to milk prices, and employed it to wipe out the tangle of economic theories incorporated in previous opinions on wage legislation. He did not propose to reverse the old opinions. In effect, he maintained, they had been reversed by the Court itself in the milk case and the door had been opened for such social legislation as reasonable persons might deem appropriate to the solution of basic economic problems. By inviting Justice Roberts to examine his own record, by attributing the strict view of the majority to economic predilections, by taking down the bars set up by the Court against such social legislation, Justice Stone presented the real issues that divided the Court and the country. His strong and muscular English admitted no double interpretation.

§

However considered as a pronouncement in law, the decision of the Supreme Court in the minimum wage case struck into sentiments that had long been expressed in contests over such social legislation and were to count heavily in the approaching presidential campaign. Intransigent feminists had fiercely objected to wage regulation that applied merely to women, considered as a sex so weak as to require special protection. They did not oppose legislative measures applicable to men and women alike. What they especially feared was that minimum wages, if binding on women alone, would become maximum wages for women or would in fact, as some experience had indicated, drive women out of many employments and make their plight worse than before. Although, on different grounds, manufacturing and other private interests rejoiced with the irreconcilable feminists in the decision of the Supreme Court invalidating the New York statute, the action of the Court aroused intense hostility. For years innumerable men and women had striven to secure protective legislation for women in industry against the opposition of employers; now their labors had been declared vain by the Court and a constitutional barrier had been set up against all such forms of protectionism.

As a climax to the Court's work for the season, the minimum wage decision presented vexatious features to those politicians who imagined that they could make the constitutional division correspond to the partisan division in the presidential campaign. Republicans in general had praised the Supreme Court for invalidating New Deal statutes and had sought to identify President Roosevelt's policies with assaults on the Constitution and with attacks on "the independence of the judiciary." In fact it had been the fashion for newspapers to treat judicial decisions in the language of the sporting page and to speak of "victories" and "knock outs." After the defeat administered to the Guffey-Snyder coal law, The New York Times summed up the play to date under the heading, "Court's New Deal Score." In the great controversies of the law, the New Deal had been twice upheld, once ambiguously, and eight times repudiated, all unquestionably and on major issues.

But the minimum wage decision did not run against any policy peculiar to the New Deal. For many years Republicans as well as Democrats, spurred on by women who championed the idea of improving the weak economic position of their sex by law, had sponsored such legislation applicable to women and children. Out of the Court's adverse ruling no mere partisan case could be made. Nor did the foes of the Roosevelt administration venture to celebrate it as a triumph of constitutionalism over haste, waste, folly, and communism. Even to them it did not demonstrate the inerrancy of judicial decisions — the truth of the proposition that the Supreme Court could never be wrong in its constitutional interpretations. If it could be wrong in one case, why not in another or many others?

For politicians who hoped to make a clear-cut constitu-

tional issue in the coming campaign, the decision in the
New York case was rendered all the more troublesome by the
dissent of the Chief Justice. It is true that minimum wage
legislation affected mainly small employers, the owners of
laundries, petty concerns, and sweatshops, that it touched
adversely few powerful business interests; still, in respect of
the constitutional question, that made no difference. Either
the judges knew the Constitution and interpreted the document correctly or they might be wrong all along the line in
glossing the vague language of the fundamental law. Now,
at the end of a season in which the Court had ruled almost
uniformly against the New Deal, the Chief Justice had
dissented from the decision and opinion put forward by the
majority. His language had been restrained. He had not
attributed to them economic predilections. He had not even
suggested that they tortured the Constitution by reading
their own theories into its language. He had stuck close to
the technics of jurisprudence. But the general public was
not given to making subtle distinctions in its judgments. It
understood simply that the Chief Justice had declared the
majority to be wrong in its constitutional law. Even The
New York Times, never associated with revolutionary ideas
save in the historical sense, said editorially that the minimum wage decision "is unfortunate in more than one
respect."

Events had so shaped affairs that at the very end of the
judicial season, at the very opening of the presidential campaign, the issue of "saving the Constitution" was blurred for
party managers by a decision and opinion in a matter that
was of slight concern to the major economic interests. Up to
that time the Supreme Court had declared the New Deal
unconstitutional in eight "first-rate" cases, sustained it
actually in one gold-clause case, and given it limited approval
in the Tennessee Valley case. Yet when analyzed, the
"score" was not as perfect as it looked on its surface. In only
one major case against the New Deal had the opinion of the
Court, as distinguished from the decision, been unanimous,

and that opinion dealt with the farm mortgage moratorium which President Roosevelt had not officially sponsored. In four of the eight vital decisions against the administration, the Court had been divided in opinion either seven to two, six to three, or five to four. Where doctors of equal learning and competence differed about a major operation, the patients and their intimate friends could hardly avoid making choices. While readers of sporting pages and helpers at filling stations probably did not go into such recondite matters as "the reasoning necessary to the decision of the case," they could scarcely scan newspapers without noting that the "score" of the Supreme Court was a subject of animated debate. Added to the disagreement in the minimum wage case, the divisions of the Court in official New Deal cases made it impossible for political engineers to make the Constitution of the United States exactly identical with the constitution of the Republican party. Even men and women of little learning could easily discover discrepancies in any such hypothesis.

Yet in the early summer of 1936 the jubilation of Roosevelt's critics was almost rapturous. Huge and fundamental sections of the New Deal had been declared invalid and, if there was strict logic in the reasoning of the majority of the judges, other sections awaiting trial were also foredoomed to destruction. Powerful economic interests, affected by actions of Congress and the President, had sought and received ultimate protection at the hands of the Supreme Court under the aegis of the Constitution, so difficult to amend. Nothing seemed to remain save the obituary of the New Deal and the vindication of the Supreme Court in the coming referendum.

§

While the Supreme Court, proceeding from its own major premises, was crushing New Deal measures in the logic of law and critics of the New Deal were celebrating, the Roosevelt administration kept on its course, promoting new legislation although somewhat bewildered by the mazes of constitutional law. Whether deemed magnificent or petty, the exercise of negative functions by the Court left the positive responsibilities of governing with the President and Congress. Though the Court had spoken, the problem of unemployment remained immense and pressing. And in his message of January 4, 1935, President Roosevelt had formulated a more systematic policy for dealing with this dilemma. Among the prime objectives of the administration he placed security of livelihood through the better use of natural resources, security against the major hazards of life, and security for homes. He proposed that the Government quit the "business of relief," restore to states and communities the care of the feeble and dependent, and provide work for able-bodied men and women still excluded from opportunities in private enterprise.

For guidance in the provision of public employment, the President laid down seven principles: all work must be useful; compensation must be above the dole level and yet not high enough to discourage individuals from entering private employment; projects should be chosen with a view to employing directly a large amount of labor; projects should compete as little as possible with private business; arrangements should be made for tapering off public work as rapidly as private enterprise could absorb the unemployed; the location of projects should be determined with reference to the amount of local unemployment and the plans devised by the National Resources Board. In response Congress authorized the appropriation of $4,800,000,000 for relief and unemployment. The supervision of expenditures was vested in the Works Progress Administration, headed by Harry Hopkins who assumed the duty of organizing work projects and handling the remaining subsidies for local relief.

Considered in terms of financial responsibility and human needs, the Works Progress Administration was a stupendous enterprise, beset by almost insurmountable obstacles. Millions of unemployed had to be classified according to talents, aptitudes, and previous training. Their geographical distribution had to be determined, connections established with state and local agencies, projects created for the several occupations, supervisors engaged, and the numerous undertakings scrutinized. Nothing of the kind had ever been done anywhere on such a scale and in such a spirit. That private interests, local politicians, and petty parasites would seek to fasten themselves upon the enterprise was to be expected. The possibility that it would be used to build up machines for the Democratic party in every community in the country was recognized. Indeed suggestions that a non-partisan or bi-partisan administration be instituted were made early in the history of the experiment. But, apart from all such knowledge and from the issue of wisdom or unwisdom in attempting public relief, millions of people were, in glaring truth, unemployed and without the means of livelihood. The Works Progress Administration represented a national effort to avoid the mere dole, to overcome the moral degradation and the deterioration of skills associated with prolonged idleness, and to provide occupations offering a semblance of self-respect. In any case the Federal Government had moved far way from the policies pursued in previous panics and depressions.

Associated in spirit with the assumption of immediate responsibility for the unemployed, but looking to the future, was the enactment of the Social Security law of August 14, 1935. By this measure Congress set up the framework for a national system of old-age and unemployment insurance, rounded out a national scheme for old-age pensions, and made various provisions for health, welfare, and security, in coöperation with the states. For the attainment of its objectives, Congress exercised its powers of taxation and appropriation. To create a fund from which to pay old-age insurance to certain classes of persons over sixty-five years of age, it laid a tax on employers and employees, beginning in 1937 and supplying accumulations to be drawn upon in and after 1942. Provision for insurance against unemployment, for the benefit of given classes of employees and for fixed periods of time, was made by the imposition of a federal excise tax on the payrolls of employers. The tax, however, was a mere device to compel the states to act, for it was stipulated that whenever a state created a system of unemployment insurance, within the frame of the national law, employers could make substantial deductions from the federal levy. Likewise conditional were the terms of the Act pertaining to old-age pensions. These terms authorized federal grants to states, up to the amount of fifteen dollars a month per person, for the purpose of encouraging state governments to give pensions to all needy individuals over sixty-five years of age, with the sum of thirty dollars a month regarded as the standard. In other words the Federal Government matched state grants, dollar for dollar, up to the maximum allowance and thus offered a stimulus to old-age pension legislation that had been developing in various parts of the country over a period of many years.

While efforts were made during the consideration of the social security measure to secure the adoption of a health insurance program, Congress was not ready for that experiment, especially in view of the hostility exhibited by members of the medical profession. In formulating the Act, Congress limited the scope of its general welfare clauses to specific grants to the states. It gave them aid in providing for needy and dependent children, promoting the health of mothers and children, especially in areas of economic distress, furnishing medical services for crippled children, maintaining public health services, and caring for homeless and neglected children. Admittedly defective in many respects, economically fantastic in authorizing the accumulation of enormous reserves in the Federal Treasury for insurance purposes, the Act none the less went a long way towards establishing some safeguards against awful hazards of fortune for approximately twenty million people. While criticized on one side for the extent of its range, it was attacked on another side for omitting millions of persons, such as employees in small concerns, domestic servants, and agricultural laborers from the insurance benefits of the law.

Treating railway employees as a special group, Congress established for them an independent pension system. After the Supreme Court invalidated in May, 1935, the pension act of the previous year, Congress sought an escape around the barrier imposed by the judicial decision. The earlier law had provided that revenues for the railway pension fund should be derived from contributions made by employers and employees. It was against this arrangement that the Court directed objections especially emphatic. Blocked in one maneuver, Congress resorted to another. By one act it granted the pension and by a second act it laid a tax on railways to provide funds for the Federal Treasury which had to foot the pension bill. It authorized the payment of graduated pensions to employees who had reached the age of sixty-five and had seen thirty years of service or had been retired for physical or mental disability.

While the social security program was still in process of formulation, President Roosevelt called on Congress on June 19, 1935, in a special message, to revise the federal tax system with a view to accelerating the movement "toward progressive taxation of wealth and of income" and "encouraging a wider distribution of wealth." Implying that wealth is not the pure fruit of individual talent and labor, the President declared: "Wealth in the modern world does not come merely from individual effort; it results from a combination of individual effort and of the manifold uses to which the community puts that effort. . . . The people in the mass have inevitably helped to make large fortunes possible. . . . The ownership of wealth represents a great public interest and a great ability to pay. . . . Our revenue laws have operated in many ways to the unfair advantage of the few, and they have done little to prevent an unjust concentration of wealth and power. . . . Social unrest and a deepening sense of unfairness are dangers to our national life which we must minimize by rigorous methods." On the basis of this social philosophy, the President suggested a heavy tax on large inheritances and on large incomes and a graduated tax on corporation incomes.

The tax message fell with a splash in the very center of national politics. In appropriate quarters it was called just a scheme for "soaking the rich." In other quarters, equally appropriate, it was hailed as a forward step toward "social justice." Senator Huey Long, then driving ahead with his share-our-wealth campaign and attacking the administration on the left flank, addressed an open letter to President Roosevelt commending this proposal. The Senator admitted that the wind had been taken out of his sails but declared consistently that if the plan were enacted into law he would "take 200,000 share-our-wealth clubs" straight into the New Deal camp. With the campaign of 1936 creeping on, this proffer of help was not to be treated as a trifle.

Other Senators, more realistic in outlook, thought the occasion fitting to reconsider the federal tax structure from top to bottom. Senator La Follette, for example, insisted that mere heavy taxes on large incomes and inheritances would not yield a revenue commensurate with the amount of political noise raised by the suggestion, nor go far toward curing the growing disease in the national budget. He countered, therefore, with a proposition to broaden the foundation of the income and inheritance taxes, to carry the tax line far down into the ranks of the middle class, and to produce revenues befitting the continuing expenditures. In the end, however, Senator La Follette was overborne. Congress did no more than raise the rates on large estates and on high incomes, make levies on the "excess profits" of corporations, tax inter-corporate dividends, and increase the rates on personal holding companies. As a revenue producer, the Act worked no wonders. As a stick to beat off the storm troops of Senator Long and Father Coughlin, it was not without force.

Among the agencies contributing to the concentration of wealth, against which the new tax program was directed, were holding companies, especially in the field of electrical utilities. Their growth and extension had been rapid in the days of the golden glow and then some of them had exploded in the days of the dissolutions, scattering casualties among millions of trusting investors. Congressional investigations had laid bare many of the questionable methods employed by financiers in promoting these corporate leviathans and had disseminated the suspicion that their sponsors had often been imprudent and in some cases deceptive, if not clearly dishonest. By the summer of 1935, the Federal Trade Commission had published in many volumes the testimony gathered during its inquiry into electrical utilities — testimony showing practices from which honorable persons might well shrink, practices intended to deceive the public, defeat reasonable legislation, and augment private profits at the consumers' expense. Persons acquainted with the documents bearing on holding companies, in particular President Roosevelt, his advisers, and informed members of Congress, knew very well that the facts in the business invited remedial action. Indeed none save the most prejudiced witnesses could dispute the necessity of federal intervention. Accordingly there was little excuse for surprise when Roosevelt put the regulation of holding companies on his program for legislation in the summer of 1935.

Shortly after the holding-company bill came before the Senate, a provision was inserted in the text calling for the dissolution by 1940 of all "intermediate concerns," that is, for an excision of many superstructures erected upon operating companies. This proposition, loosely called "the death sentence" by critics, raised a terrible din. Telegrams and letters deluged Senators and Representatives; lobbyists descended upon Washington in protest; but under the pressure of the Executive, a majority was mustered in the Senate for the measure carrying the death sentence. More amenable to the demands of critics, the House broke out in revolt and refused to approve the objectionable clause. Only after a spectacular debate, in which emotions dominated ideas, could party managers, led by Senator Burton K. Wheeler and Representative Sam Rayburn, force the House to accept the Senate's verdict against intermediate holding companies.

As finally drawn, the Holding Company Act reached out in two directions. It vested in the Federal Power Commission the authority to regulate the rates, facilities, and security issues of concerns engaged in the interstate transmission of electrical power. It stipulated that, at the end of three years, super-holding companies must be dissolved; that such corporations were thereafter to limit their operations to "single integrated systems and the business directly connected with the supply of power service to consumers." One exception was made to this rule: a holding company might continue to exist if necessary to tie together a group of operating power plants in a single region and to promote efficient operation. Inevitably the "securities" of flimsy structures sank to a low level on the stock exchanges. One section of the great American rainbow appeared to be beyond hope of restoration.

Another application of the common-law doctrine that industries affected with public interest are subject to special regulation was also made in August, 1935. For several years motor trucks and buses had been engaged in interstate traffic, utilizing the magnificent highway systems built at public expense. As usual individuals and companies rushed into the business, cutting rates, furnishing various types of service from good to bad, and often exhibiting an inability to pay damages for the destruction of lives and freight in accidents. In some respects the early history of railway transportation was repeated.

As motor traffic swelled in proportions, railways felt the keen edge of competition and lodged protests with Congress. They were strictly regulated; they could not slash rates or dodge financial responsibility; and they were heavily taxed. A large portion of their revenues went into the public treasuries from which flowed money to pay for the construction of highways. Shippers and passengers who had grievances against truck and bus lines joined their laments to the objections of railway companies. All this agitation had been going on for years, when in August, 1935, Congress took action and placed interstate buses and trucks under the Interstate Commerce Commission. It required such common carriers to secure certificates of convenience from the Commission before engaging in operations. It empowered the Commission to regulate the rates, services, issuance of securities, safety appliances, and hours of labor in this branch of transportation. In short, it put motor transportation on about the same footing as interstate commerce by rail.

A respectable tradition lent sanction to the regulation of industries affected with public interest, and shippers, passengers, and consumers approved that form of government intervention on their behalf. Government aided business with subsidies, provided tariffs for special industries, and protected property; and beneficiaries usually commended each transgression of the "natural order." A tradition that approved government interference with labor relations was also in process of development. In early days state courts had intervened to outlaw labor organizations and to penalize strikes. Gradually, over a long period of years, this practice was modified by legislation and judicial interpretations; and at length the formation of trade unions, collective bargaining, and the conduct of strikes became lawful within certain limitations, statutory and judicial. From a position of negative tolerance, circumscribed if in many respects generous, government moved to a position of positive control in the promotion of bargaining in labor relations. If direct intervention was proper in the interests of business enterprise, why not in the interests of labor? Logic offered no prohibition and the course of events, through its own compulsion, suggested an affirmative answer.

A place within the framework of law, in statutory language at least, had been given to organized labor by the Clayton Anti-Trust Act of 1914, passed during the administration of President Wilson. Lines of protection were still more firmly

drawn by the Norris-La Guardia Anti-injunction Act, signed
by President Hoover in 1932. This measure expressly stipulated that thenceforth workers were free to organize, choose
their own representatives, and negotiate with respect to terms
and conditions of employment. By the same Act the circumstances in which injunctions could be issued in labor
disputes were strictly defined. And all this was done in order
that workers "shall be free from the interference, restraint,
or coercion of employers of labor, or their agents, in the
designation of such representatives or in self-organization,
or in other concerted activities for the purpose of collective
bargaining or other mutual aid or protection." When the
draftsmen of the National Industrial Recovery Act, in the
following year, sought precedents for the clause on collective
bargaining, they had only to turn to the Norris-La Guardia
law and the debates in Congress for illumination and guidance. They made nothing new, out of whole cloth, in a
vacuum.

Nor did the labor movement stop on the day that the
Supreme Court abrogated the labor codes drawn up under the
National Industrial Recovery Act. Nor was the conduct of
collective bargaining relegated to the domain of private
negotiation. The Clayton Act and the Norris-La Guardia
Act still stood on the books. The organization of labor proceeded. And on July 5, 1935, a few weeks after the decision
of the Court in the Recovery case, Congress added to the
older statutes the Wagner-Connery Labor Relations Act.
The new law declared that it was the policy of the United
States to protect the free flow of interstate commerce by
encouraging and safeguarding workers in forming associations, electing representatives, and carrying on the practice
of collective bargaining. The policy so announced was then
expressed in terms of positive provisions. If amazing to
readers not grounded in history, it was in reality a mere
affirmation of accepted legal doctrine. To the declaration
of right, however, Congress added guarantees and an agency
of enforcement. It forbade employers to interfere with or

dominate any labor organization, such as a company union, or to refuse to bargain collectively with their employees. The administration of the Act was intrusted to the National Labor Relations Board, composed of three members, appointed by the President and the Senate. That judicial safeguards might accompany proceedings, "cease and desist" orders of the Board were made subject to judicial review. Thus an administrative agency, under judicial control, set about guaranteeing to laborers specific rights in reference to organization and collective bargaining.

In matters of procedure, the Wagner-Connery Act went beyond the labor section of the Recovery Act which the Supreme Court had invalidated. It left untouched, however, the determination of hours and wages. Responding to pressures that survived the judicial decree, Congress hunted loopholes in the close-knit texture of the judicial reasoning and was not long in finding one. The Federal Government was among industry's greatest consumers, its purchases ranging from thumb tacks to battleships. Presumably it had the power to prescribe the conditions under which its purchases were produced. So, at all events, Congress thought, for in 1936 it passed the Walsh-Healey Government Contracts Act, laying down labor terms for all producers who made contracts with the Federal Government involving amounts in excess of $10,000. Such contractors were required to pay not less than the prevailing rate of wages in the locality — in general the trade union rate; they were to maintain an eight-hour day and a forty-hour week; and they were forbidden to employ boys under sixteen years of age and girls under eighteen. In substance this law attempted to establish, within given areas of industrial enterprise, minimum standards of employment, such as the Supreme Court had destroyed the previous year in overthrowing the Recovery Act. As a supplement, Congress, by the Air Transport Labor Act of 1936, extended similar controls to common carriers by air and to all carriers engaged in transporting air mail.

As the record stood when Congress adjourned on June 21, 1936, after appropriating during its life the breath-taking sum of more than twenty billion dollars, including authorization for the payment of the Veterans' Bonus in cash, the public had notice that the adverse decisions of the Supreme Court had put no tight brake on executive intentions or legislative policies. The President had beaten no retreat. Congress had left unpassed no major measure up for consideration. It was demonstrated that judicial intervention in the course of political affairs had not stopped the movement of secular history — as the people prepared to pass judgment on the New Deal in November.

## CHAPTER VII

### *Appeals to the Ultimate Power*

THE earth turned and amid the eternal dying and becoming, which are phases of human history as well
as the history of all organic life, the season came for
a popular appraisal of the New Deal and a verdict upon its
authors, its critics, and its future. This democratic process
was provided by the Constitution to which all paid homage.
Although Chief Justice Hughes, speaking as a lawyer, had
declared that the Constitution is what the judges say it is,
the dictum was not all-comprehensive. Before his appointment a wit had remarked that the Supreme Court follows the
election returns. There was some truth in that maxim also,
and yet not the whole truth. Still further back in American
history the substance of the business was more correctly
and solemnly described by Thomas Cooley, once a member
of the Michigan Supreme Court and universally regarded as
among the three or four truly great commentators on constitutional law that the country had produced, ranking with
Kent and Story if not above them. Speaking of the written
document, Judge Cooley remarked: "We may think that

we have the Constitution all before us; but for practical
purposes the Constitution is that which the Government in its
several departments and the people in the performance of
their duties as citizens recognize and respect as such; and
nothing else is. . . . It represents at last the acts done under
it." The President, Congress, and the Supreme Court had
discharged their duties as they were given to see them. In
the summer and autumn of 1936, citizens were to perform
their duties, working their thoughts and their verdicts into
the structure of the Constitution as acts "done under it."

§

In the process of appraising and deciding, personalities as
well as laws, judicial opinions, and economic practices entered
into consideration. This too was history. The greater the
contingency, the broader the opportunity for the personality.
That had been true in the days when Napoleon liquidated
the French revolution into tyranny and when George Washington devoted his talents and energies to carrying the American revolution through the trial at arms to a settlement under
the Constitution. It was still true. The New Deal was per-
sonified in President Roosevelt, affectionately called in wide
circles "F. D." and in a circle more intimate "the Chief."
Did the Republican opposition have at command a personality competent to enlist the interests, express the ideas, and
consolidate the sentiments necessary to victory?

Ex-president Hoover was available. Yet, however distinguished his qualities, he had never been popular with the
working politicians of his party and running against him were
the memories of the panic that had come upon the country
during his administration. Martin Van Buren, with all his
personal charm and political skill, had not been able to recover power after the economic disaster of 1837. It was no
more likely that Herbert Hoover, if regarded as an unfortunate victim of history, could accomplish in 1936 a feat which
had not been achieved in the previous campaigns that had

followed panics. In private relations, Hoover excited warm loyalties. On the public hustings he lacked magnetism. Over the radio he gripped few hearts. Even the experience of eight years had effected no profound alteration in his thought or his powers of cognition, making him more competent as a leader for the campaign of 1936.

In sheer prestige, of course, no regular Republican was comparable to Hoover. His former Secretary of the Treasury, Ogden Mills, possessed talents and energy, but he was a symbol of great wealth in a country that still had six or eight million unemployed men and women and with unshakeable tenacity he clung to the attitudes of 1928. To Ogden Mills supple adaptation to changing environment was a form of inconsistency and instability and, in standing still, he invited neglect. The rock of Gibraltar might be majestic, but human history was not so geologic in nature, if equally inexorable. At the opposite end of the party was Senator William E. Borah, generally regarded as progressive in tendencies. During the upheavals of other times, Borah had remained formally in the path of party regularity while displaying all kinds of irregularities in opinions and practices. As a life-long critic of great riches and concentrated industries, he had appealed to the little man in Republican ranks. On such grounds, he was classified as a radical by the Respectability. That epithet he accepted. Declaring that he intended to break the hold of the Old Guard on his party, the Senator allowed himself to be put forward as an aspirant for the nomination and was valiantly supported by Hamilton Fish, a member of the House of Representatives, who had thus far won renown principally as a "red-baiter." But Borah was old and, though still dynamic, was beyond the age line for strenuous campaigning.

Among the younger dignitaries of the Republican party Senator Arthur Vandenberg of Michigan, reëlected despite the Democratic landslide of 1934, was considered a potential candidate. In political philosophy Vandenberg claimed to be a follower of Alexander Hamilton and an exponent of the doctrines laid down in the Federalist. In a volume entitled Alexander Hamilton, The Greatest American, published years before, the Senator had nominated Hamilton for that exalted position, apparently above Washington and Lincoln. The first Secretary of the Treasury was, he declared, "the Master Builder of the indissoluble Union, the Gladiator who saved the Constitution, the Founder of Public Credit, the Architect of Policies and Institutions, the inspired Oracle of sound American Purpose and Necessity, the Intrepid Soldier, the Great Economist, the Most Brilliant Author, the Most Fascinating Orator, and the Foremost Legal Luminary of his time." This work on Hamilton, and other writings, had helped to rank Vandenberg among "the leading statesmen and thinkers of Michigan."

After the crisis of 1933 came upon the land, the Senator recalled the days when Hamilton and Jefferson had been united in Washington's cabinet and, in remembrance of their joint labors, he had proposed a coalition of Democrats and Republicans to overcome the forces of economic dissolution. Failing in that objective, he supported several New Deal measures in the Senate, including the Stock Exchange Act and the Social Security Act, and thus revealed progressive inclinations, while asserting the right to independent criticism. Having left the school of Die Hards without passing the center line, Senator Vandenberg was talked about for the presidency in 1936, but his candidacy was not pressed. Did he smell the smoke of immediate defeat and retreat in preparation for 1940?

While Republican negotiators were casting about for the right personality as leader, a figure rose out of the plains, Governor Alfred M. Landon of Kansas. He too had escaped the Democratic landslide in his own state and thus achieved a reputation for exceptional talents. As governor he had been prudent and industrious though he had displayed no qualities of spectacular genius that in themselves attracted national attention. Had fortune not favored him, Landon might have encountered the fate of many competent governors who had shone locally for a season on the way from obscurity to oblivion. But his neighbors thought he had the calibre of executive leadership and local newspapers spoke of him as the right man to break the entanglements of the New Deal and lead America into another period of "sanity and prosperity."

Reports flew beyond the borders of Kansas and reached William Randolph Hearst, then politically disgruntled. Unable to control President Roosevelt, he had broken away from the New Deal early in its course and flung diatribes against it in his customary style. After casting about on all sides for a man who could oust President Roosevelt from the White House, Hearst came to the conclusion that Governor Landon offered the best chance. He visited the Governor in person and afterward let loose a torrent of publicity in favor of "the strong, silent man of Kansas." Almost over night, the Governor was built up as a national paragon, with the aid of Hearst's call to his millions of readers.

Two possibilities lay before the promoters of Governor Landon's candidacy for the nomination. They could present him in the role of "the Coolidge from Kansas," as he was sometimes called, make a bid for the support of conservative Democrats already forsaking their party standard, and launch a frontal attack on the New Deal all along the line. Such tactics were not entirely fanciful, for Mr. Landon had been a business man — an independent oil producer; he had amassed a small fortune; and as Governor he had been an apostle of economy, while the Federal Government poured millions into Kansas for the relief of farmers and the unemployed. The second possibility was to present him as bidding for the approval of the progressives who had flocked in large numbers to Franklin D. Roosevelt's camp. This project, too, had merits, for in 1912 Landon had forsaken Republicans of the Old Guard and joined the insurrection led by Theodore Roosevelt. Emphasis could easily be laid on that aspect of his political career. In the end, apparently through the good offices of William Allen White, the progressive tack was taken, effectively but not brusquely enough to frighten off those who preferred the image of Calvin Coolidge.

In either role, however, Governor Landon found difficulties arising from the propaganda of his leading publicizer, William Randolph Hearst. Innumerable conservative Republicans regarded Hearst as the unregenerate Catiline of 1901. To progressive Republicans he was no less offensive, for his press daily vilified everything that savored of "liberalism." Unwilling to cast off Hearst, as William Allen White urged, Governor Landon took the incubus along with the supposed aid and carried it through the convention and the campaign.

§

When the Republicans assembled in convention at Cleveland early in June only one bond united all hearts. That was opposition to President Roosevelt and all his works — an opposition ruled by fear and hatred. In seconding the nomination of Governor Landon, Senator Vandenberg voiced this antagonism : "I belong to but one bloc and it has but one slogan — stop Roosevelt." The will to revolt was expressed even more emphatically in an address by Hoover, who condemned Roosevelt and the New Deal in implacable language and called for a holy war on them both, amid the deafening cheers of the delegates. But, if united in condemnation of action already taken, the Republicans were divided in respect of future action. Their experienced party managers were conspicuous either by absence or neglect. Charles D. Hilles, David A. Reed, Ogden Mills, and J. Henry Roraback, who had driven the steam roller over many a convention, commanded no regiments, exercised no sovereign prerogatives at Cleveland. The place of finance capital in Republican counsels was taken by the representatives of business concerns, such as E. T. Weir of the steel industry, Joseph Pew of oil, and William Bell of chemicals. Though thoroughly familiar with the economic interests laboring for the control of platform and candidate, Governor Landon's political sponsors

refused to accept dictation. They pushed aside the old practitioners whose thought had crystallized in Mark Hanna's
age and the new men whose theory of politics rested on something akin to Darwinism. Convinced that at least a tinge of
progressivism, a recognition of some changes in American
economy, must go into the platform and the proceedings,
they would brook no interference with their way.

In the end the convention adopted a platform that certainly looked more like the program of the New Deal than
like the Republican formulation of 1900, and Governor Landon was presented to the country as a kind of "liberal" by a
maneuver as clever as it was ruthless. Only in the preamble
did the platform reflect emotions shared by all the delegates.
Free citizens, it declared, today for the first time are threatened by government itself. The New Deal has "dishonored
American traditions" and "betrayed" party pledges. The
powers of Congress have been "usurped" by the President.
The integrity and authority of the Supreme Court have been
"flaunted." The rights of citizens have been "violated."
The rights of states have been torn away from them. The
country has been "dishonored" by the repudiation of "its
most sacred obligations." Witnesses have been "intimidated." Citizens have been harassed by investigations. The
New Deal has "bred fear and hesitation in commerce and
industry"; it has "coerced and intimidated voters"; it has
been guilty of "tyrannical policies." The morale of many
people has been destroyed. "Appeals to passion and class
prejudice have replaced reason and tolerance." Those were
biting words — betrayal, dishonor, usurpation, coercion, and
tyranny. Even subject to the usual discounts applied to
party platforms, they expressed the inveterate passions of
the economic conflict. A reporter described the temper of the
convention in saying that "this may be the bitterest campaign since the Civil War."

When the platform makers turned from preamble to
planks, from criticism to proposals for action, divisions broke
out in the convention and irreconcilable contradictions in

matters of policies became manifest. The first plank pledged the party to resist all attempts to impair the authority of the Supreme Court and bound it to uphold the independence of the judiciary against the encroachments of the legislative and executive branches of government. Yet in a subsequent paragraph, the platform favored state legislation and inter-state compacts to abolish child labor and sweatshops and to protect women and children in the matter of wages and working conditions. "We believe," the Republicans de-clared, "that this can be done within the Constitution as it now stands."

That declaration was made on June 11. A few days before, the Supreme Court had held the New York minimum wage law invalid. The language of the majority in the Court had been specific and sweeping — all such legislation is unconsti-tutional. Chief Justice Hughes had tried to convince his colleagues of the majority that a particular kind of wage law was valid and his view they had rejected in language that was not open to any double interpretation. Therefore every person who had read the opinion of the Court, including Governor Landon, knew that a promise to enact minimum wage laws for women ran directly counter to the Constitution as interpreted by a majority of the judges; in substance, if not in theory, it flouted the authority of that high tribunal. As they engineered the plank into the platform, did old Progressives of 1912 who had once overtly denounced the judiciary laugh up their sleeves?

Passing from legal abstractions to the exposition of eco-nomic theory and promise, the Republicans framed their planks for business enterprise, conceived mainly as little enterprise. Assuming the correctness and continuity of the existing distribution of property and income, they proposed government protection against foreign competition and free-dom for private enterprise within the tariff walls. They promised a repeal of the Reciprocal Trade Act, as "futile and dangerous," and a return to the principle of "the flexible tariff." Yet tariffs were to be adjusted "with a view to promoting international trade, the stabilization of currencies, and the attainment of a proper balance between agriculture and industry." In the interest of free enterprise at home there was to be a vigorous enforcement of civil and criminal laws against monopolies and trusts and the enactment of additional legislation against restraints on trade. While promising greater freedom to private enterprise, the Republicans also recognized " the existence of a field in which government regulation is desirable and salutary." The location and area of the field were not fully specified. But there was a hint: "We favor federal regulation, within the Constitution, for the marketing of securities to protect investors . . . also of the interstate activities of public utilities."

More space was given in the platform to agriculture. After condemning New Deal practices, the Republicans made their own pledges: retirement of abandoned and non-productive lands; enlargement of the domain dedicated to public uses; benefits to farmers for coöperation in protecting and restoring land resources; aid in the development of new crops; protection against foreign competition; "as an emergency measure," during the agricultural depression, federal benefit payments within the means of the Federal Government, consistent with a balanced budget; ample farm credit at rates "as low as those enjoyed by other industries"; encouragement and development of coöperative marketing; aid to districts suffering from temporary disaster; removal of land banks from politics.

Thus far there was little divergence from the agrarian policies inaugurated before the New Deal and expanded under that dispensation. Respecting only one point was there a sharp departure. The Republicans promised government aid in disposing of surpluses abroad and advocated bargaining for foreign markets selectively as distinguished from granting favors all around on the most favored nation principle. Over this issue George N. Peek, former administrator of the Agricultural Adjustment Act, had parted with the New

Deal. He insisted on driving a hard bargain with each foreign country and was so extreme as to propose dumping abroad at any price. Although this was a game which two could play and retaliations were always possible, the Republicans paid tribute to Mr. Peek and his agrarian philosophy.

To the labor sector of economy, the Republicans repeated their old tender. Under the head of the tariff, they offered to protect American wage levels against "the destructive competition emanating from the subsidies of foreign governments and the imports from low-wage and depreciated-currency countries." If the tariff clause conformed to Republican history, the promise took cognizance of changed operating conditions in what economists were fond of calling "international economy." Turning to domestic aspects of labor, the makers of the platform caught the phrase "collective bargaining" from the political atmosphere. Labor must be protected in its right "to organize and to bargain collectively through representatives of its own choosing without interference from any source."

The phrasing seemed clear on its face, but analyzed in the light of contemporary usage it could have a double meaning. Did the words "without interference from any source" cover "outside agitators" from the American Federation of Labor or the Committee for Industrial Organization? In appropriate minds they did and thus in appearance lent countenance to company unions. Support for that interpretation came from the sentence immediately following, which bound the party to "prevent government job holders from exercising autocratic powers over labor." Members of the Federal Labor Relations Board might be included among such job holders. They had been supervising labor elections in industries and applying the provisions of the Wagner Act which outlawed company interference with the balloting of employees. At all events while Republican campaign orators pointed with pride to the collective bargaining plank in their platform, Democratic orators pointed with scorn to its ambiguity.

That the American system might not function perfectly even under their auspices, the Republicans recognized by pledging themselves to measures of social security. Real security, they said, could only come from increased productive capacity and for this boon they looked to "the energy, self-reliance and character of our people, and to our system of free enterprise." Nevertheless society had an obligation "to promote the security of the people by affording some measure of protection against involuntary unemployment and dependency in old age." This did not mean approval for the Social Security Act of the Roosevelt administration of course; that was subject to severe criticism; it omitted many classes of people from its benefits and was unworkable besides. Hence a more effective system should be created. In the matter of old-age pensions, the Federal Government should provide standards for the states and territories and make proportional contributions in money up to a fixed maximum. In the matter of unemployment insurance, the Republicans proposed to encourage states and territories to adopt "honest and practical measures for meeting the problems." The pages of history were really not to be turned back; the events of recent years were not in fact to be denied; but greater competence and more practical sense were to be concentrated on the public solution of the problems raised by old-age dependency and the casualties of unemployment. The automatic adjustments of free enterprise could no longer be the sole reliance.

Nor were the poor to stew in their own "improvidence," as in the days of normalcy: "The necessities of life must be provided for the needy." This function could not be left to private charities and local governments as President Hoover had thought proper. A compromise was necessary. Responsibility for relief administration should fall upon non-political local agencies familiar with community problems; federal public works should be planned on their merits and separated from relief activities; relief agents should be selected on grounds of merit and fitness; and state and local governments should bear their fair share of the cost. On such conditions the Federal Government should make grants-in-aid to states and territories "while the need exists." In this way, ran the argument, an end could be put to the "confusion, partisanship, waste, and incompetence" which had marked the course of the New Deal in coping with the social distress of the crisis.

With an easy-money faction led by Senator Borah to be conciliated, the Republicans walked more warily than they had done in 1896 when they threw out the silver phalanx bag and baggage. Now their provisions on finance, money, and banking were cautious, even in revealing secret wishes for a return to 1896. No mention was made of restoring immediately the gold standard at the old ratio or any ratio. "A sound currency" was to be preserved "at all hazards"; there must be no further devaluation of the dollar; authority to control the currency must be taken from the President and restored to Congress. The budget must be balanced "not by increasing taxes but by cutting expenditures, drastically and immediately." The taxing power should be employed for "raising revenue and not for punitive or political purposes." That was a seasoned principle which Democrats had repeatedly used in their constitutional arguments against the protective tariff, but in the urgency of this occasion its origins could be overlooked.

As in the case of domestic finance, the Republicans indulged in some circumlocution in their reference to international exchange: "We will coöperate with other countries toward stabilization of currencies as soon as we can do so with due regard for our national interests and as soon as other nations have sufficient stability to justify such action." With nearly all nations committed to managed currencies, tariffs, subsidies, bounties, quotas, or prohibitions, the prospects for stabilization on any terms were not flattering. Nevertheless the Republicans evidently felt that something had to be said on the subject, if only for the benefit of concerns engaged in the export business.

Careful as it was, the reference to international stabilization of currencies was partly offset by declarations on foreign policy, as well as on the protective tariff. Peace was mentioned: "We pledge ourselves to promote and maintain peace by all honorable means not leading to foreign alliances or political commitments. . . . We will coöperate with nations in the limitation of armaments and control of traffic in arms." Still there must be no collective affiliations. "Obedient to the traditional foreign policy of America and to the repeatedly expressed will of the American people, we pledge that America shall not become a member of the League of Nations, nor of the World Court, nor shall America take on any entangling alliances in foreign affairs. . . . We shall use every effort to collect the war debt due us from foreign countries, amounting to $12,000,000,000, one-third of our national debt." In a world rent by wars and rumors of war, the Republicans declared that the best promise of peace lay in international arbitration by free, independent tribunals, acting "in accordance with law, equity, and justice." Meanwhile national defenses must be "adequate."

Before the name of Governor Landon was placed in nomination, a telegram from him stating his position on certain items in the platform, "as a matter of private honor and public good faith," was read to the convention. Ingeniously the telegram cut left, then right. Landon expressed the hope that the promised protection for women and children with respect to wages, hours, and working conditions could be effected under the Constitution as it then stood, but declared that, in case this proved to be erroneous, he would, if nominated and elected, favor a constitutional amendment authorizing such legislation. Since the managers of both parties were chary of advocating any alterations in the text of the Constitution, Governor Landon's announcement was a boon to the progressives.

At the same time comfort was given to the conservative wing. The Governor interpreted the words "sound currency" to mean "a currency expressed in terms of gold and

convertible into gold." That much made a clangor which
awakened memories of 1896. But the iron ring was quickly
softened. The adoption of such a gold-based currency must
not be effected "until and unless it can be done without
penalizing our democratic economy and without injury to
our producers of agricultural products and other raw materials." If the gold faction could applaud one sentence,
the easy-money faction could applaud the second, for it imposed conditions upon the first. In addition Governor Landon broadened the party's plank commending civil service
reform. On these terms he was nominated by acclamation
after other aspirants had dropped out of the race and with
him was associated, as candidate for Vice President, Colonel
Frank Knox, a Chicago newspaper publisher.

§

The Democratic convention followed, late in June, at
Philadelphia — a monster demonstration in popular ebul-
lience. For two good and sufficient reasons it was held in
the Pennsylvania metropolis. By the choice of that city for a
gathering of the faithful, the political designs of the Democrats on the great Republican state might be forwarded. And
direct economic advantages were offered to the party chest.
In anticipation of great crowds and much spending, local
merchants had helped to raise a bounty for Postmaster
General Farley's treasury. Indeed it had been said by the
critical that he auctioned off the convention to the highest
bidder. Like most party rumors there was something in
the allegation; it merely fell short of the whole truth in the
premises. At all events immense crowds poured into the
city by train, airplane, automobile, bus, and boat, and the
convention, which had little work to do, was prolonged for
the purpose of giving the Philadelphia merchants "their
money's worth."

With nominations a matter of routine and no tangled
factional disputes to smooth out, the delegates stamped,

cheered, and whistled in the assembly hall, amid the blare of bands and speeches amplified by the radio, accepting the fact that their function scarcely rose above the dignity of that performed by a rubber stamp. Between sessions, delegates and visitors swarmed over the city, sight-seeing, buying, and seeking amusement in every place of diversion. Composed largely of job holders, political beneficiaries, and expectants, the convention had little to do beyond providing ratification, celebration, and jollification, with the aid of noises afforded by the machine age and of liquid refreshments made freely available by the repeal of the Eighteenth Amendment. Efforts of a small group to stage a demonstration in favor of Alfred E. Smith were whirled away like chaff in a cyclone. Enlivened by war whoops from the braves, the convention approved the platform and nominations in a rush and a roar. Even the time-honored rule requiring two-thirds of the delegates to make nominations was abrogated. In the long history of political meetings there had never been anything just like the Philadelphia assembly of 1936.

One resemblance to previous assemblies was to be noted however. As in nearly all conventions, the main business was determined by managers behind the scenes, in the relative quiet of little rooms — this time under instructions from the White House.

Being the party in power the Democrats, in accord with political usage, devoted a large part of the platform to the approval of their own works. Whereas the Republicans had surrendered to "the privileged few," the Democrats had restored the people to sovereignty, promoted recovery, and humanized the policies of the Federal Government. Putting aside the hoary maxim of anarchy plus the police constable, they had adopted as their overarching hypothesis: "We hold this truth to be self-evident — that government in a modern civilization has certain inescapable obligations to its citizens, among which are: (1) protection of the family and the home; (2) establishment of a democracy of opportunity for all the people; (3) aid to those overtaken by disaster."

Under this conception, pertinent measures of the New Deal were cited. There had been a drive on kidnapers and bandits, the platform asserted. In the same paragraph with the mention of criminals, perhaps not inadvertently, stood the words: "We shall continue to use the powers of government to end the activities of malefactors of great wealth who defraud and exploit the people." Stock speculation had been curbed; "the unholy practices of utility holding companies" had been checked. On the foundations of the Social Security Act "a structure of economic security for all our people" was to be erected. There must be an extension of rural electrification, an expansion of housing activities, a continuation and enlargement of the agricultural program, additional protection for labor, freedom for business from "the ravages of cutthroat competition," enforcement of antitrust laws against "monopoly and concentration of economic power," provision for the unemployed on "useful public projects," a currency stabilized so as to prevent "wide fluctuations in value," and an enlargement of the merit system in civil service.

When they came to foreign policy the draftsmen of the platform tried to encompass a wide range of hopes and fears. The issue presented by the League of Nations was moribund and they failed to mention it. The plan for entering the World Court had been defeated in the Senate and reference to that form of mondial collaboration was omitted. But many voters still clung to the idea of collective action among nations, allegedly in the interest of peace, and they were to be placated. On the other hand recent neutrality legislation had indicated a passionate desire in every section of the country to abstain from quarrels in Europe and Asia. The fruits of the world war and its victory had been too sour for popular digestion and "isolationists" had to be conciliated.

What then would the Democrats do? They would continue the policy of the good neighbor, work for peace, oppose war as an instrument of national policy, advocate the settlement of international disputes by peaceful means, resist aggression, foster foreign commerce, and seek by mutual agreement to lower trade barriers "which have been raised against our exports of agricultural and industrial products." In this bill of promises, one item was elusive. Just what was meant by the phrase "work for peace"? Since America was now at peace with all the world, the words could mean nothing more than generous sentiments — tenders of "good offices" to nations in trouble or on the verge. Or, if twisted, they could signify direct action in the nature of collaboration for war on the world stage. If the latter was intended, the phrase did not declare it in positive terms; nor had elections since 1920 warranted any such interpretation; nor did President Roosevelt's campaign speeches lend sanction to it.

Indeed several positive phrases in the Democratic platform presented a direct antithesis to the idea of working for peace by any collective underwriting of the status quo or the balance of power in Europe or Asia. "In the disputes of others," it declared, "we shall continue to observe a true neutrality." Whether that had been done during Italy's war on Ethiopia was a matter of dispute, but there stood the pledge. Bowing to the storm raised by the Nye investigation of the munitions industry and war financing, the Democrats said, somewhat cryptically, that they would "continue . . . to take the profits out of war." They would "guard against being drawn, by political commitments, international banking, or private trading, into any war which may develop anywhere." Nor was there to be anything quixotic in the lowering of trade barriers. "We shall continue . . . as in the past to give adequate protection to our farmers and manufacturers against unfair competition or the dumping on our shores of commodities and goods produced abroad by cheap labor or subsidized by foreign governments." In accepting the idea that international banking or private trading could draw the country into a foreign war, the Democrats went far beyond the Republican pronouncement on foreign affairs, while avoiding specifications. By offering adequate protection against cheap labor and dumping, they adopted Republican doctrines and repudiated the hypothesis of the "free international market" as representing a reality or as offering prospects worthy of any immediate or practical consideration.

High above all other issues, if in the background, was the Constitution of the United States under which Democrats had been acting and were proposing to act further. Along nearly all their front, the Supreme Court had erected barriers of interpretation against the exercise of federal power. Yet procedure on a national scale seemed to be made imperative by the very interlocking of great economic processes. "The Republican platform proposes to meet many pressing national problems solely by action of the separate states. We know," countered the Democrats, "that drought, dust storms, floods, minimum wages, maximum hours, child labor and working conditions in industry, monopolistic and unfair business practices cannot be adequately handled exclusively by forty-eight separate state legislatures, forty-eight separate state administrations, and forty-eight separate state courts. Transactions and activities which inevitably overflow state boundaries call for both state and federal treatment. We have sought and will continue to seek to meet these problems through legislation within the Constitution."

Nevertheless Democratic legislation designed to solve these problems had been riddled by decisions of the Supreme Court; and if principles announced by that tribunal were applied in the future, many remaining statutes and additional laws of similar character would be rendered invalid under or "within" the Constitution. For this reason some party advisers had insisted that the issue be taken up boldly and that a constitutional amendment be proposed. After some debate, their suggestion was discarded by the makers of the platform, perhaps on grounds of difficulty or timidity or with the thought that other devices might be employed after the election. At all events, the route of contingency was chosen: "If these problems cannot be effectively solved by legislation within the Constitution, we shall seek such clarifying amendment" as will permit the state and federal legislatures, within their respective spheres, to enact laws deemed necessary "adequately to regulate commerce, protect public health and safety, and safeguard economic security. Thus we propose to maintain the letter and the spirit of the Constitution."

The phraseology bore the stamp of "the sacred tradition," save for the word "clarifying." Suggested by a lawyer of singular distinction, a connoisseur of language, the term insinuated that Congress had ample powers already, that the Supreme Court had muddied the Constitution, and that in any event nothing beyond clarification was required. Having given this notification, the New Dealers, unlike Republicans in 1860 and Democrats in 1896, refrained from making any reference in the platform to a possible reconstruction of the Supreme Court.

On its face, until analyzed, the constitutional plank of the platform adopted by the Philadelphia convention seemed legible enough. The Democrats announced in substance that they were going ahead on lines already pursued and if necessary would seek to clarify the fundamental law of the land by an amendment. What implications, however, were contained in the term "necessary"? More than a hundred years before, John Marshall had explored its meaning in the case of McCulloch *vs.* Maryland and given his interpretation: "If reference be had to its use, in the common affairs of the world, or in approved authors, we find that it frequently imports no more than that one thing is convenient, or useful, or essential to another. To employ the means necessary to an end, is generally understood as employing any means calculated to produce the end, and as not being confined to those single means, without which the end would be entirely unattainable. . . . A thing may be necessary, very necessary, absolutely or indispensably necessary." In effect, therefore, the Democrats said that they would seek a clarifying amendment if they found it convenient or useful, provided they could not vault the judicial barriers in other ways.

Doubtless the Democratic management had in mind no purely formalistic conception of the Constitution and the Supreme Court, such as the lawyers of the Liberty League

had set forth as the true and only view. To this conclusion
something like positive warrant was given by the acclaim of
the convention itself. Amid ripples and roars of applause,
President Roosevelt's chosen spokesman, Senator Alben
Barkley, of Kentucky, implied as much in delivering the keynote address — that pronouncement which, according to all
realistic understanding of power politics, reveals the spirit
and animus underlying the overt terms of the platform. After
surveying the policies and achievements of the Roosevelt administration, the Senator came to the barriers: "But we are
told by the smug and cynical apostles of the status quo that
the Supreme Court has nullified some of the acts of this administration. And while anxious farmers ponder their fate,
and laboring men scan the heavens for a rainbow of hope,
and women and children look in vain for the preservation of
their lives and health, a voice from the grave at Palo Alto
[Ex-president Hoover's home] shouts: 'Thank God for the
Supreme Court.' I make no attack on the Supreme Court.
As an institution I respect it, and I would be both unfair
and unjust if I were unwilling to accord to judges on the
bench the right to their views of laws and constitutions
which I claim for myself. But . . ."

Having placed judicial lucubrations on a level with his own
opinions, as mere "views," the Senator proceeded to set forth
his interpretation of the whole business. Some three or four
outstanding acts passed during the Roosevelt administration
had been invalidated, as against twenty-one acts declared
null and void between 1920 and 1930. The three or four acts
in question had been "conceived and consummated in behalf
of labor, or agriculture, and the honest conduct of business,
and designed to constitute this a government of equal rights."
These were the measures "cast aside by the rigors of techni-
cality and the application of antiquated economic predilections in the interpretation of the document." Democrats had
taken a higher ground. "We have thought that under its
broad and generous outlines we might rescue the people from
national disaster. We have sought to treat it as a life-giving

charter, rather than as an object of curiosity on the shelf of a museum." Even so, Democrats would abide by the Court's decisions and seek to shape their program "in accordance with them. But . . ." The nine eminent judges could not agree on what the Constitution means. How then could 531 members of Congress expect to agree? On occasion five of the eminent judges have said that a law violates the Constitution and four judges "equally eminent, learned, and sincere, and equally alive to the compulsions of modern life" have said that it does not violate the Constitution. "Then we are at least relieved of any obligation to underwrite the infallibility of the five whose views prevail."

Bringing the Supreme Court to the bar of popular judgment, Senator Barkley asked: "Is the Court beyond criticism? May it be regarded as too sacred to be disagreed with?" The answers he sought in American history. Jefferson did not think so. Andrew Jackson did not think so. Abraham Lincoln did not think so. With evident relish the Senator quoted the famous passage from Lincoln's first inaugural address: "If the policy of the government on vital questions affecting the whole people is to be irrevocably fixed by the decisions of the Supreme Court the instant they are made in ordinary litigation between parties in personal actions, the people will have ceased to be their own rulers, having to that extent practically resigned their government into the hands of that eminent tribunal." This conception of the Court and the Constitution, Senator Barkley buttressed by a reference to the dissenting opinion of Justice Stone in the Agricultural Adjustment case, with which Justice Brandeis and Cardozo had concurred.

What was the conception of Chief Justice Hughes? This question must have risen in the minds of the Senator's auditors. "The Constitution," said that dignitary, during the interval when he was off the bench, "is what the judges say it is." Theodore Roosevelt did not think that the Supreme Court was above scrutiny and he had used scathing words about its decisions. Governor Landon and Colonel Knox, the very Republican candidates now offered to the people, had supported Theodore Roosevelt in 1912 in a campaign of criticism. The record of practice stood out against the pure theory of the folk lore.

As he proceeded, Senator Barkley grew ironical. "The judges have decided that, under the Constitution, the Federal Government cannot lift men, women, and children out of the degradation of unconscionable hours, wages, or working conditions, because it invades the rights of the states. They have decided that the states cannot do it, because it invades the rights of private property. I presume that this progressive and logical course will soon lead us to the conclusion that private property cannot do it, because it violates the law of gravitation." A new definition of interstate commerce was needed — an interpretation bringing commodities produced in one state and consigned to another state within the scope of that term. Thereupon the Senator placed "over against the hosannahs of Hoover for the tortured interpretation of the Constitution . . . the tortured souls and bodies of men who work and pray, of women whose God-given right is not fulfilled in a sweatshop, and of children whom we have sought to restore to the school room and the playground."

In his address accepting the renomination, President Roosevelt spoke of ultimate power only in broad and general terms. He made no specific reference to the constitutional controversy; but after charging "the economic royalists" with creating a new despotism, he accused them of wrapping it "in the robes of legal sanction. . . . In vain they seek to hide behind the flag and the Constitution." However casual these words may have seemed to the generality, no adept in power politics could miss their import.

§

As soothsayers had foretold, the campaign was both lively and acrimonious. The Presidential candidates themselves as a rule kept their part of the debate on a high level but their vocal supporters were rarely so scrupulous. Allowing Vice President Garner to play a minor role, Roosevelt went on long tours and made extensive use of the radio. His rival, Governor Landon, campaigned like a veteran, traveling west to California and east to Maine, speaking in great cities, talking at country towns, appealing over the air, and mingling with throngs in the fashion consecrated by democratic practice.

As the campaign proceeded, the tension grew tighter. Although Roosevelt discussed many issues in genial speeches, he drew the lines firmly in his Madison Square address on October 31 : "For twelve years this nation was afflicted with hear-nothing, see-nothing, do-nothing government. The nation looked to government but the government looked away. Nine mocking years with the golden calf and three long years of the scourge ! Nine crazy years at the ticker and three long years in the breadlines ! Nine mad years of mirage and three long years of despair ! Powerful influences strive today to restore that kind of government with its doctrine that that government is best which is most indifferent. For nearly four years you have had an Administration which instead of twirling its thumbs has rolled up its sleeves. We will keep our sleeves rolled up. We have had to struggle with the old enemies of peace — business and financial monopoly, speculation, reckless banking, class antagonism, sectionalism, war profiteering. They had begun to consider the Government of the United States as a mere appendage to their own affairs. We know now that government by organized money is just as dangerous as government by organized mob. Never before in all our history have these forces been so united against one candidate as they stand today. They are unanimous in their hate for me — and I welcome their hatred." After enumerating the principal measures and projects of the New Deal, the President exclaimed : "For these things, too, and for a multitude of others like them, we have only just begun to fight."

On behalf of the Republican cause Governor Landon spoke

with equal firmness, if in general with less asperity. He listed and condemned the New Deal measures in rhetoric which recalled the preamble of his party platform. But he did not align himself with mere conservative intransigence. Taking up the issue of civil liberty, in language clearer and more specific than that employed by his powerful competitor, he pleaded with the nation to keep the channels of free discussion open as the best guarantee for the perpetuity of democracy. He denounced restraints upon liberty of opinion, spurned legislation imposing special oaths upon teachers, and decried all forms of suppression and oppression. "The right of free inquiry," he declared, "is one of the essentials of free government. It is the very bed rock of democracy." Turning to the Roosevelt administration, he charged it with employing the machinery of government in propaganda designed to keep itself in power and "to bring into question the faith of the people in their way of life and in their form of government." With more than wonted verve, he quoted Thomas Jefferson's program for the University of Virginia : "This institution will be based on the illimitable freedom of the human mind. For here we are not afraid to follow truth wherever it may lead, nor to tolerate error as long as reason is left free to combat it."

In speaking of other matters Landon broke through the rigid line which Roosevelt insisted on drawing between the parties. His appeal to farmers went beyond the strict tender of his platform in promises of federal aid. Taking up the labor question, he interpreted collective bargaining more nearly in the terms of the Wagner Labor Relations Act, much to the annoyance of his followers on the extreme right. When all discounts were made, the net impression left by the Governor at the end of the campaign was that of a man who would make strenuous efforts to straighten out federal finances and to rationalize, rather than demolish, the program of social and economic legislation ascribed, not with complete justice, to the New Deal. No carping critic could find in his campaign addresses an argument for a complete return to the state of things prevailing in the days of the golden glow.

Blaring above the fray of the campaign debate was the shrill note of the constitutional issue. Elaborating their platform, Republican speakers charged their opponents, in terse, even violent, terms, with seeking to destroy the independence of the judiciary and to undermine the Constitution. In the main the answer of the Democrats was a plea of avoidance: Nothing irregular had been done. The administration had obeyed the decisions of the Supreme Court. If necessary, it would seek an amendment clarifying the sacred text. While there had been criticisms of the jurisprudence turned out by the majority of the judges, that was in accord with the Jackson-Lincoln tradition and had the sanction of time-honored practice. But such counter arguments were vague, so that the upshot of the election was inevitably controversial. Just what campaign pledge had been made by the Democrats on the court issue? Certainly it was not as transparent as President Wilson's implied promise to keep the country out of war in 1916 nor as definite as the Republican promise of prosperity in 1928; yet it gave the general impression that the method of constitutional amendment would be employed by the Democrats — only if necessary.

Against the Democratic position, Republican orators arrayed specific arguments. Though the Supreme Court had overruled most of the New Deal program, the Democrats proposed to go ahead without resorting to a constitutional amendment, unless necessary. That was no unconditional surrender to the judiciary and its Constitution. President Roosevelt had urged Congress to pass one measure in spite of doubts respecting its validity. That, the Honorable Bertrand Snell, Republican leader in the House of Representatives, had hinted, came near to the borders of an impeachable offense. The President's acrid remarks about the "horse and buggy" view of the Constitution were reiterated by critics and treated as evidence of his underlying animus against the high tribunal in the Palace of Justice. The whole legislative program of the Roosevelt Administration, they insisted, ran against the letter and spirit of the Constitution, amounted to a usurpation of powers, trampled down the rights of states.

Given this record, the refrain continued, there could be no doubt that a Democratic victory meant some kind of assault upon "the independence of the judiciary" and a re-interpretation of the Constitution under some kind of partisan pressure. In other words, Republicans informed the country, with shrewd insinuation, that the Democrats, if victorious, would in some way curb the Supreme Court; while Democrats carefully avoided exhibiting an official bill of specifications respecting their concrete intentions. Given this loose joining of issues, the Democrats could say, in 1937, with a show of justification, that the country, instructed by their opponents on the consequences of a Democratic triumph, had approved President Roosevelt's call for a re-reading of the Constitution and had given him a mandate to arrange the details of the undertaking.

In accordance with the psychology of the popular process in politics, the personalities of the candidates had a positive bearing on the outcome, entirely apart from the proposals discussed in the campaign. Whatever the intrinsic merits or defects of Governor Landon's arguments, his crusade had not advanced far when it became notorious that he was not swinging the currents of popular enthusiasm over to his side. Indeed at the outset a division over strategy added elements of weakness. One group of his advisers, including William Randolph Hearst, continued to emphasize the role of "the silent Coolidge from Kansas," and wished to rely upon the power of taciturnity in creating the image of the strong man for an hour of crisis. By keeping pen and ink away from William Henry Harrison in 1840 and confining his utterances to sententious generalities, the Whigs had been able to stem the tide of Jacksonian Democracy and gain possession of the presidency. The successful experiment might be repeated. On the other hand another group of Landon's advisers demanded an open campaign all along the line. With that idea of strategy, stern silence was incompatible. The candidate had to join the war of words, to present himself as he really was, without paint or adornment, and to pit his knowledge, thought, voice, and personality against the powers of his opponent. As the conflict proceeded, the giant once shrouded in the mystery of silence slipped out of the shades and as a sheer candidate submitted himself to popular judgment.

In the beginning of Landon's campaign, seasoned observers, Republican in sympathies, doubted whether any person enlisted under their banner could carry the country in the election. As the days of the contest ticked off, doubts increased. If the people wished to hear trenchant arguments, they were certainly not gratified by the manner of Governor Landon's speaking; his very syllables were heavy. If the people expected flaming oratory, they were disappointed; that was not in keeping with the Coolidge tradition nor was it, apparently, within the power of the Governor. The sight of the man did not magnetize audiences. His voice, in platform address and over the radio, was hesitant, even in its strength, and displayed no insinuating graces. It also lacked the resonance required for the packed amphitheater or marketplace. His reasoned counsels of prudence were burdened by awkwardness; his most effective pleas were blunted by the style of his delivery. Though long associated with plain people and following their ways naturally and without effort, the Governor did not capture "the folks" as he drove through or mingled with crowds.

Had he possessed the art rather than the substance of the popular appeal, he might have done better. Or did the people not want one of themselves in the White House now? In any case, for some reason, the solid, lymphatic man did not make headway. Perhaps no one could have done that under Republican auspices, not even another plumed knight in shining armor, if such could have been discovered and entrusted with the old banner frayed by the blasts of the depression days. Had fortune favored Alfred Landon, as it blessed Warren Harding in 1920, and had victory come to him on the wings of Mercury, he might have disclosed great qualities in the office of President; but that opportunity was in neither the omens nor the necessities of the time.

On his part, President Roosevelt conducted his campaign with improved adroitness and heightened energy. Four years before, caution had been his guardian; the promise of success lay not so much in saying the right thing as in avoiding the wrong thing. Now the scent of victory suggested belligerency. Experience had brightened his wits and enlarged his knowledge. His role as the heir of Andrew Jackson seemed to grow in his imagination and give a driving quality to his decisions. While his speeches did not resound with Webster's sonorous roll, or shimmer with the polished hardness of Woodrow Wilson's rhetoric, his prose, although sometimes dull and repetitious, often glowed with poetic warmth and was enlivened by the flight of speeding words. And through all his addresses ran the strong note of democratic humanism — the note struck in Thomas Paine's Rights of Man, kept alive in the Middle Period by the reformers, and renewed after the darkness of the civil war.

Endowed with a positive genius for the opalescent phrase, clever in forming rounded sentences, agile in springing the trap of logic, proficient in insinuation, the President sped through the whole gamut of campaign strategy, now as if in the thick of the fray, now as if judging it from afar. No son of the soil or the forge himself, he nevertheless in his travels seemed the very apotheosis of popular sentiment, as monster throngs crowded about his car or train, evincing spontaneous enthusiasm. If in writing his speeches the President had, as admitted, the aid of powerful literary advisers, nearly every passage was finally composed in his tempo, fitted his armature of thought, and expressed his gift for the artistic touch. Personality and destiny seemed fused in a single force.

§

Before the campaign had entered the final phase, "name calling" had become a favorite substitute for inquiry and reasoning. By that time an array of horrid names had been created to stigmatize opponents, and they were rotated with heat and profusion. To the Democrats, Roosevelt had given a cue in the epithet "economic royalists" and they clutched at the signal, adding accusations equally invidious and more flamboyant. In the Republican appeal to national intelligence, the repertory of damnation was also varied : communists, alien ideas, enemies of the American system, foul breath of Moscow, riot of confiscation, ought to be deported to Russia, agents of the Red international, fomenters of class war, foes of the Republic founded by Washington and consecrated by Lincoln, revolutionary attacks on American democracy, undermining the Constitution, assaults on the independence of the judiciary, preachers of hate, sowers of domestic discord, demagogues. Over and over again the phrases rolled, over and over with thrumming and plangent reiteration. If Federalists, peering over the battlements of Heaven, heard their spiritual heirs brazenly defending "democracy," which only "Jacobins and atheists" had favored in 1800, they must have thought that the world had gone mad.

So continuous and heavy was the verbal barrage against him that President Roosevelt deemed it necessary to make a well-placed speech devoted to disclaiming communism and asserting his Americanism. Yet, judging by the new outburst of criticism which followed this profession of loyalty to his country, the disclaimer was without effect on the press and Republican orators. If indeed the characterizations of the President by Republican leaders and rhetoricians were really to be taken at face value, the voters chose a Communist for the office of Chief Executive and declared in favor of a full communist program in the November election.

As a matter of fact the Socialists and Communists themselves made a poor showing in both the campaign and the election. The former, with Norman Thomas again at their head, put forward an orthodox platform, dismissed the New Deal as a capitalistic illusion, and offered a few planks of immediate demands directed to farmers and industrial workers.

By a strange turn of events, the Socialists seemed, in their orthodoxy, to be on the left of the Communists and received some support from the disciples of Trotsky at the very end of the Red wing.

Presumably instructed from Moscow as to the correct party line, the Communists were very circumspect. They refrained from making a totalitarian statement of Marxism. They declared that American economy should be made "the common property of the whole people, operated fully for the benefit of all who work." If true to party tradition, this statement fell far short of proclaiming "the revolution and the dictatorship of the proletariat." With ears turned to agrarian discontent, the Communists advocated the regulation of farm prices in a manner to guarantee cost of production — a proposal in harmony with the demands of the Farm Holiday Association. In foreign affairs, they advocated reliance upon collective security, support for the League of Nations, economic sanctions against Japan, Germany, and Italy, and a prohibition on loans and sales of supplies to nations that violate the Kellogg Pact. Even William Lemke, bidding for the farmer-labor vote as the candidate of the Union party, though milder in general philosophy, was as radical as the Communists in some of his immediate demands and in his denunciations of the "concentrated wealth" that had "impoverished the masses." At the end the combined vote of the Socialists and Communists was only about one-third of their total in 1932 and less than half the number of ballots cast under the sign of the Union ticket.

§

To the power of the actors in the campaign was added the force of the stage machinery secured by lavish outlays of money. Although the Republicans had huge campaign funds at their command, there were heavy battalions on the other side. According to the careful calculations of Dr. Louise Overacker, published in The American Political Science Review for June 1937, the Democratic outlay between January 1 and December 31, 1936, was $5,194,741, about $3,700,000 below the expenditure of the Republican National Committee during the same period. Under the astute management of Postmaster General Farley, men and women were invited to dine together for the cause at the rate of $50 or $100 a plate, and Democrats holding office or in expectancy of favors-to-come accepted invitations with alacrity. An elaborate campaign book was sold at high prices, even to heads of corporations that could not lawfully subscribe to party funds. Contractors, merchants, and industrialists advertised generously in its pages, bringing more gifts of dubious legality.

To the contributions of the "economic royalists" who happened to be in the Democratic fold and the receipts from dinners and campaign books were joined "free-will offerings" from the huge army of political job holders and relief beneficiaries. Where reluctance laid a drag, discretion suggested a spur. In possession of the federal administration, as well as state, municipal, and local machines, the Democrats had official sources of funds that were wide and rich. In other times, party workers in the lower ranges had been paid mainly from contributions collected in the upper ranges. Now millions of urban and rural voters were sustained wholly or in part by money from the Federal Treasury; millions of farmers were showered with payments for not producing crops. Even allowing the whole contention that party politics did not enter into the administration of relief and agricultural adjustment at the top, the fact remained that such beneficence had been called into being under the auspices of President Roosevelt; and the beneficiaries were not likely to forget it. Not often, if ever, in the history of popular campaigns had so much money been enlisted on the side of a party whose members owned the minor share of the national wealth.

Within the category of large campaign gifts, as Dr. Overacker's analysis of the returns shows, was visible a significant shift of economic incidence. "In 1928," she says, "both major parties depended largely upon bankers and manufacturers for their contributions, although the Republicans received a larger proportion of their funds from manufacturers than did their rivals. In 1932, although the proportion of the Democratic fund coming from manufacturers dropped appreciably, Roosevelt's promises of a New Deal had no apparent effect upon the support of the bankers, who contributed as heavily as in 1928." Four years later the scene altered. "The revolt of the bankers and brokers from the Democratic party is startling. Only 3.3 per cent of the contributions of $1000 or more came from this group, compared to 14.7 per cent in the case of the Republicans."

Among the contributors to the Republican fund were representatives of "such important New York banking and investment houses as J. P. Morgan and Co., . . . Bankers Trust, Guaranty Trust, National City Bank, Chase National Bank, . . . Kuhn, Loeb, and Company, . . . and Dillon, Read, and Co." — all of which had been recently subjected to congressional investigations. Among the manufacturers, the heaviest forces, especially steel and chemicals, were thrown on the Republican side. Oil and tobacco were more equally divided. "Chain stores and mail order houses gave the bulk of this part of the Republican fund, while none of these supported the Democrats." The economic support of great publishers went with their editorials to the Republican candidates, William Randolph Hearst leading with $50,000. On the other hand motion-picture producers, theater owners, and the professionals, such as lawyers, physicians, and authors, displayed Democratic leanings. Perhaps even more portentous in terms of power was "the emergence of labor as a factor in the financing of the Democratic party and other organizations which supported Roosevelt." From this source came "the impressive total of $770,218."

After completing a microscopic examination of all recorded contributions to national party funds, Dr. Overacker made deductions evidenced by the facts: "From this analysis of the 1936 campaign funds it seems clear that the program of the Roosevelt Administration has served to sharpen the division on economic lines. The drastic reduction in contributions made by banks to the Democratic party, the increased support which the Republicans received from manufacturers, labor's support of Roosevelt, and the very large contributions which certain wealthy families gave the Republican party all point in this direction. The Republicans became more definitely than in the past few campaigns the party of 'big business.' Their campaign was the most extravagant, and probably the most wasteful, in campaign history. Captains of finance and industry poured their dollars into the fund without stint. Mr. J. Howard Pew, himself a generous contributor, probably spoke for many of them when he said: 'Considering the importance of this campaign, I have felt it a duty and a privilege to make these contributions, and I expect to make further contributions, if necessary to the cause. The American form of government, the fundamentals of our democratic society, the economic system under which our country has become the greatest in the world, are in jeopardy.' The 'haves' rose generously to the defense of a system under which their fortunes had been made."

Yet income and property were split, if unevenly. "The Democrats, abandoned by the financiers, and with less support than usual from representatives of the larger manufacturing interests, drew heavily from the legal profession and from the liquor and tobacco interests. They also had material support from two groups whose traditional allegiance seldom falters — office holders and the South, irrespective of economic interest. Without the support of these two groups, they would have been in a sad plight indeed. Lastly, they wooed the 'little fellow' diligently and to good purpose, and won substantial support from a new quarter — organized labor. The Democratic party emerged from the campaign less definitely the party of the 'have nots' than the Republicans are the party of the 'haves,' but the 'have nots' played an important role in financing its campaign." Looking to the future, Dr. Overacker asked what would happen in case of a revolt on the part of office holders and Southern conservatives. Without funds from these sources the Democrats would be compelled to depend more heavily upon contributions from labor. Was that a handwriting on the wall or merely the flicker of a passing shadow?

§

Reflecting in some measure, perhaps, the drift of campaign contributions, great newspapers operated ostentatiously on the Republican side. A conservative estimate, based upon careful surveys by the editors of The New Republic, indicated that at least seventy per cent of the metropolitan circulation, probably more, was thrown against the candidacy of President Roosevelt. The old Pulitzer organ, The St. Louis Post-Dispatch, abandoned its ancient moorings and went over to Landon. The Baltimore Sun, unable to make a clean-cut decision, repudiated Roosevelt without embracing the Republican cause zealously. Many papers nominally committed to the Democratic leader, such as The New York Times and the Scripps-Howard chain, were lukewarm, apologetic, and querulous, rather than militant, in their support. Coupled with the shift and vacillation of journalistic opinion was a manifestation of belligerence in editorial language that signified deep-seated passions. For a fair comparison in the arts of vituperation it was necessary to go back to the campaign of 1896, indeed to the campaigns of 1796 and 1800. The metropolitan press, in the main, was not only Republican in philosophy; it was almost revolutionary in its vindictiveness.

Another striking feature of the campaign lay in the fact that nearly all the columnists were about as vindictively Republican as the majority of the prominent editors themselves. Despite an air of Olympian detachment that occasionally hung over the opening words of their articles, there was little question about the nature of their subjective irritations when the final sentences appeared. Thus special powers of elucidation, innuendo, and persuasion were enlisted on the Republican side. In addition, many editors who were nominally Democratic in policy printed daily or periodical comments and homilies from one or more of the chain writers, and in this way countered their own news selections and editorials by propaganda from the other camp. The total flow of ink in the Republican cause was, therefore, greater than the total roll of Republican newspapers indicated. Such was the power of the press to be tested by the popular verdict.

For the course taken by the metropolitan press in the campaign, economic determinists had their explanation: the newspaper business is merely one phase of "big business" in an age when large capital is required for a single publishing plant as well as for a chain of plants. In support of this hypothesis they could cite the authority of The Wall Street Journal: "A newspaper is a private enterprise, owing nothing whatever to the public, which grants it no franchise. It is therefore 'affected' with no public interest. It is emphatically the property of the owner, who is selling a manufactured product at his own risk. If the public does not like his opinions or his method of presenting news the remedy is in its own hands. It is under no obligation to buy the paper. . . . Editors, except where they own their own newspapers, take their policy from their employers. . . . But for ridiculously obvious reasons, there are many newspaper owners willing enough to encourage the public in the delusion that it is the editor of a newspaper who dictates the selection of news and the expression of opinion. He only does so subject to the correction and suggestion of the proprietor of the paper." When the ownership and economic affiliations of the newspapers opposed to President Roosevelt were tabulated, they fitted rather closely the line of division in the campaign contributions; and, if The Wall Street Journal was correct in associating opinion and news selection with proprietorship, there were some grounds for assuming that the rhetoricians of the press gave heed to the voices of the counting room.

Yet polls taken while the campaign was under way indicated that newspaper readers did not believe their own eyes or were impervious to the admonitions of their journalistic tutors. This indication, later confirmed by the election itself, led to the conclusion that newspapers had "lost their influence," and that other agencies of communication, especially the radio, had disrupted their empire over the popular mind. To some extent the conclusion was well founded. The credulity that accepted the printed word as a revelation of pure disinterestedness was doubtless diminishing. But other factors affected the influence exerted by the newspapers. It was not merely their support of the Republican candidate that alienated voters and augmented distrust; the manner of the editorial campaign also counted in the process of alienation and repudiation. Many editors were not content with analyzing and weighing arguments, with sober statements of policy, or with eloquent pleas for public sympathy. In the hysteria of the campaign their sense of fair play deteriorated. As a brash king had often weakened a strong monarchy, so intemperate editors weakened the empire of the press over national opinion.

§

Despite the clear indications revealed by preliminary polls, save that taken by The Literary Digest, the overwhelming nature of the Democratic victory at the election was a general surprise. It is true that the Institute of Public Opinion had recorded only three states as "sure for Landon" — Maine, Vermont, and New Hampshire, but it had admitted doubts as to some other states. So when the returns of the balloting gave only Maine and Vermont to the Republicans, even hard-headed politicians rubbed their scalps in amazement. Yet such was the triumph. Nothing like it had occurred in the long history of political campaigns since the victory of James Monroe in 1820, in the era of good feeling.

In popular terms, no doubt, the landslide was not so destructive. Although Roosevelt's plurality was eleven millions, in round numbers, the official poll showed that there were still nearly seventeen million Republicans left in the country — a far larger proportion of the voters than that recorded for Federalism in 1820 or for anything like Whiggery in 1836. According to any calculation, the figure was too substantial to warrant sending out the notices of a party funeral.

Nevertheless, political prognosticators, especially of the theoretical type, immediately began to speculate upon the probabilities of a new political alignment, implying the death or reconstruction of the Republican party. At last, they said, it seemed possible to have a "true" liberal or conservative party and a "true" radical party. But for this view there was little warrant in the immediate situation or the history of American politics. If logic suggested the sharp split, the realities of the popular process forbade it. The Democratic party had suffered defeats almost as drastic, in effect, as that just administered to Republicans, and yet had returned from forlorn hopes and years in the desert to hopes realized and the spoils of office. No foreclosure of history denied that possibility to the Republicans.

Any rational form of political calculation acknowledged that contingency. With Communists torn into factions, Socialists divided, Democrats at war with themselves, and Republicans ranging in type from Gerald P. Nye to Ogden Mills, two simple and unequivocal faiths for a single division, right and left, could not be formulated in words; nor were the economic interests and emotions as yet reducible to one positive set of antagonisms. Heedless orators and columnists were fond of saying that the nation could not exist half collectivist and half individualist, but, as Aristotle had pointed out more than two thousand years before, only some such an interpenetration of opposites could be called a society and stand anywhere, anytime.

A division on that line was improbable. The Republican platform and the orations of Governor Landon demonstrated the fact. Beneath words were configurations of

economy and culture. As long as American society continued
to display a wide diversity of interests, all interrelated, no
political party could hope for a victory on an appeal to a
single interest. An election map of the United States showing
two states white and all the others red did not divulge the
underlying substance of politics, and when Congress met
the next year this truth became obvious to calculators busy
with new projects for realignments. Political arithmetic was
not limited to subtraction, division, and addition. If map
students in party headquarters saw clear contours and sharp
antagonisms, front soldiers in party trenches wrestled with
mutiny and confusion.

What then was decided at the record-breaking election in
which nearly forty-six million men and women expressed
their judgments and the victorious candidate for the presidency commanded a plurality of more than eleven million
voters? On that day a few items were certainly set down in
the record and sealed with the seven seals of history. The
image of power and proposed action presented by the Republican platform and candidate had been rejected by a staggering majority. The election did not repeat the performance
of 1896, in which the Tiberius Gracchus of the agrarians,
William Jennings Bryan, after a vigorous assault on "the
money power," was decisively repudiated at the polls. Nor
did it repeat the verdict of 1912. In that year, it is true,
Woodrow Wilson denounced government by "the big bankers, the big manufacturers, the big masters of commerce, the
heads of railroad corporations and of steamship corporations," as he characterized the foe, and was elected; but
Woodrow Wilson had proposed no such program as that
offered by the New Deal and he polled only a minority of the
popular vote. And unlike Wilson, President Roosevelt was
not steeped in the philosophy of Edmund Burke whom the
fright of the French revolution had transformed into a Tory.
Not even the defeated candidate on the Republican ticket
had offered in 1936 the policies of 1896; on the contrary a
comparison showed that his platform was more like the

Progressive tender of 1912 than the once orthodox creed of his party. However interpreted, the election of 1936 was no exact repetition of any episode in history; it represented a drift of events and thought flowing through the day into the morrow.

In other respects the outcome of the election was positive. To the Democrats, whose candidate had defied the power of "organized money," the responsibilities of the Federal Government were entrusted for another season. Upon the Democrats were also bestowed again the spoils of office. They had promised to go ahead along the lines already laid down in voluminous legislation and a huge majority of the voters had approved their pledge. On the issue set by the decisions of the Supreme Court against New Deal statutes the popular verdict was likewise emphatic; the barriers interposed by that high tribunal were to be vaulted, if necessary by constitutional amendment. This much, at least, seemed written in the record of 1936, but it was in the nature of history rather than visible prophecy. Just what definite propulsions to action, if any, were set in motion by the popular decision?

That question was not answerable out of knowledge on the morning after the election. President Roosevelt was re-elected. What would he do? What, in fact, could he do? Under the Constitution, he was not the Government of the United States. Though he could propose, urge, and press, he could not legislate at will. Swept into legislative power on the same popular tide was an immense majority of Democrats with wills, temperaments, and purposes of their own. In the Senate, seventy-six Democrats were to dominate a little group composed of sixteen Republicans and a few independents; in the House of Representatives the Democrats were to mass 331 members against eighty-nine Republicans and a handful of independents. If the Chief Executive mirrored the mind of a vast national majority, the legislators of his party mirrored the minds of 331 congressional districts and many states.

On analysis this enormous legislative bloc disclosed numerous internal variations. It included members from the Solid South who had little love for the New Deal and yet were entrenched as the heads of powerful committees; it embraced also other Democrats from the Solid South who had about as little affection for their regional colleagues as for the members of the Republican delegation — on many issues, less. With the Southern groups were associated under the banner of the Democratic party in Congress a few radicals from Northern labor constituencies and a far larger number of legislators picked by the political machines of great cities or the small-town bosses of rural regions. In a strict sense, no taut line divided the Democrats from the little assembly of Republicans, and their unwieldy aggregation was criss-crossed by deep antagonisms which were bound to erupt at every crucial shift in events. If, therefore, some pages were closed in the record of history by the great decision of 1936, no legible chart was delivered, revealing the avenues of advance into the hazy land of the future, near or distant.

## CHAPTER VIII

### *The Execution of the Mandate*

As if symbolizing the hurried spirit of the age, the inauguration of President Roosevelt to succeed himself occurred on January 20, instead of March 4, in accordance with the Twentieth Amendment to the Constitution shortening the time between the popular mandate and the beginning of official action. Certainly symbolic to his critics and opponents who believed in omens were the black clouds that lowered over the city of Washington all day and the sheets of rain that poured down, dimming the bright colors of banners and streamers designed for the pageant. But for these "accidents of history," the President was in no way responsible and they could be dismissed as meaningless. Far more sibylline were two features of the occasion which he arranged to express his own sense of the proprieties. Putting aside protests from citizens and associations pacifically inclined, he decided that a military parade, not a civilian pageant, should celebrate his return to power. And he also decided that he and his immediate entourage at the White House must review the marching men, with banners and martial music, from a replica of the Hermitage, the home of Andrew Jackson, the hero of New Orleans who had worn boots and spurs in war and politics.

Although the outward signs of his installation were military, President Roosevelt's inaugural address pulsated with peaceful professions. He opened with an emphasis on the beneficent obligations of the State: "The need to find through government the instrument of our united purpose to solve for the individual the ever rising problems of a complex civilization. Repeated attempts at their solution without the aid of government had left us baffled and bewildered. For, without that aid, we had been unable to create those moral controls over the services of science which are necessary to make science a useful servant instead of a ruthless master of mankind. To do this we knew that we must find practical controls over blind economic forces and blindly selfish men. We of the Republic sensed the truth that democratic government has innate capacity to protect its people against disasters once considered inevitable — to solve problems once considered unsolvable. We would not admit that we could not find a way to master economic epidemics just as, after centuries of fatalistic suffering, we had found a way to master epidemics of disease. We refused to leave the problems of our common welfare to be solved by the winds of chance and the hurricanes of disaster." "Complex civilization . . . moral controls . . . services of science . . . master economic epidemics . . . fatalistic suffering . . . winds of chance . . . hurricanes of disaster" — these were words hard to discover in previous presidential addresses.

Long before January 20, 1937, a European philosopher, Friedrich Meinecke, had found, in the eternal conflict between the ideal and the real, the tragedy of western civilization. Whether through reading or reflection President Roosevelt had come to a similar conclusion and in his address he took account of the tragedy: "We are beginning to wipe out the line that divides the practical from the ideal, and in so doing we are fashioning an instrument of unimagined power for the establishment of a morally better world." The times are changing. "For these reasons I am justified in believing that the greatest change we have witnessed has been the change in the moral climate of America. . . . Shall we pause now and turn our back upon the road that lies ahead? . . . Timidity asks 'how difficult is the road ahead?'" The United States "can demonstrate that, under democratic methods of government, national wealth can be translated into a spreading volume of human comforts hitherto unknown — and the lowest standard of living can be raised far above the level of mere subsistence." In other words, the United States could have the material basis for a civilization shared by all; it need not rest upon slavery, servitude, or a vast body of laborers on or below the subsistence level. Its President was rejecting an argument buttressed by fifty centuries of history and disowning an explicit or tacit tradition as deep-rooted as the very idea of government and the main body of contemporary middle-class opinion.

Having thrown the weight of his intellectual and moral force on the side of resolving the tragic conflict between the ideal and the real, Roosevelt passed beyond generalities. He went on realistically and, judging by the phrases of mere thanksgiving so often uttered on such occasions, courageously, to specify the evils to be overcome. "In this nation I see tens of millions of its citizens — a substantial part of its whole population — who at this very moment are denied the greater part of what the very lowest standards of today call the necessities of life." At this point the President paused. His circle of hard-headed politicians preserved their inscrutable calm; chill winds blew gusts of rain hither and yon over the plaza in front of the Capitol; but he proceeded with his specifications: "I see millions of families trying to live on incomes so meagre that the pall of family disaster hangs over them day by day. I see millions whose daily lives in city and on farm continue under conditions labelled indecent by a so-called polite society half a century ago. I see millions denied education, recreation, and the opportunity to better their lot and the lot of their children. I see millions lacking the means to buy the products of farm and factory and by their poverty denying work and productiveness to many other millions. I see one-third of a nation ill-housed, ill-clad, ill-nourished." He also saw the other two-thirds of the nation : "In our seeking for economic and political progress as a nation, we all go up — or else we all go down — as one people."

This was not to say that a pessimist was addressing the nation : "It is not in despair that I paint you that picture. I paint it for you in hope, because the nation, seeing and understanding the injustice in it, proposes to paint it out. We are determined to make every American citizen the subject of his country's interest and concern, and we will never regard any faithful law-abiding group within our borders as superfluous. . . . If I know aught of the spirit and purpose of our nation, we will not listen to comfort, opportunism and timidity. We will carry on."

Yet across the plaza and a narrow street stood the Palace of Justice, under the clouds and in the rain. From its chamber had gone forth decrees proclaiming that vital measures of Roosevelt's first administration were forbidden by a higher power — the Constitution of the United States — whose cryptic meaning a majority of the Supreme Court could alone decipher. Since the Supreme Court had invalidated the main parts of a milder program, how could President Roosevelt expect to carry on, to achieve the larger promises? His address contained no concrete answer, merely a premonition : "The Constitution of 1787 did not make our democracy impotent."

§

Fresh from the people, with the mandate in its hand, the Seventy-fifth Congress opened with enthusiasm. Among the first measures laid before it for consideration was the Guffey-Vinson bituminous coal bill to take the place of the Coal Act which had been declared null and void by the Supreme Court in 1935. The sickness that had long plagued the coal industry had not been cured by the judicial operation. By a consensus of expert opinion, some form of coördination and collective action was necessary to keep it alive, to say nothing of restoring it to health. Congress had tried to accomplish this purpose. The Supreme Court had intervened. Congress tried again. By April 12 it completed the passage of the new coal bill and the President's signature was soon affixed to this "little National Industrial Recovery Bill." The substitute law provided for public and private collaboration in matters of marketing, price control, and trade practices throughout the industry. In deference to the Supreme Court's rulings, Congress omitted the sections of the previous law pertaining to the determination of hours and wages, but it declared collective bargaining in labor relations to be a part of the public policy governing the administration of the law.

While the coal bill was on its way to passage, Congress began the study of several measures proposed on behalf of agriculture. In the campaign of 1936 the Democrats had assured farmers and planters that they would aid them despite the adverse decisions of the Supreme Court, and the Republican candidate, Governor Landon, had outbidden them in some respects for the support of this powerful interest. Now the response of Congress to the commitments was whole-hearted and found expression in a number of enactments. A sugar-quota law applied the principles of the dead Agricultural Adjustment Act to the sugar industry. It authorized the Secretary of Agriculture to determine the amount of sugar required by consumers in the United States, fixed the proportions to be allocated to foreign and domestic producers, empowered the Secretary to make allocations of quotas among domestic producers, made specific stipulations respecting the employment of labor, and provided benefit payments to farmers who complied with the terms of the law. Neither in intentions nor designs was there any pure laissez faire in this Act. Notwithstanding the pressures and objections of particular interests, the law brought within its scope exporters, importers, farmers, workers, and manufacturers engaged in the wide-reaching sugar industry.

Almost without opposition, certainly with no concerted Republican resistance, Congress amended and reënacted several provisions of the Agricultural Adjustment Act relative to marketing orders and agreements, especially in connection with the dairy industry. In destroying the Adjustment Act, Justice Roberts had said that agriculture belonged to the states. Bowing to his decree, Congress made grants to states for carrying out its "soil-conservation program"; the President called upon state governors to press for appropriate local legislation; and a majority of state legislatures responded favorably within a few months. To this circumlocution, Congress added a new Soil Conservation Act which was a kind of preliminary to a wider measure soon to follow.

Paying heed to the alarming growth of farm tenancy, reported by a special presidential commission, Congress made at least a feint in that direction. By the Farm Tenant Act, signed July 23, 1937, it gave to the Secretary of Agriculture the power to arrange long term loans to tenants, at three per cent interest, for the purchase of homesteads, and provided for initial appropriations. In the course of such transactions the Secretary could exercise a wide discretion in retiring submarginal land and rehabilitating run-down farms. More radical than the President in rural sympathies, Congress repassed, over his veto, a bill continuing low rates of interest on farm loans. In the House sixty-two Republicans voted for over-riding the President's objections and only seven voted against it, thus displaying an almost united front in favor of the agrarian proposal. In the meantime Secretary Wallace announced the most comprehensive agricultural program yet conceived in the United States — a program including an "ever normal granary" for the storage of five great non-perishable commodities. And action was promised on this proposal at the next session.

Amid the concern for agriculture, cities were remembered. Returning to the issue raised by municipal bankruptcies in many parts of the country, Congress passed the Municipal Debt Adjustment Act to replace the Bankruptcy Act declared void by the Supreme Court. Then the ill-housed, to whom the President referred in his inaugural address, were taken into consideration. On February 24, Senator Wagner of New York introduced a broad measure authorizing a frontal attack on the problem of bad housing. Although debate was long drawn out and some opposition came from members representing rural regions, especially conservative Democrats and Republicans, Senator Wagner's bill became a law on September 1. Not without reason was it called "the most important legislation of the session."

The Act set up the United States Housing Authority in the Department of the Interior and conferred upon it the power to issue within a fixed period $500,000,000 in securities, for the purpose of financing public agencies engaged in clearing slums, repairing buildings, and erecting new dwellings. At last taking cognizance of the fact that families in the low-wage levels really could not pay a sustaining rental for decent housing, Congress provided conditional subsidies to communities. It offered them annual grants in aid of low rents if they would make contributions equal to twenty per cent of the total. As a supplement in the same interest, it authorized federal subsidies running as high as forty per cent of the construction cost, subject to the stipulation that local authorities add twenty per cent. By this means, the author of the measure expected, construction would be stimulated and economic barriers to low-rental housing would be removed.

In the preamble the Housing Act announced a departure from traditional conceptions of federal responsibilities in matters of human well-being and a pledge of national concern for the living conditions of the people. It declared the policy of the United States to be the promotion of the general welfare by helping the states and their subdivisions to alleviate unemployment, to remedy unsafe and unsanitary housing conditions, and to overcome the acute shortage of decent, safe, and healthful dwellings for families of low income in rural and urban communities. From beginning to end the Act reflected the condition of the housing industry as a branch of capitalist enterprise. In the days of the golden glow thousands of investors had put billions of dollars into the real estate bonds which had financed the feverish construction boom, and in the days of its dissolution they had lost the major portion of their "savings." Many mortgage companies were proved to be little better than pillagers. The bankruptcy proceedings that followed the great smash of 1929 had been accompanied by speculation and peculation in which lawyers, receivers, referees, and harpies had thrived on pickings from the remnants. In such circumstances private investors were in no mood to hurl more billions, if they had the money, into an industry that had despoiled them and left behind a trail of chicanery and dishonesty added to folly. Whether by throwing public credit into the breach the Wagner Act could revive a decaying trade and accomplish, on any considerable scale, the promise of the preamble remained hidden in the general fate of all capitalist enterprises.

Other great measures, proposed or supported by the Roosevelt administration in fulfillment of the mandate, were blocked in Congress as the unwieldy body of Democrats broke up into snarling factions. Both parties had bound themselves in the campaign to extend the merit system in the rapidly expanding federal service. Instead of discharging this obligation, Congress raided the civil service and created more political jobs. Leonard D. White, who retired from membership on the Civil Service Commission, mildly described the operations of the legislators: "This record discloses a scandalous disregard of a solemn undertaking and a complete indifference to the plain mandate of the American people." Even the Housing Act, while making noble professions, exempted officers, attorneys, experts, and all positions paying over $1980 a year from the restrictions of the Civil Service Act. But in the summer of 1938 President Roosevelt offset this record by broad executive orders extending the merit system to practically all positions in the federal service not expressly exempted by law.

Dragged along for weeks and finally defeated was the President's plan for the reorganization and consolidation of the scattered and often conflicting agencies of the Federal Government. To this reform both parties had long paid lip service. On the basis of a special report from a Committee on Administrative Management, Roosevelt called upon Congress to enact legislation authorizing a realignment of federal administration in the interest of efficiency and economy. Thumbs were turned down on his project. A similar fate was meted out to the President's plan for the creation of seven regional agencies, akin to the Tennessee Valley Authority, for the purpose of developing the resources of seven great watersheds in the United States. With the Tennessee experiment already under fire and the electric power interests on guard against the project, Congress laid this proposal on the shelf.

§

In some measure, although not entirely, the futilities of the Congress fresh from the triumph of 1936 were due to a controversy over judicial reform, precipitated by the President. His inaugural address gave no hint of the method to be employed in releasing the executive and legislative departments from the bonds imposed upon them by the constitutional interpretations of the Supreme Court. Yet the conflicts of preceding months and the temper of the campaign made it almost certain that some proposal would emerge from administration circles after the delivery of the popular mandate.

Acquainted with Charles G. Haines' monumental treatise on judicial conflicts and with supplementary documentation, watchers of the political scene had practical grounds for supposing that the deadlock between the Political Departments of the Government on the one side and the Judicial Department on the other, in respect of primary policies, would be relieved by some process. They remembered, for instance, that the Republican party, with Lincoln at the head, had defied the ruling of the Supreme Court in the Dred Scott case, had refused to accept it, and had carried the day. They had in mind the way in which Democrats had later condemned the Supreme Court for its five-to-four decision in the Income Tax case and, though momentarily defeated, had seen victory achieved in the Sixteenth Amendment. John Marshall had been able to strike down an obscure provision of the Judiciary Act in Marbury versus Madison without evoking effective measures in rebuttal, but the Court had never succeeded in paralyzing a statute of major interest to any great political party without encountering a powerful recoil.

The whispering galleries of Washington between the election in November and the opening of Congress buzzed with discussions of the constitutional issue. In January, soon after the inaugural, a number of liberals, including Senator Norris, issued a call for a national conference to consider the issue and to concentrate opinion on a single plan for disposing of it. Of plans there were many; of opinions there were, perhaps, even more. Congress could follow a Republican precedent of Reconstruction days and by a simple enactment strip the Supreme Court of appellate jurisdiction over constitutional cases — a procedure once upheld by the Court itself. Congress could require a majority of six or seven Justices to invalidate a statute — a proposition obscured by juristic doubts.

From statutes, opinion swung to amendments. The thought was easy to entertain. But what kind of an amendment? Many had been devised. Sticklers for propriety proposed an amendment concretely enlarging or restating the power of Congress to deal with social and economic legislation. Scoffers replied that choosing effective phraseology would be difficult and that judges of the Supreme Court could quickly riddle the provision in their classic style, as they had already riddled many plain words in the law of the land. In a second projected amendment it was proposed that Congress be given power to over-ride an adverse judicial decision by an extraordinary majority, perhaps after a congressional election had intervened. Around and around these and other schemes, debate and oratory clacked and rattled without effecting a concentration of the talents seeking a way through the constitutional impasse.

Before the liberal conference could assemble, out of a blue sky, on February 5, 1937, came President Roosevelt's proposal for cutting the Gordian knot, accompanied by a bill couched in specific terms. In substance the scheme went beyond the Supreme Court and provided for the appointment of a new federal judge whenever an incumbent failed to resign or retire within six months after reaching the age of seventy. The number of judges so to be appointed was limited to fifty, of whom not more than six could be added to the Supreme Court.

In his covering message, the President referred to past changes in the number of Supreme Court judges; to the heavy burdens carried by the Court; to long and vexatious delays in litigation; to the clogging of administrative processes by injunctions or other forms of judicial intervention; to the phenomenon of a federal law constitutional in one district and invalid in another; to the fact that years often passed before such muddles were straightened out by final adjudication in Washington. Turning to the sanction of precedent, the President cited the Act of 1919, which required him to nominate a new district or circuit judge whenever he found one permanently incapacitated, and declared that no President should be asked to pass upon the ability or disability of a particular judge. "Modern complexities," he said, "call also for a constant infusion of new blood in the courts, just as it is needed in the executive functions of the government and in private business. . . . New facts become blurred through old glasses fitted, as it were, for the needs of another generation; older men, assuming that the scene is the same as it was in the past, cease to explore or inquire into the present or the future." The essential concepts of justice, he insisted, must be applied in the light of the needs and facts of an ever-changing world.

§

The President's message on his court plan stunned friends and foes. Apparently in drafting it he had not consulted or informed party leaders in Congress, or taken counsel with all the members of his official family. If he had, no inkling of the project had reached the gossip corridors of the capital in advance of his message. When the proposal was made known, it provoked feelings of wonder, resentment, and resistance. Republicans were quick in lining up their forces for opposition. Their own offering to the public at the last election had been rejected and they were searching for an opportunity to pound some general measure that touched no specific issues so recently decided by the popular verdict. This was their chance. It was now possible for them to condemn changes in the composition of the Supreme Court without approving the action of that tribunal in striking down laws which they abhorred. True to the party instinct, they made the most of the occasion, without obtruding their thin and battered ranks too obviously upon the public gaze. True also to political use and wont, they conveniently overlooked all their party had said and done in connection with the Dred Scott case and the first Legal Tender case. Gathering up the garments of righteousness, which Democrats had worn in 1857 and 1871, they clothed themselves in the apparel of pure theory.

The formulas of their argument were age-worn and simple. They had been recited by one party or another, as occasion permitted, since the establishment of the Federal Government, and they ran in this fashion. The Constitution ordains an independent judiciary. The Supreme Court consists of honorable and competent lawyers. In passing upon the validity of a statute, the judges, or a majority of them, perform an act as certain as calculations in physics or mathematics; they merely "square" the statute by the Constitution and, according to the reading of measurement, declare it correct or void. The act so performed involves no question of personal judgment, conscience, social preference, or economic predilection — nothing save the perfect and indisputable mandate and logic of law. When a statute is declared void, the Court merely expresses the will of the people set forth in the Constitution. It is, in short, the automatic and infallible (or almost infallible) executor of the people's will as against the erroneous judgment of Congress and the President. After the Court has invalidated a statute, the one and only procedure lawfully available to Congress, the President, and the people, if dissatisfied with the verdict, is to amend the Constitution by due process — a two-thirds vote in Congress and approval by three-fourths of the states.

Thus the argument moved from unequivocal axiom to unequivocal axiom and closed with the unanswerable demonstration. As long as the tacit assumptions of the major premise were unexplored and the sociology of the axioms was left entirely out of the reckoning, the conclusion was indisputable : Loyalty to the Constitution requires the indignant repudiation of President Roosevelt's proposal for reorganizing the federal judiciary.

On both the logomachy and the merits of the case, the President's own party was torn asunder. The chief committees and the general political management in Congress were largely in the hands of conservative Democrats from the South, although the numerical weight of the party was then in the North. On the whole the sociological jurisprudence of the Southern Democrats corresponded with fair exactness to that generally prevailing in the North about 1880. Apart from pleasure over cotton and tobacco legislation, the President's Southern colleagues, with a few exceptions, had been restive under his direction and had accepted many of his other measures without cordiality and often with strong distaste. Since an hour and wage bill, devised, among other things, to abolish the low differentials of the South, was then pending, these colleagues might well rejoice in the prospect of judicial annulment.  It was not surprising, therefore, that their veteran leader, Senator Carter Glass, of Virginia, in a national broadcast, emptied the vials of his wrath upon the judiciary project, raked it from beginning to end with the fire of his powerful vituperation.  Nor was it surprising that the Vice President, John N. Garner of Texas, deliberately left the Capitol for a vacation at home and did not return until he was able to administer the death blow to the statutory proposal, at least for the current session of Congress.

The liberal wing of the President's supporters was at first bewildered and then divided into factions.  Many individuals within its fold, perhaps a majority, had hoped for a more fundamental treatment of the deadlock, on the assumption that a constitutional amendment could be adopted or that Congress could permanently alter the procedure of the Supreme Court by statutory enactment.  Personal considerations, as usual, also entered into consideration; and they were crystallized when Postmaster General Farley, Chairman of the Democratic National Committee, declaring that the votes for the bill were "in the bag," virtually ordered Senators who had ridden into power "on the President's coat tails" to obey orders from the White House.  More than one wavering mind was apparently stiffened by what seemed to be a personal insult.

Whatever motives dominated quivering minds, in the end one of the most active Senators on the Democratic side, Burton K. Wheeler, announced his resolute opposition to the Court plan and condemned it in terms scarcely less withering than those called into play by Senator Glass.  Of Mr. Wheeler's progressive orthodoxy there could be no question.  He had taken his political fate by the forelock and joined the revolt of Senator Robert M. La Follette against both parties in 1924, when Franklin D. Roosevelt had supported John W. Davis, now a beacon of the Liberty League.  For the opposition to the Court plan, Senator Wheeler was a godsend and he was taken into its fold with appreciation.

Of the other liberals who decided to support the Court plan

many were skeptical about the wisdom of the particular project but, confronting the necessity of choice, they cast their lot with the President. After all, they reasoned, it might be impossible to get an agreement in Congress upon any kind of amendment or to secure ratification by three-fourths of the states within a period of ten or fifteen years. Despite the brave arguments in favor of an amendment, there was no assurance of any gain in that direction. Perhaps the President, ingenious in interpreting popular dispositions, had correctly fixed the only practical line of advance against "the judicial oligarchy" that formed a majority of the Supreme Court. For these and other reasons, a number of "honest doubters" put aside irresolution and defended the bill to reorganize the judiciary.

Even with chances of defeat ahead, some liberals were happy to have an opportunity to debate before the whole country the issue presented by the steady advance of the federal judiciary upon the field of policy — an issue long discussed in the technical language of the law schools. Nowhere in the law journals could there be found in the austere language of jurisprudence competent support for the entire course which the Supreme Court had deliberately pursued for the preceding quarter of a century. To translate the language of adepts into the language of the street was the task assumed by the liberals who finally went over to the President's side in the conflict. Seldom if ever had they enjoyed such an opportunity to bridge the gap between erudition and popular impressions.

The division of the country on the issue presented curious contrasts with earlier conflicts. In the controversy over the judiciary that followed the Dred Scott decision in 1857, Respectability had been divided. Men of such talents and power as Abraham Lincoln and William H. Seward had led in rebuking the Court and had questioned its honor as well as its reasoning. During the debate of 1896 over the income tax decision and injunction procedures, Respectability had been mainly on the side of the angels, while criticism came from

"populists" and "anarchists," as they were called by sticklers for conformity. Now in 1937 Respectability was in
fierce discord. It is true that six New England college presidents deemed it necessary publicly to condemn the court
plan, and that the president of Princeton University went to
Washington in person to speak against it. It is true that
other eminent members of the élite openly aligned themselves
with the opposition. But talents, if not wealth, were ranged
in opposite camps. If the bulk of Excellence was antagonistic, the distinguished deans of law schools and the scholarly
students of constitutional history who favored the bill could
not be called populists and anarchists in the style of 1896. In
the lapse of time much water had run over the wheel.

As the contest advanced, the opposition adopted a definite
form of strategy. In the matter of maneuvering, on account
of numerical weakness or for less obvious reasons, the Republican management left sapping and mining mainly to the
Democratic insurgents. While quietly holding its own position, it chose to press Senator Wheeler to the front as the
strategist of the campaign rather than the titular Republican
leader, Senator McNary — who after all had voted for many
New Deal measures himself. Significantly absent now from
the Senate committee's hearings on the judiciary bill were
the "great constitutional lawyers" who the year before had
served the Liberty League in its disparagement of President
Roosevelt and all his works. Nowhere among the witnesses
that appeared before the committee was there a mighty
Joseph Choate, to declaim in the rhetoric of Webster against
"this assault on private property and the Constitution."
Eminent lawyers and distinguished citizens did file their
objections to the court bill, but none came forth from the
school of oratorical Supereminence to lodge his complaints in
person. Nor did those who protested against the Court plan
as a rule undertake to defend all the decisions of the Supreme Court that had precipitated the conflict.

Indeed one of the conspicuous features of the opposition
was the general admission that the Court had rendered

dubious or unwarranted opinions and had laid itself open to just criticism. A New England college president, in voicing his censure of the court bill, confessed that on the whole his view of the Constitution was that entertained by the dissenting minority. Senator Wheeler declared before the Senate committee that he had severely criticized some decisions of the Supreme Court, and he scorned the classic theory of judicial impeccability by advocating an amendment permitting Congress, by due process, to over-ride judicial vetoes contrary to its interpretation of the Constitution. In a speech upon the floor of the Senate, Joseph O'Mahoney, who ably seconded Senator Wheeler's attacks on the bill, declared positively that "the courts have upon occasion usurped legislative power, and that usurpation ought to be brought to an end. I have repeatedly denounced it. There can be no defense of it."

This was, of course, directly contrary to the classic doctrine that the federal courts only set forth the true meaning of the Constitution and could not possibly misinterpret it or usurp power. Nevertheless it is in the nature of politicians to accept aid even from a sworn enemy of their most precious propositions. If belief in the major axiom of judicial infallibility had been a test for membership in the opposition, the President's court bill would have quickly gone through Congress and commanded a far more general approval in the country. Agreement could have been reached on a concrete action amid differences of opinion over its meaning and consequences.

As usual in the discussion of great public questions, the contestants in the controversy over the judiciary "talked past one another," to use Karl Mannheim's phrase, for the sources of their difference in opinion did not lie entirely, if at all, in the theme of debate or the words employed in the argument. On their part, sponsors of the President's proposal declined to accept either the major axiom or the structure of the classic syllogism. They insisted on testing the purity of perfect theory by reference to historic practices.

They widened the frame of reference beyond logic to the borders of history and sociology. The Supreme Court should be independent? Has it ever been in fact wholly independent of the ideas and policies of the President and Senate that selected its members? The Supreme Court merely declares the law of the Constitution? Dissenting members of the Court, equally honorable, equally competent, have repeatedly maintained that the majority was simply reading its economic theories or predilections into the general language of the document. It is an unholy thing to change the number of federal judges for the purpose of influencing the course of constitutional interpretation? This had been done, more or less covertly — by Jefferson's Republicans, Jackson's Democrats, and Lincoln's Republicans. It is evil to think of the constitutional theories and social sympathies of possible nominees when making selections for the supreme bench? Have the President and Senate ever failed in practice to take these basic matters into account? When the Supreme Court declares a law invalid, the only way out of the impasse is a constitutional amendment? Other methods have been adopted in many cases and only once in a century and a half has Congress over-ridden an adverse decision by resorting to an amendment. Righteousness, patriotism, democracy, loyalty to the Constitution, knowledge, and logic, it has been said, are opposed to the judiciary bill. How can anyone be sure that he has sole possession of those virtues?

Taking into the reckoning the testimony and statements presented to the Senate committee for and against the bill, no monopoly of talents appeared on either side. The dean of the Columbia University Law School opposed it; the dean of the Yale Law School supported it. Against the opposition of the dean of the Michigan Law School was pitted the support of the dean of the Northwestern University Law School. For the bill, appeared the dean of the Notre Dame Law School; against it, the dean of the Fordham Law School. The dean of the New York University Law School filed stern objections ending in a prayer; the former dean of the Pennsylvania Law

School and head of the American Law Institute and the former dean of the Duke University Law School cast their influence on the side of the bill. Professor E. S. Corwin and Professor W. F. Dodd, both serious students of constitutional law and history, disagreed, the former supporting and the latter opposing the measure. Of more than passing interest was the fact that Charles Grove Haines, undoubtedly the greatest authority on judicial conflicts in American history, with the indefatigable researches of a lifetime at his command, went before the Senate committee to support the President's project for resolving the judicial conflict of 1937. Nor was it without significance that three or four outstanding masters of constitutional law, masters, as distinguished from advocates of causes, stood mute while the conflict was in progress. Above all things it was evident that a profound alteration in the climate of expert and general opinion had occurred since the great judiciary dispute of 1896.

When the Senate committee closed its hearings early in June, 1937, it decided by the narrow margin of one vote against the court bill. In its report the majority spared no words of excoriation. The summary denounced the proposed bill as a "needless, futile, and utterly dangerous abandonment of constitutional principle . . . without precedent and without justification." The bill, if enacted, would "subjugate the courts to the will of Congress and the President and thereby destroy the independence of the judiciary, the only certain shield of individual rights. . . . It points the way to the evasion of the Constitution and establishes the method whereby the people may be deprived of their right to pass upon all amendments of the fundamental law . . . a proposal that violates every sacred tradition of American democracy. Under the form of the Constitution it seeks to do that which is unconstitutional. . . . It is a measure which should be so emphatically rejected that its parallel will never again be presented to the free representatives of the free people of America." Furthermore, the bill was presented to Congress "in a most intricate form and for reasons that obscured its

real purposes." In short, the President was proposing to
evade the terms of the Constitution, subjugate the courts,
deprive the people of their rights, violate every sacred tradition of American democracy ; besides, he was guilty of deceit.
Those were contemptuous words for seven Democrats to hurl
at the leader of their party, the President of the United
States.

§

Between February and June, while the debate was raging
in Congress, in the press, over the radio, and before the
Senate committee, no sound of complaint came from the
Palace of Justice. It was a privilege of the Supreme Court to
keep secret and sacred the conflicts of opinion, conviction,
and temper which appeared at its inner council table.
Rumors might escape through solid doors, but custom forbade authentication — at least until memoirs of the dead
could safely be published. Custom likewise placed restraints
on judicial participation in public disputes. Only once during
the contest over the President's proposal was a voice heard
from behind the veil. In response to an inquiry from Senator
Wheeler, Chief Justice Hughes, with the approval of Justice
Van Devanter and Justice Brandeis, wrote a letter declaring
that the Supreme Court was "fully abreast of its work," thus
directly denying one of President Roosevelt's main contentions that it could not carry its load ; and the Chief Justice
allowed the Senator to make this communication public.
What the members of the Court thought of the court bill
and of the national uproar over it was nowhere a matter of
accessible record, but inferences from experience permitted a
guess that mighty arguments were being carried on at the
council table. Little more than a year had passed since
Justice Stone warned his colleagues, in the Agricultural
Adjustment case, that an abuse of power might destroy it,
and the forecast of fulfillment now fell athwart the Palace of
Justice. With the verdict of the November election behind
them and the President's bill in front of them, the justices

of the Supreme Court must have taken thought of the morrow.

What the justices would have done between February and June, 1937, had President Roosevelt quietly acquiesced in their previous decisions against his measures was not known, even to the justices themselves. Nor could it ever be known. History permitted no repetition of identical laboratory experiments in jurisprudence in different circumstances. The Court merely went ahead, entering its decisions and opinions upon the public record as the debate over the judiciary bill swept the forum. On March 29, by a five to four majority, the Court upheld the validity of a minimum wage law that came to it from the state of Washington. Less than a year before, the Court, by a five to four majority, the "same" Court, had declared void a similar measure from the state of New York. In the New York case, Justice Roberts had joined Justices Sutherland, Van Devanter, McReynolds, and Butler in holding that the state had no power under the Constitution to enact such legislation; while the Chief Justice had aligned himself with the dissenting Justices Stone, Brandeis, and Cardozo. In the Washington case, Justice Roberts was enrolled in the majority that sustained the minimum wage law.

To mere laymen this looked like a reversal of position but the Chief Justice, in his opinion, shrouded the transaction with the technicalities of the law, which spared his colleague the positive appearance of having changed his mind during the past ten months. But in so doing the Chief Justice did not spare the Court. In affirming the Washington statute, he declared without wincing that the contrary decision in the earlier District of Columbia case "should be, and it is, overruled." For some reason, despite the orthodox thesis, the Constitution which had not been amended in this respect was changed to mean something which it had not meant when President Roosevelt sent his court message to Congress in February. Had two plus two ceased to equal four?

A fortnight later, the Supreme Court, in another five to

four decision, upheld the Wagner Labor Relations Act designed to promote collective bargaining in industry. "Friends and Foes of Bench Change; Sweeping Progress within a Year," flamed the front page headlines of The New York Times announcing this new "victory" for the Roosevelt administration. Two years before, in the National Recovery case, the Court had held, in effect, that the regulation of industry, except where "direct effects" on interstate commerce are in evidence, belongs under the Constitution to the states. Now, in the Wagner case, it held that industries whose products enter into interstate commerce come specifically within the commerce powers of Congress. To the layman, this might have seemed to be a reversal of the position on the Recovery case; indeed, the four dissenting Justices of the Court thought it was and said as much. Yet in the refinements of judicial distinctions there was no reversal, merely a discrimination of substance and circumstance.

In vain did the minority declare that "almost anything — marriage, birth, death — may in some fashion affect commerce. . . . There must be no impairment of rights guaranteed. . . . The right to contract is fundamental and includes the privilege of selecting those with whom one is willing to assume contractual relations." The majority stood solid in upholding the constitutionality of the Labor Act and President Roosevelt revealed his jubilation in an open message to a friend. "It's been a pretty good day for all of us," he said. In truth it seemed a good day in general, for opponents of his court plan now said that the reorganization of the judiciary was wholly unnecessary, and supporters of the bill suspected that its efficacy was becoming obvious.

A third stroke came on May 24. On that day the Supreme Court held valid, by another five to four vote, the unemployment insurance tax provisions of the Social Security Act and an Alabama statute setting up a scheme of state insurance in coöperation with the Federal Government. To the inexpert mind this decision might also have seemed to be a direct reversal of the principles announced in the ruling of the Court against the Agricultural Adjustment Act. Like that measure, the Security Act laid a tax — not for revenue at all but for the purpose of inducing, indeed compelling, states to establish a certain program of insurance. In the Adjustment case, Justice Roberts had declared that agriculture was a matter reserved to the states. Was not insurance just as much a field reserved to the states? Even more, since promoting social insurance, in contrast to agriculture, was certainly not contemplated as a federal function in 1787. How could Congress constitutionally force states by punitive taxation to provide such insurance and yet not authorize the Secretary of Agriculture to enter into voluntary arrangements with farmers for crop adjustments? Had Chief Justice Hughes and Justice Roberts, who agreed in holding the Agricultural Adjustment Act unconstitutional, changed their minds? For these questions legal thought had good answers, if not real answers: namely, that the first case was no precedent for the second and that differences in facts warranted discriminations in the application of the Constitution.

Since the decisions and opinions of the Court in these cases seriously affected the general public, the inexpertness of laymen outweighed the panurgy of the legal fraternity in the formation of popular sentiments on the subject. Readers of newspapers, unskilled in the technology of the law, could readily assume from the morning headlines that the Court had reversed itself and surrendered. By many defenders of the President's court plan the new judicial rulings were read in this light, and on that ground some of them urged him to accept the substance of victory, drop or modify his project, and relax executive pressure on the judicial branch of the Government.

Opponents of the proposed Court reorganization now had mixed feelings. They still insisted upon defeating the court bill but differed as to reasons for the policy. Liberals in their ranks were inclined to approve the latest grist of constitutional law ground out by the Court and be content to let well enough alone. On the other hand, the conservative wing, still determined in its antagonism to the bill, looked upon the grist with displeasure. Could a Court that had sustained minimum wage legislation, the Wagner Labor Act, and the Social Security Act really serve as the indomitable protector of free contract, private property, and the individual liberty of possessors against the pressure of popular mandates? In ditching President Roosevelt had the Court not surrendered the very citadel of the constitutional stronghold which, after all, formed the center of the contest over the bill for the reorganization of the judiciary? Thoughts of victory over the Chief Executive were permeated by forebodings.

§

While the echoes of the Social Security decision were still resounding, another flash broke into the surcharged atmosphere of Washington. Just as the Senate committee was preparing to file its denunciation of the President's court plan, Justice Van Devanter announced his coming withdrawal from the Supreme Court. For this action Congress had recently prepared the way by passing a bill permitting retirement on full salary. That measure and the announcement of the Justice had the superficial semblance of an economic bargain, though the semblance could be regarded as deceptive. In any case Justice Van Devanter had been among the consistent opponents of recent social and economic legislation, and his return to private life gave President Roosevelt an opportunity to select his first justice for the supreme bench. That he would not choose a nominee with the exact outlook of Justice Van Devanter was a foregone conclusion. Despite the long-standing tradition that mere honor and technical competence were sufficient qualifications for a justice, it was reasonable to expect the choice of a man under eighty years of age, belonging to a more recent generation, and in general sympathy with the constitutional outlook of the Chief Executive of the Nation who was to appoint him.

After the notice of Justice Van Devanter's retirement was made public, buzzing gossip was focused on his probable successor. Long lists of available and congenial candidates were canvassed by editors and commentators. For a while it was rumored that the President, compelled to reckon with opposition in the Senate, would make a recess appointment after the adjournment of Congress. Undoubtedly he was in a trying position and his perplexity was increased by the sudden death of Senator Joseph Robinson. The Senator, though conservative in attitude and affiliations, had been a loyal leader in the upper chamber; and it had been more or less taken for granted that his reward would be an appointment to the first vacancy in the Supreme Court. At the time of his death he was engaged in a struggle to engineer through the Senate a modified court plan which would permit the President to nominate two additional Justices instead of six. Now even that project was blocked. With the passing of Senator Robinson, Vice President Garner took charge of the legislative machine, aligned himself completely with the opposition, reduced the President's proposal to mere procedural changes, and killed the provisions for a reorganization of the Supreme Court. Stung by the repudiation at the hands of his own party and knowing that any nominee for the Court might be rejected by the Senate, President Roosevelt kept his counsel and bided his time.

At length, in a stroke of dramatic suddenness, apparently without the previous knowledge of his own secretaries, the President announced the selection of Senator Hugo Black to fill Justice Van Devanter's vacant post. The very name of Senator Black caused consternation among the conservatives of both parties, since he had been a vigorous and unwavering supporter of New Deal measures in Congress and outside. As the head of Senate investigations he had conducted inquiries into the mercantile marine, aviation, and utility lobbies. He had pushed the inquisitorial powers of the Senate to the limit — beyond the limit, his critics alleged — and he had been as zealous in sustaining what he considered the public interest as Justice Pierce Butler had been in the defense of special railway interests as a practitioner at the bar. Not without reason of its own did Respectability look upon Senator Black as an injudicious man, a prosecutor rather than a judge. Respectability was also aware that he had been supported in his candidacy for the Senate by the small farmers, share croppers, and industrial workers of Alabama against a combination of industrialists, business interests, and planters.

In the ordinary course of politics, the nomination of a man like Hugo Black outside the Senate, if another such person could have been found, would have brought about searching inquiries. The Senate committee on the judiciary would have made an investigation of his character and attainments, hearing critics as well as friends. A favorable report from the committee would have been subjected to the fire of a critical debate on the floor of the Senate. But, according to a long-established theory, Senators were supposed to be well acquainted with their colleagues through close association, and under this rule of courtesy the Senate committee dispensed with wide-open hearings on Senator Black's qualifications for the Supreme Court. When the nomination came before the Senate, however, the courtesy of the gentlemen's club was somewhat relaxed. There was an exchange of inelegant words on the floor; and insinuations that the candidate was or had been a member of the Ku Klux Klan were bandied about. Still the Klan issue was not pressed. The hints were discounted. Everyone acquainted with backstairs politics in Washington knew that, if affiliations with the Klan were to be thoroughly aired, a number of Senators might actually blush. Senator Black was readily confirmed.

For the moment the President rode the crest of the waves. He had forced the conservatives of both parties in the Senate, under their own rule of courtesy, to accept, from their economic point of view, the worst possible man for the Supreme Court. Their feelings were almost beyond expression. Editors who had castigated the President during the campaign of 1936 found a new occasion for lashing out at him. But as everything had been done with due constitutional formality, there seemed to be no way of evading the dénouement.

After taking the oath of office Justice Black sailed for a vacation in Europe. He had barely reached the other side of the ocean when a Pittsburgh newspaper, belonging to the chain dominated by Paul Block, an inveterate foe of the New Deal, sprang a press mine. It published serially a number of documents and facsimiles purporting to show that Mr. Black had been a member of the Ku Klux Klan, that he had received a life membership in that association, and that he had addressed his white-robed brethren in fulsome terms. For Catholics, Jews, Negroes, and the intelligentsia generally, the revelations were certainly upsetting, to put the matter mildly. And now that the Klan was ineffectual, if not dead, in Northern states, politicians could breathe more lightly and strike at the new Justice by joining in the wholesale indictment of the organization. Justice Black was accused of duplicity for failing to acknowledge his membership while his confirmation was under consideration in the Senate. He should resign; he should be impeached, it was said by furious foes. Even his best friends were distracted. When reporters besieged the Justice abroad, he refused to conciliate them. When they raised questions in press conferences at the White House, the President declined to comment until Justice Black's return, but by the expression of his countenance gave occasion for the report that he felt embittered. Had he never thought to inquire about Mr. Black's membership in the Klan?

On his return to the United States in September, Justice Black greeted a swarm of pressmen genially, refused to make any statement, and informed them that he would present his case to the nation over the radio. To newspapers already chafing over their failure to dominate the country in 1936, this was egregious. It was indeed a dismissal of their fiction that news was and could be reported objectively. It was also another vivid demonstration of the fact that the radio was a powerful rival of the press, perhaps now superior, as a means of reaching the public without incurring the perils of editorial emphasis or distortion.

Having waved the press aside, Justice Black, on the appointed night, laid his case before an audience estimated at fifty million people. He began by a homily on the evils of religious and racial intolerance. He pointed to his congressional record in the defense of civil liberties. Then, after a breath-taking pause, the Justice quietly confessed that he had once belonged to the Klan. But he had early dissociated himself from it, he asserted, and had paid no attention to any life membership card if presented to him. After referring again to his record in Washington and his services on the side of civil liberties, the Justice bade his auditors "Good night."

Either by accident or advertence, Roosevelt was at the moment on a prolonged tour across the continent. The pressure of engagements connected with the trip or a sense of circumspection may have suggested immediate silence on the whole issue of the Supreme Court, since no utterance on that subject could have allayed the excitement over the question of the Ku Klux Klan. A tremendous diversion of popular interests to some other theme was necessary to accomplish that end. Wittingly or not, the President made the diversion on October 5, the very day that Justice Black started his work on the bench, as a throng swarmed curiously around the Palace of Justice and through the corridors. On that day Roosevelt delivered at Chicago a belligerent speech against foreign disturbers of world peace and proclaimed a "strong foreign policy." By implication he denounced Japan, Italy, and Germany as dictatorial states threatening the peace and safety of mankind, and suggested a union of democratic nations in a "quarantine" against them. In a flash this address to mankind crowded "the Black affair" into an obscure place in the newspapers. One Roman holiday was substituted for another.

Since the possibility of a second world Armageddon for democracy was offered to thought, lively imaginations could hear the war drums throbbing in the distance. The effect was instantaneous. Emotions were channeled into other outlets. Powerful newspapers that had consumed a forest of trees in rebelling against the appointment of Justice Black now joined in a shout of commendation for the President's gesture of grandeur on the world stage. Even Colonel Frank Knox who, as the Republican candidate for Vice President in 1936, had almost invoked curses on his head, now praised his statesmanship in foreign affairs. Governor Landon, not to be outdone, pronounced his benediction. Fervent advocates of "collective action" against dictatorships quieted for the moment any feelings of rage they may have nursed against Justice Black and hailed the dawn of a new day in international relations. If a multitude of people shrank from the idea of another world war, President Roosevelt's Chicago speech certainly blanketed the sullen grumblings over the Black episode.

Undisturbed, according to outward signs, by the noise in the country, the Supreme Court received Justice Black into membership and went on its way. It dismissed protests lodged against his eligibility and turned to its regular business. Finding himself shifted to the minority by recent veerings in jurisprudence, Justice Sutherland resigned near the close of the year and his place was taken by Stanley Reed who, as Solicitor General, had argued before the Court in favor of sustaining the validity of New Deal legislation. So minded and so constituted, the Supreme Court, before its adjournment in the spring of 1938, rendered a number of decisions in line with legislative tendencies, with Justice Black frequently dissenting on the ground that too much caution governed the divagation.

The Court refused to allow power companies to stop federal loans made to municipalities for the purpose of building competing plants. Setting aside a long line of reasoning, it held that certain officials and other persons connected with state and local activities were subject to federal income taxes. Utility holding companies were instructed to register with the Securities and Exchange Commission and to disclose their financial operations as provided by law. On vital points of authority, the Labor Relations Board was upheld; and the Federal Power Commission was confirmed in the right to extract information from utilities. A decision in a California rate case indicated that the Supreme Court was putting behind it old theories of valuation for rate-making purposes and preparing to accept the prudent investment theory of valuation. Most spectacular of all, however important, was the action of the Court in reversing a previous decision ninety-six years old; in 1938 it declared that federal courts must apply state law, not their own law, in suits between citizens of different states involving local matters. At the end of the term only one major statute of the New Deal remained without some form of judicial sanction, namely, the Tennessee Valley Act.

§

Although Roosevelt's plan for the reconstruction of the Supreme Court was defeated, Congress did overhaul the lower ranges of the federal judicial system by passing the Judicial Procedure Reform Act before it adjourned in August, 1937. Somewhat obscured by the fog of that debate, the Act nevertheless conceded and struck at many abuses with which the President had tried to deal. It stopped judges in the inferior courts from passing upon constitutional questions in litigation between private parties without giving the Government notice of such impending issues. By express terms federal courts were required to notify the Attorney General whenever the constitutionality of an act of Congress was drawn in question before them, and the Government was permitted to intervene as a party for the presentation of evidence and argument on the matter of validity. Single judges of lower courts were forbidden to issue injunctions on constitutional grounds at their pleasure, as in the good old days. Henceforward such actions were to be tried in courts composed of three judges, including at least one circuit judge; injunctions were to run for only sixty days; and appeals to the Supreme Court were to be expedited. Indeed, all along the line, the process of appeal to that high tribunal was accelerated in cases involving decisions against the Government on constitutional questions. The Reform Act was by no means sensational, but it did serve notice on judges and private litigants that the business of the Government was not to be held up, delayed, and befuddled by shrewd tactics pursued under constitutional theories.

Apparently the contest over the judiciary exhausted Congress. Through the hot summer it grumbled and fretted in recriminations, producing no other legislation of significance for the execution of the mandate delivered in the presidential election. The Republicans, reduced to less than one-fourth of the House and to fourteen in the Senate, could offer neither effective opposition nor constructive proposals. The Democratic factions, more impatient with one another than with the impotent Republican remnants, were unable to agree on a single major bill bearing on the economics of recovery or reform. Tired of the impasse, they adjourned and went home. So the first session dominated by the victors of 1936 came to a dreary end. The barriers raised by the Supreme Court had been beaten down; the way for law making had been opened; but the Democrats in Congress could not unite on a grand program of legislation in fulfillment of their opportunity and their mandate.

Despite the ill feelings fanned by the debate over the judiciary and against the counsel of many advisers, President Roosevelt called Congress back for a special session in November to consider three measures included in his own program under the mandate: a national hours and wages bill, a comprehensive scheme for agricultural adjustment, and a modification of the Housing Act with a view to stimulating private building. As soon as the Senators and Representatives gathered in Washington, the discontents associated with the struggle over the reorganization of the judiciary revived and were aggravated by the demand for additional labor legislation. And for several reasons, leadership in the opposition to such legislation came largely from the President's own party — to which the mandate of 1936 had been delivered by the voters.

For more than a century, Southern statesmen had fought the protective tariff as a device for exploiting the agriculture of their region in the interest of Northern manufacturers. That cause they had lost. Now even Democrats would not vote for a general and drastic reduction of the tariff, to say nothing of free trade. For the South the next best hope of economic advantage had been industrialization, and a wage scale far below the Northern rate had served as a magnet drawing capital, mills, and factories from the North. To the middle class of the South, therefore, a national wages law, even with lower rates for that section, meant a bar in the way of rapid industrialization — another historic defeat. Nor, in fact, was the business of adjusting conflicting claims among producers of cotton, tobacco, corn, rice, peanuts, and dairy products a simple proposition for "the great Democracy" which had carried forty-six states in 1936. While Republicans looked on with ill-concealed glee, faithful Democrats wrangled among themselves and Congress adjourned in December without disposing of a single problem raised by the President's instructions, except the matter of amending the Housing Act.

The difficulties encountered by the Democrats in exploring the mandate of the preceding election were increased by a decline in business, euphoniously called a "recession," which set in during the spring of 1937. A precipitous fall in stocks and industrial production marked the economic course through the summer and autumn, with no halt in sight. Whether it was a temporary drop or the signal for a deepening crisis made little difference in the psychology of the hour. However viewed, the recession was embarrassing and, indeed, alarming, to the administration.

Having proscribed many speculative practices in business and on the stock exchanges, Democrats had fancied that the capitalist system would run more smoothly and discharge more effectively its alleged function of providing prosperity.

While industry had been on the upward grade, President
Roosevelt, not unnaturally, had attributed the good fortune
to his own policies. "We planned it that way," he had said.
Yet, despite his plans, provisions, and policies, production
had slowed down rapidly, more railways had gone into bankruptcy, and the army of the unemployed had risen again to
the ten million figure and beyond. Such facts could not be
ignored and the opposition made the most of them by demanding a retreat from the New Deal. It called for a repeal
of the high tax on the undistributed profits of corporations
and the tax on capital gains, provided by the Revenue Act of
1936. Just as the Democrats had ascribed the troubles of
1933 to Republican policies, now the Republicans invited the
country to look at the fruits of the Democratic mandate.

§

When Congress reassembled early in January, 1938, it
received a mild and general message from the President. No
startling suggestions for an extension of the New Deal program, no new proposals for tackling the recession, were contained in the executive document. Had President Roosevelt
found in the mandate of 1936 no instructions to make radical
alterations in the economic system inherited from the past?
Like President Hoover in 1929, he called representatives of
capital and labor to the White House. He consulted with
Thomas Lamont of J. P. Morgan and Company, Owen D.
Young of the General Electric Company, and John L. Lewis
of the Committee for Industrial Organization. He sought
their advice on policies and measures. Yet, if any major
decisions came out of such conversations, none was made
known to the public. From the White House conference
Lamont emerged laughing, as well he might, while his associates looked dour, as well they might. The Lords of Creation
and of Labor seemed as helpless as the President of the
United States to set the economic Leviathan in motion.
Having taken counsel with big business and big labor, the

President summoned, through the Department of Commerce, a conference of little business men and women; and they almost made a riot. They scored nearly every feature of the New Deal and with a vengeance called for the establishment of laissez faire. Only with difficulty were they persuaded to adjourn and leave the formulation of their conclusions to an executive committee, which toned down their resolutions with the idea of making a program somewhat palatable, at least, to the administration. The two groaning mountains had produced one big laugh and two small mice.

During the season of "conferences," representatives of the administration mounted the platform to discuss the causes of the depression. For instance, Robert H. Jackson put the onus on monopolies and trusts and demanded sterner legislation against them. His addresses, fortified by speeches in similar vein from other members of the official family, seemed to indicate a return over the long road to a "trust-busting campaign." The way to recovery and prosperity might now be sought in a retreat, after all the ridicule, back to the days of horses, buggies, village smithies, and crossroads stores.

Yet the whole country did not seem to be enamored of the strategy. Trust-busting had been a recurring political diversion since the enactment of the Sherman Anti-Trust Act in 1890; and the charm of the results had scarcely been commensurate with the noise. Entertaining doubts on this score, Donald Richberg, formerly sponsor of the National Industrial Recovery Act, spoke genially and diffidently of coöperation with big business. But President Roosevelt countered by exclaiming at a press conference: "Why have any holding companies?" And in so doing, he gave a temporary shock to those pyramids of American economy. Although he later added that he did not mean to wage a wholesale war on all holding companies, his discourse increased the uncertainty and discomfort of leaders in high finance. One day, business was severely criticized; the next day, it was appeased. Such oscillations continued until near the middle of February when at a regular press conference the President lapsed into almost complete silence on the battle over business interests. That, at least, was a novel feature of the political scene.

If the President, pulled first one way and then the other by his advisers, was confused in his own mind in respect of the new depression and the concentration of corporate control in industry, Congress composed of 531 minds presented confusion confounded. The great machine for congressional control set up in the easy times of Joseph Cannon and Nelson Aldrich had been broken to pieces and no substitute had been devised. Democratic members of Congress who sought to lead their colleagues had no huge corporation favors at their command. They could use labor lobbies for limited purposes, but these pressure groups were not comprehensive enough to effect a general control and they were split into three factions — the independent railway unions, the American Federation of Labor, and the Committee for Industrial Organization. The principal cement for holding Democrats together was political patronage and that was mainly in executive hands. To get possession of it, leaders in the Senate and the House had to make terms with President Roosevelt or the main dispenser, Postmaster General Farley. In other words, no practical method was available for overcoming diversities of opinion and creating a self-contained unity in the legislative body. Individual members of Congress inclined to conciliate large economic interests were in constant peril of becoming entangled in the engagements between President Roosevelt, master of patronage, and the "economic royalists," as he designated opponents representing large affairs.

Although Roosevelt made concessions to "the little men" — the ardent "trust-busters" — in his administration and outside, his record showed that he did not completely share their view of American economy and the best method for putting it into efficient operation. On signing the National Industrial Recovery Bill in June, 1933, he had declared publicly: "History probably will record the National Industrial Recovery Act as the most important and far-reaching legislation ever enacted by the American Congress. It represents a supreme effort to stabilize for all time the many factors which make for the prosperity of the nation and the preservation of American standards. Its goal is the assurance of a reasonable profit to industry and living wages for labor with the elimination of the piratical methods and practices which have not only harassed honest business but also contributed to the ills of labor." In his annual message to Congress in January, 1937, he had expressed a similar conviction: "Sober second thought confirms most of us in the belief that the broad objectives of the National Recovery Act were sound. . . . The statute of N. R. A. has been outlawed. The problems have not. They are still with us." At the bottom of his mind, President Roosevelt had evidently decided that some kind of collective effort, not disruptive actions, furnished the fullest promise of success in setting economy in high speed.

In general, Congress was in a mood of hostility toward the corporate concentration which dominated large and strategic areas of economic enterprise and in this respect Republicans differed little, if any, from Democrats. As a matter of fact in the preceding campaign the Republicans had denounced monopolies and trusts more explicitly than had the Democrats and had called for drastic legislation to tear them apart and enforce competition. With such doctrines a majority of Democrats in both houses doubtless agreed. Though fifty years' experience had demonstrated that it was easier to condemn corporations and monopolies than to dissolve them or indeed put any brake on their growth, the politicians remained adamant in their opposition, at least for rhetorical purposes. Even so, a growing number of Senators and Representatives with progressive inclinations were becoming convinced that the favorite political sport of "baiting the trusts" was dangerous as well as obsolete, especially in the face of contracting capitalism and rising unemployment. Believing that capacity production could not be attained without the active participation of large corporate concerns, they were disposed to search for methods of coöperation rather than for weapons of destruction.

Recognizing the utility of caution in dealing with the central issue of the time, President Roosevelt surveyed the so-called monopoly problem from all sides, in a special message to Congress in April, 1938. In perhaps the most penetrating economic document ever drafted in the White House, the President reviewed the whole ground of concentration in corporate control and wealth and coupled the economic aspects of the situation with their significance for political democracy. He described and illustrated by figures the growing centralization of corporate power in the United States and showed that depressions had a tendency to accelerate rather than retard this movement. In the second section of his message the President dealt with the increasing centralization in financial control over industry, which made even more marked the unified character of American economy. Having presented a survey of the leading facts, Roosevelt came to "the choice before us." Under this head the importance of a thorough-going study was emphasized and a few broad suggestions were set forth: antitrust laws and procedures should be improved and strengthened, additional financial control invoked, the function of trade associations defined and clarified, patent laws amended, and taxation adjusted to the stimulation of competitive enterprise.

Although the President gave his monopoly message an antitrust cast, he spoke of that "approach" as "traditional," pointed out the need for a fundamental examination of the entire problem, and suggested to Congress ways and means of prosecuting that investigation. He warned "those who sincerely want to preserve the system of private enterprise for profit" that the inquiry was long overdue. To this warning he added a more portentous caveat: "No people, least of all a democratic people, will be content to go without work or to accept some standard of living which obviously and woefully falls short of their capacity to produce."

Nothing was more evident in the statistical returns of each day than the fact that American industry was operating at a level far below the level of capacity. It had been operating under that level even in 1928. It had thumped and dragged along near the bottom for four or five years. The revival of 1936 had been followed by another downward swoop and the precipitous drift was painfully obvious in the spring of 1938. In prosperous times President Roosevelt's reference to productive capacity might have passed as academic. In the circumstances it struck into a powerful and agitated stream of American thought.

In respect of politics, no less important than economics — parts of the same thing — President Roosevelt was also emphatic and monitory. Without mentioning the name of the author, he quoted a passage from that mighty Whig philosopher, Daniel Webster: "The freest government, if it could exist, would not be long acceptable if the tendency of the laws were to create a rapid accumulation of property in a few hands, and to render the great mass of the population dependent and penniless." That was a political axiom accepted by leading thinkers among the founders of the American republic, ranging from John Adams to Thomas Jefferson, from extreme right to extreme left. For many years, however, it had been neglected. Now Roosevelt placed it in juxtaposition with official figures showing the rapid accumulation of property in a few hands, as things stood in the fifth year of the New Deal, just after the hundred and fiftieth anniversary of the signing of the Constitution had been celebrated. Still he refrained from adding to his quotation from Webster the very next sentences of the original speech delivered in the Massachusetts convention of 1820: "In such a case [of accumulation and poverty], the popular power must break in upon the rights of property, or else the influence of property must limit and control the exercise of popular power. Universal suffrage, for example, could not long exist in a community where there was great inequality of property." Anyway it was suspected that the President had read and pondered the whole of Webster's thesis, especially as in an earlier paragraph of his message he referred to "unhappy events abroad" — the conquest of democracy by fascism.

Engrossed in their own concerns, members of Congress gave little heed to warnings from the White House. At the moment they were more inclined to spurn executive recommendations than to welcome them, except when it came to voting billions for pump priming and naval expansion. With a great display of oratory condemning dictatorships, the House of Representatives defeated the President's bill for the reorganization of administrative agencies. An anti-lynching bill was destroyed in the Senate by a filibuster of Southern members. In defiance of the President and in response to demands from private business, Congress overhauled certain features of the tax system. It modified the progressive surtax on the undistributed profits of corporations, imposed by the Revenue Act of 1936, and also moderated the tax on capital gains. While he criticized these actions in a public address, the President allowed the revenue bill of 1938 to become a law without his signature.

§

During the early days of the second regular session it looked as if the seventy-fifth Congress would waste its last period in idle bickerings but before the adjournment in the summer it reached agreements on a few fundamental proposals. The new Agricultural Adjustment Act of February, 1938, made relatively little disturbance in lobbies and committee rooms, for it included within its scope cotton, rice, and tobacco as well as wheat and corn, and thus effected a certain union of desires among the Democratic managers in Congress. In general lines the Act followed the prescriptions of the law which the Supreme Court had declared unconstitutional; namely, the assignment of production quotas to the producers of the enumerated crops and benefit payments for compliance with the terms of the allotments. Coupled with it were amendments of the Soil Conservation Act of 1936, stipulations respecting the division of payments between landlords and tenants, provisions assuring to consumers continuous

and adequate supplies (an ever normal granary), the establishment of crop insurance for wheat growers, and declarations intended to encourage the formation of coöperative
associations among agricultural producers. A number of
staple commodities, such as dairy products, were not covered
by the law and hence the chorus of agrarian approval was
accompanied by discord, but the Act proclaimed again the
resolve of farmers to follow capitalist methods and cut down
production whenever surpluses threatened them with ruin.

No new National Industrial Recovery Act was passed to
serve as a companion piece for the agrarian law. Instead,
Congress enacted a bill for the investigation of the subject.
It set up a temporary national economic committee composed
of Senators, Representatives, and persons designated by the
heads of certain executive establishments, and instructed this
body to inquire into the causes of concentration in industry,
the working of the existing price system, and the effect
of government policies upon competition, unemployment,
profits, and consumption. The committee was explicitly
directed to make recommendations respecting the improvement of antitrust policy. So far its instructions seemed to
imply a mere search for new "teeth" to be inserted in the
antitrust legislation already on the books. An added phrase,
however, implied that the committee might go beyond the
consideration of historic remedies and make suggestions for
the establishment of national standards for corporations
engaged in interstate and foreign commerce. Here, at least,
was a sign that the outcome of the inquiry might be more
than a bill for the enforcement of the jungle law in competition.

The genuflections to agriculture and industry were accompanied by references to labor. Congress established a
Maritime Labor Board charged with the duty of assisting in
the formation, interpretation, and application of agreements
between employers and employees in the shipping business —
long a storm center of labor disputes. An act creating a Civil
Air Authority provided for the development and enforcement

of regulations relative to hours, wages, and working conditions in aviation. These special stipulations were supplemented by a general law, the Fair Labor Standards Act, popularly known as the National Wages and Hours Act, designed to apply throughout the country to industries engaged in commerce under federal jurisdiction. The Act looked forward to the establishment, by gradual stages, of a national minimum of forty cents an hour and a time schedule of forty hours a week by the end of seven years. Limited discriminations based on differences in cost of production were permitted but classifications founded on age and sex were forbidden, the latter provision meeting the ultra-feminist demand. The enforcement of the law was entrusted to an administrator in the Department of Labor and the administrator was empowered to make use of temporary committees for the several industries in arriving at immediate decisions and finally reaching the goal of the law.

The measures pushed through Congress during the endless disputes between "radicals" and "reactionaries" embraced three other acts of a general nature. A more elaborate Food, Drug, and Cosmetic Act was substituted for the famous Act of 1906. Authorization was given for a system of flood-control works extending from the Merrimack River to the lower Mississippi valley and westward to the basin of the Willamette. The work relief program was expanded to take care of an increase in the ranks of the unemployed and the "pump priming" process was renewed to cope with the depression. In all, approximately $3,750,000,000 was made available for these two purposes. General in importance, if local in geographical interest, was an act of Congress providing for an investigation of the Tennessee Valley Development, then in turmoil as the result of violent controversies among members of the Board, culminating in the removal of the chairman, Arthur Morgan. Whatever the upshot of the inquiry, it was bound to throw light on the power policy of the Roosevelt administration and give indications of national developments ahead. After Congress adjourned, the Treasury announced, on June 30, 1938, that the deficit for the last fiscal year was the smallest since 1931 and that the gross public debt stood at $37,165,000,000. Careful estimates made in July placed the deficit for the coming year at $4,000,000,000 in round numbers.

In this fashion the overwhelming mandate of 1938 was executed.

## CHAPTER IX

## *Exploring Domestic Sources of Foreign Policies*

DURING the tossing and pitching about that accompanied the search for an outlet from domestic difficulties, official and private investigators stumbled upon the sharp angles of foreign affairs. In some respects the outcome was a revolution in thinking about international relations, so called, for it had long been the fashion of American writers to treat foreign policies as a separate and distinct branch of politics. Such policies, according to their thesis, originate in the efforts of the Federal Government to deal with questions raised by the conduct of other governments and to apply, to emergencies of alien origin, historic maxims, for example, the Monroe Doctrine and the Open Door in China. As a matter of fact the official business of the United States known as "foreign" was by no means so distinct and separate from domestic transactions. In reality foreign policies and domestic policies for the United States, as for all other nations, were parts of the same thing and handled by the same government.  Policies classified as "foreign" had roots in ideas and interests prevailing within the political economies and cultures of the nations which maintained relations with one another, and scattered through history were illustrations of this axiom.

For nearly fifty years previous to the domestic crash of 1929, for instance, Americans had been told by influential politicians and naval officers that the prosperity of the United States depended, basically, on operations outside the country rather than on economic practices at home.  Near the close of the nineteenth century, this thesis had been used to justify the American adventure in imperialism; that is to say, "surpluses" of agricultural produce and manufactures cannot be used by domestic consumers and profitable outlets must be found through colonial expansion, sea power, and diplomatic pressures abroad.  Later, in the years of the golden glow, the American nation was informed by trusted instructors that markets for the goods which then clogged domestic commerce would be provided by the copious lending of money in all parts of the world — by "pump-priming" beyond the seas.  When imperialist adventure and copious money-lending in all parts of the world failed to produce, in obvious reality, a continuing and expanding prosperity for the American people, other instructors who enjoyed public confidence revived the Victorian creed of international laissez faire — free trade, "lower trade barriers" — as the contrivance under which to work the miracle.  At this point in time, however, that familiar device was being undermined by tough facts.  The glut in the market which followed the economic breakdown of 1929 led even the most popular instructors of the people to doubt the possibility of escaping the domestic deadlock by foreign adventure, by colonial expansion, by selling pressures abroad, by copious money-lending, by free international capitalism, or even by the sea power.

Immersed in their economic tribulations for several years after 1929 Americans, in places high and low, reached the conclusion that the source of their trials lay somewhere else and began to search for origins at home. Representatives in Congress, through numerous official investigations, endeavored to find out just how the great economic misadventure had happened. They explored naval and shipping lobbies, foreign loans, branch factories, the advantages of empire in the Philippines, the munitions industry, aviation, the merchant marine, and other domestic enterprises, with an avidity seldom before displayed in the history of American unrest. And in their searchings they uncovered domestic sources of foreign policies more extensive and more powerful than had hitherto been imagined under the smooth and easy assumptions of inherited diplomatic formulas. To reports of official inquiries were added voluminous works by scholars, publicists, and other private investigators, who dealt with the processes by which the world war had come into being; with the settlement at Paris in which President Wilson had directly participated; and with the consequences of that vindictive experiment in pacification, economic settlement, and diplomacy. At the end, if inadvertently, the conventional picture of world history and America's role in it was badly damaged and partly reconstructed with different lineaments.

§

By one of the curious occurrences with which history is crowded the first legislative investigation into the realities of foreign policy came as an apparent accident in domestic affairs, not as an outcome of agitations by peace societies. In fact, peace societies had rather consistently, if unwittingly, avoided the idea that foreign policy might have an intimate affiliation with economic interests at home and had largely confined themselves to preaching the word of good-will — though it so often seemed ineffective. On the whole, Respectability of every type, whether engaged in pursuing peace or the main chance, deplored congressional inquiries into the operations of private interests, even when related to matters of obvious public concern. But these traditions were given a singular twist in 1929 when President Hoover, with wide popular approval, sought to extend to naval auxiliaries the principle of limitation that had been applied to capital ships at the Washington conference. Immediately large shipbuilding interests were involved and, if it had not been for a strange incident, they might have successfully managed their lobbying behind the scenes. The strange incident was a suit at law brought by one William B. Shearer against shipbuilding corporations to collect his pay for propaganda which, he alleged, he had carried on for them at Geneva, where President Coolidge's attempt to reach a naval accord had been blocked.

For the shipbuilders the incident was inopportune. For President Hoover it was a clue and an occasion. Taking advantage of the partial revelation made by the mere filing of the suit, President Hoover excoriated propaganda designed "to create international distrust and hate," called upon the Attorney General "to consider what action we can take," and suggested that a Senate committee go "to the very bottom" of the business. It was a delicate matter. All except freshmen in international politics knew very well that the British navalists had been hardnecked at Geneva, that the British government would never rip into British interests through a persistent and comprehensive parliamentary inquest, and that the revelations of a Washington inquiry would be confined to American operations. Yet, if Hoover was not to be balked in his foreign policy, something had to be done to counter opposition at home. Accordingly the Senate by resolution instructed its committee on naval affairs or any subcommittee thereof to investigate the activities of William B. Shearer and the shipbuilding interests in connection with the Geneva naval conference. The inquiry was limited and a lukewarm Senator was placed at the head of it, but despite every care the investigation produced information of the first importance for the immediate issue, for naval policy, and for American foreign policy in its largest outlines.

The testimony and documents brought out by the Shearer

investigation, occupying almost seven hundred pages of print, uncovered a huge network of personalities, interests, and concerns engaged in making naval policy for the United States — and to that extent in making foreign policy. Eminent members of the shipbuilding industry, including Charles M. Schwab, appeared before the Senate subcommittee, underwent examinations none too severe, and yet told a story enlightening even to innocence. They had unquestionably furnished money to Shearer as their "observer" at Geneva. Of that they were sure.

On other points they were uncertain. They were vague as to his commission and could not remember many transactions of prime importance to themselves. Nevertheless they recalled that they had spent thousands of dollars on lobbying activities in connection with navy and merchant-marine promotion and had employed Shearer in their stealthy campaign. They admitted that the threads of the net spread far out into industries engaged in furnishing supplies to the navy and the merchant marine. The intimate relations between merchant-marine policy and naval policy they had thoroughly understood. They had treated the two interests as one interest and had spent money lavishly in bringing pressures upon Congress in favor of enormous appropriations for both kinds of shipbuilding. With this business, officials of the United States navy were vaguely associated by witnesses at the hearings, but the Senate committee refrained from bringing the principals in to deny or corroborate. Rumors of opposition between the Navy Department and the State Department were whispered, but apparently that subject was too mysterious for Senators to fathom or the public to consider.

Despite the restraints imposed on the inquiry, the hearings at Washington definitely showed that shipbuilding corporations had "orally" employed Shearer and had paid him substantial sums; that he had been notoriously engaged in anti-British propaganda at Geneva; that he had done his best to defeat arms limitation; that he had entertained naval officers and newspaper correspondents — all "for the navy and the merchant-marine." In performing these services Shearer had sent out literature discrediting American advocates of peace and had secured the insertion of his propaganda, under the guise of news, in such reputable papers as The New York Times. For the purpose of influencing federal actions, the shipping interests had organized a lobby in Washington, spent money freely, dispensed food and drink, maintained contacts with key persons — all in support of naval and merchant-marine bills pending in Congress. As a phase of nation-wide propaganda, articles had been prepared for publication in newspapers and magazines, lecturers had addressed patriotic societies and other civic organizations, the Hearst press had been enlisted, "experts" had been employed for activities undesignated, and speeches had been "doctored" up for the American Legion, chambers of commerce, and other agencies of power engaged in creating popular opinion and bringing pressures upon the representatives of the people in Congress.

Not less educational for the intellectual hinterland were the disclosures respecting the ideology employed to screen the profit-seeking instincts so interwoven with fateful foreign policies. In a pamphlet bearing the title, The Cloak of Benedict Arnold, Mr. Shearer had named names and classified advocates of peace and naval limitations. He did not exactly call them "traitors," but the implication needed no comment. Under Mr. Shearer's philosophy, "our country was betrayed by Charles Evans Hughes"; and Dr. Nicholas Murray Butler and Secretary Frank B. Kellogg were almost as wicked. Not all opponents, Mr. Shearer generously conceded, were communists or traitors; some had been merely deluded or misinformed — victims of foreign propaganda. They belonged among the "unrealistic idealists, the unsophisticated, and the gullible," to quote the epithets put forth by the Navy League in a release to the public. The true patriots, the sophisticated, the wise, the practical makers of naval policy and pertinent foreign policy were, it seemed, the great shipbuilders, their agents, and their editors; and, if they made millions out of their activities, that was to be deemed just and incidental to the promotion of a noble cause.

According to the version of Mr. Shearer, the shipbuilders' agent, at the very heart of the opposition to naval and merchant-marine expansion was a deliberate conspiracy fomented by sinister foreign powers. "From October, 1914," he declared, "the weight of internationalism and communism was developed, the members of which, pacifists, defeatists, radicals of many hues and foreign agents, communists, I.W.W., and socialists, included in the merger, and a dozen or more organizations with impressive names designed to fool patriotic Americans and lend aid to the enemy. Associated with these agents and organizations of these anti-American bodies were statesmen, Senators, bankers, lawyers, actors, directors and writers, men and women of American birth who were used to fight the existing Government of the United States. . . . All names, records, checks from prominent people in this country, instructions from Moscow, speeches, theses, questionnaires, indeed the workings of the underground organization, working secretly through legal bodies in labor circles, in society, in professional groups, in the Army and Navy, in Congress, in the schools and colleges of the country, in banks and business concerns, among the farmers, in the motion picture industry, in fact, in nearly every walk of life — this information and authentic documentary proof of a colossal conspiracy against the United States were seized by federal officers and are in possession of the authorities."

If Mr. Shearer as the shipbuilders' agent was to be accepted as an authority, then patriotism was practically restricted to shipbuilders, professional patriots, and William Randolph Hearst. If, as he alleged, federal authorities had authentic proof of a great communist and pacifist conspiracy against the Government of the United States and yet pressed no prosecutions, those authorities made themselves parties to the conspiracy by refusing to arrest offenders and purge the official family. The thesis was too gargantuan for American credulity. It was such a tall tale that it could not elude the American sense of humor, although there was no Artemus Ward or Mr. Dooley to dress the story up in dialect for the newspapers. Naturally, in their raw forms, the confessions, assertions, allegations, and admissions of great shipbuilders and their magnificent retainer, W. B. Shearer, were enough to make people smile. And smiles changed to riotous laughter when the Senators brought out the fact that Shearer had once operated a night club, had been "taken" by the police in a liquor-dealing affair, and had failed to make an income tax return on the funds received from the shipbuilding interests. In such entanglements had grand naval policy and its accompanying foreign policy become enmeshed. Not even toplofty editors accustomed to belittle congressional inquiries as "fishing expeditions" and "scandal mongering" could accept such offscourings of shipbuilders' propaganda as "sound Americanism." The spectacle was not ennobling to contemplate, but it opened the way for more informed thought about foreign affairs.

With terrific force the disclosures of the Shearer investigation burst into the headlines of metropolitan papers, creating especial consternation in the East where certain business interests favored a naval compromise with Great Britain. The mentality displayed by the shipbuilders seemed infantile to such capitalists as were accustomed to subtler procedures in achieving results. For idealistic peace advocates the whole affair provided a basic education in realism. Long inured to the habit of regarding nations as legal and rational personalities capable of establishing international amity by written words, without reference to domestic interests, promoters of arms reduction and war outlawry were appalled when the lid was taken off the Geneva conference and they saw what lay beneath the pomp and ceremony of official circumstance. Henceforward workers for international concord and opponents of entanglements in foreign quarrels had to reckon with shipbuilders, naval bureaucrats, munitioneers, and wide-ranging supply concerns in calculating the interplay of forces and pressures. The problem of national security and good-will among the nations could never again stand forth in its old and simple form as a matter of Christian brotherhood or missionary zeal — at least to persons engaged in studying the practices involved in any theory of solution. Moreover the elementary lessons contained in the new arithmetic and philosophy of foreign relations gained wide popular currency through the firm action of President Hoover in supporting the Senate investigation and in placing the seal of his authority on publicity for the detailed analysis of the material interests functioning in the manufacture of foreign policy for which American citizens were to pay, fight, and die.

§

After the Shearer inquest had started and while the seamy story was being unfolded for public benefit, Hoover made ready for the London naval conference in circumstances more favorable than those surrounding the ill-fated Geneva affair. According to news reports, the Government issued notice to American "patriotic" organizations, such as the Daughters of the American Revolution now closely affiliated with army and navy bureaucrats, to watch their steps. According to the New York Evening Post it warned them that "their alleged connections with the anti-disarmament agencies will be ruthlessly investigated by the Department of Justice should they attempt to interfere with proceedings in London. All 'big navy' propaganda agencies in the United States are said to have been similarly warned. . . . To the shipbuilding interests which employed Shearer it has been intimated that President Hoover has legal power to withhold further contracts from private shipyards and that the President will not hesitate to exercise his power at the slightest sign of defeatist agitation. Finally, the United States navy itself has been reminded that the President is commander-in-chief and that his decision regarding future policy must override the opinions of admirals." At last even Respectability was brought to book — contrary to ordinary use and wont.

While the temperature created by the Shearer investigation was still rising, Hoover's delegates brought back from the London conference the new naval treaty providing an upper limit on the construction of auxiliary vessels until the close of 1936. The document was far from satisfactory to the American representatives at the conference. At best it was a compromise. But it gave promise of holding down the race in naval armaments for five years. Still sick from the nausea of the world war, the peoples of Great Britain, Japan, and the United States seemed to welcome a pause, even at some inconvenience for Mr. Shearer's shipbuilders.

Nevertheless, in an atmosphere thick with the Shearer scandal, the Navy League, largely founded and supported in the beginning by munitions and supply interests, unleashed its propaganda against the treaty. Perhaps smarting from the exposure of his ingrained nature by the Senate revelations, the irrepressible Hearst sprang to the support of the League's counter-activities. In his Washington Herald, it was announced on July 7, 1930: "A smashing attack on the London Naval Treaty was fired by the Navy League of the United States yesterday on the eve of the special session called by President Hoover to consider the Pact. Heretofore the League, reflecting the viewpoint of the high command of the American Navy, has withheld judgment on the treaty. . . . The statement yesterday, however, issued by Walter Bruce Howe, chairman of the board, ripped into the treaty as jeopardizing American national security." Granting that this was true to form, the consequences were unusual. Hitherto the weight of Respectability had been on the side of the Navy League. Now it was divided and the Navy League, once able to dictate headlines and intimidate private citizens, was an object of contumely in high places. Its anatomy was uncovered — with additional results in the form of public education respecting the manufacture of foreign policies for which the American people were to pay, fight, and die.

Thus the stage was being set for a dramatic contest in the Senate when the ratification of the London pact came before it for consideration. More scenery was opened to view by the hearings of the Senate committee on foreign relations in preparation for decision and action. In the course of the hearings, Senator David Reed of Pennsylvania subjected the admirals who resented ratification to a "grilling," exposed their hearts' desire for an unlimited sea power, even riddled their "expertness" in technical matters, and gave the nation an inside view of the naval bureaucracy. Despite the efforts of Senator Hiram Johnson to throw around the admirals the cloak of Hearst's inflammatory patriotism, Senator Reed dug and bored his way through the mystifications of naval ideology and showed the country the inner meaning of what they were fond of calling "adequate defense." In the end the treaty was approved and signed.

When the issue of naval construction came up later in Congress, the conflict was renewed. The Navy League again assumed its role as national instructor on foreign affairs and again berated President Hoover and his policies. It charged him with "exhibiting abysmal ignorance of why navies are maintained" and with knowingly serving British and Japanese interests "to the prejudice of analogous interests in the United States, although the responsibility of the President is primarily to and for the United States." In short the Navy League, serving as the mouthpiece for a small private organization and a faction in the official bureaucracy, came near to accusing the President of deliberate treason.

That was going far, in view of the recent testimony at the Shearer investigation. And, on behalf of the administration, a reply came in the House of Representatives from no less an authority than the chairman of the subcommittee on naval appropriations: "The issue right now becomes larger than the Navy League and resolves itself into whether or not the country shall have regard for actual naval needs and for the burdens of taxation that rest upon the people, as the President insists, or, ignoring national welfare, turn the Federal Treasury over to the exploitation of those who have personal ends to serve — navy yards and shipbuilders, aircraft and munition manufacturers — and to some extent officers who are blinded by personal interest in seeking their own ends." In the upper chamber, Senator Arthur Capper plunged into the fray and rebuked the Navy League for claiming to be a "patriotic" organization. "The country," he said, "should be grateful to President Hoover for having torn off its mask and shown it to us as the greedy commercial organization that it is — seeking to make excessive profits from the Government for steel and shipbuilding companies under the plea of superpatriotism."

For a moment prophecies were made that there was to be a congressional investigation of the underground relations between commercial interests and the naval bureaucracy in the manufacture of foreign policies. But, as if fearing the educative effect of such an inquiry upon the country, the leading participants on both sides patched up a kind of truce. Even so, Pandora's box had been torn open. In the recent history of American naval and foreign policies no President had asserted such an unqualified civilian supremacy over the Navy Department. If the public soon forgot it, the shipbuilding interests did not. In the campaign of 1932 representatives of those interests were readily enlisted against Hoover by Democratic campaign managers and their affections and hopes were transferred to Franklin D. Roosevelt who was advertised, and correctly, as "ship-minded." Although after the election of that year, the naval supply concerns received the largest golden stream from the Federal Treasury in all their history, the scars of the conflict waged under President Hoover remained in the record. If the shipbuilding concerns that financed Mr. Shearer's propaganda and later contributed to the Democratic campaign fund could gloat over bigger and better naval construction, that part of the public given to remembering in matters of domestic-foreign policy applied the knowledge they had acquired to the education of those who could endure the process.

§

Only a few days after the Shearer investigation closed, another Senate inquiry involving a phase of foreign policy was launched under the heading: "Independence of the Philippines." This also raised the question of sea power and its covering ideology in relation to the Pacific Ocean and Asia. It likewise brought out into broad daylight economic interests underlying the formulas of diplomacy and empire in the Orient. In striking contrast to the Shearer inquest, however, the examination of the Philippines situation encountered the strong and continuing opposition of President Hoover, the State Department, and the War Department, as well as of the Navy Department. Ranks once divided now merged, for the new inquest touched a network of interests and potentials far wider than any mild "limitation" of naval armaments advocated by pacifists. It promised to expose the morphology of Imperialism, America as a World Power, the White Man's Burden, and America's Coming of Age, so applauded in the martial days of William McKinley, John Hay, and Theodore Roosevelt.

The imperialists of 1898 had assured the country that trade would follow the flag and that outlets would be found for the "surpluses" of American farms and factories, but the test of experience had blasted the promise. Whatever industrial and commercial capitalists had got out of the excursion into the Philippines under the banners of war, American farmers were sure that they had got nothing; that they had, indeed, suffered severe losses from the competition of Philippine raw products in the American market. Frankly scorned by President Coolidge and treated with frosty tolerance by President Hoover, the agrarians were now resolutely bent on securing "farm relief" and they thought that the Philippines lay in the way. It was their insistence that forced the resolution for an investigation of the Philippines through the Senate, and when the hearings started their agents were present in full force.

On both sides noble sentiments respecting American outward politics were expressed to the listening Senators. Spokesmen for farmers and organized labor reminded them of the high ideals put forward when the Philippines were annexed and the insurgent revolt crushed by arms; of the pledges of independence repeatedly made by statesmen. The great principles of the Declaration of Independence were to be applied by granting full liberty to the Islands — and by erecting tariff barriers against their agricultural products.

On the other hand, agents of commercial and industrial interests placed their emphasis on "our moral obligations" in the premises, on "ethical grounds," and on "our responsibility" for defending "our" distant wards against predatory neighbors. Journalists and politicians who lifted their voices against the granting of independence to the Philippines gravely discussed the balance of power in the Pacific, the perils likely to arise from giving the natives of the Far East an example of emancipation, and the disturbing effects of experiments in democracy in that quarter of the globe. To some of them it seemed that the fate of the British Empire was at stake and that, if the United States should "scuttle and run," British and Dutch dominion in the East would be jeopardized. That state of affairs they contemplated with horror as directly involving American responsibility.

But underneath the lofty verbalism the substance of many things was visible. Speaking for the Farm Bureau Federation, Chester H. Gray presented a resolution of his organization reading as follows: "It is an idle gesture to place even high rates of duty on farm commodities and then allow such commodities or substitutes therefor to enter our markets, duty free, from our so-called colonies or dependencies. Therefore, we favor immediate independence for such dependencies." If that could not be allowed, the Federation demanded that the tariff duties on Philippine products be raised as high as those "applicable to similar products from foreign nations."

This statement was surely explicit enough. "Do not understand," Mr. Gray explained, "that the farmers of America approach this question wholly from the economic point of view. They are not forgetting the historic point of view or the humanitarian point of view," namely, the long-standing promises of independence contained in official statements scattered through the years from McKinley to Coolidge. The structure of their ideas and the structure of their interests coincided with impressive exactness. Arguments delivered by the anti-imperialists in 1900 without producing any noticeable effect on policy now seemed to have more weight with Senators of the United States.

Speaking before the committee for the American Federation of Labor, W. C. Hushing, its legislative representative, also advanced moral and economic reasons for granting independence to the Philippines. Since 1898 the Federation had consistently opposed "forcing our system of government upon an unwilling people." Later its members began to feel the pressure from commodities produced in the Islands and the competition of laborers who migrated to the United States. "The desire for cheap labor has acted like a cancer in American private and public life, destroying American ideals and preventing the development of a nation based on racial unity." A schedule taken from a publication issued by the Philippine-American Chamber of Commerce showed that the minimum daily wages of laborers in the Islands ranged from twenty cents a day for casual workers to $1.20 for mechanics. Special efforts had been made to induce Filipinos to enter the United States for the purpose of enjoying "the great prosperity existing there." Like organized agriculture, organized labor was willing to accept restrictions on imports and on immigrants, but it preferred complete independence for the Philippines. Thus two masterful interests, not to be minimized by Congress, were thrown on the side of "fulfilling the historic pledge."

To these arguments, commercial and financial concerns filed objections. They presented a case against the granting of independence — emphasizing grounds of moral responsibility. If the retention of the Islands was impossible, final adjustments should not be allowed to have an adverse effect upon their business, they contended; and four prime considerations — two of them connected with naval and military affairs — were offered in support of this claim. The erection of trade barriers between the Philippines and the United States would be "a blow at the American merchant marine." By reducing the import of coconut oil, it would strike at "a source of glycerin for the manufacture of explosives." The agrarian argument that Philippine raw materials competed with domestic products was not well founded, in their opinion; at all events business interests had as good a right to protection by the Government as the interests arrayed across the line.

With pertinent bluntness the president of the Philippine-American Chamber of Commerce declared: "Assuming for the purpose of the argument that our interests are selfish, I ask in what respect do they differ from the interests of the representatives of other organizations which have appeared before your committee?" The question was relevant and it brought forth a balance-sheet of interests in which the commercial and financial advantages of empire looked small.

In summarizing the parallel exhibits, Senator Hawes described the political upshot: "To put it on a selfish basis, if you please, 5,000,000 union [labor] men, represented by their national organizations; all the farm and dairy organizations in the United States; and, in so far as it could be given, the best sugar raisers of eleven states, the cane sugar industry of one state, and capital representing not millions, but two billions, as I understand it, of American money invested in Cuba, have all expressed their views. Put those things on a selfish basis. I hope this thing will be settled on a higher basis than that, but all those interests take a position exactly contrary to your own, on a selfish basis."

Similar economic measurements were introduced in the congressional debate on the issue of Philippine independence and an article from The Harvard Business Review, entitled A Balance Sheet of the Philippines, was spread upon the record. This article, by Rufus S. Tucker, an expert formerly in the Department of Commerce, maintained that the gain accruing to American citizens from Philippine trade was less than ten million dollars a year and that the cost of retaining the prevailing arrangements, even apart from naval expenditures, was many times the sum total of the private profits arising from commerce.

Exact weights could not be attached to the several specific interests aligned on opposite sides. Nor could the pressures of moral sentiments for and against independence be exactly gauged. What could be said with some assurance was that the combined votes of farmers and trade unions were not to be ignored by members of Congress. Things had changed since the great moral crusade of 1898 when "Americans were growing up" and America was assuming her place as "a world power." Against the stiff resistance of President Hoover, the State Department, and military and naval experts, Congress passed a bill offering independence to the Philippines. After Hoover vetoed the measure, the requisite two-thirds vote was marshaled to carry it over his protest.

When the Filipinos rejected the terms of the tender, Congress revised them and its modified bill became law with the signature of President Roosevelt in March, 1934. The new Act authorized the Filipinos to call a constitutional convention, draw up a plan of self-government, and pass upon the offer of liberty. Ten years after the fulfillment of the stipulations, American sovereignty was to be withdrawn. Pending the completion of the transaction, limitations were to be placed on certain imports and on immigration from the Islands. The question of a permanent naval base for the United States in the Philippines was left for later settlement. With such a matter of imperial strategy, neither farmers nor trade unions were much concerned, although the issues connected with that unsolved problem might be more fateful in terms of blood and treasure than anything they contemplated.

Whatever was to be the long-term effect of Philippine independence upon the shape of things to come in the Pacific Ocean, the debate over it had a profound influence upon domestic opinion. In 1898 the country had embarked upon a crusade to free Cuba and had unwittingly become involved in moral obligations in the Far East. There had been skeptics then — the anti-imperialists. But the election mandates of 1900, 1904, and 1908 had apparently, if not actually, set the seal of popular sanction upon the idea that America had "come of age" and must play a great role as a world power on the world stage in the concert of nations — for the sake of playing it, if for no other reason. The critics who had called the adventure "joining the greedy nations of Europe in a scramble for the spoils of empire" had been overborne and smothered. America became involved in the proceedings carried on by "the family of nations" — a family none too happy at the time and tragically disrupted after 1914. American sea power was to grow from naval base to naval base. Trade was to follow the flag. Outlets were to be found for the "surpluses" of American factories and farms. Such was the mirage in the good old days.

In 1933 the mirage had lost some of its charm. The outlets had not followed the flag. On the contrary, millions of farmers and trade unionists were protesting against the fruits of empire, calling them bitter and unbearable. Though the protestants may not have known or cared much about sea power, naval strategy, the concert of nations, or imperial obligations, they were positive that empire had not "paid" them and, by forcing independence upon the Philippines, they left American policy in the Far East and all its glittering phrases, such as the Open Door, hanging in a fog. By their action they also plunged naval and diplomatic bureaucrats into dismay and seemed to offer them no alternative save withdrawal upon the Alaska-Hawaii-Panama line; that is, withdrawal unless the allure of Woodrow Wilson's universal philanthropy could be employed to restore national morale for diplomatic, naval, and military excursions in Asia and Europe.

§

Before the effects of the congressional hearings and debates connected with commercial "expansion" in the Far East culminated in the offer of independence to the Philippines, the Senate committee on finance started an inquiry into another phase of empire — the sale of foreign bonds and securities in the United States. In what was lightly called the strategy of finance capitalism, territorial conquest was not always necessary to the gathering and accumulation of profits. Heavy investments in other countries — especially in "backward places" — brought returns, yielded influence over governments, and expanded trade, without the obtrusive use of the flag. If defaults led to punitive expeditions, protectorates, and annexations, State actions of that sort were mere means to larger ends.

Such was the theory of the finance empire. But the widespread defaults which followed the crash of 1929, particularly on Latin-American bonds, were followed by an upset in traditional strategy. They kindled popular indignation against domestic bankers rather than a frenzied demand for the employment of the army and navy in heroic efforts to collect from the defaulters. According to the strict logic of finance capitalism, American investors should have called for the extension of empire over the debtors and dollar diplomacy in the Caribbean had seemed to confirm that necessity. But going contrary to this line of logic American citizens insisted that American bankers be brought up on the public carpet and forced to tell how and why they had inflicted staggering losses upon "innocent investors."

It was this factual interest in the ways of American bankers, not a concern for dialectics, which dominated the finance committee of the Senate during its hearings, in the winter of 1931–32, on the sale of foreign bonds and securities in the United States. The hearings had not gone very far when they brought out evidence of an utter confusion in the minds of the bankers with respect to the benefits, significance, and consequences of their operations. Instead of making sure that the copious money-lending would redound to the economic advantage of the United States, they had been primarily absorbed in the pursuit of the main chance. Nevertheless their testimony demonstrated, if incidentally, that the promotion, flotation, and outcomes of foreign loans in the United States had a direct bearing upon the foreign policies and relations of the Federal Government.

From witnesses reluctant or voluble the Senate committee drew pieces of evidence which, when fitted together, presented a definite configuration. Collectively the fragments of testimony showed that finance capitalists, the State Department, and concession hunters operated according to a single economic hypothesis : It is the duty of the Government to promote foreign investments, concessions, and trade opportunities, in the routine course of foreign policy. Although the Senate committee could not get to the bottom of such matters as Bolivian loans and the Barco oil deal, it did discover Henry L. Stimson, the Secretary of State, acting as an intermediary in a manner neither dignified nor ceremonial. Disgruntled investors who held Bolivian bonds may not have appreciated the "diplomacy" of the transaction, but Senators and Representatives did. Readers of headlines caught glimpses of it. Editors all over the country must have been led to suspect the practical sense and fiduciary judgment of men in high official positions. Students of "foreign" affairs who were not asleep or engrossed in reciting their time-worn formulas must have been moved to reconsider some of their habitual assumptions. At all events the State Department as the attorney of private interests and the sea power as a debt-collecting agency lost some of their glamour as the public received a reëducation in the fine arts of banking, money lending, and huckstering.

§

Like the investigation of shipping and naval propaganda, the inquiry into empire-building in the Philippines, and the examination of witnesses in connection with the flotation of foreign securities in the United States, a long survey of the munitions industry commenced largely as a study of domestic affairs. For many years the American Legion and other organizations had been demanding that the profits be taken out of war, not merely to put a brake on belligerent propensities, ostensibly at least, but with a view to equalizing the sacrifices for war. A similar demand had arisen in Germany among war veterans, under the leadership of Ernst Roehm slain by Hitler in the purge of 1934; Roehm despised pacifism and saw in the limitation of profits cheaper, hence bigger and better, wars. On the other hand, genuine advocates of peace in and outside the American Legion regarded the profitable manufacture of armaments as a prolific source of international belligerency. They ascribed much of the friction and rivalry among nations to the pecuniary passions of manufacturers — "munitioneers" eager to sell their products anywhere, at any time, to any State or faction in a State, to friend or foe of their own country, to armies slaying even their own sons. Presumably, therefore, the argument ran, a reduction of profits will facilitate a curtailment of armaments and heighten the prospects for peace.

Thus many conflicting ideas could find refuge under the slogan: "Conscription of wealth and men." Even advocates of an immense army and navy for the United States and believers in "the inevitable war" found it useful for their purposes; if the populace could be marshaled against profiteering in munitions, it might be induced to approve larger military and naval plans for a total mobilization of men for war in Europe or Asia or both. Obviously no such mobilization was required for a mere defense of the United States and its adjoining sphere of interests. But for war on distant continents or in distant seas "universal service" was indispensable.

It was under pressure and with support from various directions, accordingly, that the Senate created a committee to study the munitions industry in April, 1934, with Senator Gerald P. Nye as chairman and Senators Barbour, Bone, Clark, George, Pope, and Vandenberg as colleagues. This is not to say that the project was warmly approved by the whole country. On the contrary the committee began to work in an atmosphere charged with doubts, sneers, and trepidations; accusations were even made that Senator Nye was mainly interested in turning the limelight on himself. Nevertheless, commanding a staff of competent investigators, among whom Stephen Rauschenbush was outstanding, the committee, for nearly three years, bored deeper and deeper into the ramifications of war industries, war finances, and war policies. And in opening up domestic operations, it detected corollaries in the conduct of foreign relations.

In the course of its proceedings, the Nye committee explored three special phases of the munitions industry and related activities: the structure and methods of the industry, military projects for total mobilization in the United States, and the economic background of the policies pursued just previous to America's entrance into the world war. Under each head, the committee produced pertinent papers from the files of munitions concerns, banking houses, and the State Department, and examined witnesses possessing special knowledge of transactions. In every direction the searches and presentations of the committee staff seemed to be thorough, except in respect of State Department archives. Although given access to the Department's collections of papers, the committee was limited as to the examination of witnesses and the publication of diplomatic documents. In the nature of things, the Department felt bound to protect the sensibilities of the powers associated with the United States in the world war by withholding certain transactions from public scrutiny. Consequently it was not exactly true to say, as was said at the time, that the Nye committee "went to the bottom" of munitions finance and diplomacy and gave out "all the facts in the case." Nevertheless its "revelations" were voluminous and long-hidden domestic sources of foreign policies were exposed to public view.

The evidence bearing on the structure and methods of the munitions industry, elicited by the committee, confirmed the knowledge of the subject already possessed by foreign experts and set forth in numerous European treatises. In this field of exposition the novelty lay in the American illustrations unearthed rather than in any additional practices discovered. But the total effect of the investigation was a demonstration that American munitions concerns had followed the patterns already established by European manufacturers of armaments in respect of "patriotism." American concerns had relentlessly pressed the sale of munitions to other countries wherever they could — not excluding potential enemies of the United States. They had opposed measures of pacification pursued by the State Department in Latin America and had fomented discords in the interest of sales. In the business of promotion some of them had bribed the buying agents of foreign governments or persons of influence with such governments. They had looked with disfavor upon all conferences designed to curtail armaments and had lobbied against the reduction of expenditures for munitions. American concerns had combined with foreign companies in pooling trade secrets, pushing the traffic, and distributing profits. In other words, the international character of the munitions business was once more demonstrated by a multitude of documents and witnesses. That the munitions concerns made enormous profits in supplying governments, especially in war time, was again proved by a wealth of evidence, and the practice of driving hard bargains with the Government of the United States in the midst of the world war was illustrated in detail.

During this phase of its inquiry, the Nye committee discovered that the official attitude of the War and Navy Departments in Washington did not differ fundamentally from that maintained by the military profession in European capitals. Army and navy officers favored the manufacture of munitions by private concerns, opposed the nationalization of the industry, and resisted the drastic limitation of private profits. They encouraged sales of munitions to foreign governments, on the ground, they alleged, that it kept the industry active, in constant practice, and hence in a better position to serve the needs of the United States in time of war. On such assumptions, war vessels of the United States had been moved around in foreign waters for the purpose of demonstrating the effectiveness of specific weapons and promoting sales to foreign governments. Army and navy officers, after retirement or resignation, had been given desirable berths in the munitions industry. Before the vision of officers in active service constantly loomed attractive opportunities in private enterprise. In such circumstances the spirit of coöperation prevailed. The Shearer investigation had unfolded a certain degree of affiliation between navy officers and propagandists engaged in discrediting arms limitation. By the Nye inquiry knowledge of such relations was greatly amplified, if still inadequately.

In their eagerness to secure an abundance of materials, army and navy officials had given little or no attention to the true costs of manufacture or to the gains accruing to private interests from munitions contracts. After even a limited inquiry into the matter, the Nye committee reported astounding profits in various forms of construction and supply services. It found out also that the Federal Government had little knowledge of these profits and no agencies for checking and controlling them. In one summary based on extensive investigation, the committee described the situation in respect of shipbuilding as follows: "The Navy has never examined the underlying costs or profits of the private builders. It makes no pretense of doing this. It has no staff for it. The figures studied by the Munitions Committee were all news to it. The Navy makes no attempt to examine the costs of the private companies to determine whether the profit limitation of 11.1 per cent in the Vinson-Trammell Act is enforced or evaded. That is left to the Treasury to do after three years, after a job is done." In the absence of accounting control, competition among bidders for naval construction seemed to be purely nominal. "If there were no conversations about bidding among them, there was telepathy. . . . In 1933 two shipbuilders knew and wrote down lists of the low bidders weeks in advance of the time the bids were opened. Mr. Bardo was one of them. Mr. Wilder was another" — two gentlemen who had employed the redoubtable Mr. Shearer in the campaign against naval reduction and in favor of ship construction.

Now, for the first time in American history, members of Congress in charge of military and naval affairs had before them exact patterns of the methods employed by munitions industries and the War and Navy Departments in drawing contracts and handling supplies. Furthermore, for the first time in American history, the War and Navy Departments were given a broad conspectus of the economics involved in their light-hearted transactions.

Under the glare of the evidence, testimony, papers, and figures brought out by the Nye committee, the heroic picture of many "Dollar-a-Year Patriots," so revered during American participation in the world war, shriveled into grotesques. Supply concerns which some of them "controlled" made exorbitant profits. "The committee finds, under the head of War Time Attitude of Shipbuilders, that the record of the present shipbuilding companies during the war, wherever examined, was close to being disgraceful. . . . They secured cost-plus contracts and added questionable charges to the costs. . . . They secured changes in contract dates to avoid war taxes. They bought from the Government, very cheaply, yards which had been built expensively at Government cost. In one case this was prearranged before the yard was built. One yard did not build necessary additions until it was threatened with being commandeered. Knowingly exorbitant claims were filed against the Government for cancellation. Huge bonuses were paid to officers. Profits were concealed as rentals. . . . The committee finds no assurance in the war-time history of these companies to lead it to believe that they would suddenly change their spots in case of another war." If, as argued by witnesses, large profits and high salaries were necessary to guarantee an adequate supply of war implements for the battle front, then the coloration of sacrificial patriotism was inappropriate for the heads of munitions concerns. In time of national stress, they had taken their pound of flesh — and far more.

From an examination of past practices, the Nye committee turned to plans for "the coming war." In more or less nebulous forms these schemes had been discussed since the close of the "war to end war." Before American soldiers were withdrawn from Europe, certain military officers and civilians had advocated the establishment of a large army based on universal liability to service — an army on the German and French model. Thwarted in this project, they did their best to attain their ends by the enlargement of the Regular Army, the closer unification of the National Guard, the establishment of training camps, and the wider introduction of military discipline into colleges and high schools. This increase in military effectives was supplemented by plans for mobilizing industries, labor, citizens, and relevant private agencies for a totalitarian war.

Army officers were eager. Industries, perhaps remembering the profitable experiences of the last war, were pleased to coöperate. But organized labor expressed misgivings. Advocates of civil liberty, recalling the "raids" instituted by the former Attorney General, A. Mitchell Palmer, proclaimed objections. The American Legion, while approving the plans, made some disturbance with a clamor about "taking profits out of war." Anyway the plans for a totalitarian mobilization had proceeded, were in process, and the Nye committee gave to the country a minute and accurate picture of just what was to be expected in the way of totalitarianism, Gleichgeschaltung, during "the coming war." For a nation that liked to think of itself as pacific, non-militaristic, and dedicated to liberty and democracy, the vision of its coming "day" was informing, to some extent shocking, in any event educative.

§

In the course of its inquiry the Nye committee discovered that "prior to our entry into the world war, a great deal of the sale, distribution, export, and also financing of arms and munitions of war was put into the hands of a few of our banking organizations." Under its instructions to investigate the whole range of munitions manufacture, distribution, import, export, sale, commerce, and promotion, the committee went into the financing of the munitions industries and the export business. It took up the study of such operations as they appeared just after the outbreak of the war in Europe in 1914 and traced the expansion of munitions and export banking down through the declaration of war on Germany by the United States. This procedure led into transactions of great financial establishments, especially the J. P. Morgan Company which had finally obtained a kind of monopoly over the purchases of the Allied Powers in the United States.

Inasmuch as the sale of munitions to belligerents and the granting of credits and loans to them involved pertinent policies of the United States Government, the inquiry advanced into a study of those policies in their development and of the relations of munitions-bankers to the Wilson administration. This was ticklish business. The exploration brought into consideration great personalities belonging to the period in question. It touched upon highly controversial issues and awakened slumbering passions. But the findings were of the utmost importance for the formulation of rules respecting neutrality and war trade in preparation for the possibility of another general war in Europe or Asia. And a by-product was a material revision of many historical judgments pertaining to the manner in which foreign policies were shaped.

This phase of the Nye inquiry opened with testimony and the analysis of documents bearing on the origin and expan-

sion of munitions financing after the outbreak of the war in
1914. To make clear the intimate relations between domestic
interests and foreign policies thus revealed, a somewhat
detailed recital of the committee's finding is necessary. On
August 3, the Rothschilds in Paris cabled the Morgan Company offering their services in aid of the French government
to the extent of at least a hundred million dollars, to be
devoted in part to "purchases of merchandise." To this
tender the Company replied that, owing to the uncertainties
of the moment, it was unable to take advantage of the offer
but it expressed the belief that in a little while such a transaction might be possible. August 8, 1914, Herman Harjes,
of the Morgan affiliate in Paris, cabled the Company in New
York, renewing the suggestion of a loan to the French government, though on a mere ten million dollar basis. In this
message more emphasis was laid upon the purchase of merchandise and the possible withdrawal of gold was minimized.
A small loan could be increased later. "Fear that if we do
not forestall others," ran the cable, "it is probable that such
houses as Kuhn, Loeb, and Company may try to do something for other nation."

According to the testimony of Thomas Lamont, "the
French government was then beginning to buy supplies in
the United States on a considerable scale, and they wanted
to have some ready cash available. That was the whole
thing." In terms of legal precedent, the proposed loan was
lawful, but the Morgan Company postponed decision and
cabled Paris that it was taking the question up with the
State Department in Washington. Three days later, Harjes
again cabled the Morgan Company from Paris, this time
proposing a possible twenty million dollar loan, perhaps
below par, at six per cent, to be entirely expended for goods
in the United States. Again the New York House delayed a
categorical answer and indicated a desire to observe strict
proprieties in dealing with the Government of the United
States.

Shortly after the Morgan Company lodged its inquiry

with the State Department, Secretary Bryan laid the problem before President Wilson, on August 10. He informed the President that the Company had asked "whether there would be any objection to their making a loan to the French government and also the Rothschilds — I suppose that this is intended for the French government." While the Secretary conceded that there were no legal obstacles in the way of such loans, he insisted that profound political and economic objections were involved. Loans would be taken by investors who sympathized with the respective belligerents and this would make more acute the divisions already existing in the country. "These expressions of sympathy are disturbing enough when they do not rest upon pecuniary interests — they would be still more disturbing if each group was pecuniarily interested in the success of the nation to whom its members had loaned money."

In time the divisions of public opinion might be sharpened by the money-lending influences. "The powerful financial interests which would be connected with these loans," Secretary Bryan reasoned, "would be tempted to use their influence through the newspapers to support the interests of the government to which they had loaned because the value of the security would be directly affected by the result of the war. We would thus find our newspapers violently arrayed on one side or the other, each paper supporting a financial group and pecuniary interests." With more precision no one could have described the forces of economic gravitation. "All of this influence," the Secretary continued, "would make it all the more difficult for us to maintain neutrality, as our action on various questions that would arise would affect one side or the other and powerful financial interests would be thrown into the balance" — a prophecy well fulfilled by subsequent events. Having presented his analysis, Secretary Bryan asked President Wilson: "Would the government not be justified in using its influence against the enlistment of the nation's dollars in a foreign war? The Morgans say that the money would be spent here, but the

floating of these loans would absorb the loanable funds and
might affect our ability to borrow."

Having consulted President Wilson and received his views,
Secretary Bryan placed a "ban" on loans to belligerents in
a letter to the Morgan Company on August 15, 1914: "In
the judgment of this government, loans by American bankers
to any foreign nation which is at war is inconsistent with the
true spirit of neutrality." Complying immediately with this
official dictum, the Morgan Company informed its Paris
house that it could not negotiate the loan to the French government. Besides observing the formalities of the occasion,
the Company accepted the idea that it was persona non
grata at the White House. During his campaign for nomination and election, Wilson had been put to great trouble in
disclaiming the "Morgan influences" connected with his
sponsor, Colonel George Harvey, and perhaps the personal
considerations still had weight in August, 1914. At all events,
Thomas Lamont did not think that his banking house was
regarded with special favor by the President of the United
States.

After the Morgan proposal had broken down, the question
of a loan to France passed to the care of the National City
Bank, a friendly neighbor prepared to work in a coöperative
spirit and to share its transactions with the Morgan Company. Public notice had been given that loans to belligerents
were under an official ban, but agents of the National City
Bank reopened the problem orally with the Secretary of
State. Late in September, 1914, the French ambassador,
M. Jusserand, presented France's case to Secretary Bryan
and gained the impression that the official ban on loans
would be reconsidered. On October 5 M. Jusserand informed
Frank Vanderlip, president of the National City Bank, that,
in his opinion, Secretary Bryan would not object to a lending
arrangement with the French government.

Desiring a clear and direct confirmation from the State
Department, a representative of the National City Bank
called on Secretary Bryan and received from him oral advice

to the effect that the proposed transaction had his consent. By October 18 M. Jusserand was convinced that the obstacles thrown in the way of money lending by the official declaration of August 15 had been definitely removed by the State Department. In making the private reversal of his public announcement, Secretary Bryan expressed to the National City agent "the wish that no advertisements of the forthcoming issue of French treasury bonds would be published in the press and he was assured that none would be."

Although doubly assured by oral promises coming directly from Secretary Bryan, the National City Bank, through a representative, took the question up again, on October 23, 1914, with Robert Lansing, then acting Secretary during the absence of Mr. Bryan. His oral statement the representative supplemented by a letter of that date. In the letter stress was laid on the stimulation of "the unprecedented and unusual buying that is now going on in this country by foreign governments and their nationals." But foreign credits were being depleted. "Lately we have been urged by manufacturers who are customers of the bank and in some cases by representatives of the foreign governments, to provide temporary credits for these purchases. . . . We strongly feel the necessity of aiding the situation by temporary credits of this sort, otherwise the buying power of these foreign purchasers will dry up and the business will go to Australia, Canada, Argentina, and elsewhere. . . . If we allow these purchases to go elsewhere we will have neglected our foreign trade at the time of our greatest need and greatest opportunity."

In fact the United States, at the moment, was suffering from a slump in business and, as bankers diagnosed the situation, credits to belligerents would help to relieve embarrassment all around. As Frank Vanderlip told the Nye committee in 1936, a newspaper dispatch in October, 1914, stated that "there were 100,000 steel men idle in the Pittsburgh district. That gives a picture of our industrial situation at that time. There was a large amount of idleness. There was great dullness in our industries, and there was every reason for us to stimulate those industries with an export business if we could." Other evidence of the depression lay in the fact that there had been a drop of about thirty per cent in the excess of exports over imports between June 30, 1913, and June 30, 1914. That an increase in war business, in lieu of other business, would help to lift profits and employment out of the trough was apparent to all informed observers and was a subject of general comment among negotiators.

On the evening after his conversation with the agent of the National City Bank, Mr. Lansing, as Acting Secretary, took up personally the question of money lending with President Wilson at the White House. As the result of their conversation, they worked out a formula which distinguished between "loans" to belligerents calling for bond issues and credits or arrangements for meeting debts incurred in the ordinary course of trade. The distinction was somewhat artificial but under this formula they agreed that certain obstacles, such as interference with an arrangement of credits or easy methods of exchange, should be removed. At the conclusion of their conference, President Wilson authorized Mr. Lansing to give these impressions "to such persons as were entitled to hear them, upon the express understanding that they were my own [Mr. Lansing's] impressions and that I had no authority to speak for the President or the government." The substance of this White House conversation Mr. Lansing conveyed to Willard Straight of the Morgan Company at the Metropolitan Club at 8 : 30 in the evening, October 24, 1914, and to R. L. Farnham of the National City Bank at the State Department on October 26. So the way was cleared for the flotation of French treasury obligations on November 4, 1914, and their distribution among banks in various parts of the country — the Morgan Company taking one-half the total amount and the du Pont Powder Company about half a million dollars' worth.

Thus the official ban publicly imposed on the Morgan Company by Secretary Bryan in respect of an earlier transaction was privately lifted by oral communications to bankers authorized by the President of the United States. The flood gates for the extension of credits were opened. In a short time credits grew to such proportions that President Wilson confronted the alternative of allowing them to be funded into term bonds sold to American investors or dealing with a drastic curtailment of foreign buying, if not a crash in domestic economy — that is, in "war prosperity."

Nominally Secretary Bryan's thesis stood as official. New York newspapers, it is true, announced in the middle of October, 1914, that there had been a "change of official attitude toward European loans" as "admitted in a high authoritative quarter," "on the highest authority." Yet the State Department gave out no official confirmation of this "news." On the contrary, in a letter to Senator William Stone on its money-lending policy, Secretary Bryan, over the protest of Mr. Lansing, declared on January 20, 1915, that his ruling of August 15, 1914, was still in effect. Not until March 31, 1915, was it officially and publicly stated that the Government had changed its ruling and had approved the extension of credits to belligerents while still maintaining the official ban on "loans" to belligerents. How this transformation had been effected was not made known to the public until January, 1936.

By the midsummer of 1915 the Allies had apparently stretched their short-term "credits" to the limit. At all events the British pound was slipping down. The British government and the Morgan Company either would not or could not sustain it, although the Company in fact sold sterling, thus depressing the exchange. If the pound continued to fall, British buying power would decline and American sellers would be in straits. Immediately the entourage of President Wilson began to close in. On August 14, 1915, Benjamin Strong, governor of the Federal Reserve Bank of New York, drew Colonel House's attention to the slipping sterling and to the influence "gradually growing stronger to curtail our export business." Three days later, J. B. Forgan, president of the First National Bank of Chicago, an American citizen of British birth, informed the vice-governor of the Federal Reserve Board that the Allies needed more than credits; they needed a loan. What would be the attitude of the Wilson administration? Copies of Mr. Forgan's letter reached William G. McAdoo, Secretary of the Treasury, and Robert Lansing, now in fact Secretary of State in place of William J. Bryan who had resigned. The Bryan ban on "loans" still stood, nominally at least. Should it be dropped? If so, why?

In a letter to President Wilson, Secretary McAdoo stated his views bluntly: "Our prosperity is dependent on our continued and enlarged foreign trade. To preserve that we must do everything we can to assist our customers to buy. . . . To maintain our prosperity we must finance it. Otherwise it may stop, and that would be disastrous." Secretary Lansing added his plea. He sent to the President a copy of Mr. Forgan's letter and declared unequivocally that "the large debts which result from purchases by belligerent governments require some method of funding these debts in this country."

Another hour of decision had arrived. The President of the United States was informed by his official advisers, on the basis of banking advice, that huge credits, such as he had orally approved in 1914, must now be funded into bonds sold publicly. American investors must furnish the money to pay American producers for American goods bought by the Allies. If this could not be done, the outcome would be, Secretary McAdoo declared, "disastrous."

Facing this hard dilemma, fateful for bankers, manufacturers, farmers, industrial workers, American boys who were to die in France, and all the families who were to suffer losses on the battlefields, President Wilson made his decision — that the rest of the Bryan ban should be swept away and the public flotation of term-bonds for the Allies duly sanctioned. Obliquely, as in the case of the credits in October, 1914, the President conveyed his decision on loans to Secretary Lansing on August 26, 1916: "My opinion in this matter, compendiously stated, is that we should say that 'parties [the

Government] would take no action either for or against such a transaction,' but that this should be orally conveyed, so far as we are concerned, and not put in writing. . . . Faithfully yours, W. W."

In October, 1914, Wilson's decision had been "orally" conveyed, but not as his decision, to those "entitled" to hear it, namely, a representative of the Morgan Company and a representative of the National City Bank. Now that his decision of August 26, 1915, had been orally conveyed to those entitled to hear it, the way was smoothed for bankers to issue all the bonds of belligerents that the borrowers could underpin with securities or American investors would buy either on their own motion or under the stimulus of manufacturers and bankers already entangled in war business. By the spring of 1917 the outstanding indebtedness of the Allied Powers in the United States amounted to about $2,700,000,000 — scattered widely among citizens, industries, banks, institutions, and especially concerns engaged in producing for and financing the Entente Allies. The pecuniary interests of a small group in New York had been extended to cover nearly every nook and cranny of American economy, carrying along implications for the making and enforcement of foreign policy.

Before the year 1916 closed, bankers were again having difficulty in upholding the pound sterling, despite their freedom in floating term-bonds for the Allies. In distributing loans, the Morgan Company was encountering "reluctance on the part of some institutions." Its inability to forecast British requirements and policies and to answer questions respecting the exigencies of exchange "was very disturbing to these bankers." In short, it was somewhat in the dark as to the intentions and capacities of British authorities; and in a cable to its London affiliate, the Company expressed the hope that the authorities would clarify the grave situation. "Perhaps they have," the cable ran, "some undisclosed resources that we are not aware of, but at the present rate of going they will soon exhaust all gold available or in transit

and also available American securities, even going so far as
to assume that we can possibly secure loans up to eighty per
cent of the value of these securities."

In such circumstances, the Morgan Company urged the
British government to mobilize more resources in support of
the exchange and purchases in the United States, for British
and French demand loans and floating paper had reached the
straining point. What the British government could do by
desperate effort remained unknown, but its hesitations and
delays spread gloom among financiers in Britain and in the
United States. The war boom had carried American agricultural and industrial production to a high point. Every part
of the United States, important economic institutions, all
classes were entangled in its inflated structure. A severe
break in the exchange, a sharp curtailment of Allied buying,
or a crash on the battle front would have brought a decided
recession if not a panic. Informed financiers knew this.
Government officials were likewise aware of it through their
relations, direct or remote, with American bankers, if not as
a result of their own observations. Appropriate foreign
policies might be adopted.

To evidences of this situation drawn from various sources,
the Nye committee added a summation presented to the
State Department by Walter Hines Page on March 6, 1917,
a month before the United States entered the war: "The
financial inquiries made here reveal an international condition most alarming to the American financial and industrial
outlook." Then followed a description of the strained position of the British government and a forecast of a material
reduction in Anglo-French buying in American markets.
"This will, of course, cause a panic in the United States. . . .
This condition may soon come suddenly unless action is
quickly taken to prevent it. France and England must have
a large enough credit in the United States to prevent the
collapse of world trade and of the whole European finance.
If we should go to war with Germany the greatest help we
could give the Allies would be such a credit. . . . All the

money would be kept in our own country, trade would be continued and enlarged until the war ends, and after the war Europe would continue to buy food and would buy from us also an enormous supply of things to reëquip her peace industries. We should thus reap the profit of an uninterrupted, perhaps an enlarging trade over a number of years, and we should hold their securities in payment. . . . Perhaps our going to war is the only way in which our present prominent trade position can be maintained and a panic averted. The submarine has added the last item to the danger of a financial world crash."

The situation presented by Page's message on March 6, 1917, was verbally confirmed four months afterward by a letter from the British ambassador in Washington, Sir Cecil Spring-Rice, to Secretary Lansing, on July 1, 1917. In this letter the ambassador declared that the financial position of Great Britain was "of an urgent and critical character. . . . There is danger that the ability of His Majesty's Government to effect payments in America from today onward will be in jeopardy. . . . A collapse of the exchange will be no less disastrous than a great military reverse." It would throw commercial relations between the two countries "into complete disorder," including the cotton trade, "entailing the stoppage of the entire private export business from the United States." Nor was that the climax of the British plea. "Further, the basis of financial relations of all the Allies with the rest of the world will be removed, and a general collapse of credit and of all financial confidence will inevitably result." On such grounds the Allies were able to shift a huge burden to the United States Government after it had entered the war.

Yet in 1936 the Morgan Company's representatives sought to minimize the gravity of the impending crisis. They insisted that the British government was not at the end of its resources, that an economic crash was not necessarily impending between December, 1916, and April 6, 1917. Before the Nye committee they maintained the thesis that the

British had ample resources — gold, bonds, and stocks — which they could have employed as security for additional loans in the United States. Under this hypothesis, the British government had merely delayed mobilizing its securities during the period in question, for reasons none too clear. And there were grounds for accepting the Morgan thesis on this point of finance.

Acceptance, however, raised another dilemma. British citizens still possessed huge quantities of securities representing the ownership of enormous properties scattered throughout the whole world and, in consequence, control over commercial activities in other countries, especially in Latin America. The government of Great Britain could have commandeered these securities and sent them to the United States as pledges for additional loans. But it did not see fit to risk passing these guarantees of empire to American bankers and investors. In picturing itself as on the verge of collapse in July, 1917, it apparently falsified the picture — doubtless for the purpose of unloading as much of the burden as it could upon the Government of the United States.

By either facilitating or acquiescing in that operation, the Morgan Company was, wittingly or unwittingly, a party to the transaction. With its aid or silent consent, British authorities saved the equities of their empire, dumped upon the United States Treasury the responsibility for paying off huge Allied debts in this country, placed immense obligations for financing the Allies upon the Wilson administration, took back to Great Britain a large block of securities already pledged for American private loans, and shifted to the United States about four billion dollars' worth of British government paper that later went into default. This was banking — connected with war and foreign policy.

Such were the economic interests, pressures, stresses, and strains amid which the diplomacy of the Wilson administration was waged and its foreign policies were formulated. The American stake in the financial and military strength of the Entente Allies had swelled to enormous proportions after the

Bryan bans on credits and loans were lifted by President
Wilson in response to the persistent requests of bankers. By
the end of 1916 the government of Great Britain had a
powerful weapon in its hands. If the Department of State
had been intransigent in its protests against the high-handed
manner in which the British government interfered with
neutral rights and black-listed American merchants, a sharp
contraction in buying could have brought a partial collapse
of American economy, now geared to foreign transactions.
The Secretary of the Treasury, the Secretary of State, and
prominent advisers of the administration in Washington were
fully conscious of this economic contingency. President
Wilson was repeatedly told about the peril. Even German
ministers were familiar with the prevailing conditions. Moreover President Wilson knew that the German government
would renew the submarine warfare in case he could not or
did not compel the Allies to relax the rigors of the iron
blockade.

In the light of the documentation, the renewal of the German submarine campaign early in 1917 had inescapable implications for American economy and foreign policy. It
might still be viewed as "an outrageous and immoral act of
an autocratic power"; it might have been the revolting act
that turned the balance of President Wilson's mind to war;
but it did not stand alone as a cruel deed in a moral vacuum.
Inevitably the submarine campaign made still more difficult
the shipment of Anglo-French gold and securities to the
United States in support of the exchange and the continued
buying of American goods in enormous quantities. It increased the losses of goods at sea, adding strains to insurance.
It weakened the military potential of the Allies and recipro-
cally their financial potential. If the Allies had made a sharp
reduction in purchases, a terrific blow would have been
struck at American prosperity. If the Allies had been
defeated in the war or it had dragged on indefinitely, the
losses in the United States would have been enormous in the
best of bad circumstances. Temporarily the perilous state of

economic affairs at home was relieved by the entry into the war abroad.

§

In sketching the domestic background of American foreign policy in its economic relations, the Nye committee did not ascribe President Wilson's war decision to "economic causation." It was not engaged in writing history. Under its mandate from the Senate to inquire into the adequacy or inadequacy of existing legislation for the control of traffic in munitions and implements of war, it was trying to discover the motives, interests, activities, methods, and conditions that favored such traffic and their repercussions on government policies. And the pertinence of the committee's findings was indubitable.

The Morgan Company, it is true, by its own publicity, insisted that it had been guilty of no legal improprieties and that the Nye revelations were merely sensational and unimportant. On the score of legal proprieties, it was successful in demonstrating the correctness of its procedure. The matter of "importance," however, remained in debate. With regard to this point, the Company argued, the country knew all along that the bans on credits and loans had been lifted, that an enormous trade in war supplies had sprung up, and that an economic entanglement in war destinies had come about. That was undoubtedly the case. But the country did not know, until the Nye inquest was completed, that bankers had hammered at the Wilson administration privately until they had broken down the ban on credits and then hammered at it again until they had destroyed the barrier against loans. Nor did the public know how President Wilson had made his decisions and caused them to be transmitted "orally" to privileged persons "entitled" to have the information. This was both sensational and important, if not to bankers, to everybody interested in pressure government, in foreign policy and the ways of making it, and in the practice of warfare.

In outcome the Nye committee's findings spread distrust of presidential discretion in handling foreign affairs and stimulated the popular interest that culminated in the neutrality legislation of 1935. They deepened, for a moment at least, the general resolve to avoid a repetition of such economic entanglements and "to stay out of the next war." They hastened the disintegration of ideology associated with President Wilson's "war for democracy," the League of Nations, and "close collaboration with the democratic powers of Europe."

Propaganda for that version of diplomacy had been conducted in the United States on a lofty plane of legal and abstract idealism. By disclosing the secret methods and the economic backgrounds — the interests, activities, and pressures — of the Wilson regime, the Nye committee injected realistic knowledge into the consideration of dynamic forces shaping foreign policies. Whatever the final verdict of that shadowy tribunal called "history" might be, the popular idea of Wilson as the pure idealist who went to war for the sole purpose of saving democracy was shattered beyond repair. Could "the universal philanthropy" of "the great moral crusade" launched in 1917 ever again present the same aspects to that part of the public which sought knowledge and did any thinking? Many imponderables had been let loose by the munitions investigation.

Nor was the contribution of the Nye inquiry to the economics of foreign policy as such to be treated as immaterial. The Morgan Company could point out that Americans had sold about seven billion dollars' worth of goods to the belligerents, with the aid of bankers' facilities; but simple arithmetic suggested that the war would cost the American people at least ten or twelve times this amount in the long run and that their former associates in the world war still owed ten or twelve defaulted billions on the final account. If imperialism did not furnish the outlets for the "surpluses" of American factories and farms, if armaments and war proved to be extravagantly expensive rather than profitable, could any foreign policy whatever dispose of the "surpluses" and keep American economy out of periodical collapses? The quest for an answer to that question was accelerated by the Nye investigation.

§

Another phase of domestic business brought under critical examination was the promotion of the navy and the merchant marine in relation to foreign affairs. If the generality of the people did not understand that the two sea arms were linked together and were clear and open manifestations of a foreign policy, key persons at the center of these interests were fully acquainted with the fact. In congressional hearings on the Geneva fiasco and on the London naval treaty, this acquaintance was plainly revealed. And by other inquiries it was made widely known that, in the midst of popular confusion and neglect, pertinent interests had formulated sea policies for civilians and landlubbers who sat in darkness.

"All navies," Admiral W. L. Rodgers informed a Senate committee, "relate to national policies. For many years the national platforms of both parties in this country have mentioned an adequate navy. They have not said 'adequate to what' so that the General Board [of the Navy], which has been charged since its inception with the general characteristics and size of the Navy, has been obliged to find out what the Navy is to be adequate to." In carrying out this assumed obligation, the Navy Board formulated the foreign policies to which the Navy must be related and, in effect, set the patterns for the performances of Congress in making naval and merchant marine appropriations and for the actions of the State Department in the conduct of foreign relations. For fifty years the country had been pouring millions of dollars into the Navy, without knowing why, and at last the Navy Board felt compelled to explain the hitherto mysterious transaction.

The program formulated for the country by the Navy Department was certainly as wide as the world. The Navy, it explained, should have sufficient strength to support the policies and commerce of the United States and "to guard its continental and overseas possessions." The Navy was under obligation also to exercise "ocean-wide economic pressure." It was "to make every effort, both ashore and afloat, at home and abroad, to assist the development of American interests, and especially the American merchant marine." Another responsibility assumed by the Navy Board was "to have always in mind that a system of outlying naval and commercial bases suitably distributed, developed, and defended is one of the most important elements of national strength."

Although the Navy Board, in formulating and continuing this policy, accepted the limitations imposed by naval treaties for the time being, it held fast to the center of its philosophy, namely, the sea-power doctrine of the Mahan school. By implication and by intent, the formula meant that the foreign policy of the United States was to follow the course of commercial expansion, supported by naval power, to develop a system of naval bases "suitably distributed," and to retain the "overseas" Philippines, with the corresponding obligations in the Asiatic sphere. In sum and substance, this was the straight imperialism of the British sea power, borrowed by Admiral Mahan and substituted for the older continental policy of the United States.

According to the true milk of the word, therefore, national greatness "depended" on sea power, and sea power meant overseas possessions, naval bases throughout the world, and a navy big enough "to keep the sea lanes open" in peace and war against all offenders. It was a sign that the nation "had grown up"; that little boys had become big men. For a time American "experts" in the subject had accepted a second place at sea — after Great Britain; but later they demanded supremacy. Indeed, logic required that. What, after all, was the use of having a navy inferior to any other? An inferior position, as the fate of Germany seemed to demonstrate, was about as bad as none.

As the scheme of thought and action was formulated by the Navy League, the American navy must be strong enough to impose its will on any power or combination of powers in the waters of Europe, Africa, and Asia. But the navy cost money and attached to the doctrine of the sea power was the plea that it "paid." It opened and kept open the lanes of commercial and territorial empire which furnished markets for goods and investment opportunities for capital. Trade followed the flag. Sea power was, in fine, the wonder-working Providence that assured the interminable outlets for the "surpluses" of American farms and factories. The glory of power and the pleasure of profits were thus wedded in a union of perfection.

The merchant-marine aspect of the sea power was fully developed in various congressional inquiries. When sifted and correlated, the rambling evidences on this point fitted neatly together under a simple hypothesis: A big navy is necessary to protect the merchant marine in all the waters of the world; a merchant marine is necessary to the development of American commerce abroad; merchant ships are to be armed in time of war and the number must be sufficient to supplement the increased navy. To a simple mind this amounted to a simple proposition: We must build more fighting ships to defend the merchant marine and more merchant ships to augment the power of the navy to defend the ships. Collaterally, the merchant marine was to assure bottoms for the transportation of American produce at reasonable rates in war and peace, to furnish the navy with trained sailors in time of stress, "to give steady employment to American working men in ships yards," and to afford business to the supply industries, therewith developing skill and plant for rapid expansion in all emergencies. Again powerful domestic interests were enlisted on the side of world-spanning "foreign policies," with a view to enlarging the oft-cited outlets for the "surpluses" of American farms and factories that swamped the domestic market and contributed to periodical crises in domestic economy.

When all was said and done, however, the maintenance of a merchant marine called for huge expenditures of public money and thus affected the prospects and profits of ship-building, supply, and operating concerns. As a result of the heritage left by the Wilson administration, it also involved the disposition of ships left on the hands of the Government at the close of the world war. Billions of dollars were at stake. During the Harding, Coolidge, and Hoover administrations, the pressure of ship lobbies had usually been effective in Congress and the sponsorship of the Navy Department constantly in evidence. The grant of lucrative payments for the carriage of mails made by the Jones-White Act of 1928 had induced a scramble for "mail contracts." The air was murky with agitation. One investigation after another, especially the Shearer inquiry of 1929, had uncovered the methods of ship lobbyists, and news of scandals in the Federal Shipping Board and the subsidized industry leaked into the corridors of the Capitol.

Stirred by rising expenditures, criticisms, and uncertainties, the Senate instructed a special committee, headed by Senator Hugo Black of Alabama, to investigate "air mail and ocean mail contracts." In accordance with use and wont, charges of politics, snooping, and muckraking were immediately lodged against the new Senate committee, and yet with relentless persistence it steered its way through the intricate history of the merchant marine in recent years. Another mountain of testimony and documents was heaped up for students, practitioners, and all citizens interested in the relations of merchant marine and foreign policy. Again the newspapers felt compelled to crown sensational revelations with tall headlines and that large public accustomed to deriving impressions from such sources was stirred to criticism of folly and waste.

In its quest for the "ultimate consumers" who received the Government's subsidies, the Senate committee plowed through a veritable mass of holding companies, subsidiaries, and collateral beneficiaries — an excursion bewildering even

to adepts in the mysteries of contemporary finance. Although
the story of the business was not completed, a number of
chapters were established beyond cavil. Billions of dollars,
for instance, had been poured into the bottomless hulks of
the merchant marine during the world war and the following
decade, and yet the United States had no "adequate merchant marine." In the construction of high class ships, the
country lagged far behind the other great powers. If in the
presentation of this contrast some real achievements were
minimized, the general plight of the American marine was
limned in the statistics of tonnage, in the classes of ships
afloat, in the passengers carried, and in the mileage covered.
"Although the United States ranks third in tonnage engaged
in the international carrying trade, it ranks fourth as to
speed, and last among the principal maritime countries in
regard to the age of its ships."

A third-class ranking might have been accepted with some
equanimity, had it not been for glimpses into shipping finance
afforded by the Senate committee's investigation. For example, in 1923 a steamship company bought on liberal credit
from the Federal Government at a price of $3,850,000 seven
vessels that had cost the Government approximately $29,-
000,000. For carrying mail on these ships the Company
received handsome payments from the Post Office Department. As a "service" supplementary to its operations, the
Company organized a ten thousand dollar lighterage corporation. Besides paying large salaries to its officers, who were at
the same time officers of the mail-contracting concern, the
subsidiary garnered profits of more than a million dollars in
five years. Grateful to its president for buying seven ships
on credit for a low price, the shipping Company gave him
over four hundred thousand dollars in commissions. Between 1924 and 1929, it made profits of nearly seven million
dollars on ships bought from the Government, in part out of
returns from the lucrative mail contracts won from that
generous Government. Then, after a season of good luck,
the Company defaulted on its payments to the Government

for the ships and went on making payments to its president
in appreciation of his services in buying the ships.

To the records of tangled finances, bonuses for officers, and
high profits on little or no actual investments, the Senate
committee added new chapters on the pressure politics played
by the American Steamship Owners' Association and financed
by a regular levy on the mail payments received by the companies from the Post Office Department. Money had been
pried out of the Federal Treasury by lobbies and a fixed percentage of the money so gained had been spent to support the
continuance of lobbies for the same purpose. With funds so
collected, agents of the steamship interests prepared "news
releases," formed contacts with editors, enlisted writers,
hired radio broadcasters, bought popular orators, carried on
"educational campaigns" to instruct the country in the
patriotism of ship subsidies, maintained close relations with
two mighty propagandists, William Randolph Hearst and
Arthur Brisbane, and aided Congressmen who favored generous grants of public money to shipbuilders and operators.
The "right" materials were supplied to a writer for The
Saturday Evening Post. Successful efforts were made to win
the support of General John J. Pershing. "Dope" was prepared for a high government official in the Post Office Department and then sent out as "news" through the American
Press Association. An officer of an oil company that was also
engaged in shipbuilding secured the publication of propaganda articles in a great popular magazine. Through all the
ramifications ran the slimy trail of party politics; private
interests greedy for appropriations from the Treasury could
change their political spots like a chameleon and shift their
affections from defeated Republicans to triumphant Democrats.

Magazines and journals notoriously affiliated through advertising with the shipping and importing business attempted
to dismiss the findings of the Senate committee as "sensational and unimportant," and to charge it with "wrecking
the great enterprise." But those members of Congress not

dependent on the shipyard vote or on support from ship lobbyists were certainly "edified" by the investigation. Former sponsors of "big subsidies" suffered some loss of face and confidence. The reading public was once more jarred, momentarily at least, by frank testimony and confessions showing how private interests had burrowed into the Treasury. Their conduct had scarcely measured up to the lofty theory provided for popular instruction.

After all, the shipping propaganda had dwelt heavily and continuously on the merchant marine as an arm of the navy, an instrument of national defense, and a patriotic service. It might still be represented in such terms, but when the Senate committee got through with an exploration of practice, as against the beautiful theory, the shipping business was bereft before the country of that noble, sacrificial aspect which the lobbyists had insistently portrayed. Nor were hopes for American equality or superiority in mercantile shipping raised by the findings of fact. In the circumstances, Congress, without much display of enthusiasm, merely substituted direct grants from the Treasury for what had been euphemistically called "lucrative mail contracts." However considered, such sea power did not seem to "pay," and lust for it as a symbol of "national maturity" appeared to be diminishing, if congressional debates were to be regarded as reflecting public sentiment.

§

While the Shearer inquiries and the merchant-marine explorations were being carried on, a few admirals and experts in naval affairs began to suspect the gospel truth of the sea-power doctrine handed down by Admiral Mahan with the benediction of Theodore Roosevelt; and outside the naval circles independent thought was brought to bear upon it in articles and books. Questions were asked. How big a navy would be required to keep the sea lanes open to Europe if great sea powers at war decided to close them? If desirable from any point of view, in any interest, would it be possible for the United States to build a navy big enough to impose its will in the waters of Europe, Asia, or Africa? Would not a mere start on such a program encounter effective rivalry from sea powers whose strength was threatened? These were troublesome questions touching the technology of the vast ambition.

Other questions, involving national morale and practical economy, were also asked. Should the sacrificial patriotism of officers and men be enlisted in the promotion of profit-making propensities and the protection of investments everywhere in the world? Were officers and men to accept mere salaries and wages and to offer their lives in aid of commercial adventure? Was not the main function of the army and navy to defend the continental home of the American people and adjacent spheres of interest? Besides, did world sea supremacy "pay" as promised? The state of American agriculture after 1920 and of industry after 1929, the collapse of the Philippine "outlet," the scandals of ship lobbying, and the general disillusionment of the prolonged depression challenged, even mocked, experts in the theory of marine supremacy. The dream of commercial empire "sold" to the public in 1900 had burst, cracking the solid front of the sea-power specialists.

In a sensational broadcast to the country on May 8, 1935, Admiral William S. Sims repudiated, root and branch, the doctrine that it was the function of the American Navy to maintain freedom of the seas everywhere, to keep the sea lanes open for American profit-seekers in time of war. "The point of the whole business is this," he declared. "We cannot keep out of a war and at the same time enforce the freedom of the seas — that is, the freedom to make profits out of countries engaged in a death struggle. If a war arises, we must therefore choose between two courses: between great profits, with grave risks of war, on the one hand; or smaller profits and less risk, on the other. When I say 'we' I mean not only the traders themselves but all of us, for practically our whole population benefited by this wartime trade —

though we did not understand that we were inviting disaster
for ourselves and for the world. . . . We, as a people, must
come to understand that peace is priceless; that it is worth
any reasonable sacrifice of war profits; that a decent regard
for humanity must be placed ahead of gold. Therefore, let
every citizen who has the cause of honorable peace at heart
take this stand: Our trade as a neutral must be at the risk of
the traders; our army and navy must not be used to protect
this trade. It is a choice of profits or peace. Our country
must remain at peace." In his simple and cogent statement,
Admiral Sims pierced to the very center of the Mahan sea-
power doctrine — keeping the sea lanes open for trade profits
in peace and war.

But to what extent did Admiral Sims then speak for naval
officers at large as distinguished from the inner directors of
the naval bureaucracy and its supply interests? In a search
for an answer, the World Peace Foundation addressed three
questions to admirals and captains and received responses
from 130 of them. "Do you think the application of the plan
suggested by Admiral Sims would be politically possible in
time of war?" On this point naval opinion was divided
equally; four officers felt "that business acquisitiveness and
greed were more potent than patriotism." "If politically
possible, do you think the plan desirable in the interests of
the United States?" Fifty-two officers said "Yes" without
misgivings, thirty-six answered "No," and the others expressed doubts. "Are you in favor of the adoption of the
Sims plan as a policy tending to keep us out of war?" This
question cut to the core of naval thought and the upshot was
striking: "Sixty-two are for it, without reservation. Thirty-
nine are unqualifiedly against it." Admiral Herbert O. Dunn
took the position that "Sims' views, you will find, express the
idea of the Naval service . . . a majority of thoughtful
service opinion." Judging by this referendum, the Weltpolitik
of the Mahan school was dying, if not dead, as an active
principle of naval policy.

§

To the reports of congressional investigations and frank pronouncements of high officers were added the inquiries and findings of scholars and publicists engaged in exploring recent history and the roots of foreign policies. As a huge array of books, articles, and pamphlets demonstrated, a multitude of such seekers, armed with various instruments of research, struggled with might and main to discover just how the world, including under that symbol the United States, had come into the present passage. Applying their particular methods of authentication and analysis, historians examined the vast mass of documents released from secrecy by revolutions in Europe and by congressional inquiries in the United States and filled in, with increasing minuteness, the outlines of war origins in Europe and America. Publicists delved into recent history, compared theories and performances, and made special and general reports to persons accustomed to reading and thinking.

By 1927 the fortieth and final volume of Die Grosse Politik der Europäischen Cabinette — the immense pile of documents on war origins issued under the auspices of the German Foreign Office — had been completed and published. By that year the eleventh volume of British Documents on the Origins of the War had been placed in the hands of students, and the French were busy with their Documents Diplomatiques Français, the eleventh volume of which left the printers in 1936. Meanwhile the Russians were turning out papers, books, and articles giving the background of the mighty war as seen through the archives of the Tsarist regime. Into the main stream of new information flooded other papers, memoirs, and letters revealing details and generalities that had been closed to the ordinary soldiers and civilians who had played their part under the coverage of official ideologies emitted in justification of policies, actions, and war.

Written in many languages, frequently meaningless save when placed in juxtaposition with one another, often intricate and obscure even to the most highly trained adept, these thousands of papers and volumes made their way into libraries. Long before, Jacob Burckhardt had said that the opening of royal archives to historians would mark the doom of monarchies. Now these new archives, sifted, sorted, classified, analyzed, and pieced together by a host of scholars, marked the doom of all the simple explanations under which the world war had been launched, fought, and "settled." Practitioners, as usual, resenting the findings of the scholars, insisted that they knew better, and threw themselves athwart the streams of revelation; but, as Emerson had said, the State sketches in coarse outline the progress of thought. In time distillations of historical findings reached casual editors and readers, and even crept into the arcanum of the State Department where experts guarded the national mysteries.

Also in the wide open spaces of the United States reports on domestic sources of foreign policy circulated quietly but none the less potently. From library to library, from woman's club to woman's club, from university to university, from college to high school, from high school to grade school, from private study to editorial sanctum, seeped and crept the new knowledge of what diplomats, bankers, munitions makers, statesmen, and warriors had thought, planned, contemplated, fumbled, and done. Though imponderable, this knowledge dissolved the vision of diplomacy and war that had been officially supplied to the fighting, dying, and paying populace. Despite protests from monopolists of noble sentiments, it disrupted the grand fabric of official imagination; and men of practical affairs, protesting, explaining, and correcting, might not be able to restore for the coming generation the official picture of the grand foreign policies supplied to the war generation and its heirs. Once more the cruelty and justice of history were illustrated.

That all these investigations, searchings, and inquests exerted a material influence on the making of current foreign policy was attested by the commotion which greeted the neutrality legislation of 1935. Wise or foolish, according to the assumptions of philosophers and commentators, the neutrality legislation, coupled with the granting of independence to the Philippines, signified, at least temporarily, the steep decline of the imperialism sponsored by McKinley, Mahan, Lodge, Hay, and Theodore Roosevelt, and also punctured the universal philanthropy expounded by Woodrow Wilson. The failure of empire, sea power, foreign loans, munitions selling, and a war for democracy to bring permanent outlets for "surpluses" of farms and factories or peace to the earth was so glaring that the very plow boys and bond salesmen could grasp the fact. That lust for profits, facilitated in action by bankers, had accompanied the Wilson administration on what Walter Millis called the "road to war" was equally patent to the same personnel. Beyond dispute, the intellectual and moral setting for American policy in foreign relations had altered. The configurations of American thought, the posture of European and Asiatic nations, and the nature of "world economy" presented new aspects. Neither the imperial hopes of 1900 nor the philanthropic enthusiasm of 1917 nor the unbounded expectations of 1928 could be restored as sources of motivation for easy action by the President or State Department in shaping current policy. Some new mask might be needed for the face of war.

## CHAPTER X

### *Shadows and Shapes of Foreign Policy*

B Y the numerous inquiries, official and private, into the
experiences, interests, and ideas of recent and current
history, inherited conceptions of world affairs were
swiftly and extensively modified. Congressional inquests into
the making of naval policies, the financing and results of
heavy foreign loans, the management of the munitions business, the subsidizing of the merchant marine, and the fruits of
empire as they had ripened in the Philippines helped to re-
fashion the dream of America as a grown-up nation, with its
trade ever expanding over land and sea, with its moral obligations in the four quarters of the earth mystically joined to its
commercial enterprise, with its corresponding foreign policies.
To more than one keeper of the auguries, what seemed to be
the maturity of the preceding generation now took on the
aspect of emotional adolescence. And people at large could no
longer be easily satisfied by the facile doctrines of lending,
pushing, subsidizing, shoving, and moralizing as guarantees
of practical and ideal achievements anywhere, at home or
abroad. New raw materials were thrust into the operation of

434

thinking and image-making. Over them hung the fateful question : What is all this worth ?

In whatever respect the foreign policies previously applied had affected domestic conditions, the deterioration of national economy after the application forced a reconsideration of the old tenets. Despite passionate desires and efforts, the Lords of Creation, operating under these policies, had been unable to stave off economic calamity ; they were also unable to get the machines over which they presided in motion again at anything like capacity rate. Though the State Department, the Navy Department, and the Marines were all cooperative and helpful in the enforcement of "national interests" in all parts of the earth, they could not accomplish that feat. Was it possible then that the widespread crisis in town and country could be attributed, in substantial measure, to the foreign policies that had been pursued by the Government of the United States, to the false hopes that they had raised ? Certainly neither the imperialism of 1900 nor the moral crusade of 1917 nor the feverish money lending of 1928 had led to the haven of prosperity and security. So what ?

§

In attempts to gather up the old fragments and to formulate new policy, the posture and conduct of other nations, of course, had to be taken into the reckoning. To some extent, it was highly probable, the policies of foreign governments were due to acts of commission and omission attributable to the Government of the United States. For example, the procedures of Germany, France, and Great Britain might have been different if America had joined the League of Nations; but how different, no one could say. Doubtless the outcome would have depended somewhat on the types of Americans sent to Geneva as participants in the affairs of the League. Surely proceedings there would have turned partly upon their instructions and also upon the power set up within the League. Judging by the history of American activities at

various arms and economic conferences, American membership in the League of Nations would have brought about few
drastic changes in international behavior. Going over the
League affair, however, was like quarrelling with history.

Apart from all that, European powers, since the close of the
world war, had been engaged in making adjustments in their
own style. Great Britain and France did nothing effective to
bring about the general reduction of armaments definitely
promised in the treaty of Versailles which imposed strict
limitations upon the vanquished. Nor did they strain themselves in efforts to aid the Weimar republic. After the German government had conclusively demonstrated that it
could wring no major concessions from them early in 1933,
the republic collapsed. Adolf Hitler and his party of National
Socialists seized sovereignty, set about rearmament, reoc-
cupied the Rhine zone, repudiated debts and reparations,
left the League of Nations, demanded a return of colonies,
called for a free hand in eastern Europe, persecuted Jews and
dissidents, grabbed Austria, shook the mailed fist under the
noses of Paris and London.

If such actions mainly involved the European powers,
other decisions in Germany had a distinct bearing upon trade
and diplomatic relations with the United States. In the
course of the transformation wrought by the Nazi administration, German economy was placed, to an amazing extent,
on a basis of national self-sufficiency now called "autarkie"
(autarchy). Whether this changed economy could be correctly classified as state capitalism as some alleged or as Bolshevism as others contended, it was certainly not the laissez
faire capitalism of the Cobden and Bright school and it was
unquestionably controlled by arbitrary executive decrees in
the manner of Bolshevism. Irrespective of the name given
this new Leviathan, autarchy fitted neither the money-lending proclivities of the Hoover tradition nor the free or "freer"
trade conceptions of the Roosevelt administration which
came to power shortly after the rise of Hitler to supremacy
in Berlin.

To the disturbance of "free enterprise" created by the Hitler regime were added tumults set in motion by Benito Mussolini, head of the fascist state established in Italy in 1922. Having pleased American capitalists and travelers at first by "suppressing communists" and "making trains run on time," Mussolini, at the outset of his dictatorial career, had aroused no economic alarms in Washington — any more than in Paris or London. Dr. Nicholas Murray Butler had praised his labors and policies in florid language. Thomas Lamont had visited him and the Morgans had floated a big loan for him in the United States. As Mussolini had come to terms with the Pope and at first let Jews alone, he had avoided setting the world against his system through religious and racial agitations.

But after consolidating his position at home and straining every nerve to build up his army and navy for war, which he extolled as a positive virtue in itself, Mussolini directed his energies abroad, to empire-building, like a Roman Caesar. He refused any longer to play a second political fiddle to Paris or London, or pay installments on the Italian war debt owed to Washington. He had grievances to air. By the peacemakers at Versailles in 1919, Italy had been deprived of spoils of victory, which had been promised when the Italian government, after bargaining two ways, joined the Entente Allies in the war. At that settlement the peacemakers had given the lion's share of Germany's colonial goods to Great Britain and France and had refused to enlarge the Italian empire in Africa.

Remembering this transaction, Mussolini flirted with discontented Germany, prepared the way for a Berlin-Rome axis, defied the League of Nations, looked after himself, in the historic way, by seizing the whole of Ethiopia, and joined Hitler in helping rebels in Spain to wage war on the lawfully-chosen republican government of Madrid. Earlier, in 1900, when the United States was administering the "water cure" to recalcitrant Filipinos and when Great Britain was "extending civilization" to the Boers, the Italian dictator's ac-

tion would perhaps have excited less alarm in America, but a
change in interests and attitudes had occurred during the intervening years. To a large number of Americans, in 1938,
Mussolini's defiance of France and Great Britain seemed to
be an affair of honor for the United States. It was, in fact, a
defiance of the new morality, the Stimson doctrine, and the
Good Neighbor idea.

Events in Russia likewise altered the world scene and its
implications for America. For years the Government of the
United States had refused to recognize the Soviet regime,
largely on the ground that it had repudiated debts and in
other ways outraged the ethics of the State Department.
Deceived by biased press reports from Russia, the American
people had daily expected the downfall of the Union of Socialist Republics. But expectations had not been realized. By
efforts that seemed superhuman, the Russian government
carried out a five year plan for industrialization and drafted a
program in continuation. In terms of iron, steel, and factories, the achievement was monumental, at least as compared with the economic enterprise of the Tsarist regime.

After the suppression of Leon Trotsky and other self-
dedicated makers of world revolution, Russia settled down to
"socialism in one country" under the direction of Joseph
Stalin, joined the League of Nations, and sought trade on a
business basis. With the aid of experienced officers and foreign technicians, the Soviet government also built up and
equipped a huge army in approved Western style and its representatives sitting in the conferences held by the family of
nations could command, from colleagues similarly equipped,
a certain respect for their remarks on matters of peace and
international policy. Although, later, a crisis in Stalin's
system raised suspicions as to the real strength behind the
façade, by the year 1934 Russia had won a place in the concert of the great powers. For a time, her regime presented
signs of permanence. Her economic and military strength appeared substantial. An alliance with France, as in the days
of the Tsar, gave weight to Russian policy. With Japan

growing daily more arbitrary and finally lunging into war against China, neither Great Britain nor France nor the United States could be entirely indifferent to the possibility of aid from Russia, East and West, however unpalatable the idea might be to private and public business conceived in the style of the nineteenth century.

Thought of Russia provoked more thought of Japan whence a violent shift in policies and measures had sent tremors to the banks of the Potomac, the Thames, the Seine, the Spree, and the Tiber. To some extent that shift might be ascribed to measures adopted by the United States, especially the Immigration Act of 1924. With some reluctance the Government of Japan had broken with Germany in 1914 and joined the democratic powers in their war on autocracy. Given the tradition of absolutism and the cult of emperor worship in Japan, the decision had been a wrench for the Elder Statesmen. Nevertheless it had been made, and the Japanese had been welcomed as noble comrades-in-arms by Americans, French, and British, if with some wry faces. As a Tokyo diplomat described the innovation : "We were invited to the very best parties given by the very best families in the West."

That was gratifying to Japanese pride and for several years after the war an active, if small, group of liberals in Japan exercised a genuine influence in directing the thought of the people and the government toward closer affiliation with Great Britain and the United States. While their task was arduous, they made considerable progress. Yet awkward incidents made their path harder, and whether the drift of economic and military forces in their own country could be overcome by that foreign policy was always dubious. At no time did the military interest, more provincial than the naval interest, surrender the hope of regaining supremacy and establishing an Oriental despotism in Japan and on the mainland of Asia.

At the moment when the Congress at Washington moved, in 1924, toward the enactment of the immigration bill positively excluding Japanese from the United States, the conflict of interests in Tokyo was trembling in the balance. In declaring that "grave consequences" would flow from the passage of the bill, the Japanese ambassador to America spoke with full knowledge of the contest in his native land. He did not mean, as the American yellow press insinuated, that war between the two countries would follow. He did mean that the open and specific exclusion of Japanese from the United States would enable the military party at home to whip up popular passion in favor of "Asia for the Asiatics," that is, Japanese supremacy in the Far East.

Frantically the Japanese government, then under liberal influences, sought to reach an adjustment with the United States that would save the pride of its own people. It was willing to accept the objective of exclusion if something like the "Gentlemen's Agreement" could be preserved instead of a flaunting congressional fiat to the world: No Japanese wanted. The State Department at Washington sought a middle way, but Congress would not follow its advice. Within a few days after the exclusion bill was signed, the liberal and democratic forces in Japan were started down hill to destruction by the "insult." Convinced by many educative experiences that western liberalism was a cloak for imperialist operations in the Orient, the military party in Tokyo set out to realize ends long in view — dominance over China and perhaps over Siberia to Lake Baikal. The seizure of Manchukuo in 1931 and the war of 1937 on the Nanking government were in perfect line with the logic of Japanese imperialism.

As Japanese despotism grew more belligerent in Asia, the "front" of the Western powers in relation to China, never solid or stable, showed a tendency to crumble. The policy of the United States had been pliable, if not sometimes surreptitious. American enthusiasm for the imperial adventure into the Philippines had not been universal; and now, under the pressure of agrarian interests and the disillusionment in respect of markets, it had simmered down toward the vanishing point. John Hay and William McKinley might have been willing to carve out and annex slices of China in the approved fashion followed by Tsarist Russia, Great Britain, France, and Imperial Germany, had they not known that such overt actions would make trouble for them in Congress. In the circumstances the best they could do was to adopt the formula of "the open door," supplied to them by a British representative, and make it appear as a generous homage to an all-around equality of trade. In reality it was, as Tyler Dennett said, "a form of intervention in China," though in popular understanding it merely looked like "a fair deal."

However understood in theory by the popular and missionary mind, the Open Door in China was in practice a cloak for imperialist intrigues. Nominally recognizing the territorial and administrative integrity of China, it formed a shield for constant interference in Oriental affairs by successive administrations in Washington and in other Western capitals. From start to finish, the "coöperating powers," while competing ruthlessly among themselves for favorable positions in China, showed a willingness to unite in keeping China weak. For example, they refused until 1930 to permit China to raise at will her own customs duties on imports. Had this boon, this right which China should have enjoyed as a sovereign power, been granted early in the twentieth century, the Chinese government might have secured revenues large enough to sustain an army of defense against all foreigners. In that case also it might have developed the domestic industries necessary to economic independence and military safety. This achievement would have meant a China strong enough to resist the encroachments of Japan. At the same time it would likewise have meant severe checks on the arbitrary and aggressive conduct of Western powers in Chinese waters and territory. By joining other powers in holding down Chinese tariffs, the United States had made its contribution to the weakness that yielded before militant Japan. Yet in spite of, to some extent on account of, alien interference, China steadily nourished the nationalist spirit which was inimical to the interests of foreigners accustomed to doing about as they pleased within her borders.

With China in transformation, Japanese power rising, and Great Britain caught in the web of European perils, the basis for a strong American policy in the Orient shrank rather than widened as time passed. Army and navy "games" might contemplate war in the Far Pacific, but it grew increasingly difficult to count upon popular zeal in the United States for that eventuality. Experience of more than half a century had disclosed no "ample outlets for the surpluses of American factories and farms" in that part of the world. Trade with China remained relatively trivial, notwithstanding the huge volume of wild talk about four hundred million potential customers. It was true that when the calculations of economic interest were put aside as unimpressive, the missionary interest and the traditional friendship of the United States for China could be invoked. Influential as these were, however, they lacked the unequivocal support required for effective diplomatic pressure on either China or Japan, to be backed up in final analysis by naval and military action. Some injury to American citizens, some deliberate insult, or some horrible outrage, might set the United States on fire, but by no stretch of knowledge or imagination could a rational argument be found, in practical considerations, for asserting American supremacy or rattling the sabre anywhere in the Orient. Preparations "adequate" to avenge some hypothetical affront, which might or might not occur, furnished no scheme of accountancy for the State Department and for army and navy appropriations by Congress.

§

With dissolvent effects, events at home and abroad — the cataclysm in domestic economy, the shrinkage of exports and imports, and the shift in the balance and conduct of the world powers — broke into all schools of thought concerned with American foreign policies. The oldest school, isolationism pure and simple, had originated in the administration of President Washington. It had contended that the United States could expand its trade in all parts of the world, avoid entangling alliances, and remain insulated against the endless wars in Europe. For all practical purposes this scheme of policy had been destroyed near the end of the nineteenth century when, under the leadership of William McKinley and John Hay, the isolationist creed of the early republic was abandoned and the United States Government set out on a course of imperialist conquest in the Far East and trade expansion everywhere under naval pressures.

In destroying the policy inaugurated under George Washington, the McKinley school did not, however, frankly and openly adopt the imperialist dogma in the British, French, and German style, although the deed implied the word. For this proceeding the McKinley administration felt that it lacked the support of the American nation. So it sought to combine the hazards of empire with continental security, and the correct characterization of this new policy was a bastard conception, Imperial Isolationism. With some justification its temporary vogue could be called "accidental." Taking advantage of popular enthusiasm for a movement to liberate Cuba from Spanish dominion, Theodore Roosevelt, Alfred Thayer Mahan, Henry Cabot Lodge, John Hay, Albert J. Beveridge, and other "war hawks" of 1898 turned the conflict into a war for the conquest and annexation of the Philippines and for the pursuit, they alleged, of commercial interests through the agency of the sea power. Taking advantage also of the fright induced by the bogy of Bryanism, free silver, and populist radicalism, the school of Imperial Isolation, it is true, secured the appearances of popular approval in the national election of 1900 and again in 1908. Yet as the course of events subsequently showed, the program of the school had not become a national creed rooted in the unshakeable affections of the whole people.

This was conclusively demonstrated in 1938 when Franklin D. Roosevelt's message asking for a super-navy authorization

came before Congress. In the circumstances and by its very
nature, the super-navy could be used, perhaps was intended
by some sponsors to be used, in a new imperialist war in the
Orient. But no sponsor rose in either chamber to defend it
openly on that ground. In the House of Representatives,
James W. Wadsworth, son-in-law of John Hay, and in the
Senate Frederick Hale, a surviving member of the Old Guard,
voted for the super-navy bill, but most of the Republican
contingent was opposed to it in both branches of the national
legislature, while Democrats expressly disowned all imperialist intentions, explicit or implicit, in the sea-power program.

Only in by-plays, insinuations, and occasional lines in reports, speeches, and press releases did any defenders of the
super-navy bill, Democrats or Republicans, admit that hidden in it was what the minority of the House committee on
naval affairs called "the British-Mahan sea power doctrine"
— the main support of the imperialist creed. Nevertheless
the super-navy bill passed both houses of Congress and everybody familiar with its terms and the circumstances of its
adoption knew that, whatever the people in general thought
about the transaction, experts in diplomacy and naval affairs
were fully alive to its imperialist implications and utilities.
If voters at large had little affinity for Imperial Isolationism,
persons in key positions of power held fast to their imperialist
emotions and ambitions. If bothered by events, they had
not surrendered; their creed was still operative in shaping
foreign policy.

Claiming to be intensely practical in their outlook, imperialists of the isolation persuasion operated on assumptions
about the world, which were more or less systematic in form.
They took for granted a high degree of world disorder, at
least from time to time, and believed in taking pertinacious
and prudent advantage of favorable opportunities for increasing trade, making loans, and pushing what they called
national interests. They had toyed with Hague conferences,
approved academic resolutions framed by peace advocates,
and paid occasional homage to the peace sentiment, particu-

larly, as Theodore Roosevelt remarked, when it was necessary to capture the votes of that "lunatic fringe." On the whole, however, theirs was a hard and presumably realistic view of international affairs — one which they regarded as sanctioned by human history as fact rather than by human aspiration as utopia. In their view of the universe the rivalry of imperial powers was a kind of natural law — an extension of the law of the struggle for existence within capitalist society itself. The rivalry, some imperialists conceded, might be mitigated by restraint or by limited collaboration; but competition for trade, investment opportunities, raw materials, protectorates, and prestige, they thought, would continue in the future as in the past.

According to their theory, American economy, having rounded out the continental domain and fairly completed the accumulation of capital goods for domestic uses, possessing surpluses, must widen beyond the seas in a contest with other great powers for acquisition of more profits and more capital through the disposition of the domestic surpluses and other activities. Briefly stated, an expanding foreign trade was a primary consideration of imperial isolationism. To assure success in this operation, it was the duty of the Government to utilize all the instrumentalities which rival imperial powers employed, such as tariffs, subsidies, and navies. Although this power-politics, Machtpolitik, as the German devotees named it, was not deemed as absolute by American imperial isolationists as it was by the German school of Weltmacht (world-power), it was persistent and pervasive among influential circles in America. The alternative among the German exponents was Untergang (downfall) and the American theory rather closely conformed to that rationalization and fear.

As practiced under Republican auspices during the golden glow, isolationism meant the vigorous pursuit of "national interests," identified with the support of tariffs, subsidies, and bounties at home, and appropriate use of diplomatic and naval power abroad. Earlier the promise of this policy had taken the form of ample outlets for the "surpluses" of American farms, factories, banks, and investors. Since experience, however, had brought disillusionment as to the "ample" part of the program, the phraseology was now somewhat modified, to run : "Upon these outlets abroad our prosperity depends." This being so, in the world as it actually is, pressures for the outlets must be maintained, with prudence, but persistently. Only such a policy can be followed in the world of nations as they are. Other policy is fantasy. It is possible to occupy a position as a creditor nation, to collect the war debts due the Government of the United States, and at the same time raise higher and higher the tariff barriers against the flow of manufactures and agricultural produce imported to discharge the interest on loans, to pay dividends on foreign investments, and to amortize maturing obligations. On these terms relations with other countries should be as friendly as possible and war might be safely renounced as an instrument of national policy, at least outside the Caribbean region.

In substance, this brand of isolationism was "dollar diplomacy," renewed under the more euphonious verbalism set forth by Charles E. Hughes when he was Secretary of State : "Foreign policies are not built upon abstractions. They are the result of practical conceptions of national interest arising from some immediate exigency or standing out vividly in historical perspective." Although the fruits garnered from the pursuit of this "national interest" early began to decay and drop away, it took awful reverses to shake the confidence of Respectability in that line of economic diplomacy. The reverses came with the calamities of the depression, with revolutions and loan repudiations in Europe, with upheavals and loan repudiations in South America, with the victory of imperialists in Germany, Italy, and Japan.

Scarcely less desolating, doubtless, was the impact of events upon the second school of American foreign policy — that of Collective Internationalism. At home and abroad it too encountered blow after blow. The effort of Henry L.

Stimson, as Secretary of State under President Hoover, to enlist French and British support against Japanese aggression in Manchukuo was an utter failure. Even with the support of President Franklin D. Roosevelt, the proposal that the United States adhere to the World Court, a foster child of the League of Nations, was rejected by the Senate. The withdrawal of Germany and Japan from the League, Mussolini's imperialist war against Ethiopia, the futility of the application of sanctions to Italy with the aid of President Roosevelt, the inability of the League to prevent "the little world war" in Spain — these and other occurrences made the stoutest hearts among the internationalists beat a little slower. By 1937 the morale of the League of Nations had disintegrated, for all practical purposes. Although Roosevelt's "quarantine" speech at Chicago in the autumn of that year gave the collectivists a temporary lift, the popular counterblast which greeted that address throughout the country had a tendency to explode their dreams.

Yet the image of the world on which the school of Collective Internationalism based its hopes persisted. In various respects this image represented a more realistic view of affairs than did the conception of Imperial Isolationism. It was in fact more recent in origins and more nearly in line with developments. The modern imperialist process had been started by European powers in the sixteenth century, in an age of wooden ships, and had stretched out over a three-hundred-year span of time, during which virgin continents and defenseless peoples had been exploited for the benefit of the rulers. Neither that history nor those circumstances could ever be duplicated exactly. The only imperialist hope worthy of "great politics" for the United States lay in the overthrow of the British empire and the substitution of an American empire for it, and no such prospect seemed enclosed in the contours of fate.

By contrast, Collective Internationalism was nearly up to date. It had assumed a positive configuration as late as 1919 when the League of Nations was established. As the American school of imperialists had taken advantage of an idealistic war against Cuba to impose the system of "expansion" upon the country, so the Collective Internationalists, under the leadership of President Wilson, had seized the occasion of a war that sprang largely out of imperialist rivalries to dream of imposing an idealistic scheme of permanent peace upon the world — after an imperialist settlement under military auspices at Paris. Their action, therefore, came later in time and had a closer relationship with the course of events during the midpassage.

The world image of which Collective Internationalism was a political and legal expression stemmed, in part, from the internationalism of the free trade system as conceived by Richard Cobden and John Bright in the age of Queen Victoria. The conception presupposed capitalism, especially industrial capitalism, as a final order for economic transactions, with, perhaps, modifications in the form of social legislation. It covered a number of subsidiary ideas: increasing world trade through the free exchange of commodities and raw materials; a world market as a reality; gold as the uniform medium of international exchange; world-wide freedom of commerce for individuals and corporations without government intervention; abolition or drastic reduction of tariff barriers between nations; the free flow of capital, goods, and labor under the stimulus of the best returns; automatic adjustments of exchange through the operation of the free price mechanism; liberty for efficient competition without regard to national boundaries; international division of labor, industries, and skills; acceptance of world prices, as determined by efficient competition; free and equal access to raw materials whether domestic or colonial; the international liberty for developing investment opportunities.

In other words, this image contemplated the unification of the world for economic transactions according to certain rules to be collectively accepted by the participating States. It precluded or minimized unilateral economic action by governments, the management of currencies, and the insulation of domestic price and wage levels against the world price and wage levels attained by savage world competition. Governments might vary, though presumably capitalist democracies were preferable; cultures might be diverse; internal conflicts over economic interests, even civil wars, might occur; many types of civilization might exist along the scale from primitive African villages to the fashion center of France; but free transactions among the economic atoms of the whole world could be or should be maintained. "If only" this were done, the problem of outlets for national "surpluses" would be solved; the several peoples of the earth would be constantly employed at the enterprises for which they are best fitted; economic excuses for war would disappear; and an optimum or maximum economic satisfaction would prevail in the four quarters of the globe. Departures from the norms of this world utopia were to be explained in some measure by reference to "political psychiatry" or "nationalistic insanity."

Although this world conception was seldom set forth in completeness, fragments or huge sections of it were to be found in the flood of economic writings that issued from the intellectual workshops of professors, researchers, international experts, and peace societies. With modifications and vague fringes it was the basic frame for public policy upon which the Secretary of State, Cordell Hull, operated, while President Roosevelt vibrated between plans for establishing a "sound internal economy" and quarantines for aggressors. Most of the books by outstanding professors of politics and economics who dealt with "world" affairs — Alvin Hansen, Eugene Staley, Jacob Viner, Quincy Wright, James T. Shotwell, and Charles Fenwick, for example — took for granted the essential validity and realism of the world image, if with various qualifications; and the nature of their conclusions and contentions turned upon their preliminary assumption. As was said of another intellectual proceeding, they "got out of their major premise all they put into it."

From the polishing rooms of the philosophers who kept the

world image shining, their dicta, instructions, demands, and imperatives for policy crept into marketplaces, offices of exporters and importers, women's organizations, editorial sanctums and forums of public discussion, giving appropriate and automatic turns to locution respecting foreign affairs. With the formulas and mandates of this school, as of all the others, specialists in the business became so familiar that the moment the words "world economy" or "world trade" or "world society" appeared in literature or discourse, they could immediately foretell the conclusion — lower trade barriers — with a certainty of prediction like one in celestial mechanics.

Notwithstanding all their claims to the sanction of axiomatics, the world imagists encountered rough sledding. If historians asked them just when or where the world of realities conformed to the shape of the world image, they could be lightly dismissed as antiquarians. If an economist gave a different picture of things, as did Erich Zimmermann in his book on World Resources and Industries, he could be classified as a geographer. However, events which contemplation could not banish had a way of dealing perversely with the world conception. Though statesmen guilty of perpetrating these events might be called insane chauvinists, crazy nationalists, demagogues, and flouters of "sound economic principles," practitioners themselves everywhere worked against, rather than according to, the prescriptions of the world imagery. For instance, the original home of the grand dream, England, abandoned free trade, went back to protective tariffs even for agriculture, consolidated competing railways, set up a system of control over agriculture akin to that provided by the Agricultural Adjustment Act in the United States, forcibly fused public and private electrical concerns in a common grid, went in for government housing, and nationalized the coal industry — among many other departures from the "natural order." Everywhere nations sought to attain a high degree of self-sufficiency, in part by balancing agriculture and manufacturing, and employed collective regimentation of domestic enterprises as the instrument. Even in the United States, Secretary Hull, though endowed with large powers in making reciprocity treaties, could only effect minor changes in the high tariff wall erected during the Harding-Coolidge-Hoover regime; and the domestic economic regimentation introduced by the New Deal continued apace. A barrage of facts obscured the shining face of the world image.

For the third school of foreign policy, International Communism, the events of the midpassage were also disruptive. It too had a world view — one based on a specific interpretation of history. Like Collective Internationalism, this conception, formulated by Karl Marx and elaborated by V. I. Lenin, accepted capitalism as the actuating force of domestic and world economies; but it insisted that capitalism was subject to laws of development in time, of which imperialism was the latest expression. And it went further. According to the Communist theory, after imperialism had expanded to the ends of the earth, reached the limits of extension in a series of world wars, and arrived at the time-point of its own collapse, the industrial workers of the world, consolidated by the pressures of capitalism and embittered by the sufferings of peace and war, would seize power in every country and bring about the international unification and pacification of all toiling peoples, if with scant courtesy for all who toiled not.

Such was the theory. But facts did not exactly fit it. A few years after their triumph in Russia, amid the horrors of the world war and the political upheavals which followed, true believers in world brotherhood through world revolution were expelled from the Soviet republic or shot down at mass executions. Beyond the confines of Russia, the rise of fascism marked the destruction of many communist organizations. While all this was transpiring, the Russian government concentrated its energies on domestic affairs and on what was called "building socialism in one country." As a result communists everywhere split into two or more contending factions. Interest in the defense of Russia put a damper on interest in international communism or postponed the final triumph into an indefinite future, thus disintegrating it as a single force. And in the march of events it came about that the Communist party in the United States, affiliated with the party in Russia, eagerly supported Collective Internationalists in their campaign against the fascist foes of their world image and applauded the demands of imperialists for the use of sea power to coerce Japan — the long-standing foe of Russia.

During the turmoil of events that rendered older theories of foreign policy at least somewhat obsolete, a fourth school gradually emerged, without a neatly-fitting name. Like the other systems of ideology and utopia, it had roots in the past, but its conception of American interest and genius was both divergent and critical. At the center of its philosophy was the idea that through domestic measures, adopted by the democratic process, vast improvements could be and should be effected in American civilization, where at least one-third of the nation was ill-housed, ill-clothed, ill-nourished, and ill-educated; moreover, that this civilization could be defended in its continental home under prudent policies by small but appropriate military and naval establishments. Associated with the vision was the conviction that American democracy should not attempt to carry the Atlas load of the White Man's Burden in the form of imperialism all over the earth, or assume that it had the capacity, even with the best of good-will, to settle the difficult problems of European nations encrusted in the heritages of their long and sanguinary history. Its theories and sentiments were enclosed in such phrases as: let us keep out of the next world war; mind our own business; till our own garden; create the wealth; substitute abundance for scarcity; establish a sound and efficient domestic economy; make America a work of art.

Although owing to the lack of a precise name, this fourth school of foreign policy was often described as isolationist by critics, its defenders disowned the connotations of the kind of isolationist creed which had been sponsored by Henry Cabot

Lodge, Warren G. Harding, and Calvin Coolidge. They likewise refused to be battened down by the name "nationalist," with its chauvinist and militarist associations. They did not deprecate foreign trade as such; they merely insisted that the aim of such commerce should be to supplement the national resources and that in no form whatever could foreign trade, in the very nature of things, guarantee, by its own expansion, either prosperity or security for America. Surrendering shop-worn reliance upon imperialist pressures, money lending, and huckstering abroad, they turned to the efficient, humanistic use of national resources and technical skills as a means for making a civilization on this continent more just, more stable, and more beautiful than anything yet realized. Perhaps, in a world beset by clamant ideologies, the name "continental," or "American civilization," was most appropriate, if still inadequate, to characterize the thought of the fourth school of foreign policy.

The central economic thesis of this school probably came from the writings of the British economist, John A. Hobson. The primary force in the rivalry of nations for market outlets, he said, is the inefficient distribution of wealth at home — in other words, the enormous accumulations of capital that cannot find high profits in domestic expansion and must go abroad or burst. Associated with fierce international rivalry was domestic exploitation and ill-being. And the solution for the problem of attaining well-being or "prosperity," he argued, lies not in "the world market" but in domestic economy — in the wider distribution of wealth to sustain continuous and expanding buying power among the people.

Although this doctrine was grounded in a general economic conception, like the other theories of foreign policy, the school of American civilization did not contend that its creed was universally applicable; nor did it propose to employ any diplomatic or military engines to force the faith upon other countries. Its conception embraced a plural universe — a world composed of many nations, dependencies, protectorates, colonies, spheres of interest, degrees of industrialization, forms of government, patriotic and cultural ideologies. It was not concerned with efforts to run the steam roller of capitalism, democracy, communism, or any other "system" over the world. This act of universalization was not deemed possible nor, from the angle of national or human interest, desirable.

Evangelists might yearn to set up a world system and government on some religious credo, or democrats less theological might want to reproduce the capitalist system, American style, in all the world, with a police guard. On their part the continentalists who sought to formulate an American foreign policy relegated to the domain of utopias the denationalized idea of the world imagists whether it represented evangelism, the individualism of the capitalist persuasion, or the communism of the Trotzky direction. To the adherents of this school the world did not appear as a mere aggregation of individuals engaged in production and trade, but rather as an array of ever-changing political groupings, each with historical characteristics of its own. They rejected the imperialist doctrine of war "as the law of life" and deemed the Cobden-Bright, Wilson-Trotzky ideal of world pacifism to be an illusion beyond the purview of practice. They accepted the possibility of war for limited objectives, such as continental defense, and refused to accept war as an instrument of trade promotion, colonial expansion, or ideological world pacification.

In summary, they insisted that the real interests and needs of the United States did not exactly coincide with those of any other nation and that the geographical location and domestic situation of the country must and should give a different form and direction to the foreign policy of the Government. Experience, they argued, had demonstrated the failure of dollar diplomacy to attain its announced objective, that is, ample outlets for the "surpluses" of American factories and farms. The conception of world free trade, they contended, was really nothing more than a theory flung up for the British manufacturing classes in their peculiar and temporary position at the middle of the nineteenth century — a formula embedded in classical economics and repeated by rote in the speculations of American economists as if it were valid always and everywhere. Science and technology, they maintained, had slashed into the division of labor among nations, had universalized the use of machinery, had broken national monopolies of skills, had given greater economic independence to industrial societies, and had lessened the dependence of nations upon imports of manufactures and raw materials. They also contended that agreements for collective action recently proposed were old treaties of alliance in a new guise and would probably lead to war rather than to peace.

In rejecting as unreal and inapplicable to the United States the imperialist capitalism of the Lodge-Mahan fraternity, the free-trade theories of the Cobden-Wilson-Hull school, and the universal brotherhood of Marxism, members of the American civilization school did not repudiate international coöperation, conciliation, arbitration, collective action on definite matters of general interest, the tender of good offices to nations engaged in disputes, or necessarily association with a League of Nations constituted for other purposes than the perpetuation of historic wrongs. What they objected to was lecturing other nations, constantly stirring up, in effect, warlike emotions, and using the power of the United States to force any scheme of politics or economy on other peoples. They especially opposed, as distracting and dangerous to domestic life, the propagation of the idea that any mere foreign policy could in any material respect reduce the amount of degrading poverty in the United States, set American economy in full motion, or substantially add to the well-being of the American people. Foreign policy, they held, could easily be made the instrument to stifle domestic wrongs under a blanket of militarist chauvinism, perhaps disguised by the high-sounding title of world peace.

§

When it came to pressures for the realization of designs, each of the four schools of foreign policy had the support of particular interests to some extent, consciously or instinctively. Behind the World Imagists stood cotton growers of the South, cotton brokers, cotton handlers, railways and shipping concerns, and trading centers extensively dependent upon the cotton business. Exporting and importing merchants and bankers, oceanic shipping concerns, and whole armies of dealers, factors, and their employees naturally regarded any policy that increased the movement of commodities in international exchange as "good for business and good for the country." Corn, wheat, pork, and cattle producers in the West looked with a certain favor upon any procedure that promised larger outlets for their produce in foreign markets. Unlike the cotton growers, however, producers of other crops were subject to real and potential competition from imports of agricultural commodities and they clung to tariffs written in terms of their protection, while demanding bigger foreign outlets.

Imperial Isolationism, pure or mixed, to whatever degree modified in phraseology, was also approved by particular interests: by manufacturers demanding protection, manufacturers searching for foreign markets, bankers looking for investment opportunities abroad, traders and hucksters not content with their chances and gains at home. On this side also were enrolled, with shifts in politics, powerful forces in the army and naval bureaucracy and the supply interests which sold to military and naval establishments goods to the value of hundreds of millions annually. To be sure, the army and navy stood ready to support a war for democracy in the style of the world image, if officially proclaimed, but at bottom fighting men were suspicious of romance in these days, accustomed as they were to the business of getting naval bases, pushing trade, aiding in the collection of debts, and keeping order in backward places. Although many officers had no illusions about the dubious values of such operations, considered in any terms of national interest, agitations over "our commercial rights" in the ports of the seven seas always facilitated the passage of army and navy appropriation bills through Congress, and tended to vitalize the affinity between warriors and traders.

On the lists of the American Civilization school was likewise enrolled a motley collection of interests. With the formulators of its arguments, protected manufacturers went along a certain distance, that is, until problems affecting the domestic distribution of wealth were raised. Protected labor saw in the battle for "a national standard of life," insulated against European and Oriental competition, certain and immediate advantages. Discouraged about the prospects of market expansion abroad or producing especially for the domestic market, a multitude of agrarians found more hope for themselves in "parity with industry" and the "stabilization of agricultural production" than in the offerings of the world imagists. Opponents of war, assuming that it would be possible to keep the United States out of the next world conflict, took the ground that the more entanglements were created abroad, whether through world trade, imperial pressures, or underwriting world "democracies," the greater would be the likelihood of military and naval adventures in Europe and Asia. Since the world imagists generally assailed the ideology of fascism, American citizens of German and Italian fascist sympathies, though hostile to the aims of the American Civilization school, joined it in opposing collective action "on the side of the democracies."

Despite the torrent of spoken words and the oceans of ink used in supporting the four conceptions of foreign policy, it proved impossible to determine the long-term validity of any one. Nor was it easy, even in discussion, to keep each of the conceptions in its pristine purity, to insulate it entirely against the intrusion of fragments from the other conceptions. They were all vexed by internal logical troubles and by factual discrepancies. Nor was it possible, given the pressures of the conflicting interests involved, to marshal enough voters to assure the supremacy of any single policy in practice. As in all such cases, history to come would pass judgment on the competing conceptions. History would decide which of the four, if any at all, was to correspond most precisely with long-run practice.

§

That policy or no policy, stark faith in war itself or lust for it might overcome efforts to keep the United States aloof from the frenzies of Europe was intimated by a course of events running through the years. After the Hitler government in Germany set out on its line of sheer force, publicists, agitators, and editors began to hunt a slogan for the next war. Hamilton Fish Armstrong proposed one of the formulas: "We or They." According to this dictum the world is really ruled by ideas. Economic interests, imperial aggrandizement, efforts of ruling classes to save themselves do not count at all; or not much. Ideas make history. The democratic idea is challenged to mortal combat by the fascist idea. Germany, Italy, and Japan, if not broken by economic coercion or military might, will march to the enslavement of mankind. The United States will have to help Europe "solve" this "problem."

Reasoning of that kind appealed to innumerable minds in America especially among the idealists of the middle class. And strange as it seemed at first glance, communists of the Stalinist wing came to the support of the thesis that the democracies would have to coerce the fascist nations or overcome them by arms. In the early days of the Russian revolution, they had spoken contemptuously of "rotten bourgeois democracies"; German communists had voted with and fought on the side of Hitler's troopers against the Weimar republic. They had also sneered at ideas and magnified the power of material interests in peace and war. But they had learned a lesson from Hitler, and had received orders from Moscow to line up in a "united front" with democrats, mere democrats. Russia might need the aid of the United States in a coming world war, involving Japan. And, since Japan was now "the" enemy in American war games, communists were no longer to be so despised amid preparations for the approaching trial by battle.

Paralleling in time-development the four schools of foreign policy, with wide-reaching ramifications, though commanding no large vocal following, was the school of true believers in eternal war as a necessity of life — war as the independent and perpetual invariable of all human history, irrespective of systems, political and economic. This school, if a loose aggregation of thinkers could be so denominated, recognized, if it did not rejoice in, the ancient blood lust of man — the dark and convulsive urge to physical combat, which had manifested itself in endless wars, domestic and foreign, from the dawn of history, for one cause, or another cause, or for no cause at all — just an opportunity. How potent this dynamic was among Americans there was no way of knowing. That it quivered beneath the surface of things ready for an outbreak was evident in a multitude of incidents and articles from year to year — for example, in sadistic lynchings and in paeans praising battleships and great navies, composed for the populace.

But whether the mass of men, if decently employed in works of peace, would automatically leave loom or forge or plow and rush to war combat for its own sake or the sheer joy of blood-letting, could not be discovered by any available probe of psychology. Military history recorded that governments had never been able to recruit large standing armies with ease. Only by seizing loose-footed beggars, scouring prisons, snatching apprentices, kidnaping younger sons, knocking down and dragging off laggards, and buying the serfs of feudal lords, had they managed in earlier times to corral enough men for wars. Not until the adoption of conscription — the levée en masse — and the use of wholesale coercion had they succeeded in creating the monster armies of the modern world. And, as the Russian revolution of 1917 indicated, there were new perils of terrorism underneath such huge aggregations of men experienced in violence and slaughter.

In the United States, militarism as a regular way of life had never captivated the people. Nor were the army and the navy, recruited in respect of officers mainly from the civilian population, much given to the praise of war as war. They brought relentless pressure upon Congress for more and more money, materials, and men, it is true; and they sought to inoculate schools and colleges with "the martial spirit." But the majority of officers and men doubtless knew little and thought little about the psychology of the blood bath. The difficulty of holding reserve officers in the line of training and of getting enlisted men to reënlist on the expiration of their terms suggested a lack of professional interest and a dearth of hunger for the butcheries of the battlefield.

Even so, there were many men in the United States, military and civilian alike, who deemed war forever inevitable and who were propelled by passionate emotions to choose "the next enemy" and to bend propaganda toward war against that foe, when neither national peril nor national advantage was involved in the process. Moreover such men were always near centers of power where force was a factor. It could not be truly said, therefore, that the army and navy were mere pliant instruments of national policy and nothing more. On the contrary, the army and navy, by their very existence, form, and continuous expansion, expressed foreign as well as domestic policy, wittingly or not, and policy was continuously influenced, in some measure, by the historic, dark urge to war.

Belief in and enjoyment of the undersurging blood lust as a source of policy and action in foreign affairs were by no means confined to stray groups in the military profession and its associates in thought and emotion. Manifestations of the faith appeared in various forms. Gusts of the frenzy flamed out in violent language at assemblies of the very best people, lurked under disarming phrases, fluttered through ladies' smiles. "How they hate Roosevelt!" for instance, became a by-word accurately describing the fever that raged at clubs, garden parties, week-end excursions, in drawing rooms, Pullman cars, offices, and conferences of brokers, chambers of commerce, and manufacturers. Outbursts and retaliations from politicians, agrarians, labor leaders, and agitators at labor meetings exhibited the same kind of temper. Lynching parties, floggings, police beatings, third-degree procedures, sabotage, suppressions of minorities as in Jersey City ruled by Mayor Hague, all indicated that the veneer of civilization was thin enough in wide areas of society, that the restraints of civilization might burst under exceptional strain, unchaining civil or foreign war or both, in the fashion so often illustrated in history. Replete with meaning for the future was the swift decline in the great fear of huge military establishments which the founders of the republic, deeply learned in history and experience, entertained — against which they warned their own and coming generations.

Ascribing war to basic biological sources — to surges from the deeps of the irrational, shattering in action the whole web of civilization — exponents of "the next and inevitable war" made assertions that influenced the makers of policy. Had it not been for the rise of the irrational cult to great power in Europe under the guise of fascism, such alarmists might have been dismissed as a mere irritating minority in the United States; but events in the Old World gave point to their contentions in the New World and brought "war as the invariable" into discussions of American policy, domestic and foreign. Inasmuch as exponents of fascism assigned to women the primary function of bearing and rearing babies for war, inasmuch as the war urge and its consequences affected all society from top to bottom, the sweep of the war psychosis brought women and their role in civilization to the forefront of relevant discussions. What was the relation of women to this old, now re-exalted, phenomenon of war, conceived as the overwhelming dynamic of history?

On this point, generalizations were forthcoming, often with little regard for pertinent facts. And one of the easiest of the easy generalizations, indulged in by men and women alike, was to the effect that mothers hate war because it robs them of their sons; that wives shrink from war because it takes their husbands away from the home and the children; that unmarried women loathe its cruelties because they pity the wives and mothers or are in peril of lust and destruction in the war zones. But to these assumptions, history brought the penetrating light of long experience. Within its white glare, women were seen as war lords of the most intransigent type at points in historic time when they ruled States or sought to rule States. As queens they had been as ready for war as kings. Feudal ladies were personally familiar with battle and as quick as feudal lords to welcome advantages won by arms.

Moreover the immediate history of the world war offered to memory its sharp illustrations of the feminine tendency to go along with and goad men into the ways of war. Women like men, perhaps in greater numbers than men, judging from the roll calls of peace societies, had been registered as detesting war. But when the war came, women like men gave it their allegiance. Mothers, wives, sisters, and daughters rushed to the service of war — behind the trenches, as close to the front as they could get. They scorned "shirkers"; they urged males forward to the battle line. They shouted for funds in drives to finance the war. They made munitions. They drove trucks and planes. They "entertained" soldiers and washed their wounds, often taking war romantically as an escape from the rigors of the humdrum into the excitements of deadly peril. They wrote and delivered impassioned appeals to stimulate the war spirit, making use of the venerable argument that it was all for the defense of the nation, womanhood, and the home, irrespective of war origins and aims. Before and after the war, women served as auxiliaries in associations of every kind for the promotion of armaments, the extension of military control over education, and the increase of military and naval appropriations.

None the less, in the main, fighting was a man's business in history and women had been primarily engaged in the arts of peace, the making of civil society. From primitive times, when they introduced and developed the arts of the hearth and agriculture, down to the latest hour when they worked in factories, entered civil professions, managed modern homes, and took part in civic affairs, women's interests had been on the whole pacific. Their concern had been constructive and conservational, in the main, not destructive and explosive. Consequently, if the cult of the irrational, exalting man's fighting above humanity's peace, was to spread in America, as it had in Germany, Italy, and other parts of Europe, women's role was to be transformed with the overthrow of civilian supremacy in society. Was that contingency so remote in time as to seem bizarre? Handwritings on walls implied a negative answer.

§

The first pragmatic test of President Roosevelt's foreign policy came in connection with the World Economic Conference in London, called by the League of Nations in 1932. In accepting the invitation, President Hoover had asked Congress for an appropriation to pay the expenses of participation and had received a form of legislative sanction. American delegates were then chosen to serve on the organizing committee of the League Council and American representatives were dispatched to take part in the work of the expert committee charged with the duty of arranging the agenda for the coming conference. Although the political overturn of that year increased the uncertainty of the American line, preliminaries for the London conference were completed before the close of Hoover's term and Roosevelt agreed to carry out the obligations assumed by his predecessor. Furthermore during his campaign Roosevelt had hinted that he would broaden the scope of the conference by adding a consideration of intergovernmental debts and tariffs, which had been expressly excluded by the Hoover administration as a condition of acceptance. Though in conversations with the representatives of foreign countries, held in Washington shortly after his inauguration, Roosevelt avoided specifications too exact, he gave them the impression that his coöperation would be warm-hearted.

When the agenda drawn up by the preparatory committee came out, no special discernment was necessary to discover that its frame of reference enclosed the assumptions and program of the world imagists. It contained the regular phrases of that school — "the whole system of international finance," "the normal exchange of commodities," "an improvement in the world economic situation," "an international economic system," "world economy," "recovery of an economic system threatened by bankruptcy," "bringing world economy back to a more normal condition or, at any rate, to the situation that obtained a few years ago." The experts did not factually describe the system or order of world economy to which they repeatedly referred; nor did they say whether it was the system of 1928, or 1920, or 1914, which the phrase "a few years ago" implied. In effecting a compromise of conflicting ideas and interests, the framers of the agenda were cautious in giving specifications while making clear the corollaries of their logic.

Writing on the subject after the preparation of the agenda, Sir Walter Layton, who had been associated with the committee of experts, pointed out the contradiction between "an international financial system" and "economic nationalism" with its tariffs, subsidies, quotas, bounties, and other restrictions on free trade among the individuals of all nations. His image of the "system" to be established by the coming conference was fundamentally that of free private enterprise and free trade throughout the world — the dream in which Richard Cobden had reveled long before when England was in fact the workshop of the world.

That the Roosevelt administration would give some effect to the policy of the world imagists seemed fairly certain early in the spring of 1933 — before the World Conference assembled in June. In a public address, Secretary Hull sketched the outlines of his program. Concerning the center of his affections there could be little doubt. Mr. Hull had been an ardent champion of the domestic individualism set forth in President Wilson's New Freedom and a consistent believer in low tariffs, bordering on free trade as an ideal. If there were doubts, he dispelled them, by declaring: "The restoration of fair, friendly, and normal trade relations among nations at present would not only avoid serious economic, military, and political differences between countries in the future, but would go far toward composing those now existing." He condemned the "policy of economic isolation."

Nations were in profound economic distress. How were they to get out of it? Mr. Hull had his answer: "Business recovery must be preceded by the restoration of international finance and commerce, an alternative to which is a continuance of the unsound economic policies under the operation of which the entire world since 1929 has been in the throes of an unspeakable depression." Destiny pointed to American leadership in this work of reversal and restoration. America needed nothing special: "The interests of our government and our people seem so clearly to coincide with the interests of humanity." Here the whole case of the world imagists was proclaimed: the union of universal free trade on a gold basis with professions of humanity, if not of democracy. Two weeks later, in a message to mankind, Roosevelt seemed to confirm the faith by saying that the coming London conference "must establish order in place of the present chaos by a stabilization of currencies, by freeing the flow of world trade, and by international action to raise price levels." Therewith the hopes of the world imagists were buoyed.

Speaking as head of the American delegation, Secretary Hull recited his philosophy to the World Conference. He conceded that each country could by suitable steps, "to a moderate extent, restore conditions," but his accent was on the interdependence and interrelations of nations. He derided the "isolationist" for his failure to see "the international character" of the depression. The policy of self-containment, he insisted, "has demonstrated its inability to either avoid or arrest or cure the most destroying depression in all the annals of business." Mr. Hull shrank from asserting that free trade and a stabilization of the currency would positively bring the permanent prosperity of expanding outlets for "surpluses" and spoke of "a sane, practical middle course," but the upshot of Mr. Hull's theory in terms of practice was positive : Remove all excesses in the form of trade barriers; combined with "suitable" domestic measures, this will bring restoration, recovery, and advance.

In essence, Mr. Hull's creed had the predictive assurance of a formula in exact science : "Given a test tube containing an opaque liquid, add a given chemical substance, and the compound will assume a rosy hue." Emphasis on domestic production meant, in any case, he said, a lower standard of life for the American people ; adopt the practice of reducing trade barriers and America can have the substance of prosperity. Meanwhile, at home, the Government of the United States was doing exactly what Secretary Hull derided in London ; it was attempting "by boot-strap methods" to lift itself out of its troubles — with the Agricultural Adjustment Act and the National Industrial Recovery Act.

Just what happened at the London conference was not fully disclosed to the public. In accordance with custom, records were deposited in archives. It is certain, however, that dissensions early appeared. By mentioning war debts in his ceremonial address the British premier, Ramsay MacDonald, made trouble for the American delegation. If, as alleged, some agreement could have been reached on currency stabilization after the arrival of the Assistant Secretary of State, Raymond Moley, that project collapsed. Reports of a ten per cent horizontal reduction in import duties all around brought a squall instead of harmony. Whether Great Britain and the countries still on the gold standard would actually have agreed in a final test upon a specific tariff and currency program, based on the terms of the world imagists, remained among the unsolved mysteries of the world play. Beyond question, the efforts of the "gold bloc" countries to give precedence to monetary stabilization led to irritation in the conference and in Washington. There was reason for believing at the moment that the conference might last indefinitely without reaching any fundamental conclusions or disband as a result of internal conflicts arising from the diversity of national interests represented.

The knot that could not be untied by exchanges of propositions and opinions among the delegates was cut by a message from Roosevelt early in July, declaring that it would be "a catastrophe amounting to a world tragedy, if the great conference of nations . . . should allow itself to be diverted by the proposal of a purely artificial and temporary experiment affecting the monetary exchange of a few nations only." That would be to forget "the larger purposes" for which the assembly was originally called. Having paid his respects to the gold bloc countries, the President rejected in effect the agenda prepared by the experts of the conference and also the emphasis on mondial trade which Secretary Hull had so eloquently vindicated. "The sound internal economic system of a nation," continued the President, "is a greater factor in its well-being than the price of its currency in changing terms of the currencies of other nations." As far as the formula of lower trade barriers was involved in the London debate, that doctrine had recently been thrown overboard by congressional legislation: the National Industrial Recovery Act authorized the President to raise American customs duties if necessary to insulate against the whole world the new prices and wages to be brought about by measures adopted in the domestic interest.

Thus the onus for "breaking up" the conference seemed to fall largely upon the United States. But in none of the records made available to the public, nor in the nature of the national interests represented at London, was there the slightest evidence that any substantial part of the proposed agenda could have been realized. Although the Conference adjourned amid lame remarks that it might be reassembled, nothing of the kind was really expected or happened.

To all appearances President Roosevelt had made the great decision. Emphasis was to be placed upon a "sound internal economic system" as a greater factor in national well-being than monetary devices which merely promised to enlarge the outlets for American "surpluses." Adherence to this formula of independent economic action meant a fundamental shift in American foreign policy, with inferences for military and naval affairs. Incisively the President had cut away, in effect, the outlet theory of the imperialist school and the outlet doctrine of the world imagists. He had conceded the major contention of the American civilization school, namely, that the extent of foreign outlets as far as America is concerned is limited by the necessities of economy to a small percentage of the exportable production in the United States and that the principal hope for domestic well-being in America lies in developing to the utmost, by domestic policy, the materials, skills, and resources of the American nation. How deep-seated was the President's resolve, there was no way of determining in 1933, but signs suggested that at the moment he knew the nature of his choice and made it deliberately.

§

A few months after the London Economic Conference ended in confusion, President Roosevelt delivered another blow to another doctrine of foreign policy that had been sanctioned by the diplomacy of universal philanthropy under President Wilson and the diplomacy of aggressive national interest practiced by his successors. In keeping with its conception of the war for world democracy, the Wilson administration had publicly condemned the Soviet regime in Russia as contrary to the "free will and purpose" of the Russian people and had refused to recognize it. The Soviet government, the American Secretary of State had said, refused to pay its debts and carried on a propaganda for a world system opposed to the institutions of the United States. Under Republican auspices, the custom of reading moral lectures to the Russian government and refusing to recognize that sturdy defaulter had been continued. It had been all right for the United States to join in a war for revolutionizing the domestic institutions of Germany and Austria, but the not-unexpected counterblast was deemed invidious. Such had been the logical outcome of a foreign policy that involved mondial uniformity in political and economic institutions and placed upon the Government of the United States a burden of responsibility for realizing throughout the world this posited conception of universal propriety.

Ignoring, however, the notes and lectures accumulated in the State Department and, apparently, the private objections of Secretary Hull, President Roosevelt entered into personal communications with the Soviet government late in 1933. He sought and secured pledges that Russia would guarantee legal rights and religious liberty to Americans resident in that country and would abstain from all propaganda calculated to disturb the internal affairs of the United States. The question of the unpaid debts, apart from the elimination of Russia's claims for damages done during American occupation of Siberia in 1918–1920, was postponed for discussion in subsequent negotiations. Having reached an agreement on this basis, the United States and Soviet Russia reëstablished official relations in November, 1933 — to the consternation of professional foes of "alien influences."

In taking this step, Roosevelt abandoned the policy of reading moral lectures to Moscow, took cognizance of the world as diversity, and resumed the historic practice in force before the advent of the world-power school and the school of mondial philanthropy. No doubt practical considerations had some influence. Russia might be useful against Japanese aggression in the Far Pacific; and the prospects of enlarged trade, long dangled before American eyes by Russian propagandists, might be realized. But, aside from such matters, the abandonment of the Wilson-Harding-Coolidge-Hoover policy in respect of Russia seemed to indicate that the United States was returning to the policy of limited action —

attending mainly to its own affairs, recognizing de facto governments without regard to their domestic forms and policies, abstaining from ideological judgments on other countries, and observing formalities in diplomatic intercourse. That might prove to be "impossible," as the new mondialists contended, but it was being tried, at least temporarily, by the Roosevelt administration.

With a firmness equally marked, Roosevelt renounced the strong-arm program of dollar diplomacy in dealing with American nations to the south. He had declared to Latin America that his policy would be that of "the good neighbor." As a demonstration of his policy he withdrew the marines from Nicaragua in 1933. The following year he signed with Cuba a treaty abolishing the principal features of the Platt Amendment by which the imperialists of the McKinley school had forced upon that "independent" country onerous restrictions, including the right of the United States to intervene for the preservation of domestic order.

This Amendment had been a sore point with Cubans since its inception, and had been regarded by Latin Americans generally as proof that "the colossus of the North" really intended to throw its sovereignty around the Caribbean basin. Hence deliberate surrender of the control authorized by the Amendment was more than an incident. It was a generous renunciation — a pledge that the policy of armed intervention was to be abandoned. In signing the treaty, Roosevelt declared: "This Government will make it clear that it not only opposes the policy of armed intervention but that it renounces those rights of intervention and interference in Cuba which have been bestowed upon it by treaty." From that time forward, it appeared, the pressure of the United States upon Cuban affairs was to be economic and diplomatic, not immediately military and naval. What might happen in case of another real explosion in Latin America was left to the future. For the moment dollar diplomacy and the marines were pushed into the background of theory and practice.

§

With such reformulations of policy in respect of Latin-American countries, Secretary Hull was evidently in complete sympathy. If irked by the short shrift that his President had made of the World Economic Conference and by the cavalier manner in which Roosevelt assumed responsibility for the resumption of relations with Russia, the Secretary of State nevertheless favored the release of naval pressures on nations to the south. He had long been an opponent of dollar diplomacy there; the South did not sell much cotton or tobacco to Mexico or South America. His temper was equable in ordinary negotiations. Yet in his quiet way he was invincible in pursuing objectives upon which his heart was set and those objectives included cutting down the protective tariff by any and every available process of law. Taking advantage of his influence as a former member of Congress, highly esteemed by his Democratic colleagues, the Secretary of State sought and obtained, on June 12, 1934, an amendment of the tariff act which allowed him to accomplish by his own operations some measure of his burning desire.

The new law — the Reciprocal Tariff Act — permitted the President, for a term of three years, to negotiate trade agreements with foreign countries and in so doing to increase or diminish by not more than fifty per cent the existing rates of duty. Such agreements, when duly consummated, were to go into effect without ratification by the Senate of the United States.

The business of negotiation was left to the State Department with the aid of a Trade Agreement Committee representing certain other branches of the Government. Briefly stated, the making of tariff legislation was by this maneuver transferred from Congress to Secretary Hull; and, through a gradual nation-by-nation process, he could, as far as that might be possible, effect a general reduction of the tariff without risking a frontal assault. Now the Secretary had an instrument for lowering trade barriers — and discovering whether the great powers represented at the London Economic Conference really could or would "restore the free flow of trade throughout the world."

When the term of the original Reciprocal Trade Act expired in 1937, Congress renewed it. By the end of that year Secretary Hull had consummated agreements with sixteen foreign countries, including Cuba, France, Canada, Belgium, Sweden, Brazil, Costa Rica, Haiti, and Honduras. Had the maneuver been a success? An exact statistical answer was then impossible despite extravagant claims and counterclaims. The criteria of judgment were furnished mainly by transactions with relatively small nations having peculiar economies. Excepting Canada, none of them entered into large-scale competition with the staple industries of the United States, and many enterprises in Canada were either branches of American concerns or generally represented investments of American capital. Furthermore in each case the reductions in rates were modest and frequently hedged about by quantitative restrictions on imports.

By that year, however, the Secretary had been unable or unwilling to effect agreements with such heavy competitors as Japan, Great Britain, or Germany. Prospects of an adjustment with Great Britain had been announced in Washington before the close of 1937, it is true, but that step was vigorously opposed in the United States by powerful interests and in London by British industrialists, especially by advocates of tariff preference within the Empire. Whether the British government would grant any substantial advantages to the United States in exchange for the appearances of closer political unity as against the Rome-Berlin-Tokyo bloc remained among the numerous uncertainties of the whole business. In the summer of 1938 when Hitler, after subjecting Austria to his dictatorship, threatened to take the German sector — the Sudeten — away from Czechoslovakia, Britain seemed ready to conclude the trade agreement with a view to European politics as well as to her own commerce; and before the year closed the treaty was duly signed.

In the limited circumstances the only basis of judgment on the effectiveness of the reciprocity policy — aside from Anglo-American political interests — appeared to be changes in the volume of trade between the United States and each particular country with which a reciprocity agreement had been reached. Perhaps no other criterion was available to economists. At all events one of the most distinguished experts in the subject, an economist in the State Department, Herbert Feis, employed it in reviewing "a year of the Canadian trade agreement" in the magazine Foreign Affairs for July, 1937. He concluded that "the trade in each direction continued to increase during 1936, the first year of the Agreement." Yet trade had been rising with the general upturn in commerce and production. Hence there was no absolute proof of anything in the mere continuance of the rise after the agreement had been concluded.

Certainly "more significant," as Mr. Feis said, was "the fact that during this year of world-wide commercial expansion the volume of trade between the two countries increased in greater ratio than did the volume of trade between either one of them and the rest of the world." Still this was no invincible proof of anything. Changes in the volume of trade between any two countries, over any period of time, had never mechanically corresponded to the changes in their trade with other nations, in normal conditions. And what were normal conditions? If, however, the large assumption was granted, namely that the disproportionate increase in volume of trade was due to the Reciprocal Agreement, another question arose: Did the economies of the contracting parties really benefit from the increased volume? Experts did not answer that question. Perhaps it was unanswerable. They merely assumed that an increase in the movement of goods was in itself a benefit to the people as a whole, as well as to the merchants, financiers, and factors of Canada and the United States, and represented in actuality material advances in the economic well-being of the respective countries. Adam Smith might have said that this was a fact, mysterious under the "invisible hand" of Providence but nevertheless a fact. American economists specializing in foreign trade commonly assumed it without the benefit of Providence.

To American producers little given to consulting the theories of the State Department, some fruits of the Canadian treaty presented strange aspects, however sound they might be in terms of mondial economy. For example, among the concessions granted to Canada, in exchange for concessions on her part, was a reduction in the American duty on cheese, and at that very moment American warehouses were bursting with millions of pounds of cheese for which the owners could find no outlet at all, domestic or foreign. In such circumstances the freer admission of Canadian cheese might be deemed by an inveterate theorist an act of sound economy, but to American cheese producers it certainly had the appearance of a vagary. In an age of general perversity, however, such microscopic items disappeared in the dream entertained by the supporters of reciprocal agreements for "freeing the flow of world trade." Even so, despite all the fanfare about overcoming the depression through foreign trade, at the end of Secretary Hull's three-year trial, American economy was rapidly running down in another slump and in the opening months of 1938 it was near the bottom reached under Hoover's management of affairs on other lines.

Whatever the future was to say about the invincible faith in a possible world of free and independent traders pursuing their acquisitive ways unchecked by national "politicians," the Senate of the United States, after voting for Secretary Hull's first Reciprocal Trade Bill in 1934, proceeded to vote down a measure designed to aid in mondial pacification. While the Secretary's personally conducted tour of tariff revision was in full progress, amid the applause of the world imagists, the project for taking the United States into the World Court came before the Senate for ratification, after a long delay. Immediately a throng of imperial isolationists and professional patriots descended upon wavering Senators. The Hearst press and Father Coughlin were especially vociferous in condemning the proposal. Although President Roosevelt, following the example of his predecessors, gave the scheme his personal blessing, he refrained from putting on full pressure. When the vote was taken in January, 1935, the World Court was rejected — an adverse outcome gratifying to imperial isolationists, discouraging to world imagists, and no consolation at all to the school of American civilization. It hastened the dissolution of faith in the League of Nations, already far advanced. It was also a collateral repudiation of reliance on collective action as a means of "keeping out of war." With reservations so extensive as to approach a cancellation of commitments, the World Court project actually meant little in terms of "entanglement"; nevertheless, not enough Democrats could be marshaled under the sign of Woodrow Wilson's crusade to carry the measure through the Senate.

§

Before the world imagists had recovered from the rejection of the World Court, they received a more direct and stunning blow from the Neutrality Resolution enacted in the same year, 1935. This measure was in large part an outcome of the munitions investigation and was thoroughly disliked by President Roosevelt and Secretary Hull. It had a wider background than that inquiry but the immediate impetus to action came from the revelations of the Nye committee. In express terms the Neutrality Act made it unlawful in time of war to export "arms, munitions, or implements of war" to belligerents abroad or to neutrals for the use of belligerents. It also authorized the President, when the security of the United States was in danger, to proclaim the fact and thereby place upon American citizens who traveled on the merchant vessels of belligerents full responsibility for all the risks, save under such executive rulings as might be issued. Coupled with the Johnson Act of the previous year, which cut off loans to governments in default on debts owed to the United States, the Neutrality Act struck at war booms in business such as had attended Woodrow Wilson on "the road to war." The ban was explicit and positive. Moreover it was mandatory; that is, it was to go into effect automatically when the President found a state of war existing abroad. Discretion was allowed to the Executive in deciding whether any particular form of fighting constituted war, but when war was declared by a foreign power or the President "found" a state of war, the neutrality prohibitions became immediately applicable.

Although Roosevelt signed the Resolution, he resented the spirit and letter of the Neutrality Act and clung tenaciously to the idea of intervening in the controversies of Europe, despite the abstention and equality of treatment stipulated in the Act. His personal inclinations became open knowledge on the outbreak of war between Italy and Ethiopia soon after the passage of the law. He did find a state of war existing and he did bring the Act into force against the belligerents. In application the Act ran against Italy — one of the undemocratic powers; for Ethiopia had no ships at sea, could borrow no money in the United States, and was in no position to buy munitions from American industries. Later in the year Roosevelt pledged the moral support of the United States to the policy of sanctions developed against Italy by the League of Nations, warned citizens against traveling on the ships of belligerents, in fact Italian ships, and discountenanced trade with belligerents in articles not covered by the embargo on munitions and implements of war. In other words, he made known to the world that, as far as he could, under the law, he would throw American influence on the side of the League's decision to penalize an aggressor. Obviously the Roosevelt administration intended to champion "democracies" against dictators in Europe.

Unmoved by Roosevelt's evident desire for a "free hand" in foreign affairs, Congress, in February, 1936, amended and continued the Neutrality Act. The mandatory embargo on the sale of munitions to belligerents was retained. The sale of the bonds, securities, and other obligations of belligerents was expressly forbidden within the jurisdiction of the United States; likewise prohibited were the making of loans and the granting of credits to belligerents. An exception was made of customary commercial credits and short-time obligations in aid of ordinary commerce, in case the President so decided, at his discretion. The transport of munitions on American vessels in war time was proscribed and American citizens were warned against traveling on the ships of belligerents. Remembering the Monroe Doctrine, Congress provided that the Act should not apply to any American republic at war with a non-American country, unless engaged in coöperating with a non-American state in such a conflict. Thus within a period of six months the national resolve against becoming entangled in foreign wars was strengthened, rather than diminished. The discussion which followed the first Neutrality Act had culminated in a tighter and more comprehensive measure.

The second Neutrality Act had been on the statute book only a few months when the outbreak of a civil war in Spain provided an acid test of President Roosevelt's foreign policy in respect of the conflict between democracies and dictatorships. By that time Mussolini had conquered Ethiopia and was ready for an excursion into Spanish affairs with the enthusiastic aid of Hitler. On this occasion, however, the Tory government in Great Britain, whose nationals had heavy investments in that part of Spain dominated by the rebel commander, General Franco, did not seem particularly interested in applying restraints to dictators occupied in a war on democracy. Of the circumstances, President Roosevelt took cognizance; and at his press conference in December, 1936, he suggested the extension of neutrality legislation to the civil war in Spain.

By some person in the administration — in the State Department or outside — a bill was drawn to give effect to his proposal. The bill so drafted was carried to Capitol Hill and jammed through Congress with little or no debate, early in 1937. In general terms the new Act imposed embargoes on both parties to civil conflicts deemed dangerous to the peace of the United States. In a haste so swift as to be unseemly President Roosevelt brushed aside the objections of the Spanish ambassador in Washington, Signor de los Rios, and barred the export of munitions to the Loyalist government no less than to the rebels.

From three points of view this was a strange procedure. As things stood in January, 1937, the civil war in Spain did not threaten the peace of the United States. Moreover the very essence of neutrality, as preached and practiced historically, forbade any legal change which adversely affected any belligerent after a war had started. Concerning the binding character of this principle there was no doubt anywhere among persons familiar with the law of neutrality, not even in the State Department. The embargo on munitions to Spain, imposed more than six months after the civil war had opened, was, therefore, a stark violation of a rule so rooted in history, law, and cautious policy.

Not only that; it transgressed the Treaty of Madrid consummated in 1902 between the United States and Spain and it was a slap straight in the face of the Madrid government. The Loyalist government had been and continued to be officially accepted in Washington as the lawful government of Spain. The belligerency of the insurgents had not been recognized. Under American theory and practice hitherto prevailing, the Madrid regime was entitled to buy munitions and supplies in the United States on the same terms as other foreign governments. But without notice or explanation the embargo applied by the Roosevelt administration deprived it of that right.

If Congress could be set down as consistent in its fierce resolve to stop all traffic in war materials, what could be said of the President's course? The Madrid government had come to power after a national election and was officially recognized in Washington as duly constituted. If it had the aid of Soviet Russia, it also had the open sympathy of the French ministry. Arrayed on the other side were avowed foes of democracy. The insurgent leader, General Franco, was an exponent of authoritarian government and he was notoriously assisted by the dictators of Italy and Germany. Without pretensions to secrecy, Hitler and Mussolini had dispatched soldiers to fight under General Franco's banner and had furnished aid, comfort, and supplies to his forces engaged in war on the Loyalist government. Here were the very dictators whom President Roosevelt repeatedly called enemies of democracy and foes of world peace. Yet by originating and signing the amendment to the Neutrality Act and then by putting it into immediate effect, he threw the support of the United States on the side of dictators and the professional warmongers of Europe. Even if the Madrid government had no merits whatsoever in his eyes, his action was a gratuitous favor to the Spanish rebels, to Hitler, and to Mussolini — a decided favor appreciated by the recipients, at the moment.

As the time approached for a renewal of the general Neutrality Act in 1937, the world imagists, encouraged, even led, by President Roosevelt and Secretary Hull, were well organized to riddle, if not defeat, it. Bent on having the power to determine American foreign policy themselves and to use that power in discriminating against parties to controversies abroad, according to their personal concepts of values, the President and the Secretary used their influence to secure modifications in the mandatory character of the existing neutrality legislation. Previous laws made the embargo on loans and munitions absolute as soon as the President had found a war of some magnitude raging to the peril of the United States. They did not permit him, at his own discretion, to extend or diminish the list of prohibited goods after he declared the embargo in effect. In 1937 this barrier to executive discretion was overthrown. The Act of that year continued and made mandatory the ban on loans and munitions; it empowered the President to place upon foreign belligerents responsibility for transporting goods bought in the United States — "the cash and carry" provision — and

# 480    · *AMERICA IN MIDPASSAGE*

to stop the shipment on American vessels of "certain articles or materials in addition to arms, ammunition, and implements of war" whenever he proclaimed it necessary "to promote the security or preserve the peace of the United States or to protect the lives of citizens of the United States."

By this amendment, Congress completely reversed its previous rule that made mandatory and somewhat precise the list of goods to be embargoed in case the President found a war raging abroad. In substance, it permitted the President to add anything else to the list closed to American shippers, even after a war began and the embargo had been applied. Instead of reducing his control over foreign policies, as the Acts of 1935 and 1936 originally intended, the Neutrality law of 1937 enlarged his power to favor one side or the other in any foreign conflict that might arise. In other words, the advocates of mandatory neutrality — that is, of a definitive foreign policy — were decisively beaten. What Congress actually did, in the Neutrality Act of 1937, was to give the President large power over American economic resources in the conduct of his foreign policy along lines distinctly personal, thus adding control over commerce to his control over diplomacy, the navy, and the army.

Henceforward the President, if limited as to munitions and loans, could exercise sovereign powers in other respects without asking the consent of Congress. Executive discretion, such as President Wilson had enjoyed between 1914 and 1917, was, in effect, extended over all areas of American industry and agriculture involved in foreign commerce. In commenting on this measure, John Bassett Moore, the greatest American authority on international law and diplomacy, correctly characterized its upshot: "No one who wished unlimited power to make war could ask for more than the authority, in his own discretion, to impose and revoke, and to modify and adjust, embargoes on our foreign commerce. . . . To commit to the executive the power in his discretion to adopt and prosecute measures that naturally lead to war, is virtually to transfer to him the power to make war, so that the formal declaration by Congress of the existence of a state of war would be an essentially perfunctory act." To this fiasco the effort of Congress "to keep the country out of war" had led.

§

Shortly after the passage of the third Neutrality law, in the summer of 1937, came another test of the neutrality principle — when Japan plunged into a war on China without making formal declaration of hostilities. For months the conflict raged. Huge armies were set to fighting. Thousands of lives were destroyed. Yet neither belligerent officially admitted that it was making war. Perhaps an age of undeclared wars had arrived. At all events, Roosevelt did not "find" that a state of war existed and hence the mandatory ban on loans and munitions was not put into force.

While the President delayed action under the law, the practical value of neutrality agitation and legislation was reviewed. Some citizens demanded an immediate application of the existing Act to the war in China, without reference to the merits of the contestants. Others, in sympathy with China and hostile to Japan, explored the possibilities of application and reached the conclusion that delay in enforcement would redound to the benefit of China, owing to her heavy dependence on imports for self-defense. Rebuttal came in the form of a contention that an embargo would hit the Japanese government harder on account of its larger purchases in the United States. Little concerned with theoretic arguments, economic interests in the United States made hay while the sun shone, by selling implements and the accessories of war to both sides without reference to their deserts.

As in the summer and autumn of 1914, so in the summer and autumn of 1937, American industry slowed down and the United States entered a depression of uncertain nature and duration. With domestic buying power in process of contraction, trade with China and Japan, small as it was relatively, grew in significance for American capital, agriculture, and labor. As a heavy buyer of cotton, scrap iron, oil, and other materials, Japan could intensify the crisis in America by retaliating against a ban on munitions and loans. Consequently, to matters of sentiment were joined serious economic considerations in respect of an embargo. Reviewing American foreign policy, Newton D. Baker had insisted that bankers exerted little or no influence on President Wilson and that economic interests scarcely affected his policy at all between 1914 and 1917, and almost in the same breath he declared with equal assurance that in case of another war the passion for making profits on sales to belligerents would nullify neutrality legislation. The experience with it, as Japan's war on China proceeded, apparently confirmed Mr. Baker's judgment. The pecuniary advantages of trade with belligerents were not to be destroyed by the application of an embargo designed "to keep the country out of war."

While American producers, merchants, and shippers lent to Japan all the aid and comfort for which its government could pay, President Roosevelt and the State Department veered first one way and then another. They warned Americans in China to withdraw from the perils of war areas and announced that it was not the intention of the United States to maintain military forces permanently in China for the purpose of giving protection to American citizens who insisted on staying there for their personal advantage. When American business men in Shanghai cried out against this abandonment of "American rights," the State Department declared that military and naval protection would be assured as usual to citizens of the United States in China. Against this form of Realpolitik, peace societies raised the customary objections. Then the State Department put out assurances on the other side. With Great Britain and France taxed by events on the Rhine and in the Mediterranean, with their sympathies divided over the Sino-Japanese conflict, the State Department had to pursue a checkered course through the clash of ideas and interests in the United States. But on the whole it seemed inclined to maintain a show of neutrality, to abstain from open interference in the merits of the war then raging, and yet at the same time to give moral lectures to the three "trouble makers" — Japan, Italy, and Germany — two of whom it had in fact aided in their war on Spain and the other, in a war on China.

§

Whether considered on their merits or in relation to the interests of the United States, events in Asia and Europe were exhilarating for Americans who were eager to operate on the world stage. For nearly a hundred years subsequent to the establishment of the Constitution, the Government of the United States had abstained from taking an official and risky part in European and Asiatic controversies, but the rules of caution long followed had been discarded, save by a few Americans now called "old-fashioned" or "unpatriotic." After the advent of the Mahan-Lodge-Theodore Roosevelt school of actors on the world stage, the State Department and the President adopted the habit of bursting frequently and effusively into the limelight of publicity; intervening and lecturing here and there became a fashion; and publicity served as meat for Caesar. While rejecting the phraseology and symbols of this school, President Wilson had followed the practice in many ways and combined resplendent lectures to the world audience with various forms of positive action, including intervention in Mexico and in the world war. Now in bureaucratic circles it was considered a poor day when the State Department could make no startling statement of "grand policy"; and the newspapers, ever in quest of sensations, indeed living on sensations, fed the fires of official zeal.

While lecturing, tacking, lunging, and back-tracking in response to the winds of domestic opinion, the State Department informed the nations of the earth that in fact it had a world policy. Shortly after the opening of the crisis in China, the Secretary of State emitted an address to mankind, laying down the proposition that serious hostilities anywhere, even in a remote place, affected the interests, rights, and "obligations" of every country. On its part, Secretary Hull declared, the United States advocated self-restraint, peace, and the adjustment of controversies by peaceful methods, in a spirit of mutual helpfulness and accommodation. "We advocate," he explained, "lowering or removing of excessive barriers in international trade. We seek effective equality of commercial opportunity and we urge upon all nations application of the principle of equality of treatment. We believe in limitation and reduction of armament."

Although the ink was barely dry on the official document that embargoed trade with the Loyalist government of Spain in violation of the Madrid treaty with Spain signed in 1902, the Secretary of State thought it fitting to couple with his formulation of world policy this statement: "Upholding the principle of the sanctity of treaties, we believe in modification of provisions of treaties, when need therefor arises, by orderly processes." Well aware that the preference of the country ran heavily against entangling commitments, the Secretary nevertheless ended on the note of collective action: "We believe in coöperative effort by peaceful and practicable means in support of the principles hereinbefore stated."

To this mondial manifesto, nearly all the nations of the earth made favorable responses. The spirit of the replies was characteristically reflected in the message from Albania to Secretary Hull, expressing "the whole sympathy of the Royal Government to the noble and well-wishing aims emanating from the statement in question in favor of the understanding of peoples, of the maintenance of peace, of the increase of international solidarity, and of the betterment of the world's economic situation." The government of the German Reich found itself in complete accord with Secretary Hull's lofty sentiments: "Its basic principle is, as is generally known, directed toward the regulation of international relations by pacific agreement and hence coincides with the ideas developed by the Secretary of State." The answer of

Mussolini was likewise sympathetic: "The Fascist government favors everything which may conduce to the pacification and economic reconstruction of the world." While asking for a full recognition of "the actual particular circumstances" in the Far East, the government of Japan expressed its "concurrence with the principles" contained in the Secretary's memorandum to the family of nations. Of such texture was the new diplomacy constituted.

Duly impressed no doubt by the unanimity of the nations, Roosevelt moved to the center of the world stage and in the impassioned speech delivered at Chicago on October 5, 1937, called for concerted action to quarantine and suppress disturbers of mondial harmony. His prologue described "the present reign of terror and international lawlessness," accompanied by ruthless bombing of men, women, and children without warning or justification. All civilization, he declared, was in peril of destruction: "Let no one imagine that America will escape, that it may expect mercy, that this Western Hemisphere will not be attacked." He then made pointed remarks about the disturbers of mankind. Without mentioning Japan, Germany, and Italy by name, he left no uncertainty as to the culprits. "The peace, the freedom, and the security of ninety per cent of the population of the world is being jeopardized by the remaining ten per cent." The answer? There must be a concerted effort of the peace-loving nations to restrain the marauders, and nations must seek "the removal of barriers against trade."

The Senate had repudiated the League of Nations and the World Court. Congressmen had expressed the resolve of their constituents to stay out of entanglements and wars. Nevertheless, defying both branches of the national legislature, the President, as Executive, called for direct and collective action against aggressors — for enforcing the gospel of world imagery. Instantaneously the world imagists exulted: "Roosevelt Abandons Isolation!" But other returns came in. Telegrams from members of Congress on vacation indicated disapproval in the "provinces." Opinion away from the Atlantic seaboard, as recorded by the poll-takers, was generally hostile to the terms of the Chicago address. Isolationists of all types again raised protests against entanglements. The school of American civilization repeated its formulas of antipathy for adventures likely to involve the country in another Armageddon. Instead of uniting the country, after the fashion of President Wilson's war message on April 6, 1917, the Chicago manifesto helped to divide it more acutely.

Stirred by Roosevelt's booming manifesto, the Assembly of the League of Nations, powerless to restrain offenders in Europe, showed signs of renewed life in dealing with the Far East. On the very next day it adopted a report urging League members to refrain from any action which might weaken China's powers of resistance and consider how far they could individually extend aid to China. The president of the Assembly invited the League members that had signed or adhered to the Nine-Power Treaty to initiate consultations. On the same day Secretary Hull issued a statement declaring that the action of Japan in China was contrary to the provisions of the Treaty and that the conclusions of the United States were "in general accord with those of the Assembly of the League of Nations."

A concrete outcome was a conference in Brussels attended by representatives of several interested nations, including Norman Davis, ambassador-at-large if not plenipotentiary, for the United States. The government of Great Britain was sympathetic but cautious and by no means united on any program. Badly burnt by previous experiences in Washington, British politicians wondered how far President Roosevelt would go or could go in backing up by force his Chicago pronouncement. Somewhat distraught by the suddenness and nature of the diversion, they cast out in two directions: they sent Anthony Eden to Brussels and a special agent to hold personal traffic with one of the three "disturbers of mankind," Adolf Hitler.

After many days of conversation the delegates at the

Brussels conference almost unanimously resolved that Japan had violated the Nine-Power Treaty and was to be viewed with disfavor by all right-thinking peoples. "Was it a bust?" a New York reporter asked Norman Davis on his return from the conversations. To this inquiry the Ambassador-at-large replied that it had been helpful to put the opinions of the pacific nations on record against Japanese aggression. Perhaps it had been. Still, the Chamberlain government in Great Britain soon freed Anthony Eden from his awkward position and made haste to effect a settlement with another disturber cited by Roosevelt at Chicago — namely, Benito Mussolini.

As a matter of fact there was little or no substance in the Nine-Power agreement. While it wore the guise of business, it was more evangelistic in spirit than calculative. The interest of the United States in Japanese trade was three or four times as great as its interest in Chinese trade, measured in terms of economic advantage. However conceived, the Treaty could not be enforced by the United States alone. Having what Theodore Roosevelt had called the Achilles heel in the Philippines, the Government at Washington was in no position to coerce Japan by single-handed diplomacy. With the whole-hearted aid of Great Britain, enforcement was possible, but the government of Great Britain had other perplexities to consider besides those in the Pacific. At the same time it suspected that the American State Department, no more than in John Hay's era, could enlist popular support for a naval adventure in the Chinese waters. Experience with the Philippines had been costly and disillusioning for the people of the United States. Why should they take on more troubles? Nor was the State Department at all sure of British intentions. In 1932, before the rise of Hitler in Germany and before Mussolini's imperial outburst in Ethiopia, Great Britain and France had trampled on Secretary Stimson's proposal for collective action designed to keep the door open in Manchuria. In 1937 Great Britain and France were exceedingly busy at home with their immediate neigh-

bors. So for one reason or another the United States was left
out on the limb, holding in hand the text of the Nine-Power
Treaty, with the platonic blessing of other signatories and
adherents. Such was the upshot of the Brussels conference
called from the void by President Roosevelt's speech at
Chicago.

§

For weeks after the delivery of the "quarantine" speech
at Chicago in October, 1937, Roosevelt refrained from ampli-
fications. To reporters who asked at private press conferences for additional comments, he returned curt and inane
replies. For the time being it seemed that the economic
crisis at home was enough to engross his attention. But
appearances were deceptive and with a suddenness that
flustered even his official family, he sent, on January 28, 1938,
a special message to Congress calling for an enormous increase
in armaments, including more battleships and cruisers, and
for the enactment of a mobilization bill which, in effect,
would prepare the way for a monster army. Although in one
part of his message the President declared that the naval
expansion, to cost about a billion dollars, was defensive in
nature, in another part he reverted to the "quarantine"
doctrine proclaimed at Chicago the preceding October. He
made his recommendations "specifically and solely," he said,
because the piling up of armaments in other countries involved a threat to "world peace and security." Taken in the
sense of English as understood, these words meant that the
new armament program, with its emphasis on battleships,
cruisers, airplane carriers, and mobilization, was relevant to
world policies — not merely to the defense of the American
zone of interest in the western hemisphere. However, as a cry
for more armaments had always appealed to powerful shipbuilding, munition, and supply interests, as well as to army
and navy leagues, Roosevelt could expect the usual hymns
of approval; and plans were made to pass the necessary bills
through Congress with little friction and great dispatch.

A hymn of praise arose — from defenders of the League of Nations, from "peace" advocates committed to collective security, from the seaboard press, and from the Stalinite communists bent on using the United States for Russian purposes. It was also joined by W. B. Shearer, more than famous as a professional shipbuilding lobbyist. Delighted with the prospects, he appeared at the hearings of the House committee on naval affairs, not to argue a cause already accepted by the administration, but to rejoice over a victory won without labor. Shipbuilders had contributed funds for the election of Roosevelt and they were pleased with the results. They knew that he was a lover of the sea and that as he sat in his favorite rooms in the White House his eyes rested affectionately on his ship models and marine pictures.

There was, in fact, little work for the regular armament lobbyists to do. The President had outstripped their very imagination and would soon have the satisfaction of carrying one measure through Congress in a rush. Who, save men and women lacking in patriotism, could oppose a super-navy bill? The chances for a quick passage of the bill were all the more certain because Roosevelt, by executive interference, had recently blocked an attempt to carry through the House of Representatives a proposal advanced by Louis Ludlow to make the use of American armies abroad subject to a popular referendum. Great newspapers that had assailed him as a communist in 1936 or had supported him with a lukewarmness almost contemptuous, with The New York Times in the lead, now lauded him for his armament program and urged Congress to enact it into law.

Notwithstanding the favorable setting, the play, destined to success in the end, did not come off exactly as expected, nor as soon. That a large part of the country was against the "quarantine" doctrine and against all the entanglements in foreign intrigues, quarrels, and wars to which it might lead, was quickly demonstrated. This repugnance had been expressed to the White House and the State Department in a flood of letters protesting against the Chicago speech. It had been so strong that it had silenced the President temporarily and stopped further elucidation and frank advocacy of the doctrine. Now the opposition flared up anew against the armament program, with its quarantine implications and its mobilization features.

Even kindergartners in naval affairs knew that battleships such as proposed, with a large cruising radius, were for use in distant waters, rather than for defense in American waters. In his naval message the President himself emphasized the threat to "world" peace and security in justification of his demand upon Congress. About the same time unofficial spokesmen of the British government made it known that their coöperation could be relied upon in the Far East; and the participation of American cruisers in the celebration at the opening of the Singapore naval base suggested that coöperation for other than ceremonial purposes was not entirely beyond the range of probability.

The inveterate suspicion that the armament program at bottom was intended to implement the "quarantine" doctrine or interventionism in the Orient was strengthened by the paragraph in the President's message of January 28 calling for legislation to prevent "profiteering" and equalize the "burdens of war." That paragraph rewarmed the controversy over the army and navy plan for a totalitarian mobilization for war. As originally conceived, this plan provided for huge armies to be raised by conscription, the commandeering of agriculture and industry, the regimentation of labor, the taxation of profits, and government control over all organs of opinion. As a result of criticism from the outside and disputes in Congress, the original design had been whittled down. Even so, the President's demand for it confirmed popular belief that the proposal was simply a step to the drafting of huge armies for use abroad, to the suppression of trade union activities, and the destruction of civil liberties in general. Indeed the chief totalitarian provisions, except those controlling the press, were finally incorporated in a revised measure and reported favorably to the

House of Representatives by its committee on military affairs but, as the party managers were afraid of a national outburst, they let it die unheard and unmourned.

The President's appeal on January 28 for an enlarged navy, though finally heeded, likewise encountered fervent opposition. Immediately after his message was emitted, Senator William E. Borah and Senator Hiram Johnson asked pointed questions of the State Department and, when assured that no understandings existed with Great Britain in connection with the naval bill, continued to wonder. Was this a scheme to aid the British Empire in policing the earth? Was it a renewal of American imperialism in the Orient? Was it a prelude to another war for democracy? Such questions were annoying to advocates of mere "defense."

As soon as the President's naval bill reached the House committee on naval affairs, the public hearings developed into a thorough airing of the foreign policies implicit in the measure. General Johnson Hagood and General W. C. Rivers, who had combined a study of foreign affairs with devoted military service, pressed for a definition of the policy behind the call for battleships and challenged the contention that they were planned for the defense of the United States as distinguished from the defense of imperial interests and the quarantining of recalcitrant nations. As in the fight over judicial reorganization, the Republicans at first shrank from a party attack on the armament program, but individual Republicans took up the gage, under the leadership of Ralph O. Brewster of Maine. Hamilton Fish, a steadfast opponent of an imperialistic war, East or West, went before the House committee on naval affairs and denounced the naval bill as a plan for translating into actuality Roosevelt's idea of policing the world and shackling disturbers of peace everywhere.

Though the naval bill left the committee with a favorable report, it was accompanied by a minority dissent which condemned it as unnecessary for defense and as the offspring of the quarantine doctrine headed directly to entanglements in collective action. Before the bill passed, the large subject of sea power, imperialism, and protection for American traders in war zones was discussed critically and extensively. While the measure mustered an overwhelming party support, the opposition vote in the lower House was substantial and included, besides such leading Democrats as Maury Maverick, Caroline O'Day, Herman Kopplemann, and Harry C. Luckey, about two-thirds of the Republican membership.

In the Senate the bill was subjected to a still more searching analysis, under the greater freedom of Senate procedure. Long and carefully prepared addresses were delivered against it by Senators Nye, La Follette, Vandenberg, Borah, Clark, and King, strongly supported by colleagues on both sides of the party line. Day after day critics of the super-super-navy plan, as Senator Vandenberg called the project, attacked it from every angle, as if in concert, while members who were to vote for the bill absented themselves from the chamber, sat silent, or made minor interpolations. Not until May 3 was the roll called and the proposal approved, with twenty-eight Senators recorded against it. In other words, more than three months passed between the delivery of the President's message launching the program and completed action on it by Congress.

Finally achieved, the victory of the administration was not an unalloyed pleasure. Congress had withheld the swift and almost unanimous approval so customary in cases of military and naval expansion. Nor had the debates been limited to details. The entire foreign policy of the President and State Department had been drawn into consideration in Congress and outside. Searching questions had been asked by the opposition with persistent repetition. Was the naval expansion bill framed to implement the President's quarantine doctrine — the proposal for collective action against Germany, Italy, and Japan? Was it intended to strengthen the United States navy for operations in the Far East against Japan, in support of the McKinley-Mahan imperialism that had yielded no economic fruits comparable to the costs?

What subterranean negotiations were being carried on with Great Britain, in the style of Colonel House or Robert Lansing, with a view to "collaboration" in aid of "the democracies" and especially the British empire? If, as Admiral Leahy had testified, the navy was already strong enough to keep Japan out of this hemisphere, why was it necessary to add more ships to those afloat, under construction, and authorized? The House had passed on January 21, 1938, the largest peace-time naval bill in the history of the country, granting substantially every dollar for which the Department had asked. Why had the administration suddenly decided seven days later, without previous notice, that another huge increase was necessary? Since Admiral Leahy had confessed that he did not know the answer to this question, who did? Were the war scares reported in the press during the passage of the bill inspired by bureaucrats and munitioneers or did the cries of "Wolf, Wolf" mean something real this time?

On all these questions the debates in Congress and in the press were educative. If the President did entertain at the bottom of his heart a desire to mount the world stage, support collective action in Europe, and take a strong hand in the imperialist conflicts of the Orient, the Democrats who supported the super-navy bill, with few exceptions, indignantly registered their aversion for all such policies. Although the State Department continued to emit announcements which savored of the quarantine doctrine, most vocal Representatives and Senators disclaimed any sympathy with it. To settle all doubts on that score, Senator Walsh, in defending the bill, emphatically and even somewhat poetically, iterated and reiterated the contention that the super-navy was merely designed for the defense of America in this hemisphere, not for collective action in Europe or for imperialist adventures in the Orient. As if to clinch the argument he more than once pointed out obvious facts in the situation: the super-navy bill did not appropriate a single dollar; it did not make mandatory the building of a single ship; it did no more than "authorize, without time limit, the expansion of our naval strength" — an expansion that could not occur until, at some date in the future, if ever, Congress should appropriate the money for expansion. The bill, in short, its proponents affirmed, really marked no departure from isolationism and was a mere pious resolution that might or might not be carried into execution in the dim, distant future.

So it was written on the record that members of Congress, in sponsoring the naval expansion bill, expressly disavowed the very idea of collaborating with European democracies in a quarantine against Germany, Italy, and Japan and rejected all thought of waging another imperialist war in the Orient. If the President did not cherish the idea and the thought, then why, opponents asked, approve a naval program that might add two or three billions to the steadily mounting debt of the nation? It must have been with mixed feelings, therefore, that the President received the news of his naval victory in Congress.

Nor did the adventure end with the passage of the bill. Few citizens doubtless read the hundreds of pages that recorded the debate in committee hearings and congressional chambers. But some did, especially persons worried by the growing power of the navy and army in national politics. And in the records they read trenchant criticisms of "the British-Mahan sea power doctrine," of profiteering in munitions, of bankers' interventions in American foreign policy, of waste, poor bookkeeping and imperfect accounts in armament expenditures, of secret diplomacy, of imperialist tactics ranging from the use of the navy to protect Standard Oil shipments in war zones to the employment of armed forces in upholding "trade opportunities." President Roosevelt rode down the opposition to the naval expansion bill, but in the process the romantic version of armaments, armament interests, and armament bureaucracies was badly spattered. If, as stated in the Senate debates, the Government set its secret agents upon opponents of the naval expansion bill, to spy on them, and to report against them, even its undercover police activities could not stop the criticism — for the moment. Such tactics might be successful in the future, but the day had not yet arrived.

§

Although President Roosevelt pursued the policy of "the good neighbor" in the American regions to the south, that meant no lack of attention to practical interests in Cuba and other regions. Despite the swing of revolutions in Latin-American countries toward straight military dictatorships of the conservative order, sometimes called fascist, there were few occasions for the employment of Power Diplomacy or the marines. With members of Congress stunned by the conduct of the Lords of Creation in floating bond issues for Latin-American governments in the boom days, there was not much zeal for dollar diplomacy on Capitol Hill, for the use of troops or naval pressure to collect interest and install-ments on defaulted Bolivian or Peruvian bonds. Militant capitalism was discouraged for the time being at all events. Though heavy pressures were undoubtedly exerted especially in Mexico in connection with debts, the seizure of oil proper-ties, and the expropriation of lands owned by citizens of the United States, they were not featured by open thundering or by displays of "the martial spirit" as in the days of Wil-son's philanthropy and Harding's normalcy.

Hence exchanges of good-will on the Pan-American line could be made freely without encountering a serious test of revolutionary practice. When President Roosevelt and Secre-tary Hull went in person to the Inter-American conference for the maintenance of peace at Buenos Aires in December, 1936, they were greeted by lavish manifestations of hospi-tality. Roosevelt's eloquent oration on coöperation among democratic nations for neutrality and peace called forth hearty approval from the dictator of Argentina. Still, noth-ing tangible came out of the conference, except the discovery that there was a difference in policy between the bloc in Latin America oriented toward the League of Nations and the bloc of countries outside that sisterhood.

Unquestionably Latin Americans were happy to learn that the economic coercion which they had called "Yankee imperialism" in the old days was to be relaxed. They were also pleased to see the shield of the Monroe Doctrine furbished, if in storage, as it might be useful again. Momentarily they were in little danger from interference on the part of the great European powers in the style of Wilhelminic times, and yet they feared that the sick men of the Old World might recover.

Beyond that the ceremonial exuberation had little or no meaning. If partly united in condemning coercion by the Colossus of the North and in welcoming delays in the collection of debts, Latin-American states possessed little or no fundamental solidarity of interest — intellectual, moral, or economic. As Hubert Herring, certainly well-acquainted with the facts in the case, said, "Pan-American unity" was a "myth." In commenting on the Buenos Aires demonstration, "there is," he remarked, "no Pan-Americanism. There is no sense of American unity anywhere in the Americas. . . . Not only is there no sense of unity between Latin America and the United States, but there is little if any sense of unity among the Latin Americans themselves." The lack of realism in the picture of the world imagists was duplicated by the lack of realism in the picture of the regional imagists. Geographical propinquity and trade produced many common bonds, but no solidarity. Nor did the speeches and resolutions at the Lima conference in 1938 alter materially the diversity of interests.

The only peculiar feature in the situation was the frequent reference to ties of strength that might be created between dictators in Latin America and their brethren in Germany, Italy, Spain, and Japan. Attempts were made to evoke this fright in the United States, especially after a Brazilian dictator announced the formation of "a corporative state" in 1937. However, the specter had qualities of a scarecrow. There was not much likelihood that Latin-American dictators, usually of the formal military type, would actually welcome German or Italian intervention with their affairs. They wanted to rule in their own way, without instruction or interference from lords and masters. Neither by interest nor necessity were South American countries inclined to call in Hitler or Mussolini or Franco. Mussolini's dream might include dominance over Spain, but scarcely over the "once glorious Spanish Empire in the New World." For him, as for Hitler, naval bases in Latin America, if procurable, could only be liabilities. The navies of Great Britain and the United States blocked the way of any European despots who might seek to emulate Napoleon III and his ill-fated effort to establish an empire for Maximilian in Mexico.

Such being the topography of power, the peril of "a fascist Latin America" did not appear very substantial. Since the days of Simon Bolivar, the United States had managed to twist and turn along its way in dealing with a multitude of dictators in that region, and history, with curious features and novel ideologies, might continue along a similar course. The only event likely to make a general explosion would have been a communist upheaval in Mexico or elsewhere in Latin America, but that probability sank into the background as Stalinists and Trotskyists turned from bothering others to fighting among themselves.

§

To the very end, however, nothing in the course of events in either hemisphere could quench the insatiate desire of the Roosevelt administration to issue discourses on the virtues of peace-loving democracies and the wickedness of the three great disturbers of harmony — Japan, Italy, and Germany. However hard it tried, the State Department could not refrain from breaking into the newspapers every little while with some comment, homily, or innuendo indicating that it was driven by a Weltdrang as well as a Weltschmerz. Doubtless with the approval of President Roosevelt, his Commander-in-Chief, Admiral Leahy, in defending the super-navy bill before the naval affairs committee of the House, repeatedly linked the navies of the three world offenders as if the United States must prepare for a conflict with this combination. He even referred to their compact against communism in his eagerness to show their "solidarity." In a broadcast to the British commonwealth of nations, Secretary Ickes took advantage of the occasion to comment on the line-up of the bad against the good. Not to be outdone by admirals or the Secretary of the Interior, Harry Woodring, the Secretary of War, in May, 1938, after lamenting that heavy burdens for armaments had to be laid on suffering taxpayers, served notice on the world that the American army might fight another war for democracy. In keeping with expectations, Secretary Woodring's warning produced sharp criticism in Rome and Tokyo — criticism which doubtless confirmed him in his view that still larger armaments were required by the United States. He had said in 1934 that the army was ready to "take charge" of the country in case of a social crisis. Now it might combine with great fervor the two historic functions of the military.

On the effusions that poured out of offices in Washington, Joseph Kennedy, ambassador to Great Britain, made a pertinent comment at London in March, 1938, about as emphatically as a diplomat could. He expressed the hope "that the United States would solve its own problems if it stopped worrying about Europe," and he advised both America and Great Britain "to better their economic positions." Ending on a realistic note, the Ambassador said: "Nothing else will matter much — believe me." But Mr. Kennedy was an "amateur" diplomat. The tradition of keeping the mouth shut, the face inscrutable, and the powder dry had been definitely outlawed by the Roosevelt administration. With the ardent support of powerful economic and bureaucratic interests, with the rabid endorsement of belligerent elements in peace societies and the labor movement, it could, in fair confidence, count upon over-riding the opposition provided by mild-mannered liberals of the middle class